THE DIARY OF COLONEL PETER HAWKER

VOL. II

Lt. Col: P. Hawker.

From a Bust by Wm. Behnes, Esq. Engraved by H. Robinson.

THE DIARY OF COLONEL PETER HAWKER 1802–1853

Introduction by
SIR RALPH PAYNE-GALLWEY, BART.

With a New Foreword by
COLIN LAURIE McKELVIE

IN TWO VOLUMES – VOL. II

Greenhill Books

This edition of *The Diary of Colonel Peter Hawker*
first published 1988 by Greenhill Books, Lionel Leventhal Limited,
Park House, 1 Russell Gardens, London NW11 9NN.

British Library Cataloguing in Publication Data
Hawker, P. (Peter), *1786–1853*
The Diary of Colonel Peter Hawker, 1802–1853;
Introduction by Sir Ralph Payne-Gallwey;
New Foreword by Colin Laurie McKelvie.
1. Great Britain. Sports. Shooting, 1802–1853.
I. Title 799.2′13′09

Volume I ISBN 1–85367–019–7
Volume II ISBN 1–85367–020–0

Publishing History
The Diary of Peter Hawker was first published in 1893 (Longmans, Green, and Co.) in two volumes. These are reproduced now exactly as the original edition, with the addition of a new Foreword by Colin Laurie McKelvie.

Printed by The Bath Press,
Lower Bristol Road, Bath.

LIST OF PLATES

IN

THE SECOND VOLUME

Lieut.-Colonel P. Hawker. *From a bust by Behnes.* *Frontispiece*

James Read, with his new Launching Punt, Hawker's Creek and Yarmouth. *By C. Varley* *to face p.* 16

Return to Keyhaven, after a Day's Gunning, in the Winter of 1838. *By C. Varley* . . „ 146

Mud-Launchers on the Oozes, off Lymington, shoving their Funts up to Wigeon. *By Colonel Peter Hawker* . . . . . . „ 182

THE DIARY

OF

COLONEL PETER HAWKER

CHAPTER XXII

1829

September 1*st*.—Longparish. The most deplorable first day on record. I very unwell. A wet morning with a north-east gale, that prevented our throwing off till near twelve o'clock. Only one borrowed dog to shoot with, not one breath of scent, birds most lamentably scarce, and as wild as at Christmas, and a variety of particular bad luck to boot, owing to one of my gun locks being out of order. Disappointed of all my good markers, owing to the harvest not being near over, and so nervous I could not have hit a cow but for the aid of bark and sal volatile. I contrived, by working till I was half dead, to knock down 16 brace of birds, but, having lost 5 brace out of the number in the corn, for want of a retriever, or, at all events, a better scent, I was obliged to come sneaking home with only 22 partridges, 3 hares, and 1 quail. So much for the 1st of September, 1829.

3*rd*.—Renewed my pursuit of the most miserably woeful shooting, and did wonders, considering all. I actually brought home 24 partridges, 20 of which were old ones, as grey as badgers, and two squeakers, which I killed to encourage a puppy.

Everyone is disgusted with the unprecedented bad shooting of this September, and many have already thrown aside their guns.

5*th.*—A westerly wind and a wet day. Went out a little before two in the afternoon; and, with a drizzling rain the whole time I was out, came in, before six, with 20 partridges; but, to cancel all, I missed four fair shots. This is what I rarely did in a whole month's shooting, but the present state of my digestive organs is such that I must compound for want of nerve.

7*th.*—Was out the whole day, and beat over the whole estate. I never worked harder in my life to make up a bag; but the birds were so very scarce and so very wild, that I literally never got but one really fair shot the whole time I was out; but, by blazing away at everything, and shooting as well as I could wish to shoot, I contrived to bring home 14 partridges. I shot with one of my old guns, and was far from being in prime nerve; and therefore I now impute my four vile misses on the 5th to the stock of a new gun, which I had on trial, and which, consequently, I mean to return.

Specimen of a sorry first week: 80 partridges, the average of which was about seven old ones to one young one, 7 hares, with 1 quail and 1 landrail, making but 89 head in the four days I was out. The worst week on record; and I had only a borrowed dog to shoot to, and had been so harassed by bother and business as to be quite unwell.

This looks very poor after the September of 1827, when I bagged, besides what I lost, 102 partridges and 1 hare the first day.

14*th.*—The first tolerably fine day we have had since I returned here. Went out, with my musket, and joined Captain Symonds over Mrs. Whitby's manor, round Newlands, the most beautifully wild country I ever saw, but a most severely stiff one to get about in. The most impregnable fences I ever met with, and blind ditches, six feet deep, to half the fields on the manor. We had fair sport, considering that this is not a professed partridge country. My share of the bag was 4 partridges, 1 hare, 1 rabbit, 1 landrail, 1 wood pigeon, and 1 turtle dove (all I shot at).

29th.—Got 1 hare and 2 partridges, which I wanted, and for which I have to thank Eley's cartridges, as the birds were so wild they would hardly let you enter the field with them.

Game bagged in September 1829: 105 partridges, 10 hares, 2 rabbits, 1 landrail, 1 quail. Total, 119 head.

The worst season in the memory of the oldest man; so, being in bad health and without dogs, I gave it up, as did many other sportsmen.

October 1st.—Shot in a part of Wherwell Wood. My share of the killed was 3 pheasants, 2 hares and 1 partridge, all the shots I got, and most of them long ones. As we spared hens, the whole bag, among four of us, as Lords Charles and George Paulett were with us and made up eight barrels, was 8 cock pheasants, 5 hares, 1 partridge and 1 rabbit.

6th.—Keyhaven. Toddled out without a dog of any kind to see if I could have the luck to get a snipe with my old musket, and had the extraordinary luck to drop in with such a flight as I never saw here before, and knocked down 6 couple, with one miss-fire. As it was, I made the best day on record for Keyhaven; but if I had had a proper double gun and a decent dog, I should have performed what, in this place, would have been considered a miracle.

14th.—Keyhaven. Left here by way of pleasant conveyance in a yacht. Wind changed, carried away mizen-boom. Heaviest sea known for a long time off Calshot. Gentlemen all sick and wet through with a happy mixture of rain and breakers, and a foul gale in our teeth. Lost the coach, and had to gig it home to Longparish. Horse fell down, and rolled over twice, broke a trace, and consequently the man and I had to walk a great part of the way in the rain and dirt. Relayed with a horse at Winchester that Weyhill Fair had 'taken all the shine out of,' so could only toddle along by sheer flagellation, and was almost perished by a northerly hurricane, and one of the coldest nights that ever nipped a nose.

19*th.*—Having seen all the gear &c. packed on the boat carriage, I this afternoon returned to Keyhaven. We had a narrow escape from accident with the Lymington coach. A high-couraged young horse, that 'Wiltshire' had to break in, took fright at a barrow going down hill. He kicked over the bar and dragged the coach to a ditch, into which we were all but overturned.

20*th.*—Keyhaven. Just stepped out with the musket, to see if there were any more snipes come. Found 5, 4 of which I shot at and killed. This evening, about four o'clock, the convoy arrived safe, with all my newly done-up apparatus, punt, great gun, &c.

22*nd.*—Walked the marsh again. Found nothing but my old friend the jack snipe which escaped being shot at the day before yesterday, but to-day I bagged him. I never saw a living creature in all my wet walk. In the middle of the day we had wind and rain, but about an hour before night it came on fine, so I launched the punt and rowed 'up along' ashore with the great gun; but there were no fowl.

26*th.*—A fine day, but no fowl to be seen. Tried a few shots at marks, and found the gun wonderfully improved since newly done up; but had to alter one of the new touchholes, which, merely from being too small, missed fire twice out of three times. This shows how necessary it is always to try a gun well before you go into real action with it. All the flesh and feathers I could see, by way of living targets, were 'old Francis' (a heron) and 'the parson' (a cormorant), both of which I killed, quite dead, at a good hundred yards.

29th.—Afloat all the morning, with a fine north-east wind, but never saw a chance. Fell in with Buckle, who had not yet had a shot.

November 2nd.—Went afloat again, to see if there were any fowl come, but the coast has, as yet, a very sorry appearance.

7th.—Having put all my 'gear' in most superlative order, and left everything ready for my recall, on the arrival of the fowl I this day left Keyhaven for Longparish.

9th.—Longparish. 3 partridges, got by mere random firing, while out with Ford, Lord Portsmouth's keeper, to try my puppies that he had to break. He is a capital shot, and, after coming home, he laid his gun cocked on the ground, threw up two penny pieces himself and then took up the gun, and hit one with each barrel before they fell. He could never meet with anyone who did the same, but there was some art in throwing up the money. As I have never yet been beaten, I was anxious to do the same, and I did it.

16th.—Had another day with Mr. Coles and the Lords Paulett, and though we scoured the whole of the best coverts with a regular battery of five double guns, not one fair chance occurred for killing a pheasant, and, indeed, the only shot was one that I blew off at, about eighty yards from me, and he fell wounded in the high wood. Such is the deplorable state of the shooting this year.

December.—While detained in London on particular business, I had the mortification to see a fine easterly wind, and wild fowl hawked at every corner of the streets. At last I received a pressing summons from Read, at Keyhaven, on the 6th, entreating me to come off the next day, the 10th, but I could not possibly leave town till the next day.

11th.—I mounted the 'Telegraph' at eight, and was in Keyhaven Cottage (just one hundred miles) within the twelve hours. But most wonderful and remarkably unfortunate, I had no sooner got about halfway on my journey down, than my implacable enemy the weathercock flew into the west, and it began a hurricane and rain just as I entered the gig which took me from the coach at Lymington. The gun and punt were all ready to take me afloat at nine the same night; but the weather ruined everything, and, instead of breakfasting in town, and perhaps getting a fine satchel of birds before supping at Keyhaven, I was obliged to turn into bed, and from the wetting I got, so unwell that I was indebted to some little management for not being laid up here in the very essence of misery.

12*th*.—Keyhaven. Went out for a few hours, while the tide was over the harbour, having to weather a gale in which we could scarcely 'row on end;' and had the mortification to see armies of birds travelling over the harbour on their route out of the country, solely in consequence of the brutal, abominable, ruinous, and detestable westerly wind.

14*th*.—Out from a quarter past twelve, directly the Sunday was passed, till three this morning, while the tide served well, and with a beautiful bright moon, but never saw or heard one single trip of wigeon the whole time. About nine this morning we had the blessed satisfaction to see that the weathercock had gone to the right about, and brought us back the easterly wind. We then had the pleasure to see some flocks of birds off on the tide; but it was too rough to do anything out at sea. We cruised round the harbour from one till five; all I fired at was (one barrel) at 4 curlews, all of which came into the larder. This shot, although at mere rubbish, was a satisfactory beginning.

15*th*.—Nipping white frost and fog; out from one till near four; a fine moon. Birds scattered about like fieldfares, and very 'ticklish;' got 2 wigeon out of the only 3 I could get together. Lay down till eight; off all day; but the fog and wind with it made a miserable time. Saw some wigeon on tide, and lowered 2. So came home, and 'blew myself out,' and got to bed soon after dark.

16*th*.—Read out all night, and got but 2 wigeon, the

birds were so scattered. I was out from three till near six; but the tide was out, or I should have had a fine shot. Out again from nine till three in the afternoon; bagged 4 brent geese, the first that I have heard of being killed this season. I shot them out of a small company at an immense distance, with my left-hand barrel; and this was the only shot I fired all day. But one of the mud crawlers spoiled me a superb shot at wigeon.

17*th.*—The 'dead of the nip,' and no more water this moon. Out all day and never got a shot. We tried to work the birds at sea between Hurst and the Needles; but although the punt worked as well there as a boat could have done, yet the motion was such that the birds could see into her every time the waves lifted; so we resolved to abandon this place for the future.

18*th.*—A tremendous gale with sleet and rain from the eastward; no water inside, and no living outside. Read crawled about on the mud with the 'Mudlark' punt, and brought in 5 wigeon.

19*th.*—Fine clear weather, with a north wind, but no chance for a shot, as the 'nip tides' are now on for a week, and therefore there will be no water over the harbour; and what birds there are remain out at sea till night, and then come in to the dry oozes, where nothing but mud crawling can get at them.

20*th.*—Sunday. Breakfasted at half-past three, and worked my way up, so as to get in the box of the 'Telegraph' at Southampton, and arrive at Winchester in good time to breakfast and to go to the cathedral, where the service was beautifully performed; and, after church was over, I got a hack gig and drove to Longparish.

N.B.—The very day that I left Keyhaven, there set in a heavy fall of snow, and a most beautiful frost.

22*nd.*—Took my artillery up to Lord Portsmouth's for a shot at the ducks on the park water; but there was such a heavy fall of snow that we thought it prudent to raise the siege and leave them quiet.

23rd.—Renewed the siege at Lord Portsmouth's; took but one shot, not wishing to disturb the fowl too much; but the birds were so scattered that I could only get 11, viz. 7 ducks and mallards, 2 dunbirds, 1 tufted duck, and 1 coot; some more were stopped, but they made their escape to the rushes, &c. Went up the river in the evening, and, though it was one of the severest nights that ever was weathered for wind, frost and snow, yet I never got but one chance, and then the gun missed fire. I never saw this country so ruined for sport in my life.

25th.—London. Sad accounts from many parts of Hampshire and other counties. I had this day, too, to witness horrors of another description. Having to cross the street, we just escaped the track of a coach and horses run away without a driver, and before our very faces were eight people knocked down and severely wounded, and among them two ladies weltering in blood and carried off on shutters, one with a broken thigh and apparently quite dead. The equipage came in tremendous contact with the window of Mr. Hale, the hatter, Oxford Street, corner of Regent Street, and I never heard such a horrid crash or beheld such an alarming sight. To name the people frightened and slightly hurt would be endless. The further progress of damage was prevented by the gallant behaviour of a policeman, who in seizing and holding the horses got such blows as to be taken off severely wounded.

The result of the horrid accident was that the two Misses Delisle[1] were so severely injured that one only came to her senses to-day, and the other was to have her broken thigh set for the second time by Brodie this afternoon. A French

[1] Their poor mother has been confined on the sofa for seven weeks, and the first she heard of the accident was a double knock, and her two daughters brought in on shutters apparently dead.

gentleman was dangerously wounded; six more taken to the hospital; the policeman had three of his ribs broken, and his chest beat in; and the coachman from whom the horses escaped was thrown from the box and much hurt. Add to this list many people who were knocked down and slightly bruised. Left for Longparish.

27th.—Left Longparish this afternoon, and contrived to get to Keyhaven by nine o'clock, notwithstanding the severe frost and snow.

28th.—Up at four in the morning, and afloat till five in the evening. A dead calm, and the frost so hard that our beer froze up in the bottles. Hot enough, however, what with thick clothing, rowing, &c. Gunners in every direction. Saw 17 hoopers, 1 eagle, and lots of fowl; but they were eternally chased, and I could not meet one man who had got a bird but myself. Had spoiled for me a splendid shot at 7 swans, and another prime chance at burrough ducks; and brought home 7 wigeon and 1 pintail.

29th.—A determined 'black snap,' water jugs in bedrooms all frozen. Harbour all ice, and birds all off at sea; thick snowy nights, and no time for wigeon. Out from dawn till afternoon, got three shots only. I was the only gunner who had a bird in his punt this day.

30th.—Keyhaven. The hoopers dropped into Keyhaven harbour, and I was all but 'doing them.' The water was low, and we had to go up a winding creek that showed us broadside too much. I could therefore only get within about 160 yards before they hooped and flew. I let drive both barrels into them; but no lucky shot happened to take their vitals, and therefore I only peppered their feathers.

31st.—All day in chase of the swans.

1830

January 1st.—3 brent geese and 1 old cock sheldrake, one of the finest and cleanest specimens that any museum could have shown, and therefore I sent him to the prince of ornithology, Mr. Leadbeater, to stuff for me.

2nd.—Still a severe frost, with a north-east wind. Read had been out all night, and never found a wigeon, though hundreds were travelling over, very high. I was out from dawn till dusk, and saw nothing (except what I got) but one flock of geese, at a distance, and 17 hoopers, travelling over, but they never offered to drop. So I got all I fired at, viz. 1 brent goose, 2 scaup ducks, and 1 golden-eye. All the other gunners had a blank day. Read mud-launched till Sunday came in, and got but 4 wigeon.

4th.—Knocked down 1 golden-eye with the musket, the only trigger I pulled all day. We were up, and at breakfast by five, to take the day-dawn chance, but it snowed and rained all day till the afternoon, when we turned out and saw nothing but 2 hoopers, that I lay in shot of, for two hours, and could get no water to bring the gun to bear on them. Not a fowl in all Lymington market, no chance for anyone, for want of water to clear the mud.

6th.—Read came in after a night's mud launching, with 13 wigeon, 1 pintail, and my wild swan, that I floored yesterday, which he rowed down and caught near where I shot him. I went out, with the moon; got 5 wigeon about eleven, but could do no more for want of water.

8th.—A return of northerly wind and frost. No tides again in consequence, though this is but one day before full moon. Read came in at daylight from mud crawling with 7 wigeon, and I got 6 brent geese about noon.

9th.—Shot but one barrel all day, and brought in 9 brent geese; 5 more were picked up by a sailing boat, and carried off in view of me. Out at night, a fine time; but the moment the water whitened the mud, off to sea flew every wigeon in harbour.

11th.—A severely cold gale all day from the north, with some frost. Discharged my gun but once all day. Picked up

10 brent geese. No wigeon about. Read, who had been mud crawling all the previous night from twelve o'clock, when Sunday was over, came in with only 1 wigeon and 1 goose.

12th.—Read had a blank night on the mud, and I a blank day in the harbour; a gale from the north enough to cut a man's nose off, no water inside, and no 'living' outside. Too cold for wigeon, but plenty of geese and some swans, defying all gunners.

13th.—Read came in from his nocturnal crawling bout with 5 geese and 2 wigeon. I went out in the afternoon. I got but one little shot, and picked up 7 brent geese.

14th.—A severe 'black snap' with snow. Read had a blank night, the wigeon frozen off to a milder climate. Out all day, bagged 10 brent geese.

15th.—Made a long flying shot with the musket at a lough diver, or female smew,[1] a bird that I had long wanted for my collection. Then got a shot at 3 brent geese, and 'floored' them all. It snowed most heavily, and coming home I saw about 11 of such birds as I never saw before. I put the first barrel into them, when much scattered, and hit down one. I then up with the second barrel, as they clubbed, and cut down 3 more. But one out of the 4 fell where I lost him. I followed the remainder all day, and could get no further chance but a blow off with 'Eley's cartridge' at about 300 yards, and down I fetched another. So I bagged 4 in all. They proved to be 4 white-fronted geese.[2] The most beautiful fowl that ever I saw brought home for a cabinet.

16th.—After being all the morning in Lymington, tormented with old Charles the gunmaker, I had just time to swallow my dinner, and bustle off after about 50 more of these extraordinary outlandish geese. I put both barrels into them, and picked up 12 white-fronted geese.

[1] The first I ever saw, or heard of, on our coast.

[2] Or laughing geese from Hudson's Bay. The *Anas albifrons* of Linnæus; and the *l'oye rieuse* of Buffon.

17th.—Sunday. Very severe weather, harbour frozen, and nothing to be seen in our walk with a glass after church.

18th.—14 brent geese, 3 sheldrakes, and 2 curlews; 3 geese the 1st shot, 3 sheldrakes the 2nd shot, and 9 geese and 2 curlews the 3rd shot.

19th.—Out before daylight, and near two hours cutting our way through the ice. A tremendous sea, and little to be done; blew off at 7 swans, so far that the shot was spent. Out till night; no other chance.

20th.—The most tremendous day I ever saw. Sleet, rain, deep snow, thaw, and then hard frost again, with a gale of wind from the north-east that one could hardly stand against, for fear of being blown off one's legs; every kind of outdoor work suspended, and everyone driven home to his house. Of course no shooting even on shore, much less afloat.

21st.—A calm frosty morning. Out an hour before dawn, but had to slave through ice till long after sunrise; got but two shots all day. Second shot got 2 wild swans. The two I got were fine birds, but the one that escaped was the old captain of the 6 I shot at, and the finest bird I ever saw. We were so blocked up in ice that we compounded for twelve hours' starvation, neither being able to get back nor forward, but by sheer slavery we battered our way home (about a mile) to Keyhaven. In the evening we were driven home from our second sortie by a south-west wind, with sleet and rain.

22nd.—The gale abated so much that we were enabled to get afloat very early this morning. The first game we viewed were 2 wild swans, which, having plenty of water, we set into with ease, and I cut down the old white one with the first barrel, and the young brown one with the second barrel as dead as September partridges. The next shot was at 9 of the outlandish geese, but I only got 2 of these white-fronted geese. The 3rd shot I got 3 brent geese at one shot with my musket. I never made such a shot with a popgun in all my life. I had a cartridge of 'Eley's patent,' containing but $1\frac{3}{4}$ oz.

of No. 2 shot, and there were five geese in a line; the one dead was eighty-five paces, and the two winged fell short at about a hundred paces. I never could have believed this had I not seen it, and done it myself. The 4th shot was at about 220 yards with the swivel gun, at an old single swan. I knocked him down like a cock pheasant (flying), of course with a barrel of the great gun; and, after exulting in my prize, the old scoundrel recovered, hobbled over the beach to sea, and bid us defiance. He will, of course, be a prize for some one.

23rd.—The frost returned with a 'north-easter,' and a heavy fall of snow, and fog. Out for a few hours, but could not get a chance to shoot anything.

25th.—White frost, and of course a butterfly day after. Everyone that could muster a punt was driving about, and the consequence was no one could get a good shot. I brought home 3 brent geese, which were 3 more than I expected.

27th.—Read could get no chance with his nightly mud creeping. On my return from Lymington about twelve, he had just put off and got an old swan; and I renewed the attack, and made two such shots as I never saw in my life; and the three birds all proved to be 3 old gander hoopers, one of which was five feet two long, and full eight feet from wing to wing. I had no other chance, but such birds as these were enough to content one for a week's sport. In bed by eight, out again from eleven till three; fine when we started, but came on as black as a hedge before the tide flowed.

28th.—Out from eight in the morning till a four o'clock dinner, and never discharged a gun. So many gentlemen poppers were flying about the harbour that not a bird could pitch, and the geese were absolutely banished from the place.

29th.—Captain Ward took a shot with a barrel of my gun; and bagged 3 of the white-fronted laughing geese out of 7 that dropped in off the quay, and I afterwards fired a barrel, a very long shot, and got 1 laughing goose.

30th.—Read came in with 1 wigeon, after a hard night's mud crawling, and I was out all the afternoon, and found the coast as free from fowl as at midsummer. Read crawled till twelve, and bagged 4 wigeon.

February 1st.—Out from dawn till dusk, and brought in but 2 scaup ducks, though it froze so hard we had to beat through ice for above a quarter of a mile before we could get under way. Dead tides; and the geese so wild that 500 yards was the very nearest we could get to them. Never on record was the sport so bad in a frost.

2nd.—The coldest day within the memory of any man in Keyhaven. A gale from the north-east that no boat could 'row on end' in, and such a severely nipping frost that whatever was dipped in water became petrified in a few seconds. I walked out with the musket and sprung a mallard, and my hand was so benumbed that I absolutely lost the shot, from not having power in my thumb to cock the gun. Read went off by day crawling, and he and his punt came home looking like a set-out of glass, and himself half frozen: he got only 1 dun diver and 1 wigeon out of 5 that he stopped and could not follow. Never, never did I witness such a bitterly severe day.

3rd.—The tightest snap on record. All Keyhaven harbour petrified in one night to one solid body of ice. Wind enough to bite a man's nose off. Out at dawn: four hours cutting our way through a mile of ice, and obliged to leave gunboat and all at Pennington, or be made prisoners at home till the weather changes. Fought through it like Britons, and floored 30 wigeon and 1 goose in the 3 shots we had. Pumps, pots de chambre, basins, beer, and every liquid but spirit turned into a solid body of ice.

4th.—Up at five. Tramped over the marshes to Pennington, where I had left the punt, laden like donkeys with traps and rations for the day; but the wind came on so violent that we were obliged to fight back through a heavy sea, and 'knock off' for the day before we pulled a trigger.

5th.—7 burrough ducks and 3 scaup ducks. A fine day, and birds so driven about that no good shot was to be had, insomuch that my best shot was at 4 burrough ducks, all of which I killed. Dreadfully hard labour to tramp to Pennington, and thrash for an hour through blocks of ice before we could get out or come in again.

6th.—Got but one shot all day, and bagged 7 brent geese and 5 wigeon.

7th.—Sunday. A complete break up of this unparalleled frost, with a whole day's wind and rain from the westward.

8th.—Keyhaven was itself again. No longer Iceland or Greenland, and we had the comfort of getting our craft home and ending our miserable tramps over Pennington marshes and ditches, to get afloat, and then to cut our way through ice. Such was the wind and rain that by this day it had cleared the whole harbour.

A good tide at night. Out from ten till two. Came on a fog with wind and rain, which scattered the birds. Fired one shot at random, and got but 2 wigeon.

9th.—Discharged but one barrel all day, and that with Eley's cartridge, which went like a ball (at about 250 yards) through 1 brent goose. A fine moonlight night; but the wigeon were all scattered like blackbirds and thrushes, insomuch that I, who was out from half past ten till two, got but 2 wigeon, and Read, who mud-launched from three till seven, got but 1 wigeon. Birds all in threes and twos, nothing to shoot at.

10th.—Got but one long shot all day, and just saved my blank by getting 1 brent goose. Out from 11 till 3: made one pretty little shot soon after midnight, having killed nearly all the company; got 16 wigeon and 1 curlew.

11th.—White frost, followed, as usual, by a butterfly day. Every dandy afloat, and of course no one could get a shot, so came home to do some jobs and get some rest. Out from eleven till four. A fine shot spoiled for me by a wretched mud launcher, blew off at random in self-defence and got 2 wigeon.

12*th.*—Birds attacked again by all descriptions of gunners. Nothing killed by any.

13*th.*—Read shot 2 wigeon after a whole night's mud launching, and I 2 brent geese after a whole day afloat.

15*th.*—Out from five in the morning till seven in the evening, and never got but two shots. The first I knocked down 2 brent geese (at near 300 yards), and the other was at 3 scaup ducks, all of which I brought home.

16*th.*—Out all day, and just saved a blank by making a good shot at 6 geese. A fine day, and the whole coast literally besieged with boats and punts, and, as far as I could learn, no one got so much as a bird.

17*th.*—Read had three successive blank nights crawling on the mud.

18*th.*—Our punt leaked with the unmerciful usage of this unprecedented winter, so that we were busy to-day overhauling and caulking. We dropped out for an hour or two in the afternoon, and blew off one barrel at the geese as they flew past. Killed two of them in handsome style. They were taken up before our faces by a yacht in a sea that we could not weather, and, to justify this, some fellow blew off a bullet from a popgun, which was much nearer killing us than any of the geese.

19*th.*—Read got in the night 7 wigeon mud crawling, and I made one very long shot at the geese. I fired but one barrel, expecting nothing, when down came 6 brent geese, and I had the luck to get every bird of them.

20*th.*—Read had a blank night's crawl. I got 5 brent geese and 1 wigeon out on tide by blowing away large shot at long distances. Afloat from eight till twelve: fine starlight and hard white frost: never heard but a few stray single wigeon: and not a gun was fired the whole time we were out. Symptoms of the sport being nearly over.

22*nd.*—20 brent geese; 12 one shot, and 8 the other. No

JAMES READ, WITH HIS NEW LAUNCHING-PUNT; HAWKER'S CREEK; & YARMOUTH.

Drawn by C. Varley. Engraved by H. Adlard.

London: Longman, Brown, Green & Longmans. 1844.

dandies or gunners out to-day. This shows what we can do when all is quiet.

23rd.—A very thick fog, and of course nothing to be done afloat. Out for a few hours, but the geese would not sit a minute together.

24th.—Ash Wednesday. A combination of such weather as one could hardly think possible to exist, viz. a strong breeze of wind and drizzling rain, with a fog so thick that nothing could be discerned more than 200 yards distant. The very worst weather of all for shooting afloat.

25th.—A very heavy fog again, but it cleared away about noon. We then went out, and came in with 10 brent geese; but they were so wild I had to fire 3 shots to get this number.

26th.—A happy mixture of wind, rain, and thick fog all day. A few geese came close to Keyhaven; put off to them, but in this weather, of course, could do nothing.

March 1st.—Made a successful finish of a bad season. Saw nothing all day but a small company of geese: got, in all, 7 brent geese. Coming home about six, I closed the evening and the season by killing a single old gander as dead as a hammer at 152 paces. Never was a season closed by a more splendid shot.

2nd.—Left Keyhaven this morning, and arrived at Longparish this afternoon.

4th.—Tried my 'invisible approach' (for the first time) at the few fowl that were left at Lord Portsmouth's. I got up to them with ease, and floored the whole of the lot I shot at, viz. 6 wigeon, 2 teal, 1 duck, and 1 mallard. A successful close of the wild-fowl season.

Game killed in the season: 122 partridges, 14 hares, 1 landrail, 1 quail, 3 pheasants, 3 rabbits, 38 snipes. Total 182 head.

N.B.—The worst list for many years, owing to the unprecedented scarcity of all game.

Wild fowl killed in the season: 11 ducks and mallards, 149 wigeon, 2 teal, 21 scaup ducks, 2 dunbirds, 3 golden-eyes, 2 pintails, 1 tufted duck, 1 scoter, 12 burrough ducks, 154 brent geese, 20 white-fronted geese, 9 hoopers, 29 plovers. Total, 416 head.

Grand total of game and fowl, 598—a sorry season, compared with the last.

April 3rd.—It was so cold to-day that cartloads of ice were brought in.

8th.—It was so hot by day as to be quite overpowering; and so warm at night that one could scarcely bear any clothes, beyond the sheet, over one in bed. This specimen of our climate is worthy of record.

22nd.—Routed up at two in the morning, with some rascally thieves that were caught dragging our river, and before thirteen hours had elapsed I had all their business executed, and the two miscreants in full march for Winchester.

June 28th.—London. The printing and completing of my book made it necessary for me to remain in town. Went down to see my good patron, the *ci-devant* Duke of Clarence, proclaimed King by Joe Hawker, the Richmond Herald, the latter in a dress like the knave of spades and on a piebald horse; and in my life I never was in such a long-continued and frightful mob.

July.—Busy all this month, preparing a sixth edition of my work on Guns and Shooting.[1]

August 17th.—Ended all my book labours, and this day launched the sixth edition of my sporting work, dedicated by permission to his Majesty William the Fourth, our most excellent King.

[1] 'Instructions to Young Sportsmen.'

CHAPTER XXIII

1830

September 1*st.*—Longparish. Wonderful success, all things considered, and with such a scarcity of birds as even surpassed that of last year. I went out with two wild borrowed dogs, at half-past nine, came home to dinner at half-past one, and then went out again. I bagged altogether 34 partridges, and mostly all fine full-grown young birds. On the whole, I think this one of the luckiest days on my list. No one else did anything worth speaking of, and the scarcity of game was a general complaint.

2*nd.*—Despatched for his Majesty the finest 16 young birds I ever saw together. Having cleared the larder for presents, I was obliged to take a few hours' shooting this evening, and in these few hours I had the luck to get 10 partridges.

6*th.* My new puppies came home, and I bought also a nice little setter. Went out to try them in a tremendously rough day, and with showers that wet us to the skin, and, in spite of all, I got 20 partridges and 1 quail. I never missed, and made five brilliant double shots. This, considering the weather and the scarcity, is one of the best days on my record.

11*th.*—A wonderful day, considering the scarcity. I bagged 22 partridges and 2 quails. What I killed this day were mostly all old birds, and I did something extraordinary, which was, to kill three times successively a pair of old birds with one barrel, by contriving to catch them like a billiard cannon as they crossed each other.

13*th.*—Was out from ten till six, over the Bullington and Furgo country, and literally never saw but 26 birds the whole day ; and thought myself well off to get what I did, 7 partridges and 1 quail.

16*th.*—Lord Poulett came, and we went to a roaring jollification at Sir John Pollen's.

17*th.*—Went to get some bait, and caught 365 minnows at one throw, and 406 the other.

18*th.*—Rode out with Lord Poulett, in a quiet way, till near four, and never got but one shot. Then galloped off by myself in right earnest, and in half an hour killed 8 birds and 1 heron. This shows the difference between the twaddle and the vigorous in shooting.

Game killed in September 1830: 154 partridges, 7 quails, 1 landrail, 5 hares. Total, 167 head.

Most admirable sport considering that the scarcity has even far exceeded that of last year, and I had not one good dog. I have beat everyone, and exceeded last year by one-third.

October 1*st.*—A wonderfully lucky Friday, and the greatest day I have made on my own little inclosures for many years. I bagged 4 pheasants (all I saw, and all superb large cocks) and 6 hares, besides a 7th caught by the dogs, and all without missing a shot, though several of them were at very long distances.

4*th.*—Went out for a few hours after breakfast, previously to going over to Mr. Fleming's, to meet Moscheles, and hear some delightful pianoforte playing, in order to try a new gun stock, botched up in the country, and rectified per Lancaster. Never set sight on a pheasant, but bagged all I levelled at, viz. 3 partridges, 2 hares, and 2 rabbits.

6*th.*—A curious circumstance occurred. Charles Castleman (who accompanies me shooting) put up an old hare in some thick rushes, into which he jumped upon her, broke her hind leg, and instantly seized her. This is the first time in my life that ever I heard of a man catching an old hare after she was up, and without snares.

18*th*.—Out all day to try hedgerows for hares, fields for birds, and river for snipes, and in the whole blessed day never set eyes on but two living creatures in the way of game, 1 partridge and 1 hare, both of which I pocketed, as the taking out of a game bag now would be ridiculous. Never was this country so fairly cleared as at present. What with the unprecedented scarcity, the rivalry of shooters, and the march of intellect in poaching, the game is all but extirpated.

November 9*th*.—London. The grand procession of the King and ministers going in state to the Lord Mayor's dinner was this day to have taken place, and we had excellent seats. But, in consequence of an alarming letter to the Duke of Wellington, the procession and all the unprecedented pageant was put an end to, 8,000 troops assembled round the metropolis, and everyone intimidated with the threatening horrors of revolution. And what did it all prove to be? A gang of discontented pickpockets worked up for a row by shoeblack Hunt and printer's devil Carlisle, who, after inflaming them, of course sneaked off to their beds of safety, and the affair ended in all these mighty revolutionists getting a confounded good thrashing from about 500 police, by whom those who were not active enough to escape got 'had up' and well trounced by the magistrates.

14*th*.—Longparish. Much more serious cause for alarm than the rows of the 9th. A house on fire so close to our back premises that we were on the very point of collecting what we most valued for removal. The house was burning to the ground, and most awful was the sight when I was roused from my bed about six. But providentially, and thanks to the vigilance and exertions of the police, the fire was extinguished before it caught the haylofts at the back of our house, or Lord knows what might have been the consequence.

20*th*.—Alarming riots in Hampshire, conflagration of many

of our near neighbours' property, and 300 men surrounding the farmers at Longparish.

22nd.—Longparish quiet again, in consequence of the farmers having all agreed to an increased allowance to the poor.

23rd.—Dreadful accounts from Andover, Winchester, and many other parts of Hampshire and the adjoining counties.

December 1st.—Most horrid accounts from various counties, but things looking better in Hampshire owing to the energy of the magistrates and the Duke of Wellington's rapid movements for the county arrangements.

4th.—Longparish. A half-year of public and private events such as I never had to experience before, and may never have to experience again. Death of George IV. Accession of King William. Revolution in France. Resignation of the Wellington Ministry. Riots and incendiaries all over England. Warlike preparations all over the Continent, and revolution in Belgium. A house burned down within a few yards of my town residence, and a narrow escape with my two daughters from a lamentable crush of persons, by a coach run away with on the pavement at the corner of Regent Street. In short, so many events, both public and private, that it would require more time than I can devote to a memorandum book to recollect and enumerate them all.

6th.—All the rioters dispersed, and the country perfectly quiet.

30th.—Keyhaven. Tremendous wind from south-east, only good for mud launching. Read brought in at daylight 9 wigeon and 1 goose; and in the evening 6 wigeon and 1 pintail. I got only 3 wigeon and 1 scaup duck. Westerly wind, hurricane, and rain all night.

31st.—Weathered it from eleven till three, and got 6 wigeon, 1 mallard, and 5 coots. Towards evening the gale abated, and the wind got more in to the northward. Read mud-launched from dusk till eleven, and then went afloat with me from eleven till two, but the late westerly gale had swept off all the birds to the eastward of our country.

1831

January 1*st*.—Read launched from three till seven this morning, but never found a bird. I went afloat from eleven till three in the day, and got 2 wigeon, 4 dunbirds, 1 teal, 1 laughing goose (the first seen this year), and 3 coots.

N.B.—I began the new year with a pretty little shot. I fired, under sail, a barrel at 5 dunbirds and 1 teal, and turned up all quite dead. A dunbird at Keyhaven is a *rara avis*.

4*th*.—Out, by moonlight, from two till near six; never found a bird; and Read, who launched both before and after I was out, found nothing. This is in some degree to be accounted for by two red-hot gunners having come to lodge under our noses, and being eternally mud launching. Out from two in the afternoon till dark, and never had the chance for a shot.

5*th*.—Read came in this morning, after a night's mud crawling, with 3 wigeon; and I was out all day, and all but coming home empty, when I got a long shot at a very large company and bagged 10 wigeon. A fine easterly wind set in this afternoon.

6*th*.—Read was out all night and got nothing, and I out all to-day and never pulled a trigger.

7*th*.—Read had another blank night owing to divers bad luck. I was out all day (though so poorly I could hardly sit up in the boat), and got 2 mallards and 4 golden-eyes (7 of which I fired at and stopped 6 at about 120 yards).

8*th*.—Read another blank night mud launching, and I another blank day on the water. We went off at daylight in such a cruel white frost that we had to cut our way to Hurst through one continued channel of ice, which had all frozen in one night, and to get through which took us between two and three hours ; and because the frost was a blackguard white one, not a bird was to be seen.

10*th.*—The white frost was of course too suddenly severe to last ; and yesterday was a warm damp day with south-west wind ; but to-day the weather flew into the north-east, with rain and a strong breeze. Neither Read nor I had the chance to get a shot, but the amendment of weather now gives us better hopes.

11*th.*—Read a blank night and morning mud crawling. A tremendous north-easter, and no water, so I could not get afloat to-day. Stepped into the marshlands with the popgun, and got 1 wild duck and 2 snipes.

12*th.*—Read, after a night's mud crawling, brought in 8 wigeon, but not a chance for me all to-day.

13*th.*—Read a blank night, and I just saved a blank day by getting 1 brent goose. The most execrable season on record, and all the gunners nearly starved for a livelihood, though the weather has not been so bad for gunning as in many far more abundant seasons than this.

14th.—Read a blank night's mud crawling, and I a blank day afloat ; a fine easterly wind too.

15*th.*—Read another blank night, and I just saved a blank day by knocking down 1 brent goose with a mould-shot cartridge at about 300 yards. Never, never was there such a miserable season for all kinds of shooting.

18*th.*—Not a chance to be got. The vagabond mud crawlers have totally annihilated our once fine country.

28*th.*—Out at night from nine till half-past one, and never heard or saw a bird, though a cold, frosty night, with a full moon and excellent tides.

Read has had some fair luck mud launching, having killed in the week 36 wigeon.

29*th.*—Out all day and all night and never found a wigeon ; got nothing but one golden-eye ; then Read crawled till twelve and got 5 wigeon.

31st.—Read brought in 3 wigeon after a crawling bout from two till five this morning. I was afloat all day, and never pulled a trigger. A precious pretty gunning season!

February 1st.—A tremendous gale of wind all day; harbour a complete sea; towards evening, at the ground ebb, I dropped off, and made a shot into some 100 geese.

2nd.—A tremendous hurricane, with an overwhelming fall of snow, and with the wind south-west. An extraordinary influx of fieldfares, not less than 20,000 dispersed round Keyhaven and Westhover, and so tame that you might have kept firing from morning till night, though I found it impossible to get more than 5 at a shot. After killing as many as I wanted, without even moving from the hedge I took shelter under, I weathered the storm and got 4 golden plover, besides one I wounded out of a flock, and which I followed for miles through this unmerciful weather. Went afloat in the evening and got 3 brent geese, and had not my first barrel (which had large shot) missed fire I should have had a fine bag. It was quite laughable, when the storm ceased this afternoon, to see and hear the levy *en masse* of tag-rag popgunners blazing away at the fieldfares. The whole country for a mile round was in one incessant state of siege.[1]

4th.—An absolute hurricane. Walked out all day with my gun, and was almost blown off my legs. Never set eyes on one living creature to shoot at.

5th.—As it blew too fresh to go afloat, I sallied forth to near Lymington, where I had heard of 3 cocks having been seen by the hare hunters last week, and after a long search I had the good luck to bag them all.

7th.—A heavy westerly wind. Afloat from six till ten this

[1] The next day, when the snow had changed to rain, all this enormous army of fieldfares had completely left the country. It was somewhat singular that, although these fieldfares were tamer than sparrows, yet they were fat as butter, and I never ate any more delicious birds in my life. I had about four dozen in all, and might have had a sack full if I had made a business of it. This is an occurrence that may happen once in a century.

morning; saw nothing but about 10 stray geese in a heavy sea. Read mud crawling eternally all nights, as usual, and not a chance to get a bird. Patience exhausted, and a precipitate 'bolt' decided on, so began to pack up this afternoon.

14*th.*—Longparish. Dreadful conflagration on our premises. Roused from my bed at half-past three this morning with the horrible sight of our premises on fire, as had been previously threatened by an incendiary letter. I had intended to start for London at six, which this catastrophe, of course, prevented; and most providential was it that I had not gone, for, had it not been for my incessant exertions with about six hundred people and plans of arrangement for the engines, heaven only knows what would have been the end of this. I was engaged stimulating and keeping in line to the river, after all our pumps were exhausted, several hundred people (and many most unwilling ones)[1] from half-past five in the morning till the afternoon; and then working and running about till ready to drop till near four, when the fire was got down. Among the buildings consumed were broiled to ashes the whole of our poultry, the barn and all the corn in it, and the largest and finest oat rick in the country. The coachhouse and stables were on fire, but saved by timely exertion. I was in one incessant bustle till near twelve at night, when I went to bed quite exhausted, and had no sooner fallen asleep than I was unnecessarily alarmed by another cry of 'The fire again!' which, on my getting up, proved to be another fire at a distance, which, owing to the extreme darkness of the night, appeared at first like a conflagration of our further premises.

15*th.*—In one incessant bother with business and lookers-

[1] N.B.—The two principal inventions of mine, which, I may safely say, saved 800*l.* worth of property, as the other ricks &c. ran parallel within 8 feet of the property consumed, was the drawing from the fire to the river, about 280 yards, a mob of people that would not leave the exhibition, which they came to stare at, by means of placing one cartload of beer at the river, as a counter attraction, and another batch of beer in the centre; and then combining the two engines so as for one to play into the other; and by thus prolonging the alignment only was it possible that I could continue to supply water to save my remaining property.

on concerning the destroyed premises. My night's rest spoiled again by an alarm of the watch, who had heard thieves whistle about the remaining ricks.

16th.—Harassed all day with the arrangement for, and trial of, a woman before the magistrates, on suspicion of writing the incendiary letter. She was committed to gaol for trial at the assizes. Up till twelve arranging the watch, &c. Nothing can exceed the state of apprehension everyone is in at this crisis.

17th.—Busy again all day concerning the late events, and everyone in the village in a perpetual state of jeopardy. Fellows heard about last night, though not on our premises.

22nd.—Have been now a clear week in perpetual jeopardy, and on constant watch with a gun in my hands for either incendiaries or thieves who have been heard about in several places.

Game &c. killed up to February 11th, 1831: Game—173 partridges, 7 quails, 1 landrail, 17 hares, 5 rabbits, 10 pheasants, 2 woodcocks, 23 snipes. Total, 238. Wild fowl—11 ducks and mallards, 3 teal, 103 wigeon, 12 curres, 9 geese, 2 pintails, 1 scoter, 4 golden plover. Total, 145. Grand total, 383 head.

One of the worst game seasons on record. The worst wild-fowl season on record, and the most lamentable season on record for private as well as public affairs.

Concatenation of events in the past season: Alarming state of the country, with tremendous riots and incendiarisms. An alarming fire after midnight within a few yards of us, when at our house in Upper Gloucester Place. Witnessed the horrible accident in Oxford Street. L—— seized with a paralytic stroke. My house in Boston Street broken open and near being sacked by robbers. Awful conflagration of my premises at Longparish through a diabolical incendiary. The worst shooting season in the memory of the oldest man living. The whole Continent in a state of fermentation, and nothing but confusion and discord at home. These are merely a few of the memorandums that I can immediately recollect. So much for the times up to the March quarter, which let us hope to God will commence their improvement.

April 19th.—A sharp frost and a north-easterly gale, which I had to face on the box all the way to London this day; and I am sure I owe my escape from ague to a hot bath, rhubarb, and soda, by which I cheated the doctor out of at least 10*l.* by finding myself all right the next morning.

May 12th.—Longparish. Was earnestly solicited to attack an unprecedented breed of perchers in the Bullington rookery; but as business prevented my getting off till near one in the day, and I lost two hours more in having to return to Longparish for a relay of three more guns and a larger freight of ammunition, I had in all but about 5½ hours' actual shooting, in which time I got and distributed to the poor the enormous number of 216 young rooks, and at least 100 more were picked up by outskirters and other parties.

13*th.*—After being at Andover all this morning, I slipped on my shooting jacket about six in the evening, and before dark got 6 dozen and 5 more rooks in the little rookery at Longparish. Although I hate such tame sport, yet the novelty of killing so many, and the pleasure of gratifying the poor clods with a 'blow out,' induced me to sacrifice my head and shoulders for once in a way. I think I shall have the bang of guns and caw of rooks in my ears for a week to come.

14*th.*—A north-easterly gale of wind with thick ice, and much damage done to all vegetation. A hard winter on the 14th of May.

26*th.*—I caught such a cold that this is the first day I have been about since I came up. I had an eye somewhat injured by the detonating gas from my gun, and my cold flew to it, and so inflamed it that I was advised to apply leeches, and these so swelled my face that I was laid up quite blind for several days and obliged to keep my bed, and in short a very great sufferer. Now, thank God, I begin to recover my sight again, and the first use I made of it was to go to London to see Lancaster and suggest an appendage to the cocks of all my guns, in order to prevent, in future, the escape of detonating gas.

June 20th.—London. Having lodged the money for my son's commission and done divers business, I heard with ecstasy the wonderful Paganini.

30*th.*—Keyhaven. Took a sail to the Needle rocks this afternoon, and brought home 30 willocks, which is the best sport of any one gun here this season. The birds had been driven all day by four other parties and were very wild, and the boy that I sent aloft to drive them out of the cliffs turned frightened, and would not go near enough to throw over the bell and string. I had therefore every disadvantage, or should have got perhaps treble the number I did.

August 1st.—Started for town at six this morning, but the grand uproar of the King opening London Bridge suspended all business.

9*th.*—Peter was gazetted.

13*th.*—Mary and Sophy arrived in town, to resume their studies at school.

16*th.*—Peter arrived, bag and baggage, from Dieppe about seven o'clock this evening.

24*th.*—Peter was presented this day to the King at the Levee (by me).

25*th.*—Peter left town for Longparish, and I attended Lord Hill's Levee to return thanks for his commission.

31*st.*—After having been very unwell with the influenza, that has, more or less, affected everyone this season, I this day went down to Longparish for a few days' change of air, but in poor trim for what little shooting there is.

CHAPTER XXIV

1831

September 1st.—An incessant pour of rain from daylight till dark, which put a stop to all shooting, and which I had reason to exult at, as I was so unwell all night that a day's hard fagging might have laid me up with a fever.

2nd.—A stormy day, with thunder and lightning and tremendous showers. Went out at eleven with Peter, and my bag was ten brace of birds, which, though the worst first day on record, was vastly well for the little we found, as wild as the birds were. So little as I got, I did as well as it was possible for anyone to have done.

3rd.—14 partridges, all I shot at. Birds scarce and extremely wild.

4th.—Sunday. Was at Hurstbourne Park and Andover, where, as far as I could learn, all the other sportsmen were far more unsuccessful than ourselves, so the complaint of scarcity appears general in this country.

Mr. Fellowes informed me that the sport has been so bad that instead of sending off baskets of game, as usual, he was sending off letters to his friends, to say that none was likely to be got this season, beyond the immediate consumption of the house, and that an excellent sportsman had been sent out the whole day, and only get seven shots on Lord Portsmouth's best property.

6th.—Wet again. Shot after twelve o'clock, and bagged 14 partridges, having missed nothing, either far or near.

During my stay at Longparish, I have killed just 21 brace of birds without once missing a shot.

N.B.—On the evening of the 6th, the day before my return to town, a man of our village just come home from Winchester gaol, confessed to me that he had in the spring destroyed above a hundred partridges' nests, and another man had feasted on above 200 partridges' eggs, besides destroying others, and all this they confessed was done to spite the lord of the manor, who is universally disliked. Thus all our shooting is to be annihilated for the sake of spiting one individual.

7th.—Returned to London, heartily glad to get away from such dull sport, and to prepare for our campaign with the militia at Winchester. All London in an uproar, preparing for the coronation to-morrow. An incessant rattle of carriages all night.

8th.—Up at five, in order to get to the United Service Club before any dangerous crowd was likely to be assembled. Doors opened at eight, and the procession passed about a quarter before eleven, and returned again at a few minutes past four. I never saw so many people together in my life, nor did I ever before witness so grand a cortège. The state carriage surpassed description for its happy combination of profuse splendour and chaste good taste. I never before saw a profusion of excessive finery without some approach to what is tawdry. But here everything was good taste in the extreme. What with the time occupied in seeing the lions, durance vile, and working home through mobs, we could not get home till past six, and then, after a late dinner, we had a few shillings' worth of Jarvey to see the illuminations.

9th.—Busy all the morning with parchments and other troublesome concerns. I have not had a day's leisure, or a comfortable night's rest, for these three weeks.

October 11th.—Winchester. My regiment completed their twenty-eight days' training. The performance of our regiment was the astonishment of everyone, and particularly the military, as, with a very few exceptions, the men were all from the ploughtail, and our officers entire beginners, except nine, who were all, more or less, on the sick list, so that I was so incessantly occupied that I had scarcely time to get even sustenance. This, however, arose chiefly from the lamentable waste of time at mess, as is the custom in all trainings, and what with jollifications, invitations, balls, plays, shoals of visitors, drunkards, guttlers, and idlers, we were in one eternal scene of confusion and interruption. The town was for the twenty-eight days in a bustle like a field of battle. The Duke of Wellington had finally settled to review us and the 90th Regiment, and to dine with us, but the 90th received a sudden and mysterious route for Scotland, and the Duke was prevented from leaving London. So that the climax of our hard labour was a finishing field day to astonish the natives. I had the command for the last week, while Lord Rodney was absent on the Reform Bill, and was literally obliged to go through it with a plaster on my chest and suffering from severe cold.

12*th.*—London. The whole town running wild about the rejection of the Reform Bill. Many noblemen assaulted, and nothing thought of but politics.

November 7th.—Received a most polite note from the Chancellor of the Exchequer, Lord Althorp, in approbation of my publication and suggestions for improvement in the Game Laws.

8*th.*—Received a letter from my son Peter to inform me of his arrival with his regiment, the 74th, at Templemore, in Ireland, on the 1st.

December 8th.—Went out the only dry hour in the day, with a cold and sore throat, to try for a snipe for a sick friend; got 3 jack snipes, all I sprung, saw, or heard of.

9*th.*—More frightful fires again, lighting the atmosphere before our windows; one last night again at Sir Henry Wilson's large farm; another two nights before at Bourne, and another at Abbot's Ann. How truly shocking is this renewal of the hellish system of last year! The night of the 12th was the most terrific I ever remember here; a hurricane, a deluge of rain, and tremendous thunder and lightning nearly all night.

14th.—I crawled out for the first time since my illness, and with a black dose to work off in the field, bagged 2 pheasants, 1 jack snipe, and 1 hare, all I saw.

1832

January 2nd.—Keyhaven. 5 wigeon, 1 dunbird, 1 golden-eye, and 1 coot. Out from daybreak till dark, and began the new year well, by firing a long shot at 2 wigeon and bagging them both, and finished the first day of it well by shooting at a dunbird and a golden-eye flying with the big gun, and bagging both of them at one shot. A fine easterly breeze, and a fair show of fowl off at sea.

3rd.—At it again all day, after a candlelight breakfast; got 7 wigeon and 2 coots, besides some cripples lost. Had extremely bad luck in getting our shots spoiled by continual poppers and sail boats.

4th.—South-west wind again; out all day; got but one little shot; picked up 3 plover and 24 dunlins, nearly all the company.

5th.—4 wigeon and 1 brent goose.

6th.—8 wigeon, 3 brent geese, and 1 pintail. Killed two of the geese with one shot, and all the rest with the other.

7th.—Read made one little shot at last, after crawling on the mud every night since I came here, and brought in 6 wigeon. I was out fourteen hours and killed but 2 ducks; lost a splendid chance at a large flock of wigeon close to me, owing to both my cartridges 'balling,' and besides this I got in the worst mess I ever was in by shipping a hollow sea.

9th.—A wet day and a westerly wind; weathered it afloat in the afternoon, and just saved my blank by knocking down a single wigeon with the popgun.

10*th.*—Wet all the forenoon. Went into Lymington, and heard universal complaints about there not being a wild fowl to be bought. Went afloat all the evening, and again just saved my blank by getting 1 golden-eye. Strong westerly wind and thick rain; a woeful time for sending all the birds out of this country.

11*th.*—More rotten weather; a regular emetic of rain, with a brutal west wind; gaol birds all day, with damp, smoke, and all other nastiness. Read crawled on the mud, and got 4 wigeon in the previous night, but we could not attempt to go out to-day.

12*th.*—It having held up a little in the night, Read had his nocturnal crawl, and came in this morning with 4 wigeon.

13*th.*—Read had some luck in crawling at last; he came in this morning with 19 wigeon, 15 of which he got at one shot. I was afloat all day, but never saw a chance.

14*th.*—Read had a whole night's crawl for nothing. Out myself from morning till night, and got but 1 wigeon.

16*th.*—Read brought in, by crawling from one till six this morning, 6 wigeon. We were then out from daybreak till five, and got but 1 wigeon and 1 goose, all we shot at. A fog, and consequently nothing to be done. Read crawling all night as usual, but got nothing.

17*th.*—5 geese; the only shot I got, though afloat all day. Out from eight till two in the night, but the harbour was, as is usual at full moon, cleared of fowl by the shore poppers before the tide made over the mud.

18*th.*—Had a good shot at last. After Parson Harrison's gunner (old Head) had been fumbling after the geese for about three hours, without being able to get within a quarter of a mile of them, and had given them up in despair, I caught them just at the ground ebb, and blew both barrels into them with mould shot, and although at an immense distance (Read thought near 200 yards) I knocked down, short on the spot,

28.[1] I was left in a state of jeopardy on the mud after this shot; my dog being nearly drowned was of no use to me, and I actually lost some dead birds that I had in my hand, and I should have lost more had I not taken off my neck-cloth to tie them together with. Read had much trouble to save the punt from being left aground, and several pirates availed themselves of our distress to take away birds, except Sam Singer, who kindly assisted us. The best shot this that I have ever known to be made in our Lymington district.

30*th.*—Read was out from two till daylight, and never got a chance to shoot; and I was out from daylight till three in the afternoon, and never pulled a trigger. A dead tide and no birds.

31*st.*—A precise repetition of what we did yesterday.

February 1*st.*—New moon, a high tide, and a southerly wind. Read had another blank night, but I, by firing long shots, saved my blank to-day by getting 2 geese and 2 curlews.

2*nd.*—Read had another blank night. Not a wigeon in the country; the rain and squalls have banished the wigeon from the coast. I was out all day and was coming home empty, when I got 2 golden-eyes.

3*rd.*—Afloat all day, and got but one shot at a few straggling geese (all I saw), and just saved my blank with 1 brent goose. Not a bird to be heard of in all the markets; a westerly wind, and the season dying away to a dull finale.

6*th.*—Busy all day putting away the shooting gear &c. preparative to quitting Keyhaven.

9*th.*—Longparish. Took my 'invisible approach' up to Lord Portsmouth's to try and get a couple of tufted ducks

[1] Making 40 wild geese at one shot, as was afterwards proved by 12 more being picked up.

N.B.—I saved the dog from drowning by tying up 12 geese with my neckerchief to make an island for him; and to prevent its floating off, I stuck the pole into the mud. My patten string broke, and I was in a miserable predicament, though in the midst of a glorious massacre.

for Mr. Fellowes. Bagged 5 tufted ducks and 2 dunbirds, besides losing 2 more tufted ducks and another dunbird.

N.B.—I first shot at 10 fowl and stopped 7. The other 3 then pitched, and I wheeled up to them and bagged them all. These were all the birds there, except a few wild ducks that flew off before I began operations.

13*th*.—A cold easterly wind, and weather that would be worth a guinea an hour at Keyhaven. Was there ever anything so truly provoking?

15*th*.—Alresford. Up at five, though not in bed till one, with the hope of a little finishing shot here. The only fowl on the lake were 6 tufted ducks, which swam in good shot of my ambush, and I was only waiting to let them swim altogether (which they were just about to do) when 2 great swans flew in and drove them off; so I finished with a blank morning, and took my leave of Alresford pond. My system here was enough to wear me to death, having a large party in the house to play the amiable with till after midnight, and then to steal out of the mansion and walk a mile in the dark every morning, as the fowl seldom remained on the pond when the people began to pass for their daily work, particularly as there were then occasional flight poppers near the high road. No lord chancellor was more in need of a little quiet repose than I am. Left Alresford this day at twelve o'clock by the 'Age' coach, and arrived (by the new route viâ Guildford &c.) in London about half-past six, where I found all well.

N.B.—The very night I arrived in London there set in the most beautiful hard frost, with a continuance of the north-east wind. Nothing can exceed my bad luck in weather. It always happens that I am never to be at Keyhaven in the only weather that suits that place.

Game &c. killed up to February 15th: 56 partridges, 1 hare, 1 rabbit, 2 pheasants, 13 snipes. Total, 73 head game. 95 wigeon, 38 geese, 5 curres, 3 dunbirds, 10 tufted ducks, 1 pintail, 7 ducks, 3 teal. Total, 162 head wild fowl. Grand total, 235 head only.

N.B.—Owing to the almost annihilation of game, I never had so little shooting at Longparish for many years.

23rd.—Got a letter from Read, by which I heard that, notwithstanding the beautiful frost we have had almost ever since my departure from Keyhaven, there has been no fowl worth naming at that place. This was very satisfactory to me, who had so regretted having left the coast at the only time the weather had suited all this winter.

March.—Busy all this month about remanufacturing and again bringing out my 'patent hand-moulds' for the piano.

29th.—Went to the funeral of Clementi at Westminster Abbey.

May 1st.—The trouble, vexation, and business that I have had pressed on me all at once, through the whole of the past month, would have driven many people crazy. What with people breaking in my debt, tenants not paying, my landlord absconding, trouble and sickness in my various establishments, incessant bother with all the workmen about my patent, which is now out, books to correct for press, frequently twelve miles a day to go besides, &c., I have often gone without a dinner, and been so exhausted and worried as scarcely to close my eyes the whole night.

June 20th.—Left Keyhaven at half-past four, and arrived in London at half-past four in the afternoon, and then had to proceed with much troublesome business relative to the delay of solicitor about lease, &c., and to prepare for removing into another town house.

24th.—Sunday. Driven about all yesterday like a mad dog, with beginning to move house, and the negotiation all in confusion owing to the delay of the gentleman's lawyer. Tormented with troublesome concerns about Longparish, where I ought to be, and unpleasant accounts from Keyhaven, where I ought to be also. In pain morning, noon and night with my wound, which I had not felt for sixteen years before, and on the eve of moving all my furniture to-morrow, and summoned to sit on a horrible special jury that very day. When am I to have no more than man's average lot of botheration?

25*th*.—Got up in cruel pain, and in the midst of house moving (which had been going on ever since five o'clock), and had to be down at Westminster Hall by nine; kept there in constant pain till near seven in the evening, and I was so ill that during a part of two other trials I was obliged to go out and lie on the floor. On my arrival home I threw myself on the only sofa then left in the house; and, by way of refreshment (as I of course had to starve the whole time), I received a perplexing letter about the Longparish concerns, a melancholy letter from Keyhaven, and a bothering communication with a gun about some new-fangled patent, a letter from Mr. Roberts about the insurance and other things of the new house; one from Coutts about the sale of stock, and by which I had not given the order precisely as it should have been. Shepherd wanting me for the examination and discharge of some bills he had paid on the old house, and various orders relative to discharging all rates, taxes &c. of the new one. Wanted for many other trifles; and, in short, worried to death, I sat down to a morsel that I had no stomach to eat, and then, after having many little items to do, I followed the furniture and my family to No. 2 Dorset Place, where I went to bed, and what with pain and bother, scarcely closed my eyes the whole night; and at half-past seven on the 26th had to get up and be off again for Westminster Hall, where I was luckily soon dismissed, and paid a guinea as foreman of the special jury. I then took the said guinea to Brodie, who prescribed for me and sent me off to doctor myself.

N.B.—I was summoned on Saturday night; and the next day being Sunday, and Brodie not to be seen, I could get no certificate to escape the jury, and therefore had the option of getting saddled with an incompetent doctor for the sake of his certificate, or being liable to 100*l.* penalty for non-attendance.

July 3rd.—Having had bother enough to drive a fellow crazy, with an obbligato accompaniment of pain and illness, I this day left London for Longparish, preparative to my entering a second series of trouble, bother, and business about my property in the country.

4th.—Caught an immense freight of trout by means of hauling at about eleven at night, when these fish are so stupid that they lie for the net to take them up, and without even requiring a stop net as by day. This is the way that night poachers can so easily clear a river if free from weeds.

5th.—Keyhaven. No sooner had I arrived at Keyhaven than the wind and rain set in. I told everyone it would, and they laughed at my superstition, as there never was a more apparent set in for the finest weather ; but I never yet have failed to the best of my recollection in bringing on rain when I came to Keyhaven.

12th.—Incessant westerly winds till this day, consequently all coasting pleasures were embargoed, and the only pastime for exercise was with a casting net in the marshes, where I occasionally had plenty of fun with such rubbish as shoals of roach, small eels, little flat fish, &c. But to-day we had a regular butterfly morning, and took another sail to the rocks. The birds were not so plentiful as on my last cruise, but I succeeded admirably in getting them under way from the 600 feet precipice by means of my old invention of sending aloft a strong-headed fellow to lower a bell and flag with 100 yards of pot line. Nothing, however, was attempted till we had been out nearly six hours imprisoned, or rather drifting off to sea, in a dead calm, during which time I had a great treat in boarding a 'Torbayman,' to whose freight of fish Billingsgate was a mere stall. Towards evening there came on a pretty breeze, when I soon killed 5 couple of willocks; no sooner had we got into the marrow of the sport, than there appeared such an awful approach of weather that we were obliged to make all sail for home. But before we had even fetched back to the Needles, there opened on us a complete battery of thunder and lightning, and such a gale of wind as made the very timbers shake; and all the way from there to Keyhaven this running fire, more or less, continued, with such a pouring torrent of rain as not a sailor on board had ever before witnessed. But we providentially got safe into port (all, of course, drenched to the skin) about seven in the evening, when, at the moment of our landing, I could compare the thunder and lightning to nothing but a field of battle, and the thunderbolts to cannon balls flying about our heads.

29*th.*—London. People dying in every direction with this dreadful cholera, and many of them close to my own town residence.

30*th.*—Left London for Longparish, to see about the building of Bullington, and also about the building of a new punt, for which Buckle is now here. Wet weather, and the corn not in; but a fair account as to the breed of birds. Disease here as everywhere else. Poor Peter, the blacksmith close by, was last night enjoying his pipe in company, and at six this morning was found a corpse in his bed.

31*st.*—I was obliged to go over to Tom Langstaff to get something to put false life in me, or could not attempt to go shooting the next day.

CHAPTER XXV

1832

September 1st.—42 partridges and 3 hares.

A wonderful day considering I was hemmed in on all sides by contending parties, and so weak and ill that I could take nothing but an egg with a little brandy and milk to support me. I, however, shot most capitally, and never had better reason to be pleased; and the masterly manner in which I outmanœuvred the green-livered lawyer and his gang, who made every attempt to ruin my beat, was even better sport than the shooting itself, and worthy, I trust, of any cavalry and infantry general.

3rd.—Had too many things to attend to of more consequence than the shooting; but found time to bag 19 partridges, 1 hare, 4 quails, and 1 landrail.

5th.—46 partridges and 1 hare; one of the best days on record, when we consider how the lawyer has injured the country. My 56 brace in former times, when with a large army and free from all nuisances, was nothing in comparison to this. I never missed, except three long random shots.

6th.—Cavalry, infantry, and dogs all done up. A fresh army called on to harass the enemy. Goodchilde and another bloody shot arrived at ten with fresh dogs; and I sent them into the inclosures to have a day's sharp-shooting, we having pretty well scoured the hills.

N.B.—They bagged 15 brace and 1 hare, having worked from morning till night.

8th.—Out the whole day; and though I slaved like a horse and missed nothing, I could only bag 16 partridges and

1 hare, which was the greater part of what I found. This shows the effect of that blockheaded, green-livered lawyer going to war about the game, and never allowing it a day's rest. The consequence is that what is not shot must be banished from within his boundary.

Game killed the first week, or rather in the first 4 days' shooting: 123 partridges, 6 hares, 4 quails, 1 landrail. Total, 134 head.

Excellent sport considering the innumerable disadvantages.

10*th*.—20 fine full-grown young partridges, after gloriously outflanking the lawyer, and slaving all day till I was quite exhausted. This bag is miraculous considering the annihilated state of the only beat I could take.

21*st*.—Out all day and never saw but two small coveys of birds, and those very wild. Bagged 3 partridges and 1 hare, which was all I fired at. This shows how soon our shooting is at an end in this country, until the winter sets in, and the shooting parties and foxhounds drive out a little more game from the preserves and coppices.

October 1*st*.—Wet weather at last. Started with a chosen banditti to try if my estate would afford 1 pheasant. Out from seven in the morning, and wet to the skin, till a five o'clock dinner. All the pheasants I set eyes on the whole day were 3 splendid cocks and 1 fine young hen. I knocked down every one of them, and all long brilliant shots, but lost one for want of poor old Rover, whom Joe had the mishap to shoot in the hind leg when firing at a rabbit, and whom we sent home on the pony to be fomented and nursed. My bag was 3 pheasants, 2 rabbits, and 1 jack snipe, the latter a proof that emigrants are moving; and these, with the cock pheasant shot and lost, were all I fired at, and indeed all I saw; so that our 1st of October was a very satisfactory day.

2*nd*.—Went up to London to procure some things for the new punt, and to get some repairs done to the locks and breechings of my great gun; also to pay some bills, and see about my sporting book, which is already out of print again.

18*th.*—Returned with all my traps to Longparish, and was nearly losing my life by a frightful accident in Whitchurch. On my way home I drove to a shop for Monk (my old Peninsular servant) to run in and get a few Whitchurch biscuits; and while he was gone in I was about to turn the chaise round, when the wheel caught in something near the step and broke it, on which the horse plunged forward and overturned the chaise with such violence that I was thrown out and stunned; and there I lay entangled with a gun and a dog in a chain between my legs, while the horse was kicking everything to pieces, except the dog and me, who were repeatedly grazed by his very heels. I succeeded, however, in saving myself, with some severe bruises, and the gun with some little damage; but was so benumbed with the shock, that it was some time before I could tell whether my bones were broken or not. Monk came out of the shop, and was just in time to save further mischief, at the risk of his own life; and I had for some time been lying where no one dare come to help me. However, I, thank God, had a most providential escape, and arrived at Longparish with the wreck about seven o'clock at night. I fomented and physicked, and passed a miserable night; but in the morning I sent for Dr. Perry to cup me in the back, where I was hurt, and was then so far better as to be able to get across the room with the help of two sticks. I omitted to say that in this accident I was rendered helpless by having to hold a gun, as well as whip and reins, and a dog in a chain between my legs. Moreover, the reins broke in the very plunge that the horse made.

19*th.*—In bed and on the sofa all day, and occasionally in much pain. It is somewhat curious, too, that I should have received a blow precisely on the spot where I was shot in Spain.

21*st.*—Able to go without sticks. This evening Read

arrived, to arrange the final trimming and sailing of the new punt.

23rd.—Continuing to improve, and, indeed, pretty comfortable, except the soreness of the old wound that was torn. Hobbled down to the river, crawled into the punt, and tried her trim, &c. Sent Monk on horseback to Southampton for more copper work, as Read is crazy to get off to Keyhaven this splendid easterly wind.

24th.—All hands on from daybreak till about half-past four in the afternoon, when we started the punt on the boat carriage for Bullington, in order to avoid the danger of that vile road in the dark; and I arranged that Read and two helpers should leave this, with a fresh horse, after midnight, and then take on the punt with good turnpike roads in order to save his tide to-morrow morning, in sailing her from Southampton. We were so hard run to get her off that I had to take a 'trap' or two from the 'Lion' and varnish her after she was on the carriage, so as for her to be drying and travelling at the same time, the weather being so favourable that there was neither dust nor dirt.

25th.—The expedition started, with the punt on the carriage, at two o'clock this morning; that is *après minuit*, as the French more properly call it.

I was again hopping about all day among the workmen, getting some *ne plus ultra* 'wrinkles' done for the great gun, covers, &c., and also hard on about repairing the wreck of the chaise, and taking the opportunity of greatly improving the way in which the body was fixed on the carriage.

Read got under way from Southampton quay by half-past ten, and sailed off for Keyhaven with a beautiful breeze and tide in his favour. The weather was delightful, and nothing could have been better managed. The crowd, as usual, was no common one, on the arrival in a strange port of one of my punts.

29th.—Received a despatch from Read to announce the safe arrival of himself and the new punt at Keyhaven.

30th.—Returned to town, in order to prepare about 150 pages of my seventh edition, the sixth being out, and the booksellers crying out for copy to begin reprinting, as many orders could not be executed till another edition was ready. Good luck and great honour, but a miserably inconvenient time for me.

November 9th.—Having done enough to leave the printers employed for a few weeks, and having corrected the two first proofs, I this day left London for Longparish, with a view of collecting all my traps together for the coast, that being their proper station, and I never had such a pinching cold journey before.

10th.—South-east rain from morning till night, and a regular doctor's and undertaker's day.

13th.—Followed my shooting outfit to Keyhaven ; arrived there about eight this evening, and found that everything had got down safely and comfortably. No prospect of sport ; indeed, I knew this before I came, but my grand object was to try all the tackle, having (except the gun, newly done up) an entire new set-out, on a somewhat different, and, I hope, improved plan.

N.B.—The greatest number of wild fowl yet killed by any gunner all this season that I have heard of was three wigeon. Quite marvellous, when in former years I have known hundreds killed in October.

The tide did not serve till nearly four this afternoon, when the rain ceased, and the wind continued to blow most furiously. This was the very time to try the new punt, and we were just ready by the time the tide was. She answered splendidly at all tacks, and we had the great good luck to see a little trip of wigeon. I blew off both barrels together, and knocked down 7 at an immense distance, which was most unexpected, and a very lucky start for the first shot of the season and the first of the new set-out. My new invention of a landing, or rather cripple, net, decidedly saved me two of the birds I got.

15*th.*—Our good luck attended us, though the coast was all but destitute, as the only three living creatures we saw were 3 brent geese, all 3 of which I brought home to Keyhaven Cottage. They had been heard of, and seen for weeks, and tried by many, but without success. I followed them for nearly the whole time we were out, and at last got them near a creek, where I turned up 2 with the first barrel, and the other with the second.

17*th.*—Out from an hour before daylight till twelve, and never saw one single fowl.

19*th.*—As there was nothing worth going afloat for, I amused myself with a little in Mr. Pryce's mudlands with old Rover and the popgun, and in a few hours cleared off all that was there, viz. 9 coots, 7 moorhens, 1 snipe, and 1 jack snipe, without missing a single shot, and sent to Mr. Pryce, to make him a substantial pie for his vassals.

20*th.*—Paltry as our sport has been, I have got more birds than all the gunners on the coast for the whole season have done, put together; and never fired a blank shot. Having had a most satisfactory trial of all my new set-out, I this day put my things by till there shall be better weather and better sport, for London, where I was much wanted, for a week or two at least, to see to my seventh edition, now at press.

22*nd.*—London. A beautiful north-east wind, now that I have left Keyhaven. This is always the case, but my book could not go on without me, and therefore I was obliged to come up, if only for a week.

December 6*th.*—I this day, thank God, got to the end of preparing for a seventh edition between 500 and 600 pages of my sporting book, having, for the last several days, worked about fourteen hours out of the twenty-four.

11*th.*—Having worked in right good earnest all yesterday and to-day, as chairman of Mr. Portman's Christchurch division committee, and hunted up the various electors for the poll, I, among my numerous brother constituents, had the pleasure to see him hailed this evening at the illuminated 'Yorkshire Stingo,' tea garden public-house, by a triumphant majority of 997, above even Sir William Horne, the other deservedly popular candidate, for whom I had also voted.

12*th.*—Attended Mr. Portman and Sir Samuel Hawker (his nominator), to the hustings, where we had a royal noise, but no serious disorder, and where Mr. Portman and Sir William Horne were this day most ably and eloquently proclaimed by Sir Peter Laurie, the Lord Mayor (though here in the more humble capacity of returning officer), as duly elected for the borough of Marylebone. As this is the leading borough of England, let us hope that it will be an example to all others; first for its good order and peaceable conduct throughout the whole of the polling, and though last, not least, for its good sense in neither being humbugged by the ranting 'Rads' on one hand nor the Joe-Surface-hypocrite 'Conservatives' on the other.

26*th.*—Went down to Keyhaven, but not with the least idea of gunning, as there had not been a single fowl killed since I left the coast. A scarcity to this degree is a phenomenon, even let the weather be what it will.

Not a bird even seen by anyone up to the very last day of this year; a circumstance that, even in the mild weather, no one can account for.

1833

January 1*st.*—1 tufted duck was seen in the marsh. I took my double gun, and got him, and also 2 snipes, all I fired at, and this made a very lucky, though a very small, beginning of the new year.

Found in the garden the nest of a 'long-tailed Dick,' with 3 eggs.

Received the first copy of my seventh edition of 'Instructions to Young Sportsmen' this day from Longman & Co.

7th.—Longparish. The wind having continued north-east ever since I came away to spend some days here, and I having received a despatch from Keyhaven to say some birds were come, I this day mounted the Oxford coach and returned to Keyhaven.

8th.—Keyhaven. Got afloat again at last. Fired a long shot with one barrel, and got 4 wigeon, which was as good luck as could possibly be expected. No one had yet done so well. Out from ten at night till two A.M. Heard a 'fair show' of wigeon, but all left as the tide 'creamed' the mud. Read on from two till six, and never heard a bird, the effects of the unmerciful way in which this harbour has been treated.

9th.—Got 1 brent goose. No other chance all day. Tried the beach flight at night, but no one there got a shot, though the number of people coming home was like a congregation from a church or chapel. A fine easterly wind, and yet no sport for anyone; indeed, my goose was the only bird shot all day.

10*th.*—Read, after mud launching all night, went with me all the way to Hampstead Ledge, where we landed in the Isle of Wight. We then came full sail, in such a sea as no other punt would have lived in, across to Pitt's Deep, four miles below Lymington, and then home. We saw but very little, though got 6 wigeon and 1 merganser.

11*th.*—2 wigeon. A deplorable show of birds considering the easterly wind; but the harbour has been ruined. Only 2 birds in all the Lymington poulterers' shops to-day, when I was there on divers commissions.

14*th.*—Out from five in the morning till half-past five in the evening and never got a shot, though a strong easterly wind. This proves the ruin of our coast.

15*th.*—Out some hours before daybreak; got 4 wigeon (all I shot at). Boarded Buckle, who came in his craft to lie here, but had done nothing, and complained that the gunners everywhere were starving, though we have had, and now have, as fine an easterly wind as ever blew.

17th.—Out all night. Shooters out of number, and not one shot for anyone, and yet a fine wind.

Game &c. killed in the season to February 28th : 149 partridges, 7 hares, 4 quails, 1 landrail, 3 rabbits, 3 pheasants, 5 snipes. Total, 172 head. Wild fowl : 4 ducks and mallards, 19 wigeon, 4 geese, 1 merganser. Total, 28 head. Grand total, 200 head.

April 10th.—Longparish. Engaged with a party of fishing gentlemen who unexpectedly popped in on me. Three of us killed 50 brace of trout in a little more than four hours.

14th.—Very poorly ; half London indisposed with the influenza, and literally not one sound inmate in the whole of my establishment.

16th.—Had the honour of a private audience with his Majesty, to thank him for the high compliment of my being permitted to dedicate to him my work on 'Guns and Shooting,' and to present him with an elegantly bound copy of the seventh edition, of which his Majesty expressed his approbation, and received me with his usual kindness and condescension.

May 3rd.—Longparish. We had a capital morning's trout fishing. General Sir S. Hawker got 11 brace. I got 16 brace in about three hours.

18th.—We have now had the weather so intensely hot for this last week that the water is everywhere tepid, and we cannot bear even the sheet alone to cover us in bed. Never in my life did I feel the heat so oppressive ; perhaps from the sudden transition after the winter that we had late in spring.

August.—In an excursion this month to that paradise, Alum Bay, where I took a gun to get a few dozen of those delicious birds the wheatears, I knocked down a curious owl that Groves, on whose ground we were shooting, had been long trying to get ; so I made him a present of it in return for his civility. On my getting home and referring to the unrivalled engravings of Bewick, it appears to be either a short-eared specimen of the horn owl or the short-eared owl, which he describes as rare and valuable. At all events I gave away what I may never again, perhaps, shoot for my own collection.

CHAPTER XXVI

1833

September 2nd.—Longparish. The wind rather abated, but the birds were as wild as hawks; and I never in my life saw a worse show of game on the first day. We, however, did wonders considering all circumstances, as our bag was 30 partridges and 1 hare; no doubt by far the best day's work that has been done in this country. The green-livered lawyer with his myrmidons, as usual, drove the whole country before us, but found himself, as he always has been, well beat, and heartily laughed at.

7th.—17 partridges.

N.B.—Splendid shooting and a wonderful bag considering that the birds were wilder and more scarce than they generally are in December. A gale of dry easterly wind the whole week, and the ground as dry as Lundyfoot snuff. Not a wheat stubble in the whole country that afforded more lay than an average barley stubble and not a turnip large enough to hide a squeaker.

9th.—21 partridges; five double shots, and not a blank shot fired.

Game killed the first week, or rather in the first four days' shooting: 97 partridges, 3 hares. Total, 100 head.

Strong north-east wind all the week. Only one dog. Birds driven off the feed every morning by the green-livered lawyer's gang on purpose to spoil my sport. But, in spite of all, I never shot so well in my life, having literally missed but one fair shot in the whole campaign, and beat all the other fellows to atoms, though they had the whole country and fresh hands and dogs every day.

October 7th.—Went out with Joe and ratcatcher Siney on a forlorn hope, to get a little game for friends, and had, to our utter astonishment, a miraculous day, viz. 10 partridges, 2 hares, 2 rabbits, 1 snipe, and 1 old cock pheasant; the latter we drove out of covert into the village and chased for two hours, and at last bagged, after a harder run and more noise than we could have had with any average fox hunt.

11*th.*—Left Keyhaven at half-past eight this morning, and arrived at Longparish House at a quarter-past four P.M., making about forty-five miles in seven hours, with the little grey mare and gig, without a whip; and she wanted to run away with me the last stage. It poured with rain, and my umbrella broke all to pieces, so I had a luxurious drive of it. I fed at a pothouse in Redbridge, the 'Ship,' and had a delicious lunch and exquisite ale for a shilling, in a room with a Broadwood piano, and the best works of Clementi, Cramer, and Herz, which were the practice of the landlady's daughters. Here we have a specimen of the 'march of intellect' in the highest degree.

12*th.*—Got up at half-past six, took my fresh horse to Basingstoke in an hour and a half (fifteen miles), and mounted the box of the Odiham coach. Arrived in Dorset Place about a quarter before three, and, thank God, found Mary considerably better. Had two droll catastrophes on the road: first, an old woman, while gone in for a drink at an inn, had her barrow of vegetables capsized and gorged by a drove of bullocks; and second, young Thurnwood, who drove for Goodchilde, ran foul of a stone cart, which fell backwards, and hung the horse up by the neck till we had driven almost out of sight, when we just saw him come tumbling down like a cock pheasant.

30*th.*—Had a whole day's rifle shooting at Chalk Farm with Long, the crack rifle shot, and discovered that my rifle shooting was quite equal to my other shooting; we never missed the target the whole day; made a great many bulls'-eyes, and the four last shots I fired (without a rest) at 150 yards, and put into the space of an apple two shots out of the four.

December 2nd.—Received a letter from Read to say the fowl were come in great plenty at Keyhaven.

4th.—Ran down to Keyhaven; but I had scarcely reached Staines when a westerly hurricane and rain attacked me the whole way, and on the 5th it blew great guns all day, with repeated squalls of rain. Every fowl was swept off the face of the coast, and, after having done what business I had, I was the whole day immured in a kind of imprisonment that Newgate would have been preferable to.

31st.—Longparish. From the day of my return up to this very night, we have scarcely had any intermission from the most determined hurricanes and constant wet days I ever remember. Let us hope that all the troubles of the past year will evaporate in this sweeping tempest.

1834

January 1st.—Longparish House. So much trouble and business that I have only taken five days' shooting up to this New Year's Day, and it's over with the sport now unless the winter fowl come. Incessant rain, and country most desolate up to the last night of the old year. 107 partridges, 5 hares, 2 rabbits, 1 pheasant, and 1 snipe, is the list up to 1834; of course a very poor one compared to former seasons, though quite satisfactory, because I did wonders for the few chances that I had, and I never shot better in my life.

7th.—Walked out with Mr. Griesbach in the forlorn hope of finding a snipe or two, but saw nothing, though I saved my blank by shooting 3 trout at a shot, and one of them was in good condition. The east end of the village all in excitement about 2 wild geese being over in the fields, and how Fiddler Blake and Miller Dance (who missed them, a fair shot) had driven them away. I rode off at once with the pony and a telescope, and after a very long reconnoitre I spied one of these geese about a quarter of a mile off in an open field. After much manœuvring and crawling (to the very earth) like a toad for two gunshots and more, I got so near as to give him such a sickener with the first barrel that I made him 'haul his wind,' and fall a dead shot to the second. In my whole life I never was more proud of my shooting generalship than in bringing home this said grey goose.

N.B.—On seeing Leadbeater in town, who has my goose to stuff, he told me that it was a very curious and a very valuable species that he never saw before; and that this bird has completely 'floored' him in his ornithological knowledge, which we all know to be about the best in Europe.

28th.—Received a most deplorable account of the incessant rain and hurricanes at Keyhaven, and of the total banishment for these last six weeks of every fowl from the coast. Read congratulated me also on the narrow escape of my two splendid punts, the 'Dart' and the 'Petrel,' by their providentially not having been put into the boathouse, which was blown down, and consequently everything within it annihilated. Two of my worn-out punts were in the ruins, but this was of no consequence.

29th.—The first fine day that we have had for several weeks.

As a relief from being constantly confined to the house, I went out occasionally during the last week in a drizzling breeze, and exercised myself with fly fishing. The trout rose well, and we always got enough, that were in fair condition, to make a good fry for dinner. Had we made a determined chase of it, we should, no doubt, have done enough, for the month of January, to make a chatter for half the clubs in London. Left for Windsor.

31st.—Saw the Castle. Paid a visit to dear old Eton College.

March 13th.—Poor Leech departed for 'another and a better world' at about four o'clock this morning.

N.B.—I am not over-superstitious, but it was a singular occurrence that about half-past one, shortly before Leech died, the bells in our town house rang so as to alarm all the neighbours and the police, and not a soul was about, though our people got up to see; and the previous night Longparish House was literally assailed and attacked at the windows by a screech owl—a bird I had not heard of or seen there for many years.[1]

20th.—The greatest trial of all—the following my poor dear friend to the grave. When the hearse drove up to bear away his last remains from the house where he was for fifty years cherished in the bosoms of my family, I had to undergo what may be easier imagined than described.

Nothing could be more satisfactory than the result of all our business, and the excellent arrangements throughout the funeral of my dear departed friend.

N.B.—Within about these last twenty months I have taken the same white cambric handkerchief to four funerals of those who were dear to me.

April 4th. Keyhaven. A day's peace and quietness. My first for many many months.

7th.—Availed myself of a most beautiful day to take a sail round the Needles and to Alum Bay; and not having fired a gun the whole winter, I took my little 'cripple stopper' and popped off a roost of wheatears, &c. The very

[1] Since my writing this, my daughter Mary received a note from her mother in London, in which she added a P.S. to observe that towards four o'clock on the morning of the 13th she was awoke by a most tremendous rattling of her shutters, without anyone or any wind occasioning it; and that she was dreadfully frightened, and observed that 'some one was going to die!' she knowing nothing of what had occurred here. These mysteries are facts, to be accounted for as we please.

first day's healthy pleasure I have enjoyed the whole season, and no small relief to my eternally worried mind.

May 1st.—London. Busy with Spottiswoode's printers, *vice* my poor old friend Davison deceased, about the fourth edition of my little book on music.

28th.—Keyhaven. Having done all I had to do, I treated myself to a day's pleasure, as every poor chimney sweeper has a holiday in May, and a royal day I had of it, having made the best day's rock-bird shooting in the annals of Keyhaven. I brought home 42 willocks, 3 puffins, and 1 razorbill; and I never missed a shot except one, when the shrouds of the boat were in the way of the gun. My day is quite an event here.

July 15th.—Being anxious to see about my son Peter, who has been very ill in Ireland, I took my place for Holyhead by the 'Wonder' coach, and got a lift down to St. Albans.

16th.—Went on by the 'Wonder' coach to Shrewsbury, where I arrived about ten at night. The very best coach I ever travelled by. It does the 154 miles within 15 hours, including breakfast, lunch, and a hasty though well-managed dinner at Birmingham. Fare only 1*l.*

17th.—Proceeded at seven by the branch 'Wonder.' Had the very best breakfast I ever ate at Llangollen (30 miles), with, of course, a Welsh harper to accompany it. Had the box seat with the coachman's full explanation through all the splendid scenery of North Wales, which country, for about 85 miles that we travelled in it, has such roads, in the hands of Government, as may defy all Europe. They are for the most part cut through solid rocks, and are flanked by stone walls the whole way to Holyhead. The gates are all of one tasteful fancy pattern, and the milestones as neat as monuments. The vale of Llangollen, the descent from the mountains into the valley, the terrific 'Swallow' waterfall, the fine view of the majestic Snowdon within four miles of the road at Capel Curig, and, above all, the 'eighth wonder of the world,' the Menai Bridge, were sights any one of which were worth the whole journey. The counties we went through were Denbigh, Merioneth, Caernarvon, and Anglesea. The weather was delightful, and I had the luck to fall in with my old friend Mr. Vaughan, the celebrated singer, who travelled with us all the way to Capel Curig, where he was met by another old friend of mine, Mr. Gaven, who took him and his daughter off to his country seat, and wanted me to go too. The dinner at the 'Penryn Arms,' Bangor, was worthy of a duke—salmon taken from just before the windows, exquisite Welsh mutton, and everything first-rate.

We got to Holyhead, 106 miles, about half-past eight. In one minute after we entered the inn all the fine weather suddenly changed as if by magic. There set in a drenching pour of rain with the heaviest thunder and lightning I ever yet beheld. Instead of these memorandums I should write an octavo volume, even to name all the beauties I had seen; but when we have most to do and to see, is just when we have the least time to write.

Embarked at ten this night on board the 'Escape' packet and went off in a tremendous night of thunder, lightning, wind, and rain, and had a heavy sea, particularly on the Irish side of the Channel. I was stowed in the only vacant berth, near the steam boiler and furnace; and should have been sweated to death or suffocated had I remained there the whole passage. So I crawled out and lay on the cabin floor, surrounded by seasick passengers, and bombarded by the brisk fire of chairs, boxes, and other 'traps,' that were all in confusion from the neglect, to everything and everyone, of the beastly steward, who took all the money the moment we got on board, with a regular charge of half-a-crown for himself, and then left us all adrift.

18*th*.—Landed at Kingstown about half-past six in the morning, in a constant pour of rain, and amidst a scrambling mob, whose noise I could compare to nothing but some hundred irritated curs at a badger bait. Was whisked to Dublin, nine miles, in the 'Royal Mail,' by a red-hot coachee, who was all but giving us a royal somerset by furiously charging round three sharp corners.

Got into Macken's Hotel, Dawson Street, and found that Peter had got better, and bolted off to join his regiment at Belfast. So there was another journey for me. Had I known this, I'd have seen 'dear Ireland' at the 'divvel' before I'd have ever set my foot on her 'elegant' shore.

A regular downright thorough wet day from morn till night. Saw what I could of Dublin, by means of jaunting cars and umbrella. Took a copy of my book on music to my old friend and master, Logier, and was petrified with the performance in his unrivalled academy. Booked the box seat, the inside being full, for the Belfast morning mail of to-morrow.

19*th.*—Heavy rain continued. One incessant gale and water-spout in our faces all the way to Newry, 50 Irish miles, where an inside became vacant, and I took it, though not before I was wet to the skin, and where I ate sparingly of the worst dinner that could be imagined. But little to remark on this miserable journey through a miserable country, except the deplorable state of the ragged and lousy peasantry, and the wretched stye-cabins which they and their pigs and poultry inhabit.

On the side of the agreeable I have to note that superb trout and salmon, just out of the river, were offered round the coach at about twopence per pound. Dundalk is a beautiful and a very sporting-looking place, with a fine coast for wild fowl and grand mountains for grouse.

The coachman, guard, and mail were nearly as good as in England; but the horsekeepers and all other attendants ragged and barefooted. Distance 80 Irish (that is 103 English) miles.

On my arrival at Belfast (which, by the way, is worth all the rest of the country put together), I was met by Peter, who, although he had been nearly dying, was so recovered as to have resumed his duty, and been out in the rain all night with his regiment in getting down a tremendous fire. My cares about him were therefore at an end, thank God, and I had only to spend a day or two to enjoy the company of him and his brother officers before I went home.

The rain kept on, and continued pouring away all night. I escaped cold by rubbing myself all over with whisky, and having a warm bed and hot tea.

20th.—Went up to the barracks, and spent the whole day with the officers, and never got back to my hotel till between one and two in the morning, as we sat seven hours at the mess. In the afternoon I marched to church with the regiment, this day being Sunday, and then took a drive to see the country. Much delighted with the 74th's excellent kind fellows; capital mess, splendid band, and in every respect a regiment that I felt proud to have placed my son in.

21st.—Went to the parade with the Colonel; made a minute inspection through the ranks of the regiment, and no corps could be in more beautiful order and discipline. Attended the practice of the band for two hours, and they played me a symphony of Mozart and another of Haydn in the first style. The drums, bugles, and bagpipes were also capitally drilled by Signor Mazocchi, the bandmaster. Peter being on duty, I took another drive with Mr. Davies. We went to Carrickfergus, and inspected the celebrated old castle, where the 74th have a detachment, and from the bomb-proof summit of which we could see all over the opposite coast of Scotland with the naked eye. The distance there and back is just twenty-two English miles. My enjoyment of all this beautiful scenery was much damped by the severe pain I was in with a bad foot, and my consequently being so lame I could but with difficulty limp on a stick. I was obliged to hire a car to go to and from my hotel to the mess, and another to get back at night. Had a sober party and an early 'bolt,' which was well suited to my unpleasant situation.

22nd.—Discharged my little bill at the Commercial Hotel, which, by the way, proved one of the very best houses I ever ate or slept in, and after breakfasting there with Peter, who came down to see me off, I embarked on board the 'Corsair,' trading steamer, and got under way for Liverpool about half-past eleven o'clock.

I write this at sea.

Delightful heavenly weather, sea like a mirror, with just air enough to fill our two long-sails. About 20 miles from Belfast we passed the Copeland Islands on our left, and ran close alongside the picturesque little harbour of Donaghadee, the passage from which is 20 miles across to Portpatrick, in Scotland, the land of which was quite visible to the naked eye. About eight in the evening we ran close alongside the Isle of Man, where our captain fired two rounds of cannon to delight us with the grand echo through the continuation of majestically bold rocks that surround this beautiful and picturesque island.[1] No sooner had daylight disappeared than there rose directly ahead of us a most beautiful moon, within a day or two of the full, and our passage was more like a gondola party or a Venetian water serenade than a commercial steamer for Liverpool. The captain, Mr. Gowan, was a most obliging and pleasant man. We had excellent attendance, splendid cabin, boarded all the way, and bill only 6*s.*, which, added to half a crown for the steward and 1*l.* 1*s.* passage, cleared me for 1*l.* 9*s.* 6*d.* except giving a shilling to a most obliging cabin boy, who made me up a prime bed on a large horsehair sofa, where I lay as well as in a hotel, and had my regular dress, shave &c. in the morning.

[1] I made a sketch with a pen while flying by at twelve miles an hour, and at all events it is more like the Isle of Man than St. Paul's Church is.

23rd.—Dropped anchor in the beautiful harbour of Liverpool at half-past seven this morning, making a delightful passage of nineteen hours. Landed in a boat at *6d.* each, and was then driven in a thing (an old coach put across two wheels) to the Royal Hotel. Breakfasted, and had above an hour to see the town, in a car, being too lame to walk. Much delighted with Royal Exchange and public room. Thought Nelson's monument the *chef-d'œuvre* of all English productions. It literally made me cry, there was so much feeling in the composition. Admired St. Luke's Church and the cemetery, where was Huskisson's monument, though, as yet, poor and unfinished. Thought much more of Liverpool than of Dublin, there was not that poverty-struck, beggarly look about it.

Went per omnibus to railroad about ten. Started five minutes after, and flew to Manchester (32 miles) in an hour and five minutes, deducting two minutes' stoppage halfway for greasing, and setting down passengers for Newton and its neighbourhood.

Terrific travelling, as I was, by my own choice, allowed to leave my seat and be perched on the summit of the mail carriage, where I had to lower my head on entering the subterraneous causeway. Fortunately I had a pair of spectacles, and by 'shipping' them I had such an awful view of the whole concern as no other place could have afforded. But had I not been provided with these my eyes never could have borne the intense current of air and the occasional volley of black dust that flew from the engine. The guard of the mail has a place on purpose with his back to the train, and well sheltered by his letter box. I am delighted at having sat where I did, now, thank God, it is all safe over, but they'll not catch me there again; it was more awful to me than anything I have weathered at sea.

Lost the only feeding hour I had, hopping about in search of my first music master, Cudmore, who had moved and was not to be found ; so I left a book I had for him to the mercy of the porter of the inn.

Proceeded for Birmingham at a quarter-past twelve by a coach called the 'Railway,' in order to avoid having to stay in the putrid air of this most filthy town till the night travelling began. This coach went by way of Stockport, Congleton, Macclesfield, and Stafford, where we stopped at the 'Swan' inn, Mr. Meeson (his name ought to be recorded), and where we had the worst dinner, the worst attendance, and the least civility of any place in my memory. Passed all the country where the potteries are ; this made a variety, as we had here another kind of smoke and stink. Arrived in Birmingham soon after ten at night. No coach on to town, so booked for the first in the morning, and went to get a few hours' rest at the 'Castle,' where I sat, till my bed was ready, with a pleasant intelligent bagsman, over 'cold-without-sugar' and a cigar. Fair inn, tidy bed, no bugs, reasonable charges.

24th.—Left Birmingham by the 'Tally-ho' coach at seven this morning, and arrived at the coach office in Islington at half-past six in the evening (108 miles).

CHAPTER XXVII

1834

September 1st.—Deplorable prospect for a field day. A heavy pour of rain till near eleven, when it held up for about two hours with a strong gale of wind, and then it poured away again till half-past four. Country all day as wet as a river; and birds, of course, continually on the run. Only one dog, poor old Bess; but by sheer slavery, luck, and good shooting, got 18 partridges, wholly through splitting one immense covey over two large fields. I gave up my bitch (the only other dog I had) to Joe, to work the inclosures, and he got 5 brace and 1 hare, so that our day was 14 brace. We had our usual spree of outflanking and racing round the green-livered lawyer, who had a whole platoon of cock-a-doodle shooters as usual, and did all he could to spoil our sport.

2nd.—Splendid sport, considering the birds were as wild as hawks, and the dogs were so tired that we were obliged to tread the ground ourselves. I bagged 27 partridges and 4 hares, and Joe 7 brace and 2 hares, making in all 41 birds and 6 hares.

3rd.—Wind as usual, with more wet weather again. Got but 11 partridges and 1 hare, though we shot most brilliantly. Lawyer's party not out, so we conclude dead beat; and all of us, with our animals, properly knocked up.

4th.—Lawyer rallied and out again in full force, so I raced out instead of resting. Did capitally; I bagged 14 partridges and 1 hare without firing one blank shot, though I had some very long ones.

N.B.—I this day shot with Lancaster's new 'patent primers' for the first time, which he had put to my favourite and celebrated old flint gun of Joe Manton's, and a better tool was never handled by sportsman.

5th.—Rested, and physicked the lawyer by sending out a friend to shoot (a dead shot), who got 8 brace.

20th.—3 snipes, 1 duck, and 5 partridges. So oppressively hot that I fainted away in the snipe bog and missed 3 shots, two of them close under my feet. I never suffered so in my life, nor ever before was so overcome by the heat.

30th.—Feeling better I went out on the pony to try for a few birds, and got 7 partridges, but I soon became so faint that I shot miserably, or should have killed 3 or 4 brace besides these, as we found more birds than I had seen before any day since the first week.

Game killed in September: 105 partridges, 6 hares, 11 snipes, 1 duck. Total, 123 head.

October 1st.—Breakfast prepared at seven, old Siney and his curs in attendance, and the usual preparation for the 1st of October; but the result was that not a single pheasant could be found on the estate. We, of course, never expected above 2 or 3, but a sheer blank day is what we never before witnessed. I was so ill that I gave Joe the command of the first sortie, and all that came in then was a huge polecat, caught by terrier 'Trip.' I then put myself at the head of the banditti, and we worked till night. The bag was 3 partridges and 1 hare.

What with a bad night's rest from illness and the fatigue of this day, I was completely done up. So much for the 1st of October, 1834.

2nd.—Better, though still weak. Rode out and got 3 partridges that I wanted, though the birds were very wild, notwithstanding the weather was as hot as in the dog days.

3rd.—Drove down to a retired stream below Bransbury, and had some good pastime with my casting net. In less than an hour I caught 17 dozen and 7 immensely large gudgeon, besides a quantity of dace and some fine trout.

4th.—Took a few hours' shooting in Wherwell Wood, and my share of the bag (the best of the party) was 1 partridge and the only 4 pheasants I fired at.

6th.—Got kidnapped into a most deplorable shooting excursion in the miserable deserts of Wiltshire with Mr. Montague Gore, and instead of loading a cart, as I was led to expect, I never discharged my gun but ten times; I got 6 partridges and 1 hare. Fired two divided shots (both of which were bagged) with another gentleman, and hit a bird, a long shot, that towered, but was not bagged. I went off at eight in the morning, and never got home till near ten at night, and the poor mare had, I think, above fifty miles of it in the gig before her day's work was completed; and I may bless myself that I was not lost on the downs, and consigned to a bivouac for the night in getting home again. Of all the horrible counties I ever saw, I think the Wiltshire downs have a decided claim to pre-eminence.

17th.—London. Went to see the ruins of the Houses of Lords and Commons, burnt down last night and still burning.

30th.—London. Up to now constantly on about my troublesome property, but received this day a flaming despatch from Read about the quantity of fowl arrived at Keyhaven; so I decided on starting without loss of time, if it was only for change of air and peace to cure my cough, though I told everyone I should bring a westerly wind, as I always have done.

31st.—Started per 'Telegraph' at eight, and arrived at Keyhaven about a quarter before eight this evening, and I *did* bring a westerly wind.

November 1st.—After bustling about to get all my traps in order from daybreak till past nine, as I had not been in the new punt since the early part of the winter before last, I went afloat nearly all day; and, as a matter of course, the change of wind had cleared the coast. The only 2 birds we fell in with were a single brent goose that I killed handsomely with a barrel of the long-laid-aside stanchion gun, and a large grey plover that I made a very long shot at with the cripple stopper, after crawling on my knees for about 300 yards. So, sorry as the bag was, I at all events began capitally with the little I saw for the first day of my season.

3rd.—Availed myself of a calm day to explore the whole coast. Started in the 'Petrel' punt at eight, and landed on the quay at Cowes (15 miles) in about two hours and a half. My set-out raised a complete mob among the Royal Yacht population of this place. After taking refreshment and passing about an hour in the town, we rowed the punt down tide along the whole coast, and all we saw was one large flock of wigeon, high in the air and travelling back to the eastward. This proves how soon the wrong weather puts an end to the chance of getting fowl.

4th.—Made another survey, but to no purpose; never saw a single bird of any kind, so finished the afternoon with paying all my little bills that were due here, and getting rid of all the business I had preparative to mounting the coach to-morrow morning.

5th.—A precious comfortable trip up to Longparish from Keyhaven to-day. Was told to meet the 'Pilot' coach at Everton at a quarter past eight. Walked there by soon after eight, but had been misinformed as to time, as the coach was gone, so had to tramp in 'double quick' for Lymington till within half a mile of the town, where I gave a warren boy a shilling to put me up with his rabbits and try to catch the coach. Horse no goer, so we failed altogether. Took a pony and gig and got to Hythe, twelve miles, in an hour and five minutes. Crossed the ferry, nearly three miles, in a quarter of an hour. A gale of wind, and should have been capsized and drowned by a squall had I not seized and let go the sheet.[1] Ran all up Southampton streets and got to the office a quarter of an hour before the coach came in. Wonderful quick work. Got to Winchester soon after twelve to see lawyer Bird, but he was not at home. Mounted a two-horse slow coach at two, from which out got Bird, and after a hasty interview with him in the thorough draught of a gateway, I went on by this *adagio* conveyance. A tremendous hurricane and heavy driving rain all the way to my farm at Furgo, the nearest point to which I was set down. The farmer out, so left my wet trunk for a countryman to bring on to Longparish. Umbrella broke and useless in the gale. Paddled it over the wet fields, with a gale and waterspout all the way, that I could scarcely make head against, to Longparish, where I arrived, wholly unexpected, and as 'wet as a shag,' a little before five, and was put naked into a warm bed till my clothes could be got at and dried, and some sustenance provided. I shall not in a hurry fail to 'remember the fifth of November.'

6th.—Went to try for a cock that I fancied I saw, but found nothing. Then worked down by the river, where I got a cold bath. On riding over Redmoor dyke 'bridge' old Bob, my horse, shied aside, and down we both came from a bridge of some height into about three feet of water, I under and old Bob on me, and I could not get above water till my breath was nearly gone. We were both completely out of sight for some seconds, as the markers informed me. But I stood true vermin and tried the islands afterwards for snipe, while Siney galloped home to get fresh clothes ready. Saw but one jack snipe, bagged him, and dined on him in commemoration of the event; and had an evening's employ to clean up my watch, and every other article that was kept under water with the old 'horse' and 'his rider.'

[1] While the sailor was engrossed in a long yarn about the wonderful exploits of 'Colonel Hawker, the great gunner,' little aware that he could have quoted Nathan and said, 'Thou art the man.'

20th.—Keyhaven. A tremendous gale of wind from the north-east all night and all day, and all night again. No boat could row on end. Dead tides, and some geese off, on the mud, near the breakers.

22nd.—Gale and rain continued. Sick of being a prisoner. Fought our way out in the punt, and waited from daylight till near twelve on board a salt lighter, then dropped down on the fowl: got 1 brent goose and 8 wigeon. My pattens came untied on the mud, and I came home in miserable mess, that took us four hours to clean up and rectify.

24th.—A cutting north-easter. Up at four, but it 'blew great guns,' and all we could do was to work through 'Stivers' creek, and 'make fast' the punt to windward, so as to be able to drop down outside without having to face a wave. No birds at all; so went home, overland, and returned to our craft at midday. Beat the marshes for snipes in the meantime, but no sport. Sadly slack crisis; no water inside from dead tides, and no facing the wind outside, and all the birds slipped off, Lord knows where, though weather most beautiful for fowl. Home to Longparish to-day.

27th.—Having left my punts &c. all ready for my immediate return, I drove off on my way back to Keyhaven, as the most ominous of all bad weather, a severe white frost, gave me warning that I had but a few more days to embrace. Indeed the change seemed, at one time, so near at hand, that I had all but turned off my gig, and proceeded up the Winchester road to London. However, my destiny was to proceed; and not wishing to bother the old mare with another forced march, I left her and Monk to 'take it easy' at Redbridge, and mounted the 'Pilot' branch coach with Jemmy Judd, who set me down at Everton, from whence I toddled with my pack at my back to Keyhaven, and saved five shillings' worth of fly. I arrived before I was expected; and Read, who was knocked out of his bed, where he had gone to bottle himself up for a mud launch, told me there had been a splendid show of birds the very two days I was away, and gave me brilliant hopes for the morrow; but, alas! Old Nick's wind came on in the night, and the pinching 'sniveller' was changed to a tempest. We, however, got under way on the 28th, as the tide was well over the harbour, and had a cruise down to below Lymington, in which we saw nothing except Buckle and two of his brother gunners anchored in the very bull's-eye of our beat. In short I never pulled a trigger, except blowing off a barrel and killing 10 shore birds, that were settled on a new-invented raft of mine, the very first tide after Read had moored it. If we could only have weather and water, how this raft would do the plover!

December 1st.—Keyhaven. Cruel weather. Tired of being a prisoner. Drove to Christchurch, and while the mare was feeding, inspected the beautiful church there, which, from its deviation from correct order, affords, perhaps, more interesting variety than any cathedral I know. In short, it is well worth seeing. I then drove on to my old rendezvous, Poole, where I was amused with seeing all the brother gunners of my infancy, who were delighted to see 'the Captain' again, as they called me, and did some commissions in salt fish, and attempts about getting a real St. John's dog &c., and, in short, anything to kill the monotony of a west-wind embargo, and with some hopes of changing the weathercock. Returned late to Keyhaven.

3rd.—A butterfly May day. Out all the morning, and saw nothing but a small flock of geese, which were so well fed, and so wild, that they would not sit for ten minutes at a time in any one place. Was informed that all the birds, by thousands, had got into Sowley Pond, where keepers were on watch, day and night, to preserve them for the 'pleasure' of Lord Montague looking at them.

4th.—Having given up the gunning for a 'bad job' till the weather changes, I went into Lymington to do some business, and then drove on to look at Lord Montague's 'thousands' of birds on Sowley Pond, of course with a popgun and cartridges, but the 'thousands' turned out to be one small company of wigeon, about 7 straggling ducks, and nearly 1,000 coots. The wild fowl were out of shot; so I discharged a barrel for the public good, and drove them off to sea, and then drove myself home.

5*th.*—Read, who was out all night mud crawling, got 6 wigeon, having shot, some time after midnight, at a company which, from place and number, I can almost swear were the birds I had started out of my lord's nursery at Sowley Pond.

8*th.*—Longparish. Availed myself of a few hours' leisure from business this afternoon to try for a snipe, and had excellent luck. I bagged the only 8 snipes I saw, and 1 woodcock that had long outwitted everyone here, and at which I made a most brilliant shot, after some masterly manœuvring, and a sharp chase of nearly an hour.

10*th.*—Returned to London. No schoolboy was more happy to escape from birch, Latin, and mutton, than I was to return to Dorset Place.

17*th.*—By way of a climax to my worry of mind with lawyers, I was this day sentenced to an awful operation by surgeons. I called on my friend Sir Benjamin Brodie, the head of the profession, who examined me, and said, if I wished to live, I must suffer this, and be ready for him about half-past two on the third day. All this day, after eleven, all the 18th, and till about twenty minutes to three on the 19th, was I kept in a state that may be easier imagined than described. At last the awful rap at the door announced the arrival of the carriage with Sir Benjamin and his assistant. The operation lasted about thirteen minutes. No pen can describe the agony I suffered, though I was highly complimented on bearing it as I did.

For about fourteen hours I lay in such excruciating pain that all opiates were unavailable, and I kept getting worse and worse, till, at last, I was quite resigned to lose my life.

23rd.—Sir Benjamin, who had attended me every day, came a little before seven this evening, when he thought me so far safe as to postpone his next visit till the day after to-morrow.

Game &c. killed up till the end of December 1834: 118 partridges, 8 hares, 4 pheasants, 25 snipes, 1 duck, 2 brent geese, 10 wigeon, 7 teal. Total, 175 head.

1835

January.—London. Here begins the new year, and God send I may have a pleasanter one than the last, which brought me throughout a series of afflictions and difficulties.

1st.—Just downstairs, after having been confined to my bed and room for above a fortnight.

12th.—On taking up my paper this morning I was much hurt, and could scarcely eat my breakfast, at reading the death of another old and highly esteemed friend and brother 'gunner,' Captain Ward, whom I had met in excellent health, and just going to prepare his yacht and punt for fowling, but three days before I came up to town.

April 16th.—Black frost and snow.

17th.—Good Friday. Black 'north-easter' with a stiff breeze, and with frost and snow. Absolute winter.

18th.—The few days' severe weather ceased, and it became spring again. What a climate is ours! Went down to Stoke Newington House to see Mr. Wood relative to his relieving me of Longparish House for a twelvemonth. Mr. Wood was here on a visit to the rich heiress, Miss Crawshay, who, house and all, is to become the property of the curate. Lucky dog! Leave a parson alone for getting the best of everything.

20th.—From morning till night in a bustle, owing to all things coming in a clash, as is invariably the case, and raced about like a hard-driven bullock in a mob. Booked Mr. Wood's and my places for Wednesday to go to inspect

Longparish. No sooner up than down, but *n'importe* in a good cause.

22nd.—Went down with Mr. Wood, and made every preparation for delivering to him Longparish House.

23rd.—While I was fishing (I got 25 trout), the carpenter and my men were employed relative to examinations, inventories, &c.; and on Mr. Wood, after a more minute inspection, doubting whether I had a sufficient supply of articles to suit his style of living, and finding the place not in such good order as Mrs. Wood would require, he declined proceeding any further in the affair unless I could make an immediate outlay that would at once swallow up the whole year's rent.

24th.—Thus have I had all this trouble and a journey for nothing. So much for house and land property. If you want to kill a chap humanely, shoot him at once; but if you want to worry his life out with successive years' plague without profit, give him land, in the present times, and some unoccupied houses.

May 7th.—London. The best performed opera I ever saw. We were taken to the box of Grisi, whose acting surpassed even Pasta. The opera was 'Otello,' and her Desdemona was perfect. Rubini, Tamburini, Lablache, and Ivanhof were never greater than this night; nor did I ever hear the orchestra go to such true perfection. I seldom notice town spectacles, but this was one in a thousand.

14th.—The most intensely crowded Drawing Room I ever was at, and a deluge of north-east rain from morning till night. The fight of carriages in Grafton Street was awful, and my 'Jarvey' cracked like a lobster. I expected a wreck every moment, and blessed myself that I had no females in charge. All the servants half drowned, and I could get no escape without the drenching of all my finery, till at last I bribed a chairman to work me to a Jarvey stand, where he shipped me from his sedan to a coach, a precious wet one too, insomuch that I dare not sit down in it, but crouched and held on all the way home. So much for being a courtier this wet day.

June 16th.—Longparish. Netted the river for the King. Killed 63 brace of trout in two drags, besides as many thrown in, and about a bushel of large dace.

July 15th.—London. After being all the morning at the concert of Benedict, which was by far the best of the season, I this day adjourned from the Opera House to the Freemasons' Tavern, where was given the grand farewell dinner to John Cramer. Much as I abominate a public feast, or rather public fast, I must admit this to have been a real intellectual treat. On the whole, nothing could be better conducted, nor could any man living have had a more cordial reception than my old and talented friend John Baptiste Cramer.

27th.—Left London and arrived at Longparish. Found the country completely burnt up by the long-continued easterly winds and overbearing heat; and, in short, not a degree cooler than London, where the heat has long been such that it was impossible to get a night's rest, at least for me, without lying on a mattress without any covering whatever.

28th.—Busy all day regulating the cellar and other things, and cleaning and varnishing all the pictures in the house. In the evening we had a tremendous storm, with thunder and lightning, and such a deluge of rain that half the rooms in the house were wetted through the ceiling.

August 7th.—Fly-fished for several hours in a good wind, and got but one fair brace of trout. Never in my whole life did I see the fish so sulky in good angling weather. They were all at the bottom running for minnows. Tried the river for fowl; got 1 duck and 1 snipe, the only two shots I had. This was Friday, and I thought I could defy the spell by the goodness of my gun and shooting; but Friday would be Friday. I fell down in the river, filled my gun, got a ducking, and consequently a miss-fire at a most beautiful shot. And then 2 more ducks passed me while I was 'done out of' my gun.

18*th.*—Started for a few days' inspection of Jersey and Guernsey, having never seen either of these islands. I got a berth in the custom-house boat, and dropped down the Lymington river just as it grew dark, and had not the officers fired three pistols for the captain to 'heave to,' the packet would not have stopped for me, and I should have had to go back, like a fool, in the middle of the night. As it was, however, all was well; I got safe on board the 'Liverpool,' and had one of the finest passages imaginable in the very best steamer I ever set foot in. We left the Channel about nine.

19*th.*—Brought up close alongside Guernsey about seven in the morning. Here we waited an hour, and, as the weather was so delightful, I determined on embracing a good passage to go on and see Jersey first. We got under way at eight, and dropped anchor off Jersey (thirty miles more) at eleven; but, owing to the multiplicity of passengers in both this packet and an inferior one called the 'Ariadne,' added to the negligent scarcity of boats, we were imprisoned under a broiling sun, and peppered with the blacks from the evaporating steam for the greater part of an hour, and in a state of exhaustion and starvation for want of a good breakfast. The chief beauty to remark on our passage was a view of rocks called the Caskets, which we opened about half-past four, and of which I took a hasty flying sketch, such as it is. But as to attempting to sketch, or even describe, the *coup d'œil* of St. Peter's, the only town in Guernsey, it would be too long a job. Suffice it to say that it presents such an endless detail of bold rocks, and innumerable houses of all sorts and colours, that nothing short of a hard laboured panorama would give a proper idea of it. An intelligent gentleman who had long resided there told me that in the island of Guernsey there were no reptiles of any kind, though they were common in Jersey as in England.

On our left going to Jersey we had a fine view of the island of Sark, and, in short, went along a coast of the boldest, and, of course, the most dangerous rocks I ever saw. On landing at Jersey I went to the 'Albion' hotel, a passable tavern for such a place as St. Helier's, the capital and great seaport of this island. The passage, the seamen said, was 140 miles; 110 from off Lymington to Guernsey, and thirty more from quay to quay afterwards. Fare, in best cabin, only 11*s.* 6*d.* including a shilling for the steward.

20th.—Having yesterday seen the town of St. Helier's, I got up this morning, and with a one-horse car made a minute survey of the country round, with which I was not a little delighted. First I went to Grouville, where the chief subject for a sketch was the church; we then went to the village of Gourey, and ascended to the celebrated old castle called 'Mount Orgueil,' in which Charles II. was secreted, and from which he made his escape to France by a passage through the solid rock, on which this splendid ruin stands, and by the excavation of which it is chiefly formed. The view of and from this castle is magnificent. We then proceeded to a delightful little rendezvous for pleasure called 'Prince's Tower,' which commands a panorama of the whole island, and which is fitted up and laid out around with more taste and neatness than any public refreshment place I ever met with. There is a winding gravel path by which you ascend to the tower, and then a most commodious winding staircase which leads to little octagon eating-rooms in every storey, from which you have windows to see over the island in all directions. We then drove back to St. Helier's in the evening, and ascended the ramparts of the fortified rock, where you have a view equally fine in its way. Here is a memorandum of the views; now for a short summary of observations.

People civil and obliging. Things about half the price of England. No taxes, no duties, and a free port for all commerce. First-rate fruit, as cheap as dirt. Capital market.

Town much like a French one, but far cleaner. Religion chiefly Protestant, the service performed in French, both languages fluently spoken in every shop, though with an accent peculiar to the natives. Town and country swarming with apples. Farmers all in a very small way, but for the most part freeholders. Plenty of employ for the people, and I never saw or heard of a beggar in the place. Only one other town besides the capital, and the only public conveyance on the island is from 'town,' as they of course call St. Helier's, to this place, St. Austin. You have a fine 'currency' profit on either English gold or Bank of England notes, being allowed 21*s.* 8*d.* for every pound, and 13*d.* for every shilling. This, and the total release from every duty of either excise or customs, is what makes Jersey, and I believe Guernsey too, so much cheaper than France and other foreign places.

21*st.*—Made a further reconnoitre of everything in and about the town. Found the prices of everything a mere nothing; for instance, best French brandy 1*s.* 4*d.* a bottle, that is 1*s.* 3*d.* English; tea, 3*s.* per lb.; snuff, 1*s.* per lb.; India silk handkerchiefs, 4*s.* each, and less if taken by the piece, and, in short, almost every article in the same proportion. While inspecting the fish market (which, although not in great repute, abounded with coarse fish, such as conger eels, and was fairly supplied with good fish of most kinds) I met the old Adjutant of the 14th Dragoons, Ben Shotten, who had settled in Jersey, and told me he could live for within one-third here of what it cost him in England. In the afternoon I took a small boat with one man, and rowed over to Elizabeth Castle, where I spent some time, and saw the armoury, King Charles's boots, &c.; and we then rowed to the hermitage close by, where, after such a climbing of rocks as I never before had to encounter, I mounted up to the old cave of St. Helier, the ancient hermit, after whom the capital was named, and got home just in time to escape a most terrific thunder storm, in consequence of which I gave up an expedition that I had in view, of going in a hired oyster smack to survey the Choissée Islands, a place with about twelve inhabitants, and swarming with birds of all kinds, and about twenty-seven miles south of Jersey. The storm threw such a darkness over the whole country and town, that we were obliged to light a candle before I could see to pen down these memorandums. This evening the whole town was in a royal uproar with a grand dinner, given by the officers of the Jersey militia to the General, Sir Colin Campbell, in honour of his Majesty's birthday, at the 'Sun' inn, which was close adjoining my quarters. Cannons, drums, trumpets, guns, two hundred jolly boys getting uproariously drunk, with incessant hurrahing and singing, bands of music, fireworks, rabbles of boys by hundreds screaming ready to split the rocks, and, in short, such a spree as could not be surpassed if Old Nick's dominions were broken loose.

22nd.—As I wished to land on and go over the island of Guernsey on my way home, I had no other alternative of doing so than embarking about half-past eleven last night on board the 'Ivanhoe' Weymouth and Guernsey post-office packet, and there waiting in durance vile till three this morning in a beastly craft only fit to convey Irish pigs across the Severn, till there was water to float her out of harbour. At this hour we got under way, and were above four hours doing the passage, which the 'Liverpool' would have done in three. As in all post-office packets, the accommodation was vile; the ladies were so little separated from the gentlemen as made it quite indecent, and, as there was no female attendant on board, nor indeed any but a superannuated old steward, the gentlemen who had their ladies there were obliged to go in to assist them where others were. We had a rough passage, with some heavy rain, a rolling vessel, and an almost general mess of sickness. We 'fetched' Guernsey soon after seven, and there I put up at the 'Crown' inn on the north pier. As soon as I had refreshed myself with an indifferent breakfast, I went to the celebrated market, in order to see it early, and therefore in full perfection. Nothing could be more abundant, but things were not so cheap as in Jersey, the people much more inclined to cheat, and the currency money allowed here is only ½*d.* in the 1*s.* The fruit market was superb, the fish market immense, but for the greater part consisting of colossal shell fish. In the poultry market turkeys were 6*s.* a couple, and young pigs 16*s.* a couple. What delighted me the most was to see the English gentlemen, like sensible fellows, choosing and buying their own things, instead of trusting to and having to be encumbered with a set of beastly lazy, idle, discontented servants, overfed and underworked, and, in short, live lumber. Here I met the half-pay officers and other refugees from English plunder and humbug, with their market basket in one hand and a lobster in the other, the wife with the fruit, and the child with the flowers, and so on. What I call the height of independence and domestic happiness. The streets here are more like the French, and not so pleasant as those of Jersey. About twelve o'clock I took a car with a most intelligent and loquacious driver, and started for a tour round the whole island about twenty-four miles, and there was no house, person, or thing but what this fellow was perfectly acquainted with, and volunteered the history of. We first mounted the immense hill of streets that leads to the fashionable part of the town, passing by the house of Lord Saumarez, the college, the hospital, and all the fine houses of the rich merchants, to Fort George. From thence we went half a mile and back out of our way to the famous tower erected to the late General Sir John Doyle for making the roads, and this I ascended by a winding staircase in total darkness, to enjoy perhaps the finest view that all this part of the world can afford—on the one half circle the whole island of Guernsey, and on the other the islands of Jersey, Sark, Herm, Jethou, and Alderney, with the coast of France in the background. Country afterwards not very picturesque, more for a farmer than a painter. Rich land, small proprietors of about from six to ten acres each. Country all divided in small crofts, with either stone walls or banks, all fortified with strong furze. Wheat put up in stacks of about two to the acre. A great deal of mangel wurzel, parsnips, beetroot, and brocoli in fields. Ploughing done twenty inches deep for this, and sometimes 14 beasts required to one plough, either French horses or bullocks, or both. No cows but those of Alderney admitted, and these were larger than what we call Alderney cows in England, and the very finest I ever saw, some giving, the guide told me, forty quarts a day. Passed village of 'Forest,' and near there drank wines a penny a glass and paid a penny for a stiff brandy grog for dinner. Continued round by the villages of St. Martin, and St. Peter's in the Wood, having afterwards on our left a fine view of the 'Rock in Bay,' Richmond barracks (now sold for the land) and the island of Leo. There are ten parishes in the island, with one church and either two or three dissenting chapels to each. French language for Divine service and everything is used throughout the country part of the island, though both languages universal to all ranks of people in town. Put in at the 'Royal Oak' at St. Saviour's, a noted, indeed the only, house for eating and pleasure parties out of the capital. Here we refreshed and rested ourselves and horse, and saw an enormous ox, and some very large and well-shaped pigs. We then put to the horse and started on our other round for the capital, St. Peter's Port, through the village of King's Mill, where at the house of a Mr. Moulin there were the very largest sized oranges growing against the wall, adjoining the parlour window, and there were in most places very fine myrtles, and aloes nearly as large as in Portugal. Near this place there is erected a manufactory for distilling brandy from potatoes. After then we passed the village of Vale, and re-entered the town on the north side without having to descend the huge hill we had mounted, and drove by the seaside and esplanade home again to my quarters, where, by the way, the windows of both my bedroom and sitting room looked off from a rock directly into the sea, and over the most superb view of the town, Cornet Castle, and the distant islands, that could be imagined. I took a kind of tea-supper, and went to bed as tired as a dog between nine and ten, having had no rest the previous night. My reason for thus making such a toil of a pleasure was to secure the 'Liverpool' for Monday, and the intervening day being Sunday, when it is not much the custom to travel about here. But after all, I found the 'Liverpool' had been suddenly bought up for a voyage to Spain or Portugal,[1] and there would be no packet for England till Tuesday.

23rd.—After a good night's rest, of which I was sadly in want, I got up to pen down these memorandums, which I was too tired to do, as usual, at night, and went to St. Peter's Church, which is so precisely the same, both in the building and the service, with our chapels in London, as to need no description. The canopy of the pulpit was formed like an immense oyster shell, and sloping from behind the preacher, which had a novel effect, and perhaps assisted in throwing out his voice. The Sabbath is kept here even more strictly than in England. Not an article of any kind to be bought, and there is no fish market on Monday because the fishing on Sunday is prohibited.

24th.—Had intended to cross over to inspect the island of Sark ; but a heavy sea, through which I might not have been able to get back, prevented my going this 9 miles passage. So I devoted the day to exploring everything in and about the town, and, amongst other things, I was much pleased with the college and the hospital. The former is a splendid building, and beautifully regulated. The latter has many well-contrived advantages for doing, by mechanical means, all that is necessary in the baking, cooking, washing, and other labours of an establishment of about 300 patients.

25th.—Having now seen all I wanted to see, or rather all that my limited time and the contrary winds would allow me

[1] Sold, as I since heard, for 11,160*l.* to run from Falmouth to Lisbon.

to see, I this morning put up my things, previous to another sortie in the town, an early dinner, and a start by the afternoon packet for England; and never did I feel more regret at leaving a strange place where I was unknown, than I do at leaving the two islands I have visited. I came to them out of mere curiosity, and for the benefit to my health of a sea voyage to where it would cost me the least, and where I expected to find a place only fit for poverty-struck refugees. But, to my agreeable surprise, I found everything so far before either France or England that I should have no objection to take my leave of both, and end my days in either of these well-regulated, independent, and happy islands.

26th.—I remained packed up for the steamer, but the wind was so strong and contrary that she never came in all yesterday, being wind-bound at St. Malo. Here I am, therefore, and cannot go far out of the way lest she should be in and out again. Saw a fine haul of fish close to the town, and the moment the fish were caught and collected in one great heap, a horse, with two large panniers, was brought down to take them as quickly as possible to the market, where alone fish is here to be sold. About six this evening the 'Beresford,' the long-detained Southampton packet, appeared, and a little before eight she arrived off the harbour, and everyone said we must hasten on board, as she would not stop many minutes. Off went I and the other passengers; but instead of her bringing up to take us in, she ran 'right into the docks,' owing to some damage, as they said, done to her in the bad passage, from which she could not proceed till early to-morrow morning; so I had to pay porters and boatmen for nothing and return to my hotel, which I was not sorry for, as I prefer a day passage to one in such a night as this.

27th.—The packet was to leave at five this morning, and I gave orders to be called a quarter before four. Woke up, looked at watch, wanted only ten minutes to five, and not a soul up. Flew from my bed to the street, and luckily a little shift of wind had penned the tide, so that the dock could not float out the packet till six, or my passage must have been lost. As it was we got under way at half-past six, and came into the Channel off Hurst at half-past five in the evening, after making a rapid passage, in spite of having a breeze directly against us for the greater part of the way. We had for the first three hours a rough, and afterwards a very pleasant, passage. At one time, near Alderney, we steamed seventeen miles in the hour. On arriving off Yarmouth, I sadly feared I should not get a boat to see our signal, and indeed none did; but most fortunately a boy in a Freshwater boat cut across to us just in time, and gave me a passage to Lymington; otherwise I should have been dragged all the way to Southampton, and kept by the custom house till perhaps past the Lymington coach time of the next morning. But as it luckily was, I landed unobserved, walked over the marsh to Keyhaven, and had all my things brought safe to me, with my own cart, early next morning. Thus ended my amusing, cheap, and satisfactory excursion, and, I thank God, found the children well, and that they had been well amused with our good neighbours during my absence from Keyhaven.

CHAPTER XXVIII

1835

September 1*st.*—A good show of birds, but scarcely a point to be got the whole day. County as bare as a seashore, and we were forced to walk up (wild as hawks) all we killed; not even the dispersed birds would stay a moment where they pitched, unless in hedges. Joe and I shot together, and both performed splendidly, indeed never better. We bagged 22 brace and 1 hare between us.

2*nd.*—In a bustle all the morning packing off birds and notes; my usual occupation the second day. Walked out after dinner to get a brace of birds I wanted. Fagged hard to get seven long shots; bagged 5 partridges and lost another. The green-livered venomous reptile of a lawyer and his myrmidons were on, of course, from morning till night as usual, but have no chance against us, though they have the whole manor, and we are confined to our own fields.

3*rd.*—20 partridges. We have, as usual, beat all the country hollow; but the shooting is sheer slavery. The ground like hot cinders, the heat like India, and getting a point out of the question. All must be done by walking the barren lands with both barrels cocked, and popping at all distances the moment the birds top the stubble. We all came home so exhausted as scarcely to be able to move.

5*th.*—Slaved all day and got but 6 partridges. A perfect farce to go out, everyone giving it up as unprofitable slavery.

7*th.*—14 partridges, and Joe 13. We gave up the bitch

and our marker to Goodchilde and his friend, who worked from morning till night and bagged 23 between them. We saw nothing of the lawyer to-day, though we gave him a royal benefit between our three parties, killing just 50 birds.

9th.—A very stormy day, and birds wilder than ever. I got 15 partridges. N.B.—I owe my bag to-day to two extraordinary shots. I began with firing at 5 birds, and bagging 4 of them with one barrel; and finished my evening with springing 4 birds on an oat stubble, and blowing all 4 of them down at one shot; 3 fell short, and the old cock flew and towered and was also bagged. These extraordinary shots occurred, I conceive, owing to the tremendous gale of wind, and my having taken out my miraculous 'Old Joe,' a gun which I can pitch with more rapidity than any other I have, and am, therefore, frequently able to catch the birds before they have time to divide. Add to which this gun cuts out all my others for throwing a regular circle of shot.

11th.—I was out from one till six, and of all the years I ever was a sportsman I never saw such a bad day's shooting; it was a real Friday. The birds got up regularly at about 100 yards, and there was such a tempest the whole afternoon that I could hardly keep my hat on my head.

14th.—I fagged from ten till seven, and never got but 7 shots. We had a fine 'spree,' as the lawyer was between both our beats, and I worked round him as a cooper would round a barrel, while he got little or nothing.

18th.—A prisoner with physic; a wet day, and the lawyer hard on at shooting, but I flew out and flanked him, and got 2 birds and wet to the skin.

25th—A fine butterfly day at last; I got 10 partridges. Splendid sport. The green-livered son of a —— the lawyer drove my preserve, but I flanked him and beat him handsomely.

29th.—A capital day for fishing. I killed 12 of the largest trout I have seen this year within the hour; and, had

I not been engaged, and therefore obliged to go, I might have done something extraordinary.

Game &c. killed up to Sept. 30.—238 partridges, 12 hares, 2 rabbits, 1 quail, 6 ducks, 18 snipes. Total, 277 head.

October 1st.—Up to breakfast at six, and out the whole of a stormy day, till near six in the evening, and a fourth of the time standing under shelter of trees, to avoid being wet through. Had an army of myrmidons and curs to scour every inch of wood or hedge that I could sport on; and, in the whole day, only set eyes on 3 pheasants, all of which I killed in brilliant style, just as they were flying out of bounds, and bagged instantly the first time of springing them. Under all circumstances I never had a more satisfactory little day's sport.

2nd.[1]—The first time for some years, I was this day jackass enough to be kidnapped into a downright country visit; and what follows is a specimen of this 'pleasure.' I was to have previously gone over to shoot 'a splendid bag of game,' but luckily a wet morning prevented my joining the sportsmen, who, although good shots, I believe, got but 7 head between four of them. Now to the set-out. The girls and I, in order to meet my old musical friend, the well-known Signor Sola, accepted a kind and friendly invitation at Quarley House, a pretty seat in a desert seven miles beyond Andover, with an obbligato accompaniment of bad roads. The girls, women-like, were all agog for the 'spree' as soon as the rain had stopped, and the treacherous sun began to show his phiz; but when it was too late to retreat, the pitiless storms, as I predicted, began to pepper away on us and our uncovered vehicles. We made a short halt in Andover in order to pick up the life and soul of all sport, Tom Langstaff, who had borrowed the brewer's pony phaeton, and 'prime' grey prad. Whether the 'sturdy beast' had had too much grains or not enough, it matters but little; as all required for

[1] A bad attempt at the much-about-nothing style of Walter Scott's novels.

my journal is to say that he was considerably slower than a good tidy donkey; and in spite of whipping, whistling, chirruping, and charming him with all the hands and mouth that I could muster, his pace was no more than five miles an hour. We arrived at Quarley about four, and, according to the feeling and roaring of my 'chitterlings,' I guess it must have been near eight o'clock before we sat down to a grand dinner, which had waited long for the return of the chasseurs and their light bag of game. Nothing could be more kind or hospitable than the friendly treatment of our host and hostess; indeed we were so regaled as to be unfit for music in any other way than for merriment; and, had we not 'fought shy,' should have 'all been drunk together.' After a batch of rattling play, jolly singing, buffoonery, waltzing, quadrilling, and joke cracking, we proposed ringing for our vehicles, and were thought quite unsociable for 'cutting our sticks' so early as a quarter past one o'clock. Up drove our carriages, escorted by a party of men with flambeaux, which was headed by the Squire himself, and he ran with us very fast till we got through a new cut to the turnpike road. I should observe that the shipping and starting of the cargo was worthy of a picture by Hogarth, what with the music, changing of clothes, fiddle, guitar, and all such like; while my mouth was alternately occupied in blowing a mail horn and puffing a cigar, and my two hands in full occupation to put life into the brewer's 'prad.' To do him justice, however, we did coax him into a much better pace; and this I impute partly to his being 'homeward bound' and partly to a 'jolly blow-out' of the Squire's corn and beans, which of course took the shine out of all his former grain diet—perhaps unavoidable mixture of cocculus indicus and other brewer's fare. Well, we got to Andover, bid good night to Tom Langstaff and his Cremona, and I then got behind my own horse, 'Old Samson,' and rattled along at the rate of twelve miles an hour, till there came on a dense fog that it was not only extremely difficult, but even dangerous, to proceed in; and our laughter was soon changed to horror by seeing the whole horizon in a blaze of awful fire, and this in the direct line of my own property, which, thank God, it proved not to be. We reached Longparish House soon after three o'clock, and smelt of smoke as strong as if we had been attending the engines; though, from the intervening hill, we could not till next day ascertain where was the conflagration. We got to bed exactly at four, and were all quite sick and unwell the next day. So much for country visiting.

3rd.—On being called about half-past eight this morning, I was shocked to learn that there had been no less than three fires since midnight on the property of my friend Lord Portsmouth—two at Hurstbourne, within less than a quarter of a mile of where we turned off, and one at Tufton, about a mile farther, in which three horses were destroyed, and the carter had the narrowest possible escape of being burnt to death. The Andover engine, it appears, came directly after us, as it did not arrive till about three o'clock. Went, in a pouring wet afternoon, to view the remains of the fires, and the awful sight of four beautiful horses that lay broiled to death, and found that all four of the carters were so burnt that they escaped absolutely naked, though providentially with not very serious injury done to themselves, except the loss of all they had. Called at Hurstbourne House to offer any assistance in my power to my friend Mr. Fellowes, and was detained a little time stopping a row and bloody fight in Hurstbourne.

In the evening Signor Sola and Tom Langstaff arrived to dinner for a 'spree' and a glut of music, which we had in perfection till twelve o'clock.

5th.—Out all day, and, in spite of good weather and good shooting, could only get 4 partridges and 2 jack snipes, the only two I saw. The birds are now so wild that it is an absolute waste of time to slave after them.

6th.—Went to Southampton.

7th.—Got into the morning packet for Ryde, and in taking a glass of soda at Cowes, where I landed for about a quarter of an hour, the cork, which the chemist cut the string of, flew into the ball of my right eye, which at first I thought was blinded for ever, and the sensation was like a pickaxe striking through my head. I was blind in this eye all day, and in great pain, but I proceeded to Ryde, which place I never saw before and had now only one eye to see with, and was quite delighted with this most beautiful of all watering places.

November 3rd.—London. I went into our United Service Club to get some soup about four o'clock, and Sir F. Egerton came in and said he had just marked down a woodcock in the little shrubs of the park, close to the club house; and, had it not been so late, General Mundy would have gone to the ranger and got leave for me to go and kill the woodcock for the King. What a novelty this would have been!

6th.—An easterly wind and a good report from Read. Took the box of the 'Eclipse.'

7th.—Left London at eleven and got to Keyhaven at eleven. Of course I changed the weathercock. The wind had been all the week north-east, and I turned the cock to south-west and rain before I reached Winchester. There had been birds, and Read had had some sport.

10*th.*—A fine gale of wind from the eastward. Had the punt up to Pennington, but as yet seeing no birds off at sea we would not go off in the wash on an uncertainty, so brought her back dry and comfortable. I shot a green scarfe shag with the cripple stopper, and had fine sport with him and my terrier; but lest the dog should swim his very heart out, I settled this crippled parson with my second barrel.

11*th.*—The gale abated and we had a fine day, in which I was at sea from nine till past six, and never found a bird on tide. We walked ashore to Sowley Pond, where we saw a few dunbirds, &c. Never discharged a gun, except a shot with which I got a heron, coming home.

12th.—Read crawled on the mud since midnight, and came home this morning with 7 wigeon. Though a strong north-easter, there was not a bird off to-day.

14th.—Had a precious day's excursion; not for sport, but business. Having received a note from Joe yesterday to say that my waggon would be in Southampton early this morning for a load of coals, and would bring there an old punt that I wanted and a new pianoforte that I had bought, I drove into Lymington, and then mounted the box of Judd's coach to Southampton because I particularly wanted to see my faithful old carter, John Reeves, who had irretrievably hooked himself into the service of the lawyer—that marplot of everyone and everything in the parish. Well, having done my business with John and some other commissions, the next thing was how to get the punt and piano to Keyhaven. I hired a little coaster for 15*s.* and away I went with my cargo about one o'clock, with every prospect of reaching Keyhaven about four or half-past; but, alas! the uncertainty of wind and water. In order to save the tide I was obliged to 'dine with Duke Humphrey,' and content myself with a few buns and a bottle of porter, that I dare not wait to touch till we had got clear of the harbour. Before we had gone far we were suddenly becalmed, and, in short, the result was we dare not attempt to land at Keyhaven, as we never got to off Hurst till near seven, and then in total darkness. We there dropped anchor nearly half a mile from the beach, and had the delightful option of either starving on board all night, or taking to the old punt, which was not caulked and therefore leaked like a basket, with the vessel's two huge oars by way of paddles. Preferring liberty on any terms, we trusted to Providence that we should gain the shore before the punt could fill, and off went I with the captain and his mate like three unfortunates escaping from a wreck. We reached the beach, ran up for help, and the only boat we could get was a little thing just fit for two men to row in. We went off to the vessel, got out the piano, and off we came with such a freight of us that I really expected every moment we should sink. However, we fetched Keyhaven, with an awful roll of the piano and the two heavy fellows who rowed me ashore. So much for anyone but a slave being condemned to make a trip in a coaster.

15*th.*—Sunday. Nothing occurred to-day, except we heard of the captain and his mate having 'held on' and 'lushed it' ashore all night, leaving the boy on board to satisfy his appetite with sleep, in a cold easterly wind. The boy volunteered to see the coast. Query, will he volunteer again?

16*th.*—Afloat all day; went about twenty-four miles, and never found a bird, though a beautiful northerly wind. Heard from the Itchen Ferry men, who came down to drag for oysters, that they had not seen a bird all the way from the Southampton river to off Lymington, and that the whole of the gunners at Southampton, who regularly come to our West Channel, had only brought in one bird among them during the whole of last week. The coast is ruined till there comes frost enough to bite one's nose off, and snow to bleach up all inland vegetation.

17*th.*—A westerly wind. Went out in the punt, without the great gun, merely to try a rifle, and could not even get a gull to shoot at. Had no other arms on board but the popgun, loaded with small shot for the chance of dunlins, and set close up to 3 wild ducks, which I peppered with this feeble concern, and all 3 of which I must have killed dead had I had the great gun on board. How ridiculous, and yet provoking, that the only shot all the week occurred when I had no proper gun to shoot with. But it always is so.

December 9*th.*—Having been worried out of sleep and appetite, I resolved on a few days' sea air before I returned to town; so sent Monk, my coachman, on to Southampton last evening to have the mare and gig fresh and clean. Made for the eleven o'clock coach at Bullington, and, after wasting half an hour, found that both coaches had ceased running, and my only chance was to catch the one o'clock coach at Winchester, which I could do only by driving our slow sulky pony and butcher's cart about eight miles in the hour, and this I did, with five minutes to spare, by the persuasive argument of a blackthorn stick that I cut, as the only tool that would tell on the pony's buffalo hide. On my reaching Southampton, Monk, instead of being quite ready as ordered, had wandered away with a pot companion, and kept me waiting an hour all but three minutes; so, out of all patience, I was just driving off alone, leaving word for him to follow at his own expense per coach, as a salutary lesson for him, when he just met me turning the corner, with his face like that of a red lion, and his eyes blinking like an owl in the sun. I got to Keyhaven about seven, instead of four, as I ought to have done.

N.B.—I always change the weathercock when I go to the coast. I came off (not thinking about shooting this time) in a westerly wind, and before morning we had a north-easter and a hard black frost.

10*th*. In the afternoon I shipped the great gun in the punt and took a cruise. It blew a heavy gale, so that I could not go far out, but I saw off at sea about a dozen geese, and a fine trip of wigeon, such as I had not seen before this season.

14*th*.—A calm day with a south-east wind; took a rush-light breakfast, and started at daylight for a long cruise up to the mouth of the Beaulieu river. Bagged 8 wigeon: the first lot of birds I saw was 4, which I got close to, and bagged all of them with one barrel; the second, a large company that were very wild, and into which I pulled both barrels, flying, and got 4 more; if I had had large shot, proper for

150 yards, I think I should have knocked down 20. We did not get home till half-past six.

16th.—Went into Lymington with my punt having a few jobs to get done there, but never set eyes on a bird, though we had good weather. Fell in with a fleet of professional gunners, who had done nothing for this fortnight. Last night a stormy petrel flew against Hurst lighthouse, and was taken alive; I bought him for a shilling, and had him booked per coach to Leadbeater to stuff for my collection.

17th.—'Knocked off' for the present, and cleaned up and put away all the gear preparative to returning to town.

N.B.—Read was mud crawling every night, and during the whole time I was here brought in but 2 wigeon. We have to thank the mud crawlers for the ruin of our coast.

20th.—London. Sunday. Sadly disappointed. Had made up my mind to go and hear again my favourite preacher Dr. Dibdin, the Paganini of the parsons, who had through debts and difficulties been a long time absent, but my cold was so bad I dare not go to church, and was obliged to sit prisoner, with a poultice to my neck, and aching bones, all owing to yesterday's horrible woman, who would have a thorough draught in the coach in the coldest weather that had been felt for years. To-day we have frost and snow in right earnest; the very weather for geese, and even hoopers.

21st.—Splendid weather, and I much worse. The swelling in my neck quite insupportable, though I supposed it to be a mere boil. Went to Brodie, who pronounced it to be a carbuncle, and said it was the wisest thing I ever did to come to him just in time, or I might have lost my life, as Colonel Broughton did, by not having it opened in time. Sir Benjamin performed the operation immediately, and a pretty severe one it was, and then sent me home to be laid up for a day or two, with poultices &c., and with every hope of my getting well in the course of a week.

N.B.—How singular! Last year I was operated on upon

December 19, and laid up all Christmas, and this year on December 21 again for a totally different case. And both times during the only good wild-fowl frosts that we have had for some years.

27th.—Sunday. After church and some visits, I went to the Regent's Park to see the immense mob that were admitted for skating ; and if all the cattle in Smithfield had enjoyed a month's run there, they could not have done more damage to the grass &c. than was caused by this free admission. The trees that had been white with powder-frost for eight days were now beginning to thaw, and the wind was getting to the west, which I told all the philosophers it would of course do when I was near getting to Keyhaven.

28th.—Left London per Southampton 'Telegraph' at a quarter past eight this morning, and drove up to the door at Keyhaven Cottage at a quarter past eight this evening, making the journey, as usual, in just twelve hours and just 100 miles. A westerly wind.

N.B.—During the past week the sport has been excellent, though merely with ducks, mallards, and wigeon, as scarcely any geese or other more northerly birds had appeared, which was the best possible proof that the very severe weather would not last. And when the west wind set in, the country was, as usual, clear of all wild fowl.

31st.—A south-east wind. Went afloat, and saw nothing but a mallard.

1836

January.—I write this at Keyhaven, where I came just too late for the good weather, having been detained in town by illness

2nd.—A fall of snow, and a sudden change of wind in the night, has brought down a fine show of birds, though they are wild and scattered, and consequently I could not kill many at a shot. But by working from morning till night, we brought in 12 wigeon, 4 mallards, 4 teal, 5 godwits, and 1 knot plover. I refused a shot at 5 pintails within forty yards, while setting up to about 150 wigeon, that I must have done wonders with had not 3 wretched curlews sprung from a creek and frightened them to sea.

3rd.—Sunday. The wind shifted back to the miserable west again. Read, our mud 'worm,' indulged in his hobby of 'launching' till after midnight, though brought in but 1 wigeon.

4th.—A tremendous gale from the west all night. Read got 3 wigeon before daylight, and we went off, on a forlorn hope, as far as we dare go, and I brought in 3 ducks and 3 mallards, which were 6 birds more than I expected. Out at night from ten till past one; but though a full moon and west wind, we had not tide enough to get near what few birds remained for the high water. Read never went to bed, but crawled on the mud till morning, and came in with 10 wigeon. We then went off for the whole day again, the 5th, but never saw a chance for sport, though out till dark. Miserably dull day for everything, except a rich jaw between mud crawler Read and Buckle, who met afloat after a previous quarrel.

6th.—Out from soon after eight till dark. A splendid calm for the open sea, so went about ten miles up, and landed near Gurnet Bay, in the most desolate part of the Isle of Wight; and, if I had had a dog, might have poached some game while two hours waiting for the ebb, which did nothing for us, as the swarms of birds that were here yesterday had shifted to Christchurch Bay; and, in short, we had a blank day, and brought home everything we took out, except the victuals.

7th.—A south wind, with heavy drizzling rain. Went up Channel to take a rope to Buckle, and lunched with him, in his floating den, on fried sprats. Put off from his craft and got 1 brent goose; a very long shot, and the only one I have had a shot at this year, as the geese appear to have forsaken our coast altogether. Coming home in a heavy rain, I had the great good luck to bag 6 pintails at a shot with the one barrel of the swivel gun, and in my life I never had so long a chase as I this day had with one of these birds. There were about 13 in the company, and I think I should have floored them all if the wet weather had not induced me to neglect loading the other barrel. Turned into bed from eight till ten. Off from eleven till four in the morning, but the birds all left the harbour directly there was water over the ground (their old trick, unless they are 'young comers,' or the weather is hard). So I proved that night shooting now is time and rest lost, except for a mud crawler like Read.

8th.—A wet day. Out in the evening, though saw nothing except a good show of wigeon at flight time, all of which flew too high, and appeared to be bound far to the eastward. Read crawled all night, and came in at daylight with 3 wigeon.

9th.—Another wet day. Went 'well breeched' for the evening flight, but the birds all went over in some fresh place, instead of where we saw them last night.

10th.—Sunday. A splendid hurricane from the east, and a right glorious fall of snow the whole day.

11th.—Out several hours before daylight, and Read like a madman with his confidence of an immense day; and, after all, there was not a bird to go after. The swarms of fowl that appeared (lost in the snow) yesterday had all gone out to Christchurch Bay, and, in short, we gave it up, and came home, in a dense fog, about twelve. I then proceeded to look at Sowley Pond, which had been black with fowl in the snow storm. Had a precious wet drive home, with the weathercock south-west and a heavy gale. And thus ended the beautiful hard frost and snow that had raised our hopes of grand sport.

12th.—Out at daybreak, and again all the evening. Got but 4 wigeon, and did wonderfully well in killing even them.

14*th*.—A terrific westerly gale, and a blank day.

15*th*.—A most ferocious gale of wind from the west the whole night. We thought our house would come down; it literally shook our beds. About eight this morning the gale was beat down by heavy rain; it then moderated, and we went off, unluckily, just ten minutes too late for water, to one of the finest shots I should have ever had. We got nothing, and came in about twelve.

16*th*.—A sharp white frost, with a northerly wind and fine day. Out from daybreak till evening, and never got a chance for a fowl. Read, who was out all night, got 2 wigeon.

17*th*.—Sunday. A pinching white frost with a butterfly day.

18*th*.—A westerly gale and a blank day.

19*th*.—A sudden change from west to east. A few birds down, and with them a host of blundering blockheads from Itchen Ferry, who drove them to sea. Never fired a shot.

20*th*.—A south wind. Out all day, and found only 6, and got 3, brent geese, in the very middle of all the Southampton gunners. I should have got the other 3 with the other barrel had it not been that one of these fellows attempted to paddle up to them where they had pitched near their shot companions.

21*st*.—A south-west heavy gale, and a blank day. Boarded Buckle in the afternoon, and even he had not got a bird the whole week.

23*rd*.—A precious excursion. Up at five to pack and breakfast. Walked to Everton in a gale of wind and drizzling rain to mount Judd's coach at eight. Misinformed as to time, and was ten minutes too late; so had to tramp three long miles more (with a part of my things at my back, and Tommy Chissel carrying my trunk) in wind and rain to Lymington. Coach, of course, gone; no other conveyance till evening, so obliged to hire a fly, as soon as I had ascertained there were no letters for me at the post office. Just as I was preparing to start, with the fly at the door, the Keyhaven postman ran up to me with a basket, which I opened in great haste, and alongside a goose which came in it was a letter from Peter, to say he had received an extension of his leave, and was therefore ready to join me at Keyhaven. Well, I stood at the flyman's door for some minutes, hesitating whether to drive back to Keyhaven or on for Longparish; and, as I had some business there, decided on the latter in order to get rid of it. Went a good pace in order to be in Southampton by twelve to save Dalton's coach to Winchester, where my gig was to be in readiness. Got in a quarter before twelve, and floored again. No more Dalton, his coach had just stopped for the winter, and no conveyance till night except a hired one. So had to work on in a hack gig to Winchester, where I found Monk and the mare. After having walked the first five miles on a turnpike road, an inch deep in slush, and gone the other thirty miles with damp feet, and a shirt ringing wet with perspiration at the price of a shilling a mile, besides the drivers and gates, and in a day that no humane man would have turned out his dog in, I got to Longparish about half-past four.

24th.—Sunday. Shivering like a dog in a wet sack from the miserable damp and cold I had to undergo yesterday.

30th.—Met Colonel Sheddon of Lymington, who was delighted yet panic-struck to see me, as his son, in a letter received the previous day, had informed him of my being drowned off Lymington on Monday night, when I was at Longparish, playing duets with Bill Griesbach.

February 7th.—Keyhaven. Mild as April, and all the birds singing. This (being Sunday too) was no day for shooting, and the accounts of the gunning were miserable, as Read and his opponent Buckle by incessantly opposing each other had nearly banished the wild fowl, without getting anything worth their labour.

8th.—Took a cruise in the punt, to try my rifle, though

never got a chance, and get some sea air, but would not disgrace myself by putting the great gun together for nothing, so took 'old Fullerd' for the fun of popping at a passing 'parson' or bagging a few dunlins for a pudding. What should I see, however, but 9 geese, which happened to pitch on the mud 108 yards from where we had water. Up we went on a forlorn hope, and off I fired the gun, with the bare possibility of stopping one by some lucky shot, when, to my utter astonishment, down came 4 of them. One, however, recovered, after we had all but got him, and joined the company, but the other 3 geese we brought home. About two o'clock it set in a wet day, and coming home, we fell in with the other six, a splendid shot for a stanchion, but (for want of water only) a little too far for 'old Fullerd.' I tried them, but it was no go.

9th.—Out again for the day, and had reason to repent the want of the swivel gun. We got within a hundred yards of about 60 geese, and they all drew up in one solid cluster, with their necks stretched up like a bundle of asparagus. But just as I rose up to discharge the shoulder gun, they all sprung and dispersed into the wind. I fired after them and beat down 4, but it was so rough that after nearly filling the punt with the breakers in the shallow water, I bagged but 3 brent geese. We therefore decided on shipping the great gun to-morrow, though I suppose when we are 'well breeched' there will be no more chances for great sport.

10th.—Put off with the great gun in the afternoon, and saw about 70 geese off Pennington Spit, but there came on such a gale and heavy sea that we were too happy to give them up, and make our escape home, through Stivers Creek.

12th.—The large company of geese were in view with a glass from our window, off Pennington Spit. Off we went in a strong breeze, and down we dropped on them, but on approaching the flock we got into such a heavy hollow sea that we had more to mind the breakers than the birds. I blew off at them at about 250 yards, and knocked down 1, but we were obliged to raise the siege and pull into shelter, with about a hogshead of water on board, and make a vow that we would abandon the cruise for these birds till we had either 'water over the ground,' or a more moderate time for 'the outside.' Any punt but mine would have been filled and washed on 'the edge,' with a comfortable sousing of gear and all hands.

13*th.*—The first fine moderate morning since I came, and, as the devil would have it, that stupid scarecrow, Dan'l Paine of Itchen had arrived last night at the Hurst pothouse, to disturb our harbour at daybreak, which he did so effectually by popping at ox-birds that, before the water was up for a stanchion, not a living creature remained. We were therefore 'done out of' everything. I, however, saved my blank by bringing in 1 duck and 1 golden-eye, the only two shots I had, except killing 1 superb spotted diver with the popgun. In the evening I went to a late dinner, with Mr. and Mrs. West, at Arwood's Lodge, a stretch of friendship that very few are favoured with by me, and as a matter of course I paid rather dearly for my pleasure. I did not leave till about twelve o'clock, when I had to drive home, about three miles, in the gig, and it was so dark that, for the greater part of the way, I was obliged to walk in front, and literally feel the way lest we should be lost or capsized among the innumerable ditches and pitch-dark turnings on this ram's-horn road, and to make it all the more agreeable we had no lamps, and there came on a cold thick drizzling rain which we had to weather with that virtue, patience, all the way to Keyhaven at the pace of a 'black job.' I of course caught cold. Here is another specimen of the delights of dining out in winter in the country, a thing I generally avoid as I would a mad dog.

15*th.*—Fine weather, and off all day, but nothing to be seen.

16*th.*—Not a chance to be seen.

17*th and* 18*th.*—Such a ferocious north-easter that not a boat could row on end, and I booked for London on the

H 2

19th. Here again we have the very essence of my turning the weathercock.

19th.—Arrived in town by the 'Eclipse,' almost perished with cold, and in the finest gunning weather we have had this year—a black frost, and a gale from the north-east. And by way of a pleasant home to leave for in the very fine weather I had been praying to have, I was assailed with a concatenation of annoyances in private and other matters that made my situation like that of a toad under a harrow, or a cat among a pack of dogs.

20th.—On the tramp, and at work with head and heels all day.

21st.—Called on the park keeper relative to presenting to the commissioners a beautiful goose that I had spared from the first shot I made at Keyhaven, and kept in my garden the whole time I was last there, and brought up with me, as we could no longer stand the damage he did to the cabbage plants. He lived on the grass, but was for ever marching about, and his feet were the ruin of everything.

22nd.—Turned the goose off on the ice in the Regent's Park this morning. Accounts in town of the awful devastation on the northerly coasts occasioned by the late unprecedented hurricanes, and among them the wreck of a kind and worthy man, named Paxton, whom I had just got a situation for at Scarborough, and who was on his passage from Lymington, where I had just taken leave of him. The crew, however, were saved, and let me hope, at least, some of the property too, though this I could not learn at Lloyd's, but the secretary promised to send me word when known.

29th.—Had the satisfaction to learn, from Lloyd's Norfolk agent, that Paxton and his property were saved from the wreck. So busy that I was obliged to go about all day with blue pills in me. Busy in the afternoon about Joe Manton's tombstone, for which I was solicited to write the inscription.[1]

[1] To the memory of Joseph Manton, who died, universally regretted, on the

In the evening I went to the new theatre of our unrivalled vocalist Braham, which I consider as decidedly the most chaste and neatest I ever saw at home or abroad.

March 2nd.—Mounted the box of the 'Telegraph,' and ran down to Keyhaven. I merely did this to recover myself after the worry I had in town; but, hearing there were still some geese about, and my punt not being yet taken from her moorings, I had my gun put together.

3rd.—A south-wester, and very wet all the morning. Went out for a few hours in the afternoon, but could expect nothing, as the coast was lined with an army of periwinkle pickers, who were preparing for a vessel, that was to sail for London to-night, fifteen tons of winkles; and may they get a quick passage out of our country, say I.

4th.—Out all day and went a long distance, but never saw anything, though heard that a great many geese had been seen last week, and that 3 had been killed by that bungler, Dan'l Paine, of Itchen. In the evening there set in another heavy gale from the south-west.

8th.—A fine northerly breeze, so we sailed in the punt all the way to off Leap. But the late gales had swept every fowl off the coast, and we came home just before dark with a blank day, though after a most delightful and healthy sail.

N.B.—My great gun was loaded last Thursday morning, and though it remained afloat till this afternoon (Tuesday) in such seas, rains, and hurricanes as we seldom see, yet on discharging the barrels, both went off as well and as smart as a clean gun the 1st of September.

9th.—Went on a miserable though satisfactory expedition. Having sent on an old punt to Christchurch, I started very

29th day of June, 1835, aged 69. This humble tablet is placed here by his afflicted family, merely to mark where are deposited his mortal remains. But one everlasting monument to his unrivalled genius is already established in every quarter of the globe by his celebrity as the greatest artist in firearms that ever the world produced; as the founder and the father of the modern gun trade; and as a most scientific inventor in other departments, not only for the benefit of his friends and the sporting world, but for the good of his King and country.

early this morning in the gig with Read, to row all over and inspect the harbour, from the Haven House at Mudeford up to the town of Christchurch. We started in a humbugging white frost, which appeared all very well for our purpose, as a dead calm suited it best; but no sooner had we got to within about three miles of Mudeford than there set in the most beastly gale of wind, with heavy rain, that the clouds could vomit up, and this continued for the whole day without one moment's intermission. Determined not to be bullied by the weather, after driving ten miles of heavy road, we got into the punt, with two shoulder guns, and went all over the harbour, till we landed in the town of Christchurch, where I had some fun at hearing of my own fame from the barber bird-stuffer and others who knew me not, but from whence we could not return against the torrent of water that the wind had brewed up. So we left the punt, and tramped by land, in water boots, two miles, with all our gear at our backs, and then drove home to Keyhaven in one eternal torrent of rain and raging blast of wind. But we were repaid for our misery by finding the harbour such as to be well worth trying on a future season, or even driving over to with a shoulder gun any fine day.

10*th.*—A strong westerly wind and rain nearly all day again. Busy taking the great punt and gun into store, and cleaning up and putting away all the gear thereunto belonging; as every fowl has now left our coast, and we have only to 'knock off' for the season.

Game &c. killed in the season up to March 15th, 1836 (a general failure all over the coast, and every gunner in disgust; the geese appear to be banished altogether): 130 partridges, 1 hare, 3 rabbits, 3 pheasants, 21 snipes. Total, 158 head. 20 ducks, 54 wigeon, 6 pintails, 6 teal, 2 golden-eyes, 8 geese, 13 plover. Total, 109. Game, 158; fowl, 109. Grand total, only 267.

24*th.*—London. Went down to Kidbrooke to see Mr.

J——, but as he was from home, I gained nothing for my lost morning but a trial of the new Deptford railroad, by which I returned, and which I found far inferior to that between Liverpool and Manchester, because the road was rather on the curve and the wheels were too high, from which circumstances the motion was not so easy as that on the other railroad, and our pace was much slower, as we were eight and a half minutes doing a little more than two miles, while on the other railroad we went about double the pace, and with half the motion.

April 25th.—To London from Southampton by the 'Eclipse' coach. We had for a travelling companion the celebrated Lord Stuart de Rothsay, who generally works up and down outside this coach in the garb of an old skipper, and either in the name of his valet or with no name at all. Though I remembered him at Eton, and had once dined with him when an ambassador, I also preserved my *incog.* lest I should have annoyed him by a recognition.

29th.—Winter. Frost and snow. Alone from morning till night, and I have not passed so pleasant a day for these fifteen years; what with writing, reading, and strapping hard at my long-lost music, I could have stayed up till daylight next morning. 'A man ought never to be so little alone as when he is alone.' I this day received a letter from Mr. Black, the great publisher in Edinburgh, offering me twenty guineas a sheet to write for the 'Encyclopædia Britannica,' but my engagements with Messrs. Longman & Co. and the extreme pressure of private business obliged me to decline this handsome offer and high honour.

May 13th.—Went to Longparish to see and decide how to proceed with the new lake that I have begun, and also to get some more of my rents in.

14th.—Longparish. A cold white frost this morning. Tried a fresh-bored duck gun ('Old Egg'), and found that it shot one-third closer, and with double the strength, since Lancaster rebored the calibre to my order. Having done this, and all the business I could do for the present, I indulged in an afternoon's 'spree' with Mr. W. Griesbach. We dragged four baskets of trout out of Mole's Hole; shot as many rooks as we could tell what to do with, and ended the evening with a 'flare up' at the bats, and then a batch of duet playing.

15*th.*—Ran down to Keyhaven to see my stone walk complete, which proved to surpass anything I ever saw, and to be the admiration of the whole country. This is one of the many things I was thought a madman for attempting, and afterwards worshipped for having done. What short-sighted asses most people are!

21*st.*—Drove to Christchurch to see Charles Tucker about doing up my old punt I had left there, and then drank tea and spent the evening at Mudeford, in order to see the salmon fishing, but was here disappointed, as not a fish was caught while I was there, though several had been taken within these three days, and some 20-lb. fish. Old Joy of Christchurch had, however, a royal catch of mullet, of which I took a few. He caught 14 cwt. in one evening. I finished my day with a drive along the beautiful shore of Mudeford, and an inspection of an old steam packet that is hauled up on an eminence and let into the cliff, by way of a fancy summer house for Lord Stuart de Rothsay, who employs a caretaker and showman to take care of the concern.

28*th.*—Returned to London, half starved with the cold winterly weather, and much gratified with meeting the beautiful procession of King's birthday mails, as well as with Williams's dexterous driving of our coach through the crowd occasioned by these and the equipages returning from the Drawing Room.

29*th.*—Influenza everywhere, owing to burning sun and chilling north-easters. Vegetation all but annihilated. Came home from bank in steam omnibus in half the time of the others. Nothing could go better.

June 30*th*.—London. Up to the end of this month I had scarcely a moment to enjoy a meal; what with bother, business &c. I was seldom in bed till one, and awake again writing down memorandum at daylight. The heat was so intense that at night one could not even bear a sheet as a cover. *Quantus equis, quantus adest viris sudor.* Horace, hem!

July 1*st*.—We went this evening to the benefit of the tenth muse, or goddess of the stage, Malibran, and so intense was the heat in the boxes that my very skin was stained from the dye of my blue coat. So no more benefits for me this season.

5*th*.—The weather has become so intensely hot and oppressive that it is even difficult to breathe. Talk of winter, it's all nonsense; this is the weather to make a man a cripple.

6*th*.—I hopping all over the town in pain that made me holloa out. All our places booked for leaving town. What with pain, packing, bill-paying, and bustle, the confusion was awful. Every servant so occupied there was no one to help the cripples, and the doctor not to be found, and most probably again in a sponging house.

7*th*.—So bad that I was obliged to ring up Charles to dress me in time to be stuck on the box of the 'Telegraph;' in short, a regular second edition of the old journey from Talavera to Lisbon, when I spent a week among the mountains with a bullet in my carcase. Got helped into a jolting fly on my arrival at Lymington, and crawled out of it at Keyhaven about eight this evening.

8*th*.—Having scarcely been able to lie otherwise than on my back all night, I was so stiff to-day as to be a complete cripple, the rheumatism having, as I before forgot to mention, set into the very part where I was wounded.

18*th*.—The worst Overton Fair for many years; and I was

obliged to think myself very lucky to sell eight score of lambs at 16*s.* 6*d.* instead of 1*l.* 6*s.*

August 1st.—Mounted the 'Red Rover' for a few days' visit to Lord Rodney at Alresford. A house full of company, and all the luxuries that could possibly be thought of.

3rd.—Left the dinner table about ten for a couple of hours' eel fishing, to be shown the way they fish at Naples. It is to have a row of lamps in front of a broad punt, by which you see the eels when they cannot see you, and then kill them with a spear. The night was too rough, and hardly dark enough; so that the bailiff despaired of my seeing enough to learn the plan; but, in spite of all, I did manage to kill 1 fine eel, and had a stroke at 2 or 3 more, which I could not see sufficiently to kill. Lord Rodney tells me he has killed 30 or 40 sometimes in a few hours' cruise. Nothing can be more novel or beautiful than this pastime; and it was so clean and dry that I need not have unshipped my dandy dinner dress.

4th.—Left Alresford, after having as usual received the greatest kindness and hospitality, and drove home by an improved road through Lord Ashburton's park. We came home on 13 miles of beautiful road instead of having to travel 21 miles of hilly turnpike with two gates to pay, and a heavy drag through the whole town of Winchester.

5th.—Busy all day with farmers, lawyers, horse dealers, clods, workmen, and other bores.

7th.—Sunday. Sailed to Yarmouth, and heard a parson who could preach, the Rev. George Burrard.

19th.—Keyhaven. Lord Chief Justice Tindall walked down from Newlands expressly for the purpose of seeing my punts, guns, and gear, which he entered into the spirit of with observations worthy of a judge; and went away evidently much pleased with my divers originalities.

20th.—After a series of fine days, of which we profited by seeing everything in the neighbourhood, both by sea and land, we had this day a westerly wind and rain. In the evening it cleared up, and we saw a splendid frigate put back owing to bad weather, and anchor off Yarmouth. Off we went to see her. It proved to be the 'Madagascar,' 46 guns, whose captain, Sir John Peyton, knew both Mrs. Hawker and myself, and whose hospitality was unbounded. The band played while we took tea, and the middies waltzed and quadrilled. We then adjourned to a splendid cabin aft with a capital Broadwood piano; in short, we had a regular merry soirée on board, and did not leave till past nine, when the marine drums struck up their watch-setting. We had a contrary wind back, and through breaking an oar and other reverses did not get home till near midnight.

22nd.—Went in the yacht of Colonel Sheddon and Mr. Hare to a grand regatta at Cowes. The King's prize was won easy by Mr. Lyons's yacht, the 'Breeze.'

31st.—Proceeded by the midday coach for Longparish; and, on the coach setting me down, I had the mortification to find that, while I was waylaid by two loungers in Winchester, a green sub. of some padnagging regiment had walked off with my portmanteau instead of his own; so I was obliged to send the only man I had for everything, in consequence of the harvest, off to Winchester with a cart and the very horse I wanted for to-morrow, and luckily he got back with my trunk a few minutes before ten at night. But the green man had the worst of it, as all his shooting things were gone off to Reading.

CHAPTER XXIX

1836

September 1*st*.—A dry gale of wind all day, and not one breath of scent. Birds ran away from almost every point, and were as wild as hawks. Nothing could have been done, but for the thin barley, in which we severely punished them in the afternoon; and though at one o'clock I had only got 6 birds, our day wound up with just 42 partridges.

N.B.—My last 3 birds I shot so late that I could not see the gun, so that I never was so hard run to get a 'butchers' halloo,' or three cheers for 20 brace. One thing I did that was worthy of my youngest days; I charged a covey against a high wind till they dropped exhausted, when I sprung from my horse, à la Ducrow, without stopping, and bagged one with the first, and two with the second barrel, leaving the horse to proceed *solus* at full speed, till Mr. Griesbach charged after him on the grey and caught him. Under all circumstances we consider this as one of our most miraculous days on record.

2*nd*.—Friday. A wet day, a glorious godsend against the blockheads who can't resist driving the birds the second day. Fine in the evening, when the green-livered son of a —— the lawyer turned out 'full drive;' so I flew out, flanked him, and bagged 8 brace.

3*rd*.—Another splendid day. I bagged 30 partridges besides 4 lost; and Joe Hawker, who was with me, and this day shot beautifully, got 27. Our combined bag was 60 head.

We worked round the lawyer's grand party as coopers would work round a barrel.

N.B.—On finding I had 29 birds, I slaved hard to make up a round number (that sounds fuller in the mouth), but without success, and had given it up as it grew dark; when, on leaving the very last field, a covey sprung from the feed, and I shot one through the head, which fell and was bagged at about 80 yards. To-morrow being Sunday, I was up till past midnight—game distributing, note writing &c. though tired as a dog, and had not dined till near ten.

4th.—Sunday. Heard all their bulletins, and found I had 'beat' all the country 'hollow.'

5th.—A wet morning, and a gale of wind all day. Went out quietly at twelve, and came home to a late dinner with 13 partridges and 2 hares, besides having lost 4 birds in the barley, and never fired but one blank shot the whole day. I shot capitally.

N.B.—The birds are now so wild that we may take our leave of all further chance for great bags; and, having now supplied all my requisitions, I shall either give up shooting or merely ride out to get a few birds when wanted.

7th.—Got 20 partridges, and never fired but one blank shot.

Game bagged the first week (I was out but three whole days and one half day): 103 partridges, 2 hares, 1 snipe. Total, 106 head, which, with 80 birds, besides 2 hares, 2 snipes, and 1 rabbit, got by Joe, who shot every day, makes the combined lot 191 head—exclusive of an unusual proportion shot and lost in standing corn for want of scent as well as of a retriever.

10th.—A splendid little 'spree' with the lawyer. While I was detained with people on business till half-past twelve, he bombarded all the best beat that is now left for me to shoot on, and had planted his marker under my firs to watch the birds that he had made up his mind to shoot in my tenant's corn; when, at about two o'clock, I made a rapid charge of cavalry, by which I completely cut him out, and at five came home with 20 partridges (besides 2 lost), 1 hare, and 1 quail, the only one I have seen or heard of this year; all of which he had driven from his own ground, and most of which I killed before his marker's face, and without missing a shot, which was extraordinary, because I was so unwell that I was scarcely able to fag. This is one of the prettiest little bits of shooting I ever made in all my sporting career.

12th.—In one constant row like a house on fire from the moment I got up till three in the afternoon, when I rode over to Bullington to announce to the keeper the surrender of Mr. Gore's lease and do other business at that place. I took a gun in my hand, but it appeared useless, as all the country was cleared, and it blew a bleak blast from the north. All I shot at therefore and got was 1 hare, so I rode home to prepare for blowing out some neighbours with a haunch of venison; and, just at the last hour, who should I see but my old friend the lawyer, so I made a rapid charge to leeward of him, and picked up 9 partridges, besides 1 lost.

21st.—Keyhaven. Went across to Mr. Guy's 'mudlands,' and got 3 snipes and 3 jack snipes. I never saw so many jack snipes in so small a space before; about a dozen kept getting up under my feet one after the other. But I was so unwell that I missed several shots, and was obliged to go home instead of following up the sport. If I had been well, and had had two double guns and one good dog, I really think that, by working all day, I might have got 15 or 20 couple; a phenomenon for Keyhaven, where 3 couple in a day is thought brilliant sport.

22nd.—Tried the bog again; but, as is always the case, the great flight of snipes had taken their departure.

28th.—I read to-day with tears of the death of the unrivalled Malibran; and I also lost my beautiful Newfoundland dog, of the distemper.

October 1st.—A most ferocious gale with a deluge of rain. But no disappointment to me, as my spies of last evening had looked round the feed near every wood or hedgerow I have, and not a single pheasant was to be seen or heard of.

7th.—Went down to Chatham and found my son Peter, thank God, in excellent health. Had a pour of rain all night and all day, and felt sadly damaged by cold and being harassed. I dined with him and slept at a kind of canteen hotel, where the noise was awful, all the windows rattling with the wind and rain; a church clock so close that it vibrated my very bed, and at daylight the bugle boys of 'the Rifles' came to learn their lesson under my window.

8th.—'Turned out' at seven, breakfasted at eight, took a hasty inspection of the dockyard till near ten. Then mounted the coach, when the rain set in again, and got worked up to Blackheath; sent on my trunk to town and ran down the dirty fields for an hour's heavy business at Kidbrooke. Then ran down to Deptford and just caught the coach; worked my way through the borough just in time to send off Peter's money before Coutts' had closed (to-morrow being Sunday, and Peter to march for embarkation before post on Monday), and then flew up to Dorset Place just in time to answer an important letter by the last moment of the post. A list of commissions ready for me as long as a carpenter's bill, but too exhausted to do more than a few of them this wet night.

9th.—Sunday. Quite unwell and without appetite; but no rest for me, even on the Sabbath day, for the moment I had got out of church I was obliged to cab it, omnibus it and run it the whole morning, to do calls on business with people that I could only catch, or find time for, on a Sunday.

10th.—On incessantly from seven in the morning till ten at night, and only a quarter of an hour to each meal. Did more in a day than all my servants would in a week. Peter countermanded, and another officer allowed per Adjutant-

General to take his place, so he will return to the depot at Perth. What a godsend that I did not give 300*l.* for his exchange, as he wished!

11*th.*—London. One hour's pleasure while here—Moscheles played me his new pieces when I called to see him.

17*th.*—Longparish. Hunted like a wild boar from eight in the morning till a six o'clock dinner. I was literally bombarded with a rushing of people on business all in a heap. Surveyor about my plans for letting the farms. The doctor about my health. Buckle, just arrived from the coast, about punts and guns. Keele about divers jobs. Dance to settle his rent, and argue for divers more things wanted. The parson, on a mission from the hospital, and his brother, to see my 'lions.' Lieutenant Criswick on a visit (who had not met me for years). J—— on divers jobs. M—— about several items. L—— about some bills. Mr. Earle, the lawyer, with all his memorandums of agreements for tenants, business about the pond, and divers letters to write for the post. Worst of all, 2 pheasants in the wood, and obliged to send Joe to kill them, which he happily did, I not having one minute in the whole day, and even losing my music with Langstaff, who was all adrift without me. This they call amusement. Lord deliver me from the delights of a country clod squire. On again after dinner with persecution and botheration, and in short was not in bed till one o'clock in the morning, and obliged to wind up with a pill, though booked for more business to-morrow.

Memorandum of game &c. killed this season: 135 partridges, 1 quail, 4 hares, 10 snipes. Total, 150. Coast birds, 10 godwits, 3 knot plover. Total, 13. Grand total, 163 head.

N.B.—Had no time for shooting.

18*th.*—Prisoner from illness and slave with business. A partridge pitched in our lawn, and I walked down in my great coat, and made a brilliant shot at him.

19*th.*—A couple of wigeon pitched by my pond before I

was up, and I sent Buckle with my right barrel, that was left loaded yesterday, to blow them over, which he easily did and brought them in. All day I was baited again, with people of six different trades. 1 cock pheasant was heard of, and I went and bagged him after a 3 hours' chase, for which loss of time I had to lose all the comfort of my dinner. *Mais n'importe*, as I've no appetite.

20*th*.—Busy all day completing my new-invented paddles for the punt, which worked beautifully, though I have my doubts as to whether the birds will stand them better than sculling.

27*th*.—I got to Keyhaven to-day about eight, and found a delightful relief from business, and a fine change of air, though, as I never yet failed to do, I turned the weathercock from a lovely north-east to a dirty westerly gale. Heard that there had been a good show of wigeon and geese last week, so put the 'Petrel' punt afloat, and cleaned up all, in hopes of fair weather to try for a shot. On all the afternoon, and got everything for gunning put together and in order for the season.

29*th*.—A tremendous gale of wind all day from the north with a little sleet and snow. The very weather we are glad to see, though dare not venture out in, and so now let us hope to have not only leisure but weather for birds.

31*st*.—Out on tide all day and never got a shot; as an Itchen blackguard, yclept Dan'l Paine, had employed himself all yesterday to drive away every flock of birds that had collected here, and he kept banging about all the Sabbath day for 1 goose and 1 plover. I'll 'serve him out' for it with a threat of the penalty if he thus annoys us again.

November 8*th*.—Longparish. Got a half-holiday to-day; and started with my unrivalled 'Paganini' gun and old rat-catcher Siney to try our wood about two o'clock, but our day ended in a 'chapter of accidents,' owing to the first head of game started—a gigantic wild cat that ran to earth in a badger hole. To begin, I had a tremendous fall and broke the splendid and beautifully fitting stock of Paganini, which was worse than any injury to myself short of a broken bone. We then had a battle of dogs, in which old Hillery's sheep dog was all but killed; we then heard the screams of old Hillery's boy, who was all but killed by his ferocious old father for joining us; and the day ended with a three hours' digging for the cat, which was at last got at, and fought its way through the whole pack of dogs and mounted a tree. Charles Castleman then ran home for Siney's old musket, and blew the infernal old 'warmunt' out of the tree and brought her home in triumph. She weighed above 12 lb.

10*th.*—On from morning till night, with about a dozen active fellows well primed with beer, weathering some heavy showers, at planting round my pond; and it was like magic, the rapid change we made in the appearance of the place. I had to gallop backward and forward to the men cutting stakes and pulling trees in our wood; and while the men were at dinner, the only hour I could spare, I rode to the bog and found 4 snipes, 3 of which I got.

29*th.*—Keyhaven. The most savage hurricane I ever beheld. Went in water boots to view the terrific sea, which ran as high as a church; and such was the hurricane that the noise of the waves was completely silenced by the wind. The sea had made a breach in the beach, and we prepared 'all hands' to remove property for a flood, as in 1802; but, providentially, the wind shifted so far in as to prevent any further apprehension of serious consequences.

December 6th.—Longparish. I had the luck to find that I had sustained no very serious damage by the late unprecedented hurricane, that has laid so many places in ruins, and caused the loss of so many lives in both town and country as well as all over the coast. It was quite awful to see the damage on each side of the road all the way from Lymington to some miles beyond Southampton.

21st.—Up before daylight, and opened the flood hatches of my new pond by ten o'clock for the first time; and the effect of the pond when flooded, with the little waterfalls, amply repaid all my long trouble by answering to a focus in every respect, and even surpassing my expectations in its splendid appearance.

22nd.—On all day in Southampton. Went over in the new floating bridge to Itchen, and spent a delightful evening at the pianoforte with the Apollo of the place, Mr. William Griesbach.

24th.—Busy with solicitor and banker at Andover. Finished the new punt and finished the pond and all the inclosure; and this evening (that of my birthday) paid off every bill, and discharged all the workmen employed for this pond and inclosure, so that to-morrow, Christmas Day, I can look at this greatest improvement that has ever been made on the estate, and fairly call it my own property, as well as my own invention.

25th.—Sunday and also Christmas Day. Splendid frost and heavy snow. Crazy to be off to the coast.

26th.—The severest frost and heaviest fall of driving snow that I have seen for several years. Monk went off in advance for Keyhaven at two this morning, and, as all this day has turned out, with a drive that could only be surpassed by a Russian campaign. Everything, and even the pond, frozen over; so we finished our 8 months and 3 days' hard labour just in time, as the severe weather set in Christmas Day, the very day after the work was completed and the men paid off.

This afternoon the snow was in all the by-roads level with the hedges, and consequently in many places eight feet deep. No coaches passed, and all travelling stopped. A gale of wind from the north-east, and many degrees colder than I ever felt it in all the course of my life. Absolutely petrifying. My following Monk for Keyhaven to-day was impossible; and I have no guess how far he got before the overwhelming snow hurricane came on, though he started with hard roads and fair hard weather.

27th.—The only coach that passed to-day was the mail from London, which had to work over a bridge near here by the help of shovels. My boat lashed on the boat carriage, and I 'all hot' to be at Keyhaven; but no prospect of getting out of prison. Snow eight feet deep on the turnpike.

28th.—Imitated the only man I condescend to imitate—Buonaparte. A second Moscow business, though without the failure. The turnpike from near Sutton to Winchester being, for six or eight miles, up to the tops of the hedges filled with snow averaging seven feet deep, I started a direct steeplechase for Winchester by crossing the turnpike at the only passable place, and then taking my boat on the carriage across the fields like a foxhunt, avoiding the turnpike as death and destruction, though keeping it in view as a beacon of direction. I had twelve men altogether, and every hedge we came to, we had to cut through a block of snow about six or eight feet high; then cut the hedge through and assist the carriage over it with all hands, and then drive away over about half a mile of clear arable country, where we could proceed above four miles an hour. My man Charles and I took it by turns to gallop forward on a rough-shod fast horse, and, with one pioneer behind, to probe and ascertain the next safe breach to be made, while the rest of the troop were cutting the previous one. Nothing had passed. Everyone defied me, and swore I was mad. Had we failed, the Lord help us; as I doubt if we could have been quite sure of completing our retreat, when within two miles of Winchester, before dark. At last we came to the grand difficulty, an impassable dyke and a wood, when I, who was in advance as pioneer and surveyor, was hailed by a gentleman shooting; so I advanced towards him, and he directed us all one field to the right, where we had only to cut through for about ten yards in five feet of snow, and then enter the turnpike road at about a mile and a quarter from Winchester, where there had been a levy *en masse* to clear the snow in order to rescue Parson Dallas, who had been blocked there in his carriage, and could only be saved by this great undertaking. We then entered the town of Winchester in glorious triumph, to the utter astonishment of everyone who heard of us; and after giving my old horse the good cheer he deserved, as well as all the men (a man should always take care of his horse first), I drove comfortably on to Southampton, where I left him for the night to follow with the boat carriage, and proceeded by the 'Tally-ho' coach to Keyhaven, where I arrived safe, after all my unparalleled difficulties, about ten o'clock at night Thanks to God for my safety, and for having done what has perhaps never been done before, at all events among the Hampshire hogs.

N.B.—I had only time to swallow two buns and a glass of beer, as the only half-hour I had in Southampton was to run about, on commissions, in water boots, in which, by the way, I had travelled all the way from Longparish, and nothing like them to keep one from cold.

29*th.*—Longparish. Castleman brought in the boat carriage and horse about one o'clock, after being detained so long at the custom house (for the licence) that I was afraid some accident had happened to prevent the perfect success of the expedition. I could not get afloat till near three, when it was very rough. The new punt answered beautifully, though I only used her as a following boat, because I took the grand set-out of all, the 'Petrel.' I got one little shot only, and brought in 4 wigeon and 1 scaup duck; for we had just time only to make a beginning and get back before it was 'pitch dark.'

30*th.*—Very severe weather. Plenty of birds off at sea, but too rough to attempt getting there. Fired but one very long shot, and got 2 wigeon.

31st.—Weather so severe that the mud was frozen, in consequence of the tides (being just now at the 'dead of the neap') not flowing over it, and the birds were all at sea feeding on the floating weeds. Too much sea to shoot in the Channel, so that there was this day no sport for a punt; and last night not a chance for Read with his 'launching.' I went out about one o'clock, and all I saw was 14 geese, at which I made a capital shot while bobbing on the waves. I pulled off one barrel at them (with mould shot) and knocked down 8. A pretty little shot to finish the old year, and, please God, to lead to success in the new one.

1837

January 2nd.—Began the new year very well. Read mud-launched from two till dawn and brought in 11 wigeon; and I went outside of Hurst, and brought in 17 wigeon.

3rd.—No fowl to-day. Read had no chance with his nightly mud crawl, and a little shift of wind had driven the birds westward. My gun missed fire at the geese. But I came home early in order to despatch baskets of fowl for his Majesty and others.

4th.—A mild, calm day. Off at sea from morning till the afternoon, and then in the creeks with my new punt, which answers beautifully. Brought home 19 wigeon and 4 geese; 15 the first shot, 4 the second shot; and the geese with the shoulder gun from a creek, where I had to launch and then crawl for an hour. I never had such a filthy, laborious job, and never in my life made so long a shot with a shoulder gun. There were five punts and boats innumerable off in the mirror calm, but not a bird did any of them get, except, I believe, 'nabbing' a few of my cripples.

5th.—A south wind. Too rough to go off in Channel for wigeon, and no chance for geese to-day, so all I got was 6 birds.

6th.—A westerly gale and heavy rain, with high tides.

Dropped down to off Lymington, and had a shot with one barrel of the swivel gun only ; picked up 9 wigeon, and let some more go, rather than risk my life by facing the breakers. I never made a better shot in my life, considering I had scarcely more than two dozen birds to shoot at.

7th.—9 geese and 1 wigeon in two shots, as it blew so hard I was obliged to abandon half my dead birds, rather than run a risk of being swamped by following them to sea. A strong westerly wind with fine tides, and a good show of geese, though extremely wild. Read has 'launched' every night, and never got a bird.

9th.—Gave up my whole tide for shooting to the pursuit of a splendid eagle that appeared off Hurst. I had all but got him, when a lubber rushed out with a musket and scared him away. He, however, returned in a few hours, and gave me a second chance by sitting on Hurst beach within range of my great gun while afloat, but the baker drove by and put him up, when he flew several miles westward. I therefore came home, much disappointed, and left word with the boys to hoist me a signal if he appeared, as I found he had been seen three days in succession within a few hundred yards of the same place.

10th.—Tremendous wind and rain all night and all day. Nothing more heard about the eagle. Busy till two rectifying gear and cleaning up. Lots of geese off, but no getting at them in the rain, which always makes them restless. Put off for an hour or two, and got 2 wigeon.

11th.—Gale turned to dead calm and nipping white frost with north wind. Every fellow turned gunner, and no chance to be got from the birds being so disturbed. Just saved my blank by bagging an extraordinary fine old cock wigeon with the 'cripple stopper,' and had another distant view of the eagle, hovering off the Isle of Wight ; and, no doubt, driven from his old haunt here by the rabble of poppers afloat at Hurst.

12th.—Out long before daylight, but not so much as a little pop shot to be seen, though hundreds of birds were travelling over, cannon-shot high. In about eleven, when a most savage south-wester set in, and peppered away its deluge of heavy rain.

13th.—Gale of wind and rain all night, and nearly all this day.

14th.—Sudden change from west to a cold north gale. No water inside. Too much sea off. Fired but one shot, and that with the shoulder gun at about 100 yards, and just saved my blank by bagging 1 goose.

15th.—The eagle came again on the beach, as if he knew it was Sunday.

16th.—Out from daylight till dark, and just saved my blank with 1 mallard; not a wigeon to be seen. Read mud-crawled all night, and never heard a bird.

18th.—2 geese; the only shot I got, and that at above 200 yards, besides 2 more that got away. Not a wigeon or other fowl to be seen. But Read at last, about midnight, got a shot on the mud, and bagged 9 wigeon.

21st.—Longparish. Never was there so much illness as now. Twenty-six people lying dead at Southampton of the influenza.

22nd.—Sunday. Confined to my bed from last evening till this afternoon with this influenza.

23rd.—Half the village and three-fourths of my men thrown out of work by this infernal disorder.

24th.—Well enough to get out, though very weak from the influenza. I got on the pony and rode to the common, where I found 7 snipes, and never left one to tell the story. No bad work for a fellow scarcely able to crawl.

25th and 26th.—Still poorly. Incessant cold, then raw, rotten rain, and almost everybody more or less unwell.

27th to 30th.—Continued rotten weather, and this influenza everywhere, though I got better.

31st.—I started for the coach, and this evening arrived at

Keyhaven, hoping to get into a healthy change of air. But, on my arrival on the coast, I found that since I left the sickness had been even worse than inland, and the deaths far more numerous. Read, his family, all the tradesmen, preventive men, coasters, in short, everyone has been or is now suffering from the universal influenza.

February 4th.—The summer weather changed to a stiff easterly wind; so I put the great gun in the 'Petrel,' and tried another cruise. Fell in with 12 geese, and gave them both barrels while tossing on a heavy sea; knocked down 2 with the first, and 4 with the second barrel. We then emptied several gallons out of the punt, got dry mats &c. and sallied off again, when we saw above 100 more geese; but such was the sea that we dare not attempt to shoot any more this afternoon.

6th.—Having sprained my trigger finger while showing some things to Sir W. Symonds yesterday, I turned out today with some inconvenience, and it was still too rough for sport; but I continued to bring home again 4 geese.

7th.—Afloat, but did not get a shot; the geese kept shifting every ten minutes from one place to another, and then went off ten miles to the eastward.

8th.—Out again, and killed an enormous large diver with the shoulder gun; but the setting in of a south wind, with a determined wet day, drove us home; and Read finished this pleasant trip with first getting wet through and changing, and then going down to moor the punt off, and falling overboard and having to change again.

9th.—Off all day, and never saw the shadow of a chance; the only flock of geese that the unfavourable change of wind had left would not let us get within a quarter of a mile of them. Read has mud-crawled for a fortnight and never heard a wigeon; and Buckle, who has been about here for some weeks, is totally sickened with blank days. In short, it appears now to be 'all up' with coast gunning.

10*th*.—A ferocious dirty south-wester all day and all night. Rain spattering the windows like the drums of a padnagging regiment, and the wind howling like a pack of hungry wolves. No moving on land, much less on water.

28*th*.—Went up to London to settle a load of accounts and business that had accumulated in my long absence from town, and to show my injured finger to Sir B. Brodie.

March 2nd and 3rd.—Busy from morning till night; scarcely time to eat a meal, as I worked doubly hard in order to get over the misery of being in town in a fine north-east wind with a lame finger.

4*th*.—London swarming with wild fowl; wigeon as low as 1*s*. a couple in the streets.

13*th to* 15*th*.—Keyhaven. An incessant gale and the most piercing cold north-east wind. In short, winter in spring, which I long ago predicted. This weather about three months ago would have been worth a guinea a puff, but now it is an absolute nuisance, as it precludes the possibility of going on the water (for healthy air and the only flock of geese that remain), and is too late even to stop, much less to bring, other wild fowl.

16*th*.—Rough, but more moderate than it was, so went afloat, and, as the devil would have it, all the Billingsgate periwinklers were out this day, and thronged the shore for nine miles, so good-bye to the 150 geese, and adieu to shooting for this season.

20*th*.—Bitter winter, frost, snow, and a black north-east gale of wind, but all of no more use than a kneebuckle to a Highlander. Too late. Birds gone long ago, so we have our noses bit off for nothing.

22*nd*.—Game &c. killed in the season: 136 partridges (never shot at a partridge after September, except 1 that pitched in the lawn and I bagged), 1 quail, 5 hares, 5 rabbits, 1 pheasant, 24 snipes. Total, 172. 5 ducks and mallards, 1 burrough duck, 1 scaup duck, 81 wigeon, 33 geese, 15 godwits, 3 plover. Total, 139. Grand total, 311 head.

N.B.—As poor a season as ever was known, except one good week just after the snow. The coast is ruined, and we have no game shooting after September.

23rd.—Longparish. The incessant snow ceased about three this afternoon, when I was at last able to get out of the house. I therefore waded off in water boots, and took my gun for the chance of a snipe. I saw at least 40 all in a flock like plover, but at such a time one never can get within a hundred yards of them.

April 11th.—Keyhaven. Loaded my heaviest shoulder gun, and tried to get to the eastward, but was soon driven back by strong wind and heavy snow. Fell in with a small detachment of the geese, which let us get well in shot, but they were so scattered on the waves that I could only shoot 1, and that I dare not follow, so I came in, and spent the evening in revising the drama that I brought here for that purpose.

May 18th.—London. Flying about like a dog in a fair to stir up divers people, lest all things should not be in in time for the girls, and after a general action with plumassiers, dressmakers, barber, tailor, jobman, and Lord knows what besides, I shuffled on my finery and drove off 'as big as bull beef' with the girls for the Drawing Room, where they were presented by Lady Rodney to the King, and to the Princess Augusta, who presided for the Queen, as she was invalided at Windsor. We got over the operation without accidents or fainting fits, and arrived back at Dorset Place soon after four, when I shifted my things, and posted off to a filthy den in search of a journeyman who is making my new-invented tambourine; his residence was in a dirty court very far in Westminster, but he having just 'shot the moon,' I had to follow him to a cockloft in St. Giles's, which made a happy variety just after the Court of St. James's.

29th.—As the King and Queen were both too ill to attend

to-day, the Princess Augusta did all the duty at Court; and of all the mobs I ever was in, I never met a more uncomfortable place than the Drawing Room was to-day. I thought it never would be over, and so badly were the carriages regulated, that the ladies were obliged to walk out among the mob like girls at a fair, and I only got home just in time to bolt my dinner and shuffle on a coat and waistcoat for the Philharmonic concert.

30*th.*—A most glorious treble concerto of Bach at the concert of Moscheles, who played it with Thalberg and Benedict.

31*st.*—Dined with Moscheles to meet Thalberg, Madame Schroeder, Devrient, Galtz, Moeser, and others, who gave me an evening of absolute enchantment.

June 1*st.*—Out from nine to-night till near five in the morning, at the grand carnival in the opera house for the benefit of the Spitalfields weavers. It was the grandest ball and the greatest assemblage of fine folks that I ever saw. The Court was nothing to it. But I went to support the concern, as I have property in Spitalfields, and to please the girls, who were charmed with the spectacle, otherwise I should have made a more agreeable use of my time and money.

13*th.*—After being busy every day, and much engaged with taking my daughters about to enjoy the splendid musical talent that now swarms in town, and after being up nearly all night through having to go to the last most glorious Philharmonic, where Thalberg almost drove me crazy with delight, I this day got on the box of the 'Light Salisbury' and went down to Longparish.

21*st.*—Keyhaven. Received a 'Morning Herald' announcing the death of our beloved sovereign and my kindest benefactor, King William the Fourth, whom it pleased the Almighty to take to 'another and a better world' between two and three o'clock yesterday morning. Although this sad event was what we had reason to dread every day, yet I felt it so much as to be unable to do anything.

23rd.—Availed myself of the first fine day to sail to Alum Bay and ascend the heights in order to see young Coleraine descend the cliffs for young birds, &c. The way he does it is this. He has two very long ropes each about an inch in diameter. The one he fastens to an iron bar, which is driven into the ground, a few yards from the awful precipice, and the other he ties round his body. He then descends, clinging with his hands and feet to that rope which is fastened to the bar, in order to lighten the weight on the other rope that is made fast round his middle, and held by his partner, with a lad in reserve, in case of wanting further assistance. When he has taken anything, he stows it between his shirt and his breast, and gives a jerk to the rope that is held by the man as a signal to be hauled up again. The only danger that I could see, and which alone deterred me from trying the experiment, was the risk of getting injured by stones and pieces of chalk that might fall before the usual caution of 'Look out!' could be heard through the roar of the sea and the noise of the parent birds. This I would obviate by a kind of cap that I could invent. I would not have missed this sight for 5*l.*, though for want of wind we did not get home till eleven at night.

In the afternoon I sailed off to the back of the Isle of Wight, in order to have a view from below of Coleraine, who appeared by appointment at four o'clock, and descended the cliffs, where I was close under with a large telescope, so I saw him take 4 more gulls (that we brought home) as well as if I had been on the rope with him.

28th.—Went up to London per 'Salisbury,' and on my arrival was informed that General Sir S. Hawker had been sent for express by our good King, and arrived from Boulogne in time to pass two days with him previously to his dissolution; and that his Majesty desired to be affectionately remembered to me, my son, and my daughters.

July 8th.—A most dismal day in town, with every shop and almost every house shut up for the funeral of his late beloved Majesty, which took place in Windsor at eight o'clock this night. I should have been one of the procession, had not Lord Munster been deprived of all influence in the arrangements. I might have gone with a ticket as a mere looker-on, but this, of course, I declined; as a funeral, and particularly the one of a sincere friend, is the last thing I should wish to undergo as a mere exhibition. From nine till eleven this night it was truly afflicting to hear the minute guns and bells all over the metropolis announcing the departure to their last resting place of our dear King's mortal remains.

9th.—Sunday. I was taken so sick and unwell all night, that I expected to be laid up to-day; but fortunately I got relief, and was well enough to go and hear a most beautiful sermon by Dr. Dibdin on the death of our lamented monarch, the whole of which, as well as the service, was a severe trial to the feelings of anyone, much more of those who had long enjoyed the kind friendship of his late Majesty.

13*th.*—Put the prads in the britchska at twelve, and arrived with them at Keyhaven at half-past nine at night, as fresh as larks.

N.B.—Everyone gloried in my driving to the coast, as the country was half ruined by long easterly winds and dry hot weather; and it never yet failed to turn the cock and bring rain. I did turn the cock, and brought about an hour's light rain.

24*th.*—Into Andover, but business out of the question till the afternoon, on account of the election; which, although there was no contest, turned out to be one of the most amusing uproars I ever wasted my time at, thanks to Mr. Marsh, who spoke admirably and showed consummate ability, by the ready wit that he shot off at the blackguards whenever they dared to interrupt him.

31*st.*—Hard on in the City from breakfast till six, and then out again till near bedtime. One of my jobs was to choose some port and sherry in the docks, where the port-wine cellar alone is nine acres and a half of ground.

August 10*th.*—All in a bustle, preparing for 'the family' and their awful freight of baggage, which (except enough for a regiment) was coming on per Jones's 'Fly' waggon first, and then by the Odiham coach this morning from London. Willum Watts, our clod carter, left at daylight with rat-catcher Siney, as a baggage guard, to drag home the trunks &c. Monk left at eight, with old Samson and my cart, to 'bring into port' the maids and the lighter 'traps;' and I left at eleven with the prads and britchska, to drive home 'the ladies' from Basingstoke. All had a good passage but myself, who had a narrow escape of getting my neck broken. My horse 'Tom Brown' shied at a road waggon, and then 'took the rust,' which I fetched out of him instanter. He then plunged and broke the splinter bar. Here I was done; and left *solus* on the road, without a prospect of anything passing. At last I made the trace fast to the stump of the bar, cut off the strings of my flannel drawers to prevent it slipping, and thus toddled into Whitchurch, where I lashed on a piece of timber, proceeded to Basingstoke, and brought my cargo home in triumph. The whole army were safely lodged in quarters before dusk, and, thank God, without any further accident.

19*th.*—Ran down to Keyhaven to recruit myself with rest and sea air for the shooting fag of September.

N.B.—I just kept my charter, as we had heavy rain for the last six miles into Southampton, and a strong westerly wind at Keyhaven.

21*st.*—Rain set in in the evening, and we had wind and rain all night; so the farmers, who prayed that I might go to Keyhaven to bring rain, for the turnips and all that was burnt up, were quite right, and I successful in their petition.

28*th.*—Though I had been out sailing in the Channel every day, yet it was too rough to weather the back of the island till this day, when at last I had good weather to try the rock birds again. But on reaching the cliffs we found that every bird had left the country, and after a long day's beautiful sail I returned without pulling a single trigger. This is unusually early for all the birds to be gone.

CHAPTER XXX

1837

September 1*st.*—Longparish. A cold, stormy day; no lay for the birds, which were as wild as hawks, and of which there proved but a sorry breed. But in all my life I never shot better nor saw my dogs behave better; in short, the performance was perfection, though the supply was poor. I bagged 24 partridges and 2 hares without one miss, and I made seven brilliant double shots.

The dogs caught besides 2 birds and 1 leveret; and Joe, who had the advantage of the inclosed country to himself, bagged 26 partridges, so that our spread on the table was, in all, 52 birds and 3 hares. One of our very worst first days for number, but one of our very best for good shooting.

2*nd.*—Wonderful work again; a stormy day with showers, but to-morrow being Sunday I took the field, contrary to my custom, the second day, though did not begin till one o'clock in the afternoon, and was home to dinner soon after six I bagged 20 partridges and 1 landrail; I never fired a shot without bagging, and made five glorious doublets of the greatest difficulty. Having once 'made a cannon' at 2 birds crossing, and consequently got 3 with my two barrels, I bagged 21 head of game in 20 shots.

Joe shot like an angel also; he discharged ten rounds and pocketed his 10 birds in brilliant style. What care we for all Europe?

4*th.*—Wonderful work again considering the lamentable

scarcity of birds. I bagged 20 partridges and 1 snipe. But I this day missed one shot, the first miss I have made this season, and up to which I had bagged 65 head, including fourteen double shots without one miss. I was very lucky in 'making cannons'[1] to-day, as I got 2 at a shot three times, and 3 at a shot once. This is the most consummate beauty and difficulty of the art, and always more than covers the misses of any good shot.

6th.—Miraculous shooting again, warmer weather, and bagged about the half of what I saw. I was out from ten till five, and came in with 22 partridges and 1 hare, without missing even a long shot or losing a bird. I made five doublets, and, by means of three 'cannons,' got my 23 head in twenty shots, and many very long shots among them.

9th.—Better, and meant to shoot, but there came on a hurricane of wind with showers every two hours; so, not wishing to look little with an empty bag, I shipped my sou'-wester and went fishing, and had a most glorious bit of sport. The 3 first fish I landed weighed 6½ lb., and I came home with 11 brace, besides throwing in about 9 brace more that were rather too small to kill when I had such an abundance of first-rate ones. I was about four hours at it, and left the water while they were taking like bulldogs, because I thought it a shame to kill more than I knew what to do with.

11th.—A tremendous stormy day. I attacked the trout again, and brought home 12 splendid fish, besides throwing in nearly as many more. I was scarcely three hours at the river.

12th.—Too busy to go out till two in the afternoon, and a stormy day; but I wanted a bird or two for the house, and I could only get 3 partridges by means of very long shots. I killed a cuckoo that flew past me like an arrow, and

[1] Catching 2 birds as they cross, and then firing so quick as not to allow them to open again.

I took him for a hawk, as I never saw a cuckoo so late before. I killed also a little wheatear, which here is a *rara avis*.

13*th*.—Called down to the lower common this afternoon with a report that 2 or 3 dozen of snipes had been there yesterday, though only found 6, and those very wild. I then took the rod and caught another splendid dish of trout. I, however, kept but 4 brace, as I wanted no more, and my best fish was 2¼ lb. good weight.

15*th*.—6 partridges, with another wheatear, and had a providential escape from being killed and mutilated. My horse fell at full gallop and pitched head over heels, and nothing but my crawling off with the rapidity of a weasel saved me from being pounded to a mummy by the revolving croup of the horse.

16*th*.—An exquisite musical treat. Thalberg at Winchester, with Mori, Albertazzi, and others. Busy in assisting about the concert, but unfortunately could not get either Mori or Thalberg to come home with me, as the one was obliged to post all night for Birmingham, and the other was obliged to proceed to London the moment he had finished his most exquisitely splendid performance. It seemed like a romance to have such gods among the Hampshire hogs.

Game killed in September: 103 partridges, 4 hares, 1 landrail, 1 rabbit, 3 snipes. I never shot better, and never shot so little. I killed 91 head of game with only one miss, and made seventeen double shots out of eighteen. What with incessant business and the scarcity of game I have had no season at all. Total, 112 head.

October 2nd.—I never saw a pheasant, though I beat all our prime places with a good squad of men and dogs, and all I got was 1 rabbit and 2 partridges, as I was so unwell I was obliged to leave the chase and come home to lie down.

4*th*.—Got on the coach and ran down to Keyhaven to get my punts there put in order for the winter.

7*th*.—We paddled out at dawn and at dusk, but saw no

K 2

fowl, though there had been some in the late east wind. Now we have it west with rain, keeping up my charter.

21st.—Having put all things in order, I went afloat the whole day, but never saw a fowl. The day was so hot I could scarcely bear my shooting jacket, much less a gunning dress.

24th.—A hurricane from the west all last night. Calm this morning. Out at daylight; got only 1 pintail and 1 curlew.

25th.—Out at daylight, but driven home by heavy rain and high wind.

26th.—Went all the way to Pitt's Deep, and found the coast destitute of everything, and never discharged my gun. Buckle and I came home in despair, and gave it up till better winds blow.

November 8th.—London. I attended the Horse Guards' Levee to-day to lay before the Commander-in-Chief my claims for an honour, and was most kindly received by Lord Fitzroy Somerset.

9th.—Had a capital place at the United Service Club, and a comfortable stare at her Majesty and all her procession on their way to the City banquet.

14th.—Longparish. Received this day the kindliest memorials in my behalf from Lord Combermere, our general of cavalry, and my friend Sir John Elley, who was Adjutant-General, which I this day forwarded copies of for General Hawker, my former Lieutenant-Colonel, to lay before the Commander-in-Chief.

16th.—Went to Southampton, and saw the remains of the awful conflagration, where twenty-one persons were burnt to death.

18th.—Keyhaven. A bitter cold white frost, but a north-east wind, and a looking-glass calm. Up by candlelight, and got all my great set-out afloat. Went all the way to Cowes before I saw a bird. About to land for some lunch, when we saw about 40 ducks a mile off. Sculled for them half seas over, when we saw the most sudden change of weather that we had ever seen or heard of; so gave up Cowes and the ducks, and made for the shore near Eaglehurst, and got on the safe side just before there set in a strong wind with rain from the west; and, in short, we had to work ourselves all the way to Keyhaven, about eighteen miles, close to the shore, against the wind, because the Channel became so rough that we dare not take the tide back as intended. We got back some hours after dark, and in all our lives we never had such a severe blank day. Not a shot, and 'wet as shags.' Had I lunched at Cowes, I must have slept and spent the Sunday there. This is a lesson never to trust to a frost again when there is any white in it.

28th.—I this day got a letter from General Hawker, inclosing one from Lord Hill, to express his regret that it was against rule to give me the Order of the Bath, because I had left the army. Most glorious letter to 'show off' with, but no order to be got as yet.

December 5th.—Longparish. Very cold easterly wind. Having half a day to spare, I scoured the whole country both for game and snipes, and all I saw was 1 hare and 1 rabbit. This shows how completely the shooting here is now annihilated.

7th.—Extraordinary weather. Wind east, with snow and sleet, though without frost, and yet so chilling that I literally could not play on the piano, the keys were so cold, and it was so dark as to require candles at half-past three. Every labourer was complaining that even his work would not keep him warm; and as for me, I have been petrified ever since I was bit by the white frost on Saturday, and should like to have returned this day to the more genial climate of the coast.

9th.—Went to Keyhaven, and the change was like magic; the report of the gunning, however, was miserable. Read had been on day and night mud crawling in his small punt, with cold winds, and even snow, and had not got a bird.

11*th.*—Lovely weather, and out all day, but not a bird in the country except a few geese, that would not stay three minutes in a place from having been so persecuted by the bullets of the lubbers from Itchen Ferry. Read out all night with a splendid full moon, and never saw a fowl.

12*th.*—Out from daybreak till a late dinner; and the only shot I got was at 2 golden-eyes, both of which came home to the larder.

13*th.*—Out from dawn till night, and never saw a chance. Read crawling on the mud all night, with a beautiful full moon, and never saw a single wigeon. The scarcity is unaccountable.

14*th.*—Persevered, but nothing done; and there came on a south-west wind. Read crawled all night and found nothing. I was off all day, and soon after daylight had a tolerable shot at about 20 geese; and, for the first time these four seasons, my great gun missed fire. Really, such gunning is enough to tire the patience of Job.

15*th.*—Nothing for Read all night, and no shot to-day, though the rough weather gave me a view of about 100 geese in the wash.

16*th.*—Read another blank night. I dropped down with the wash, and took a snap shot at the geese, and knocked down 9, and had the luck at last to bring home some geese, thanks to my new cartridge, as nothing else would have reached them.

21*st.*—Moderate, with a north-easter; but not a bird in the country. Busy, on the mud, about a contract for cutting a lake through Stivers, and direct from our harbour to the West Channel.

22*nd.*—Read crawled all night in his mud punt, and never saw a chance. We then turned to and cleaned up all the gear, preparative to my returning to Longparish for

Christmas. Never, never did we see such a blank time for fowl as this.

31*st.*—Longparish. Sunday. I have been so employed with business, friends, and music, from breakfast till after midnight every day this week, that I was quite indifferent to the week's rainy and unpleasant weather that we have had, and if we, please God, enjoy the new year as we have done the last week of the old one, we shall have no reason to complain.

1838

January 1*st.*—In spite of wind and wet weather, we had a glorious New Year's Day, by sending the tilted cart for Tom Langstaff and his fiddle, and playing from one in the day to one in the night, except at our meals, where, with Signor Sola's merry face and jokes, we were not a moment free from glee and harmony.

2*nd.*—As at Sola's earnest entreaty we had a dish of trout for New Year's Day (which, to my astonishment, were in fair season), I this day took about half an hour's fishing, and killed as many as we could eat for dinner, and some of them were as red as salmon. This shows the mildness of the winter.

4*th.*—Obliged to be up two hours before daylight, and in Winchester before nine o'clock this morning, on two vexatious actions, by Parson Cockerton and Bill Wickham, against Charles Heath, my tenant, in both of which we came off triumphant, thanks entirely to the splendid talent of Mr. Smike, our leading counsel, whom we primed at every point with strong facts to bother our opponents, who looked as if they had been over-dosed with emetics and jalap. By this sudden call to court I lost all my morning's music with Langstaff, who came over again, and I only got home just in time to dress for my dinner party. Up till two in the morning, with music, singing, fun, and dancing, so that my incessant excitement continued for twenty-one hours.

5*th.*—Badgered away from a batch of Beethoven to go

after a cursed cock pheasant that I never found, but I saved my blank with a rabbit, which was all I saw in four hours.

6th.—Signor Sola left us for London, after delighting us for a fortnight with his good performance and useful assistance in music till after midnight every evening.

8th.—A glorious black frost and north-easter. In Keyhaven soon after eight; no time to eat, and could only get through my jobs by running in 'double quick' instead of walking.

9th.—Keyhaven. Lovely weather. Pumps and water jugs frozen, and a furious easterly gale. Read was out yesterday, and his gun missed fire three times; and once he was so eager to pull off his worsted glove to shoot, that he seized it with his mouth, and literally pulled out one of his teeth, which fell into the punt.

To-day the birds were not in such swarms as yesterday. I fired my two barrels in a heavy sea, and stopped 2 mallards, 1 duck, 2 pintails, 5 wigeon, 2 teal, 2 plover, and 5 dunlins. We came home wet and frozen, and yet perspiring with bustle and excitement.

10th.—Intense frost and snow, but wind more moderate. Lots of shooters out; but nothing done, and thousands of birds frightened off to sea. I got only 2 wigeon, 1 duck, and 2 godwits.

11th.—Made a capital shot, having, from one barrel only, picked up, from one shot, 21 curlews. We had a chase on the frozen mud for two hours. These birds were so heavy, and the frozen mud in such a state, that we were obliged to go back to the punt for a rope to drag them along. My second barrel missed fire, by the cock catching the gun cloth, or I might have doubled the shot. Got also an enormous eider duck. Intensely hard weather, but wigeon so driven by boats that they were not allowed time to give us a chance.

12th.—I got 4 golden-eyes and 1 wigeon. Only out from dawn till midday, having business. To bed at six, out at eleven, stopped by snow. Read crawled from two till four, but heard nothing.

13*th.*—Intense frost; up and at breakfast by seven. Gale of wind from east, so could not get out till three in the afternoon, when I could pass through Stivers and drop down from Pennington to the Camber. Had one scrambling shot in a rough sea, and, to my surprise, bagged 6 wigeon.

14*th.*—Sunday. Read had been out till twelve last night crawling, but not a bird could live on the frozen mud; so now all must be day work. Never did a treadmill man hail the Sabbath as a day of rest more gladly than I did this day, for, what with incessant gunning, furbishing, and being my own servant here, no galley slave ever worked harder than I have done this week, though I am, thank God, all the better for it.

15*th.*—Capital day work: 1 duck, 1 goose, 38 wigeon, 32 plover, and 2 godwits. The first shot I got 18 wigeon and 1 goose; the second, 17 plover and 2 godwits; the third, 18 wigeon. The others were little pop shots. So exhausted when I came home at night, that I was obliged to swallow two glasses of sherry before I could stand to clean up my gear, in order to turn out again by midnight, should the weather permit.

16*th.*—Entreated by Read to go out from midnight till four this morning, but I told him it was too cold for birds at night, and I was right, as I had all but a blank; the birds in were a mere nothing, and all scattered. Up again at seven to prepare, and started as soon after as I could eat a breakfast. Out till dark, but little to be done, as the report of my sport, of which there were plenty of witnesses and exaggerators, had called every boat in requisition; and the order of the day was dandy bullet shooters, who, of course, got nothing, but they drove every flock to sea, and the Channel was literally barren. I, however, got one shot at a flock of geese above 200 yards, and, to my surprise, knocked down 6 geese.

17th and 18th.—Ashore all day in consequence of a part of my detonating lock having so worn away that I had three miss-fires on the 16th. Mr. Clayton, the gunmaker from Lymington, and I were on, by candlelight, on the 17th and best part of the 18th, forging and filing in our kitchen, and I hope with success. I had also a severe press of business on other matters, and was raced about the house all day. I sent Read off, and he brought me in 5 wigeon and 1 goose.

19th.—A day's work equivalent to the treadmill as to exercise and diet. From seven till eleven working with pickaxe and shovel to get to the water with the great gun and punt, and then cutting away the ice for half a mile to get out of harbour. Afloat all day; both our meat and our beer so frozen we could not eat the one or get a single suck at the other. Landed at Hurst just as night set in, and walked in the dark three miles home in water boots and with heavy lots at our backs, two miles of which was on shingles, that were the only things not frozen; and consequently as heavy as in open weather. The gun did well after the repairs, as far as we tried it, which was two shots; our bag was 7 geese and 6 wigeon.

20th.—Up hours before daylight, and tramped round the beach to Hurst. Made a glorious shot: 42 wigeon and 9 geese at one shot, and had not my primer missed fire, should have had about 30 geese at another shot. The boats helping themselves to my fleet of cripples off at sea with popguns, put an end to shooting for the rest of the day; or I might have got 100 birds, and must have hired a cart to bring them home.

21st.—Sunday, but, what with baskets, letters, church &c. I could hardly call it a day of rest. Indeed, I was up at daybreak, in order neither to neglect my commissions nor to miss going to church.

22nd.—Up at five and tramped again to Hurst by daylight. A general thaw and weather turned mild with a strong south wind. Birds, as is usual on the break up, congregated in immense flocks; but so harassed by sail boats that I could only get three flying shots, with which I sacked 15 geese, all at above 200 yards with heavy mould shot. At three in the afternoon we sailed home to our own quay at Keyhaven, and were 'hard on' cleaning up all the transported gear till eight in the evening.

23rd.—Off at daylight; much embarrassed with floating pans of ice, but got extricated by shipping sail. Fired a shot about eight o'clock, and cut down 22 geese and 1 wigeon; but such a heavy sea that I lost several both of the dead geese and wigeon. A cold easterly wind again.

24th.—A candlelight breakfast as usual, but such a tremendous hurricane from the east, that nothing could move to windward; and the ice that came to leeward blocked us up for the day, while 16 wild swans sat and bade me defiance before my very windows. On like a slave, with five hands cutting away the ice, while the wild fowl were flying round me every minute; but having greater objects in view than popping down single birds as they flew over the quay, I stuck to my work of ice cutting, cartridge making &c. Several other little trips of swans were flying about, and so tame that two were killed by the common shore poppers with their miserable muskets.

25th.—Gale continued, swans blown to leeward, and 24 more travelled over from Poole. Much trouble to get to windward. Dropped down on a host of fowl; both barrels missed fire; they pitched again and both barrels missed again. Made for shore and drew the charge. Found that Read had put wadding first and powder after; sorry blunder. Off again; refused a fine shot because 5 swans were to leeward; got close to them while all in one solid cluster; must have killed all dead, but flint flashed in pan; up they flew, all abroad; caught two as they crossed, with other barrel, and only No. 1 shot; cut both down short in high style, but one, the old cock, managed to reach the beach and go off to sea ; so, instead of clearing the harbour of the only 5 swans in it to-day, I had the mortification to come in with only 1 wild swan ;[1] after rectifying the flint barrel again, I blew it off at a long distance, and got 1 goose, 2 ducks, 2 wigeon, 1 golden-eye, and 1 burrough duck ; a curious mixture at one shot.

26th.—Strong wind, but not so furious but we could row against it. Brought in 3 wild swans ; 1st shot at five close to us, but in so heavy a 'lop' that the splash took off the shot ; 2nd shot at 7, got 2, both splendid old birds, and another fell dead, off at sea ; the latter was a very long shot, as the birds were old and wary. We were on with three boats for two hours before we caught the old captain of the swans, as he took to the breakers and made for Yarmouth. No other shot to-day,[2] as we gave up all fowl for the glorious sport of killing the hoopers.

27th.—Most glorious sport ; 49 geese and 2 such splendid wild swans that 1 weighed 20 lb. all but 3 oz. Another old swan fell dead at sea. I had only four shots ; the first, a single swan a long way off ; the second at 10 swans, an immense distance, when I killed 2 with the 1 lost at sea ; the third, shot 20 geese and sacked all ; the fourth, shot 29 geese and sacked every bird. I had three punts to cut off every cripple from reaching the Channel.[3] Never was there a more satisfactory day to finish a week.

28th.—Sunday. Severe work writing, basket packing, bill paying, church, &c. A general thaw with strong south wind and heavy rain this evening.

29th.—Very high tide all the forenoon, and the harbour besieged like a field of battle with bullet spitters in boats, and

[1] Two more wild swans picked up on beach since this entry.

[2] Our bag to-day was gigantic : 3 swans, and an enormous conger eel as thick as my thigh.

[3] The cripples were so thick that I sailed into 4 and blew down 2 with the first barrel, and another 2 with the second, of my 'cripple stopper.'

absolute legions of snobs on every point of the shore, one incessant fire the whole day, and not a single bird knocked down. Having had several narrow escapes of bullets while attempting to approach the geese, I went quietly home and gave up all further attempts till the ragamuffins had had their 'whack' of popping off blank shots, and at four in the afternoon I took the 'ground ebb' and landed 23 geese, 15 one shot and 8 the other. Weather mild the whole day, and wigeon all at sea. No more wild swans seen or heard of.

30*th.*—A dense fog, so did not go afloat, but took a stroll alongshore with Captain Vassal and some young gentlemen. A fine wild swan flew over our heads within shot, and pitched close to Highlea Point. The gents watched him till I came off with the punt, and, after setting near a mile to him, while he kept swimming away, we at last got up and I shot him as dead as mutton, and gave him to the captain. We then heard some geese and paddled off to them, and fired off one barrel only (as I could not see to shoot the other for fog). I knocked down 16 geese and sacked 'every man John' of them. I then ran into my house for a lunch; but when I came back to the punt there were no more fowl about, but I blew off a barrel at some mixed shore birds that sat on the mud thrown up by Dowden's work at my leak, and the filth that I had to wallow in to catch them. Considering the distance of the three shots and the disadvantage of the fog, I consider this the most satisfactory day of the campaign.

31*st.*—25 geese. Afloat from ten till three, and about two o'clock we got about 2,000 geese in a place where we could not fail to get a shot, when a rascally shore snob popped up his black shoulders and popped them all off. In my whole life I never saw so fair a chance to kill 100 geese at a shot, as we had a perfect ambush, and the birds were all standing in a phalanx. As it was, I blew after them and got 4. I then came home, as the harbour swarmed with bullet poppers afloat and snobs ashore, and when they were got rid of I went out for two hours just before dark, got one shot, and picked up 21 geese, making in all the above 25 fowl to-day.

February 1st.—19 geese; had but two shots all day, as the harbour was besieged with poppers afloat and ashore. One of these two shots, I got 12 so near home that the shot rattled on the slating of my house. I sent Read to crawl at night, and he got in all 14 wigeon.

2nd.—Sail boats off all day, looking for cripples, so I stayed in till half-past three in the afternoon, but there set in a north wind that cut the tides, and enabled all the geese except a few to go to the high mud, five miles off. I fell in with a fair lot about sunset; but just as I was within a minute of shooting, up jumped the geese, and 'bang' went the gun of Buckle, who cut down 5. I should have had about 15. I then steered for home, resigned to a blank evening, when I saw a few birds under the little moon. I got close to them and fired, but not one rose, and when we rowed in there lay dead 12 geese, so I annihilated the whole company of them, and this on the very edge of my own new-cut leak. So after all I came home again in triumph.

3rd.—20 geese the first shot, 3 geese (a long random flying shot) the second shot, and 34 geese the third shot.[1] The latter splendid shot was made under a curious circumstance. I had given up shooting for the day to open my new leak through the mud, just finished, to pay for it, and to lush the Keyhavenites with four gallons of swill; and while we were waiting for water to go through the leak, about four in the afternoon, the grand company of geese took the mud, when I put off to them, and shot flying as the tide was too late to shoot sitting, and sacked the above lot in presence of all the procession. It was consequently moonlight before we entered the leak, and I should have had a second cut at the geese under the moon had not a shore snob popped off his piece.

[1] Making 57 geese brought in to-day (in three shots), besides many of my dead birds that were bagged by the boats and shore sharks.

We then, with flags flying, and all the guns in Keyhaven firing, and three hearty cheers, opened the passage, and 'all hands' adjourned to the pothouse to wind up Saturday and drink 'luck to Colonel Hawker's leak.'

4th.—Sunday. The sharp frost continued. Busy sending off a corn sack stuffed with geese for my North Hants tenants, lots of baskets, letters, &c. What with church and all, I had enough to do between early rising and a candlelight gentleman's dinner on a fat goose.

5th.—Intense weather. Off at daybreak. First shot 6 enormous milk-white old wild swans, with the flint barrel, the detonator having missed fire,[1] or I should have had 12 more. Second shot very long, 2 wild swans; third shot, 10 geese, with the detonator, the flint having missed fire. These were the only three shots I had, as I was so taken up with the swans that I literally went through 2,000 wigeon in musket shot, and in getting the last of the above 6 swans I never in all my sport was in such danger, as I went over my knees, and saved myself from sinking by making a handle of my shoulder gun by laying it crossways on the mud. I was over my knees and my pattens buried every step, and so exhausted that I made for the shore and lay down on the ground before I could recover to proceed home. I then washed out my gun, and swallowed some porter, and got taken back to my punt in the custom-house boat.

6th.—What with dead tides at dawn, and dusk and floating bullet poppers all day, there was little to be seen except 400 yards in on mud; all the shots I had were two. I got another splendid old wild swan (besides hitting 2 more down that the snobs finished), and with the other shot I bagged 6 geese at an immense distance, as they crossed me on my way home at night.

[1] Another white one picked up dead on the beach, and a brown one knocked down with an oar (by some boatmen) half a mile off, making 8 at one shot of one barrel, though only six fairly sacked. We had a cart to bring the 6 up (and also the other 2 shot), as they all averaged 20 lb., making about 160 lb. besides the 10 geese, which brought the sack to just about 200 lb. cargo.

7th.—A general thaw with tremendous south wind all last night and all to-day and heavy rain. Went a little way down the harbour in the afternoon, and just saved my blank by popping down with the great gun 7 geese as a small flock rapidly crossed me to go out for the night.

8th.—Tremendous westerly gale all day, with a heavy pour of rain. Kept ready from morning till sunset, but no birds in and no living out of harbour. Read crawled at night, but got only 2 wigeon and 1 burrough duck.

9th.—A wet hurricane all day, so went off to pay visits and bills, but at four P.M. the storms abated, so we weathered it till dusk. I got one shot in a rough sea a long way off, and knocked down and bagged 13 wigeon.

10th.—Extraordinary change of weather. Up before daylight, and all was deep in snow, with a hurricane from the north-east. Ready all day, but snow and wind too much to weather. Went off in the evening, but thought it prudent to return, though discharged one barrel, a very long shot, and got 4 beautiful burrough ducks, making just 600 different birds fairly bagged up to this (Saturday) night [1] since I came here on January 8, just a month ago! and of which list 459 are ducks and geese.

11th.—Read, who would crawl in his pig trough last night, got but 1 wigeon.

12th.—A hard white frost; out at half-past six; got one shot and bagged 12 geese. Came in to lunch at one, and went out again, but the whole coast was so swarming with sunshine poppers that I gave it up, and went to assist Dowden in putting the booms to my new leak, which is now complete.

13th.—Out at daybreak; coast so bombarded I could only bag 3 geese. Went out again at three P.M.; 'Sams' all tired; got a fine shot, and bagged 8 geese and 16 wigeon. Read crawled at night, and in two shots got 14 wigeon.

14th.—Intensely cold gale of wind from the east-south-

[1] Fowl 459, waders 141. Total, 600.

east. Prisoners till three in the afternoon; got one long shot, and killed 8 wigeon. The main army of geese never came in to-day.

15*th*.—A ferocious hurricane from the east-south-east all day, so that nothing could 'live' afloat, and one could hardly stand on one's legs ashore, and most intensely cold to boot. I therefore amused myself with jobbing, writing, music &c. and took my dinner at three. About half-past four I was just stepping out to Read's house, when 4 splendid old swans passed over from the sea and pitched inland; I flew to arms, and was off like a greyhound, but already about thirty shore snobs were in full chase. They, however, all being 'green,' raced in competition to windward, and I, who was last, ran to leeward, knowing the birds would smell the snobs and come over me. Up they got, out of all reach of their pursuers; down I lay on my back; over they came, and down I brought the old captain of the four swans as flat as a flounder and dead as a hammer, and this saved my blank for to-day with my 19th wild swan. It was impossible to do better, as the 4 birds were all apart, and away flew the 3 others to sea. I never did anything in all my shooting that pleased me better than this.

16*th*.—A tremendous hurricane from the south-east all night and all day, with snow, rain, hail, and sleet. Shooting, even on land, out of the question.

17*th*.—Most extraordinary weather. A gale of wind, with severe frost all night; at six o'clock in the morning everything was frozen; at seven the cock flew to the west and it poured with warm rain, and before ten it was as mild as in May; and about the middle of the day the sun shone, and it was so hot we were obliged to 'douse' a part of our gunning cloths. At 4 P.M. we had a cold, wet evening, and before dark it was dry and mild. We were out from ten till six, but the birds were all at sea, and we brought nothing home except a crested grebe, killed with the popgun, the fifth that I have got this season, though I never saw one in this country before. I fired one long shot at a swan two miles at sea, and hit him very hard, and marked him drop on the mud, and afterwards saw three men hunting him down, and then killing him. I should have had one good shot of geese, but an ass blew a bullet at them just before we had arrived in shot. Read crawled till midnight, and got 4 wigeon. A white frost.

19*th*.—Up at three, hoping to catch the wigeon in harbour, but it came on so dark and so windy from east-south-east that we would not start till daybreak. Dead tides, and scarcely any birds, so got but 2 geese all day.

20*th*.—Out at daylight, but all the birds were gone about twelve miles to the eastward. The coast was destitute.

Memorandum of fowl killed to end of February 1838:

1837, old year.—In mild weather: Waders—3 curlews, 8 plover, 25 dunlins. Wild fowl—3 wigeon, 1 pintail, 3 golden-eyes, 6 geese. Total, 49.

1838, new year, from January 9 to end of February.—In (and after) severe weather: Waders—31 curlews, 48 plover, 5 godwits, 1 redshank, 64 dunlins. Fowl—217 wigeon, 2 pintails, 5 wild ducks, 2 teal, 6 burrough teal, 1 eider duck, 1 tufted duck, 5 golden-eye ducks, 4 dunbirds, 298 geese, 19 swans. Grand total for winter campaign at Keyhaven, 758, of which 573 are ducks and geese.

Best shots: 28 curlews—42 wigeon and 9 geese—20 geese—28 geese—23 geese—34 geese—8 swans (1 barrel).

N.B.—In 18 of the days shooting 262 geese and 18 swans.

March 12*th*.—A fine sunny day; off from about eight till three. Not a bird of any kind to be seen or heard of, except about two dozen very wild geese, at which I took a long shot, hoping to get a couple to make up my 300 in the new year, and to my surprise down came 6 geese, to add to the above list; thus I closed a splendid season with a capital little shot,

RETURN TO KEYHAVEN, AFTER A DAYS GUNNING, IN THE WINTER OF 1838.

Drawn by C. Varley. Engraved by H. Adlard.

London: Longman, Brown, Green & Longmans,

and retired from the coast without leaving as much as a plover to look after.

19th to 21st.—London. On like a slave from early in the morning till late at night, with lawyers, booksellers, bankers, creditors, debtors, artists, tenants, gunmakers, workmen, &c.

22nd.—Returned to Longparish ; most heartily glad to get out of town, and came inside the coach, being still so unwell with a settled cold, that such a brutal day as this outside might have been the death of me. Nothing but cold, petrifying, sour storms, most wet and furious, from the north-west.

23rd.—Bitter winter. Heavy snow, and piercing cold winds ; and all of no avail, as 'gunning' is over, and all foreign fowl have left our part of the country.

April 19th.—London. Piercing cold, with snow almost every day, which I was obliged to bustle about in, preparing the eighth edition of my sporting book.

30th.—Out on a stick for the first time after being confined to my bed for ten days.

May 8th.—Keyhaven. Read, Buckle and myself, all cripples. Most singular, all the three great gunners cripples, and plenty of whimbrels about and quite tame.

10th.—Up to the eyes in model working and book revising. Heavenly weather and sea looking like a paradise, though a brisk north-easter. What a climate is that of England ! Yesterday insufferably hot ; this evening frost, and obliged to light a fire.

23rd.—London. My illness and my business just admitted of my going this day, for the first time, to her Majesty's Levee, which was immensely full. I was presented by General Lord Combermere, as my Colonel, Lord Rodney was unwell in the country.

31st.—Every day occupied with divers artists, bringing out my book ; and much bothered, as I had to destroy some sketches done all wrong while I was away, and to insist on having my old able friend Cornelius Varley again. Splendid theatrical, musical, and operatic treats this month ; though too busy or ill to accept half the tickets offered me.

June 21st.—The last Drawing Room of the season ; so of course an awful crowd and a vapour bath. Had to wait above three hours for carriage, therefore could not get home till ten minutes before seven. Found a ticket waiting for me for Grisi's box at the opera. Galloped off in a cab to ask Lady Rodney in Pall Mall how we were to go. Answer : 'No more Court costumes now.' So had to strip, and bolt my dinner, and got there by half-past eight ; but a row in the house had luckily kept back the performance half an hour. Fullest house I ever saw. Home exactly at two ; so had a day's real town life—what they call 'pleasure.'

22nd.—Hunted like a wild boar from the time I got up till eleven at night, and then obliged to work for the press till a quarter before three in the morning.

25th.—Had a dinner party at home, and afterwards a music party, and everyone present voted it the merriest they had passed for years. We did not break up till past two ; and I had then to work for the printers till half-past four, as they wanted the sheets per eight o'clock post.

28th.—The Coronation. Up at five in order to get down to the club by seven, after which time the streets would be scarcely passable for ladies. So numerous were the applications for seats at our United Service Club, that there had above a week ago been a kind of raffle for good seats, bad seats, or no seats at all. I had the luck to win the very best for my girls, and of all the pageants that it was possible to behold, this was the most magnificently splendid. We had a sumptuous banquet at the club, and did not get home till near seven, and were in sad confusion owing to a man not bringing the lamps we required for the illumination ; but I made shift without them, and then sallied off till near one to view all the grand illuminations, fireworks, &c., which surpassed anything I ever saw before ; and, in short, it was nearly daylight before we got to bed, so that my bustle and excitement this glorious day continued little short of twenty-four hours.

29th.—Took the girls to the large Coronation Fair in Hyde Park, which is to be kept up three days; but found it more of a place to amuse the lower orders than to attract the fashionables, though the drives round the outside of it were thronged with carriages, and the bustle of the West End made the streets quite a misery to get through with ladies.

July 4th.—Westminster Abbey being open to the public gratis, and even without tickets, I went this day, the last of the two days it was open, to see it; and a most awful crowd I had to encounter, though the sight was gorgeous in the extreme.

12th.—Persecuted with printers, and other bothering book fellows, in the City all day; and then on from half-past three in the afternoon till three o'clock after midnight compiling and copying fair a list of contents, plates, and various other matter for my book, and other business concerning it. Who would be an author, if it was always to be like this? Formerly I had good help in all the dry mechanical labour; but with the printer's gang of careless jackasses I may as well ask for help from Bedlam.

14th.—Saturday night. Sent in the last proof sheet. Of all the happy deliveries I ever had to offer up my thanks for, this is one of the most emancipating. In short, what with printers and engravers, and the bustle of this crazy season in town, I have been in one absolute state of effervescence for three months.

23rd.—Worked my way to Longparish in order to dine with Mr. Fellowes, who wished me to meet Lord Brougham and Sir Richard Sutton, the celebrated great shot and sportsman.

August 15th.—Longparish. A reconciliation took place between me and my old enemy, the lawyer, through the friendly intervention of Mr. Fellowes, so that all scrambles and skirmishes in the field of sport will be happily at an end; and they never would have occurred at all but for the mischief-making lies of gamekeepers, who have since left the lawyer's service, and to whom he had unfortunately given credit, without giving me a chance for explanation. Hence arose all the war. And now for peace when I have hardly health and spirits to enjoy it.

27th.—Keyhaven. A grand day with the Yacht Club; dining at Hurst Castle, I went under sail with the girls in the 'Petrel' punt, which excited more curiosity than any bark upon the Channel, as people could see nothing but ourselves, the sail, and flags, there being just breeze enough to make the punt invisible at a moderate distance.

CHAPTER XXXI

1838

September 1st.—Too unwell to begin shooting till near twelve o'clock, and never did I see a worse first day, birds as wild as hawks, small in size, and so much heavy corn standing that the shooting ought to have been put off for at least a fortnight. I, however, shot capitally in spite of all, and bagged 25 partridges, besides 3 more lost, and never missed a bird, except two long random shots, and I made five brilliant double shots. Dogs behaved as well as they could do, considering a vile scent and birds on the run all day.

3rd.—Rather better, and out all day; and though I shot most gloriously I only brought home 11 partridges and 1 hare. I lost 3 birds, and Charles, who was with me and shot capitally, added 4 brace more birds to the bag. We met Mr. Fellowes's party just going home, and all they got in the whole day was 4 old birds and 4 very young ones, and they pronounced this to be the vilest shooting season on record. So, miserable as my bag has been, I have far surpassed all my competitors.

N.B.—Though I beat my whole estate I did not see so many birds as, in former times, I've bagged in a day.

8th.—A cold north wind, and the very few birds to be found as wild as at Christmas. I got seven shots, and only one fair one among them, and bagged 6 partridges. What a vile first week, and yet I believe no one has beat me.

10th.—As Monday, after the rest on Sunday, is generally

the best day in the week, I went mounted over the open country all the morning, but all I could bag was 7 partridges. So wild were the birds that I fired seven blank shots, and yet I feel confident that I shot straight every time I fired. The season is so bad that going after game this year is a toil instead of a pleasure.

14*th.*—Left for Keyhaven to join the girls, who had returned there from their visits in that neighbourhood, and attended the benefit of our friend Miss Chambers at the Southampton Theatre this evening. Never was a town so crowded, four public meetings and a morning concert besides. I could not get a seat in the coffee room of the inn, as even this was filled with men, women, and children, it being the day, both out and in, for packets.

28*th.*—Went from Lymington per steamer to Portsmouth to find out the monument to my great-grandfather, and see my friend Captain Symonds, now a patient in Haslar Hospital. Found a rich ancient tablet in the garrison chapel, which I ordered to be repaired at my own expense, and surprised the clerk not a little when I made myself known and showed the crest on my seal as corresponding with that on the monument.[1]

Game bagged in September: only 52 partridges and 1 hare, though I never shot better. Out but five times, and found the birds so scarce that I gave it up and returned to the coast. The same complaint all over our country, insomuch that I killed the most of anyone the first day.

[1] Richly carved in marble with arms and crest over, and inscribed as follows:

'Near this
place lyeth the body of the
Honble Colonel
Peter Hawker,
Late Lt Governor of
Portsmouth,
Who departed this life
the 5th of Jan^{y},
1732, in the 60th year
of his age.'

October 1*st.*—Keyhaven. Took a hard day's fag with Mr. West over his wild rough country at Arnwood, accompanied by Major Keppel. My share (the best) was 6 partridges, 2 cock pheasants, and 3 hares.

4*th.*—A strong north-easter, and some wigeon come: so I launched the 'Petrel' and the great gun, so as to get out for a few hours in the afternoon, and I should have had a good shot if I could have been ready about an hour sooner. I did get in shot of about 50 wigeon, but the tide sunk so low I could not bear the gun on the birds.

8*th.*—The wigeon have kept about here ever since the 4th, but were always on a 'lop of the sea.' I was out from six till three P.M., when just as I sat down to dinner the wigeon appeared. I left my dinner and put off, and got close in to them, where I lay for near half an hour, but they were all scattered abroad. But when I saw them in the act of 'jumping,' I caught 3 together and took another with the second barrel, and brought in these 4 wigeon. There were other gunners about, or I would rather have left them till I could have caught them properly placed for a shot, and perhaps cut up two-thirds of the company.

21*st.*—Longparish. On my way to call at Lord Portsmouth's after church to-day, I witnessed the scene where the frightful accident occurred yesterday with the Salisbury coach at Hurstbourne.

25*th.*—Longparish. Up for a candlelight breakfast. Went for the first time on the new railway: did 38 miles in an hour and thirty-one minutes: in town soon after twelve.

30*th.*—London. Off to Bank; sold some consols about half-past eleven, but had to wait till one while papers for New York stock were preparing. Being for this time a prisoner, I wished to amuse myself with an inspection of all the Bank; so went to my friend Timothy Curtis, the Governor-in-Chief, who was delighted to see me, and said I never could have hit on a better time, as the Prince Louis Napoleon, Buonaparte's talented nephew, was expected every moment to see all the machinery of the Bank, by appointment. Waited till one, but no prince; so went and completed all my American transaction just in time to save an outward-bound ship with the papers. Back again to Curtis; prince and all his staff come, and on my being introduced, he was quite delighted, as he said he had long wished to know the author of his favourite study on the *chasse*; nothing could be more flattering or agreeable. Saw all the bullion, machinery, bank-note making, steam engines &c. Had bags holding 1,000 sovereigns each in my hand (they weighed 21 lb. each bag), and then had 3,000,000*l.* in my hand in 1,000*l.* bank notes. Had a splendid luncheon with Curtis, his ladies, and the prince and staff, and then flew to Coutts's to execute my power of attorney at four. The prince walked out with me to his carriage, with all the staff following behind, and the street was so mobbed to see this new 'lion,' *vice* old Soult, that we could scarcely proceed any pace. His highness then entered a splendid carriage, and I flew off in a cab, not having time to crawl along in an omnibus. Indeed, such has been the pressure of my business that I never could have got through it in the time I've been in town, had I not cabbed it on most occasions. Now, thank God, I've done all in a most satisfactory manner, and booked my place for leaving town to-morrow morning. Up to the eyes in accounts from half-past six this evening till twelve at night.

31*st.*—Returned to Longparish by Salisbury coach, and viâ railway. On arrival found notices for a lawsuit, and a requisition for my coming to see my jobs done at Keyhaven. Never at rest.

November 5*th.*—Up before daylight; off early to Winchester; long consultation with solicitor about lawsuits; on to Southampton; down to Northam about Ward's punt, &c. busy with Buckle and gunmaker Burnett, and heaps of commissions. On per 'Pilot' coach, and at Keyhaven Cottage about half-past eight in the evening, the tranquillity of which peaceable place, after the incessant bustle I have been in ever since I left it, was a relief that was like a heaven on earth. No birds.

15*th.*—Keyhaven. There being no birds on the coast, though an easterly wind, I never took up a gun till to-day, when I went up to Arnwood to try for a cock with my friend Mr. West, who with his keepers and a cry of spaniels beat all his best country, but the only cock we saw the whole day flew into my very face, a close open shot, just after I had discharged both barrels, and I never could find him again, though I beat for hours.

23*rd.*—Longparish. I had, thank God, the satisfaction to hear that my son Peter was just getting under way with a fair wind, and in a capital transport (the 'Elizabeth') with a very pleasant party, and he wrote in good spirits. May God protect him wherever he goes.

26*th.*—Deadly cold, with an easterly wind and a fall of snow. I had such a bad cold that I could not get warm in bed or up, and got warm by a strange recipe. I was busy at accounts, and was suddenly called off after a woodcock; away I went in the snow, got wet through, and at the same time perspired with heat from the tremendous long chase I had with 2 woodcocks, which kept all my banditti on the run for nearly three hours, as they were so very wild, but I bagged them both at last.

29*th.*—Ferocious weather still on day and night. No stirring out without a tattered umbrella and a drenching to the skin. Every chimney choking with smoke, and every tree in danger with the gale. We pray to God that Peter may, ere this, have either reached a different atmosphere or put into some foreign port.

December 1*st.*—On to Keyhaven, and long before I reached Southampton all the wind and rain returned. Got to the Cottage about nine, all the coaches being late owing to the bad roads. On my arrival found that everyone had been having fine sport during the easterly wind, but the awful south gale last week had not only put an end to the shooting, but caused a serious flood, insomuch that all my things were of necessity moved to the upper floor, and the villagers, and even their pigs, were obliged to be sheltered in the bedrooms. Luckily, however, I sustained no damage worth naming.

8th.—A fine day at last, so I completed my chief business at Keyhaven for this cruise, which was to place all the booms in another new leak that I had cut by contract (at my own expense) through 'Stivers' mud for nearly half a mile, in order to get to 'Pennington Leak' without going round by Hurst. The job was completed for 8*l.*, which I paid old Dowden the navigator the moment I landed, and ordered two gallons of 'heavy wet' for the men to drink success to my 'new cut.' Mrs. Whitby was kind enough to present me with the booms, fresh cut, from her own plantations.

9th.—Sunday. Most awful accounts of the disasters in the late terrific hurricane, and among them the narrow escape of the 'Barossa' transport, the one that followed the 'Elizabeth' a few days after she had sailed with Peter. My anxiety about him, therefore, must be intense, till I, please God, hear some tidings of the latter ship, in which he sailed.

20th.—Returned to Longparish.

N.B.—Such was the scarcity of wild fowl on the coast, that while at Keyhaven for nineteen days I saw five gunners 'on' day and night, and in the whole time they only got 3 wigeon among them all. I therefore withheld launching my grand set-out for two reasons; the one that I would not waste my time and the wear and tear of gear for nothing, the other that I would not have it said that the poor gunners were half starved because my great gun had driven away all the fowl. I therefore devoted my time to the completion of my new leaks through the mud, and other preparations for a better prospect of good sport.

30*th.*—Received a letter announcing the death of General Sir Samuel Hawker, which took place in town on the 27th, and which melancholy event will restrain our gaieties and put us in mourning.

1839

January 5th.—As a specimen of what the shooting here now is, I must record that Mr. Sola, who was eager to have a day's sport, was obliged to amuse himself with the killing of sparrows and other small birds, as he could not get even a blackbird, much less a head of game.

9*th.*—Frost. Off for Keyhaven.

10*th.*—Scarcely any birds yet. All the better, as it will take me a few days to recover my strength, after being confined so long to the house.

N.B.—Not above three couple of birds killed here during my twenty days' absence at Longparish.

11*th.*—Frost ended in a set in of dirty 'sou'-wester,' with a constant batch of wind and rain.

19*th.*—Another tremendous gale and pour of rain all day, after the usual forerunner, a most petrifying white frost; weather that of course puts a stop to gunning, and the chance of birds. Read has persevered mud crawling night after night, and never saw the least chance for a shot. My gear continues still in store.

22*nd.*—A fine day at last, north wind, clear sky, and a little black frost.

31*st.*—From the 22nd up to this day we have had the most unpleasant weather, and the coast has been so destitute of birds that the poor gunners cannot earn even a few shillings a week. Nothing but white frosts, followed by westerly hurricanes. This morning, however, there set in a severe black frost, with a strong northerly gale and snow, so I got my small punt, and a light single stanchion gun, in order, not thinking it worth while to launch the grand set-out unless some good flocks of birds made their appearance.

February 1st.—A black frost, with wind north-north-west; but not a bird in the country, except a few geese that Read tried and could not get within a quarter of a mile of. He was out all last night with a bright moon, and never saw or heard a single fowl.

2nd.—Read crawled all night, and not a bird was to be seen or heard, either by night or day, on the whole coast. I availed myself of a fine sunshiny dead calm to try two shots at a mark with a new cartridge in my light stanchion, and the result was such that we had only to regret the want of a living target, on which to repeat our experiments. But the coast is done, totally done, for this season.

3rd.—Sunday. A warm bird-singing day.

4th.—A rotten wet day.

5th.—A May morning, ending in an afternoon and all night wet and windy sou'-wester.

6th.—Rotten heavy weather, but more calm.

7th.—Rotten wind and rain all day. Had a general furbish of all my 'traps' preparative to 'bolting' the day after to-morrow, as I could weather it no longer and had plenty of business in hand.

8th.—Savage wind and rain from the south-west. Called on all the good neighbours, and ordered my fly to take me off for to-morrow morning's coach.

9th.—Arrived at Longparish.

13th.—Went up to London.

21st.—After an incessant round of business with lawyers, bankers, executors, brokers, book publishers, binders, musicians, artists, gunmakers, and other tradesmen, attendance at the Horse Guards' Levee and the Queen's Levee &c., I this day returned (doing the thirty-eight miles railway in an hour and twenty minutes) per 'light Salisbury' coach to Longparish.

22nd.—A letter from Peter, who, thank God, had weathered all the awful hurricanes and landed safe in Barbadoes on December 20, after a passage of only four weeks and four days.

Lamentable list. The worst season in the memory of man. Game &c. killed up to November 26 only, as I never got a shot after, there being no game worth going out for, and the awful and destructive hurricanes, which began towards the end of this month, having driven home all the wild fowl from the coast:

Wild fowl: 1 teal, 5 wigeon (young birds in October). Total, 6. Waders in September: 2 godwits, 2 plover, 1 curlew. Total, 5.

N.B.—Seeing the failure of all the gunners, I never launched my punt this season.[1]

Game: 58 partridges, 6 hares, 7 pheasants, 8 rabbits, 1 woodcock, 4 snipes. Total, 84 head. Grand (or rather paltry) total, 95 head only.

March 4th.—Left Longparish for Keyhaven, not for shooting, as there is none this year, but for change of air, for this influenza that I and almost every one have suffered with. When in Winchester on my way through to-day I found that the assize court was crowded to excess, and would be all this day taken up with the case of Sir John Milbank stabbing the Southampton attorney, Mr. Pocock.

5th.—Found myself quite another man already from the change of air, and there came on a dry easterly wind.

9th.—Frost and snow, with a strong north wind; in short the weather of a proper, hard, healthy winter, though too late in the season to do any good. I went out to see if this set-in of fine hard weather had brought any fowl, and if so I should have launched at least my small swivel gun next day. But nothing was to be seen, except about 100 geese that would not let you get within a quarter of a mile of them. So much

[1] N.B.—Scarcity universal, and London supplied from Holland.

for fine weather setting in 'a day after the fair,' though it was sadly wanted for the health of the people, as I found that half this neighbourhood was laid up with the influenza. The effect of the hard winter and sea air acted like magic in curing me, and did me more good than all the medicines and warm baths I had taken.

7th.—Rowed out again, accompanied by Read, Payne, and Guy, in hopes of their driving the geese over my head by surrounding them on the mud; and I perhaps might have got one, but Buckle set into them with his stanchion gun, fired a blank shot, and away they all went. On my return home to dinner I had the mortification to receive a letter from my solicitor stating that the jury, for want of a better judge, had been humbugged into a wrong view of my legal case, and Charles, as well as my tenant, Farmer Diddams, was ordered three months' imprisonment. A most rascally, ignorant, and unheard-of piece of injustice. So much for the villanous laws of this country.

9th.—Fine hard winter still, but nothing afloat. Followed a flock of golden plover over a stiff country for four hours; but, at last, could only catch them so dispersed that I had the option of one or none as the last chance, so let fly and brought in 1 golden plover.

11*th.*—Out all day again in search of the plover; but the wind having shifted from north to east, they were not to be found. Intensely cold weather, and half the neighbourhood under the doctors with influenza. Fired some shots at small birds, all I could get to shoot at, with a self-priming copper-cap musket, that Westley Richards sent me as a present to try before he submitted it to Government. But although ingenious, I fear it will be too complex and not waterproof enough for the service.

18*th.*—Left Keyhaven in a piercing north-east wind and snow (though we literally had summer only three days ago) for Winchester, where I was all the forenoon employed in seeing my man Charles in gaol, relative to steps against the perjured blackguards who got him in there. Arrived at Longparish almost frozen at six in the evening, and had the satisfaction to receive another letter from Peter saying he was quite well, and had just weathered a severe earthquake.

31*st.*—Longparish. Very unwell ever since I came, from the general and horrible complaint called 'influenza.'

April 1*st.*—Winter. A bitter cold easterly wind with snow and rain. 7 wild geese were seen flying over to-day.

2*nd.*—Though the piercing cold continued, I this day saw 3 swallows flying up and down the river. A curious circumstance—grey geese and swallows in the country at the same time.

18*th.*—London. On returning from a call on Sir Benjamin Brodie, I ran foul of the grand wedding of Lord Douro, and got a capital post to view all the great dons, and the great ladies with their grace, lace, and giblets.

May 9*th.*—Cold as at Christmas again, whereas three days ago we were broiled with heat.

10*th.*—Intensely cold, with a north-east gale. People driven to great coats and furs again.

12*th.*—Sunday. Bitter cold. It was just thirty years ago from this day that our affair of the Douro took place.

14*th.*—Yesterday it was as hot as in July; to-day it was as cold as in winter, with occasional sleet and snow.

15*th.*—Epsom races, and actually snow at the 'Derby.'

23*rd.*—Ran down to Longparish. Tried trolling for a couple of hours this evening with Lord Saltoun's brass 'kill-devil,' the only artificial bait that I ever found to take in our river. It answered well; and though a vile evening for fishing, I killed 5 brace of large trout, besides what I threw in.

24*th.*—In my life, I never saw the vegetation so cut up as by the late winter, that we had about a week ago; when there were three days' snow, with ice half an inch thick. The oldest person never saw the like before.

25th.—Frost at night, cutting north-easter all day with a bright sun. Lovely weather for wild swans and geese ; but the very devil for vegetation. Proceeded to Keyhaven to order some jobbing, repairs, painting &c., and on passing through the New Forest observed the greatest part of the trees appeared as if they had been set fire to, owing to the foliage being killed by the late severe weather.

28th.—Off from morning till night between Hordle and Christchurch with my large net, that I've had for three years, and never before wetted. We did pretty well, having brought home just 20 brace of fish, viz. 14 bass (largest 7 lb.), 3 mullets (best 2 lb.), 12 flounders, 4 small turbots, 1 sole, 6 very large gore fish.

29th.—A few hauls with net on our own shore ; but the weeds were so thick, and my cadgers so drunk from the profits of yesterday, that we did but little and gave it up. We got only 5 bass (one 9½ lb.), 1 flounder, 1 gore fish, and 1 monster called a cuttlefish, which I never saw before (common as the shell is for pounce). We cut him open and threw him into the sea, and he made half an acre of water black with his ink ; which, after he was thrown away, my cadgers told me was very valuable.

June 1st.—Took a day's sail to that delightful place, Alum Bay, and then round the Isle of Wight cliffs. Had my gun with me, but there was so little wind under and off the heights, that it was impossible to sail in quick enough to shoot the rock birds. Several parties were out on purpose, and I could not see that they got a single bird. I did contrive to bring home a few.

5th.—Longparish. Rose betimes and bustled along to Hartley Row for fear of being too late for the railway from there for town, but found it went at one instead of twelve, so had to kill an hour. This gave me an opportunity of walking about half a mile to see the arches that have lately fallen in, and one of which I had gone over one journey in the 'Hampshire Hunt' coach. The engineer, it appears, perseveres in establishing tunnels through stuff like brown sugar, instead of cutting a ravine and building a suspension, or, if no good ground to hold it, a common bridge. A stupid fellow.

20th.—I was taken so ill, that I despaired of being able to go to Hampton Court to-day to attend a picnic given by my old regiment, the 14th Light Dragoons. I, however, got the doctor to quack me up for a makeshift, and we started. We got down to Hampton Court just time enough for me to inspect the Palace &c. before dinner, and I was not a little gratified by the kind reception I met from my old regiment, though there was not one officer and very few of the men that had been in when I was with the 14th.[1]

July 6th.—Keyhaven. Took a refreshing sail to the back of the island, and on passing the Needles I observed a large boat at anchor with five men in it, two of whom were constantly winding away in a manner similar to drawing water from a deep well. I gave the order to 'lower sail,' and go up to this boat, which proved to be one on a diving speculation, and the diving man, who was some fathoms under water and had already been there an hour and three-quarters, was to come up again at the end of two hours, so I of course waited the other quarter of an hour to see the diver and hear what he had done. The winding apparatus that I saw incessantly at work was very finely manufactured, and made for the purpose of inflating air into the diving machine, or rather waterproof diving dress, of the man who was working under the sea. At last the diver came up rather exhausted, and as soon as he recovered his weakness he drew out from his large bag pockets several articles that were of no value except for a

[1] Brown, the bandmaster, Heatley, the trumpet major (a piccolo boy in the band in my time), and Fitzhenry, an old mungo and pupil of mine on the tambourine, soon proclaimed me as the officer whose squadron won the trophy of the 'Douro' (which they were wearing), and the respect shown to me by 'all hands' was such as I could not but feel; and particularly the honour of my health being given (with a statement of the circumstance) the first toast (after that of 'the ladies') when the dinner cloth was removed.

mere curiosity ; the best prizes having already been taken up, as the vessel which went down there close to the Needles was the 'Pomone' frigate, wrecked thirty years ago. The 'hands' of the boat then said, 'Sir, please to remember the diver,' so I gave them a shilling and said, 'I shall still longer remember him if he gives me a bit of the copper, or anything worth a farthing, as a trophy of what I have seen,' on which the diver gave me a little thing as portable as he could find.

11*th to* 13*th*.—Immured in the town of Winchester with all my witnesses during the infernal uproar and row of the Assizes. Mr. Smith had to fly like a bird on the railroad repeatedly up and down from London. On one occasion he left at one in the night, and was back and at breakfast in Winchester by twelve in the day (eleven hours) with deeds and documents collected. Mr. Earle opened my case, and was answered by a terrific jaw from Mr. Butt, who, in order to preclude the fulminating reply of Mr. Earle, declined calling any of his witnesses, and consequently left all their lies and romances uncontradicted. As God's mercy would have it, I had insisted on a special jury (all thorough gentlemen, who were above the influence of a counsel's humbug), and they gave a verdict in my favour. The expense of course must be serious ; but what am I to do if people will rob me and won't listen to proposals of fair arbitration ?

20*th*.—London. Battle of Waterloo from morning till midnight preparative to our leaving town early on Monday morning, the 21st being Sunday. A severe day, too, on Sunday. Had to get up very early to read prayers and do business besides, as the only chance I had to get a pair of horses (which I was quite at a loss for want of) was at eleven (church time) this day, when I bought a pair of greys. While the horses were being shown off to me, the Wesleyan Methodists were in full cry in a chapel over the mews. Tried the horses in a spare omnibus (the only vehicle to be borrowed), then trotted and galloped each over town and country, then tried each separate in a gig, and in short bought them, and gave orders for their leaving town next day. I then flew off to Moscheles (the only day he could do business), and had a long and most satisfactory discussion with him on a trial of my 'hand-moulds,' after waiting till he had played three fugues and a concerto of Mendelssohn for his Sunday's practice. Then made a string of indispensable visits, that I could not catch a moment to do before. Read the evening prayers. Baited with bills, packing, and 'good-bye-ers' till twelve at night, and went to bed as tired as an old dog after the 1st of September.

22nd.—Flew by the rail to Basingstoke in two hours. We then posted home to Longparish House.

This evening at dusk a curious bird, that all the clods have been after for weeks, flew over me. I ran in and had to put a gun together, as all my things were dismantled. I shot the bird. It was quite white with a few yellow marks, and appeared more like a white canary than anything else. Perhaps a bird strayed from a cage; but I'll send it to Leadbeater, and 'time will show' what it is.

25th.—Had over Tom Langstaff with his fiddle, and enjoyed the first day's leisure and pleasure that incessant worry would allow me for several weeks past.

August 3rd.—Keyhaven. Fine weather at last; so I was enabled to take a delightful sail. Put into Hurst in order to inspect and bring away a specimen of the new paving composition, for the manufactory of which 'Crusoe's' beach cottage is let to a London man. This material is made from a stuff called 'bitumen,' like lava, which, from being pliant and somewhat sticky, is rendered as hard as iron by the process of boiling it with a certain composition; and it may then be ornamented with beach pebbles ground up so as to look like granite. The man employed in it showed me several specimens laid out in squares, stars &c. as ornamental paving for halls and such like.

20th.—An eventful day for exertion, grandeur, novelty, &c. At half-past one, being disappointed of my donkey chaise, I had to amble at a jackass trot to catch the coach before it passed Everton. I proceeded to the excellent little inn of Mrs. Osbaldeston at Redbridge, to dress in my best, and join the splendid gala of Captain Colt at Rownam's house. I then drove on in my carriage, and arrived about half-past five, just as the innumerable host of fashionables were sat down to a banquet similar to that of a lord mayor. The wines flew at an awful pace, and the speeches after dinner were like a meeting in parliament, and I had the honour of being kindly victimised on the occasion by our hospitable host as the leader of the shooting world. We then had a concert till near eleven, fireworks equal to Vauxhall till twelve under the able directions of Captain Rich, dancing till two, then a gorgeous sitting supper, and a finale with dancing till half-past three, when the carriage came again from Redbridge and took us worn out to our beds at the inn. Vercellini, who had no refuge to fly to but a night's lodging under a hedge, as every sofa in the house as well as every inn in the neighbourhood was crammed with visitors, lay on the inn sofa for the night, and we almost burst with laughter at the account of the concatenation of troubles he was in through arriving before us at the inn without his 'cue,' and being taken for a madman or wandering impostor.

21st.—This morning Vercellini was as lively as a lark, and singing his roulades in the garden. We then turned to at music till breakfast, and sang a grand duet of Donizetti. To relate all the fun and catastrophes that occurred during this expedition would fill a novel for Colburn, but my head is too distracted to write more than a sorry memorandum.

CHAPTER XXXII

1839

September 1st.—Longparish. Sunday. Shooting, such as it now is at Longparish, postponed, owing to the corn not being cut, and a good job too, as it's a disgrace to the laws to begin so early.

2nd.—After tremendous gales and showers for three days we had this day a regular set in of rain as well as wind, so while the tyros were getting their wet jackets and almost empty bags I went to do all my commissions.

3rd.—More wet weather, and the wind raging enough to blow one's teeth down one's throat. A sorry time for those who would not postpone their shooting.

5th.—Went to inspect Mr. Weld's champion yacht, the 'Alarm.'

10th.—Took the field about eleven o'clock to-day, and of all the sorry first days I ever had at Longparish this was the worst. It's all over with our partridge shooting. Had I brought home every head of game I saw, my number would not have amounted to what was a few years ago an average bag. Though I never shot better than to-day, I only got 13 partridges and 1 hare. I missed but one shot, and that was in attempting to secure a quail with my second barrel, at which my first had missed fire. The other shooters, as far as I could learn, had even worse sport than I had, though the weather, for the first time this month, was tolerably fine. Good-bye to good sport on the Longparish estate, till our surrounding neighbours have less mercy on the vermin and poachers, and more mercy on the game.

11*th.*—Rested myself and dogs, *and dined with the lawyer* at seven. He had been all over his best preserve, with Lords George and William Poulett, and their three pair of barrels got but 7 brace among them, so it proved that I had done no worse than my neighbours.

18*th.*—A windy day with a few showers. Took out my gun to try if it were possible to get a few birds for the house, and, to the astonishment of all, I brought home 18 prime partridges, and I lost another in the high turnips. I only fired my gun twenty-one times, and the only two blank shots were out of reach. In short, I never shot better, and considering the season is the worst on record, I never had a more astonishing day. I only started at twelve, and was home a quarter before five. But I was lucky in dispersing birds in the wind.

20*th.*—A treat worth all the game shooting in the world. Thalberg at Winchester for his farewell performance. Drove the girls over, and a delightful treat we had, as he was far more extraordinary than when we last heard him in town; his miraculous combination of working in four parts with intense feeling and electrifying execution decidedly proves him to be the greatest pianist that ever sat before the public.

Ran down for a change of air to Keyhaven.

N.B.—No sooner had I reached Southampton than the wet weather set in again.

26*th.*—As some trips of wigeon had been seen, I availed myself of this the first fine day, though a strong westerly wind, to launch my light punt, the 'Dart,' with the single stanchion gun, and took a long cruise beyond Pilewell, where I fell in with 9 wigeon; but the coastguard were at exercise and drove them away. Coming home 5 more travelled past, but did not stop. I saw a rare bird in the marsh, a phalarope, and got him with the cripple stopper.

Game killed in September (shooting so bad that I went

out but four times, and then only for half a day): 40 partridges, 1 hare, 1 landrail. Total, only 42 head.

Our shooting has been all but annihilated by the taking of eggs, the severe weather in May, the destruction of hedges and turf banks for firing, and the mowing of the wheat.

October 1*st*.—As we have not had any pheasants, except by chance a stray one, at Longparish for several years, the 1st of October is no longer an eventful day for me.

16*th*.—London. Saw that splendid invention, the daguerreotype.

18*th*.—Returned to Longparish after knocking off what some twaddlers would take three weeks to do in three clear days.

Universal complaints about the scarcity of game with all the gunmakers, powder men &c. in London.

19*th*.—Longparish. After being baited with business till near one, I turned out for a bit of pleasure with as fine a brigade of men and dogs as ever took the field, and did wonders, considering the scarcity. We found five pheasants, all in the country I believe, and every bird of them came home to the larder.

November 21*st*.—This is the grand day for the meeting on Chambers's (my bankers) bankruptcy; but as I had sent a power of attorney with my vote against that scorpion, old M——, and the other diabolical assignees, I had no occasion to go up on purpose, though should have much enjoyed the baiting of these scamps had my lawsuit called me to town about the same time. So I started in a pour of rain to Keyhaven, not a little delighted to get there.

25*th to* 27*th*.—Bad weather, which was rather *à propos*, as I have been three days a prisoner with illness.

28*th*.—Better, but sick and weak still. Buckle came ashore to see me, after having earned only 4*s*. 6*d*. the whole month. I took a little walk with him for some air; we saw a cock wigeon in the 'mudlands,' so Buckle hauled his punt over the bank, and I got the bird with the popgun just before there set in a wet afternoon.

December 6th.—All the wild fowl in the whole of the large town of Southampton to-day was one stinking 'curre' duck. Not even a decoy-caught wild duck in the town or market. What can be worse than these beastly white frosts; or, in other words, petrified, poisonous fogs? Not a bird at Keyhaven.

7th.—A cold damp southerly wind. Too much sea to go out.

8th.—Sunday. A strong easterly wind, but damp and deadly cold instead of bracing, and so dark I could not see to read in church, nor, by the way, hear either, for the constant coughs and sneezes of the congregation.

9th.—A cold damp east wind. Took the punt to bring home some things for the house from Lymington, but brought back again the charge that had been put into my single stanchion gun on last Saturday fortnight. Not even a chance for a shot.

10th.—Bitter cold, and damp east wind. No fowl; a sure sign that this east wind is only a humbug, and 'bound' for a south-wester and rain. Blew off my gun, which went like lightning, though loaded 18 days.

16th.—A fine day at last. Afloat at daybreak, but never saw a fowl, and came home with nothing but an old crow that I knocked over with the popgun. A pinching white frost at night.

17th.—The white frost broke into a damp southerly gale. Not a bird to be seen.

N.B.—I this day saw, by mere accident, the following article, under the head of different regiments, in the 'Naval and Military Gazette' of the 14th inst.:

'74th. Lieutenant Hawker is about to return from the West Indies on sick leave. He is son to Colonel Hawker, whose "Hints to Sportsmen" have gained a just celebrity.'

I at once wrote to my agent in town to go and learn particulars, as I had not heard from Peter, though I wrote every foreign post day, and yet received no letter since one on September 24, when he was in good health, and had been having grand sport with the tobago plover and other birds.

21*st.*—A fine day at last, though a heavy south-wester. Had a general furbish of all the gear and stores, and put them away, preparative to going inland for Christmas, after the most barren year for sport in the memory of the oldest person living.

25*th*—Longparish. Went (Christmas Day) to our church, where Mr. Greene read a prayer for fair weather. The church is beautifully ornamented and altered ; a fine painted window over the altar, and some fine specimens of carving from the Continent, all of which is presented by our worthy vicar, Mr. Greene.

26*th.*—The pinching white frost that bit our noses all last night, turned this morning into another most determined wet day. Accounts from Peter to November 5, when he was, thank God, 'quite well.' So the news in the paper was all false.

27*th.*—Wet again, but outwitted the weather by having a jolly good day with Tom Langstaff and his fiddle.

28*th and* 29*th.*—Sunday. Petrifying white frosts.

30*th.*—Ditto, and so deadly cold that one could get no warmth in bed, up, in doors or out of doors. Everyone complaining of chills. This night, soon after ten, began Mr. Fellowes's grand ball at Hurstbourne Park, when I dressed up and went, though so unwell I could hardly stand, and shivering with cold 'like a dog in a wet sack.' Never was anything more handsomely done, and the sitting supper for all (above one hundred of the *élite* of the county) was quite the best I ever saw. We went in a bitter cold white frost, and came away, about three, in a pour of rain.

1840

January 9th.—Keyhaven. Everyone complaining of chills, and nearly all the gunners ill from the late poisonous weather. Not a bird yet come to the coast.

13*th.*—Longparish. Unprecedented weather, and, what I never saw before, eight white frosts running, with wind south-south-east. So deadly cold that everyone complained of not being able to get warm, even with exercise; and not so much as a fieldfare or a few larks, much less a head of game, to be seen or heard of. The dullness of the country now is absolutely lamentable so far as concerns outdoor amusement.

18*th.*—Bitter white frost. Started, bag and baggage, with the whole family, in the Whitchurch chariot and my carriage at half-past eight this morning for Basingstoke. The roads were so vile that we were nearly three hours doing the 15 miles. We had nineteen heavy packages, besides innumerable little things, and all was shipped with the regularity of clockwork by means of my patent plan of not only numbering, as most wise people do, but by tying a piece of scarlet binding to distinguish every article that belonged to my party. What a contrast between the awful freight of a batch of females, and a gent with his one portmanteau!

22*nd.*—London. Rain and a hurricane all day; tiles and chimney pots flying about like Waterloo. Few men have had a sharper day's work than I to-day, viz. after paying bills and doing several commissions in the City, I was with Parkinson having a tooth drawn at eleven. Then a long business with Chambers, my former banker, in the Fleet Prison; ditto at the 'Times' office; then down to the Court of Exchequer in Westminster Hall, where I had a consultation with counsel about my lawsuit, expected on every day. Then an interview with several officers at our club about getting Long the appointment of furbisher at the Tower; then with Mr. Hatch, the secretary of the Army and Navy Club, about Peter's concerns. Then with Jones about a clever six-barrel pistol; with Eley about cartridges, and with Lancaster and Long about guns. Then up to H——, near Tottenham Court Road. Then down to Mr. Gunther's at Camden Town on the business of a new piano for Keyhaven, and on transferring to him my 'hand-mould' business. Then a long visit at Moscheles' about musical lessons and divers musical novelties. Then to settle a bill and give some orders in Park Road, and home just in time to save the post with some letters on business to the country. Swallowed my dinner about six, and afterwards had a stiff pianoforte lesson from Bertini, who by mere chance dropped in and invited me to a good 'strap. Went to bed at eleven, as tired as a dog after the 1st of September.

24*th*.—Ferocious weather and another deluge of rain all day. At Westminster again to-day, but trial not to come on, and to-morrow the judges will be all occupied on the point (of our humbugging laws) which relates to the notorious Frost.

25*th*.—No lawsuit till about Tuesday, as the Court of Exchequer is occupied to day with the case of the notorious Frost, and will not resume equity cases till next week.

29*th*.—The rain ceased. Judges decided against Frost. I was directed to be in the Exchequer Court this day at two, and when I arrived my trial was over; so unexpectedly did it come on that Wickham's leading counsel (Butt) and his solicitor and my solicitor were all too late, but both my counsel, Earle and Smirke, were there, as was also Mr. Smith, my solicitor's clerk, who gave us a full report. Judgment was deferred till the judges had conferred together, and Mr. Butt got leave to have a new trial in case their verdict did not suit him. Judges Park and Alderson took my part, but I am fearful as to Judges Gurney and Coleridge. We were much amused at the blustering Mr. Butt arriving too late to spit out his jaw. Here ends my business in London for the present.

31*st.*—Went down, viâ railway and Salisbury coach, to Longparish, where I cut through all my bills, inspections of work done &c. with railway speed, and with only a few hours' sleep, in order to get out of the place before the damp of it should make me unwell again.

Lamentable list of game up to February 1, 1840: 42 partridges, 1 landrail, 3 hares, 3 rabbits, 4 pheasants (all I saw), 8 snipes (all in one day). Total, 61 head only.

The fact was that the game season was so bad I gave up shooting, and resigned to Charles Heath, my keeper, the hard labour of getting about 5 head a week for the table. I never shot better; but there was nothing to shoot owing to the destroyed breed, and then the floods and hurricanes.

February 3rd.—Keyhaven. In a bustle since this early morning putting things to rights, unpacking the new piano &c. when about 30 geese dropped inside below Pennington. We left one bustle for another, dried some powder, launched the 'Dart,' the light single-gun punt &c. in hopes of catching the geese before the ground ebb; but, after all, we were about a quarter of an hour too late, and they left us for the eastward.

4*th.*—Weather more awful than ever; a tremendous hurricane and an awful flood. It came on last night at twelve. My punt the 'Dart' was torn from her moorings and washed inland, but saved by the coastguard. To-day at high water (eleven o'clock), the sea swallowed up the whole quay, and I galloped off for help from Milford; but at one the waters happily abated sufficiently to induce us to withhold the removal of further articles from the ground floor, and we now remain all anxiety about the tide of this night, with a raging hurricane and a pour of rain, though, thank God, a few more points from the awful south. After remaining on guard, 'all hands,' till past twelve at night, when it was as dark as it possibly could be, we retired to bed in safety, as the change of wind had providentially arrested all further danger.

5*th.*—In the morning all was as well as if nothing had happened, save a few shillingsworth of damage to gear &c. A strong north-wester all day. Had I not been here, I should most likely have had one of my splendid punts knocked to pieces, as I had her carried into the yard in spite of Read and others, who advised me to let her swing near the quay, where, soon after I rescued her, there was a fall of water like Niagara, and she must have caught the current and been dashed down a fall of about eight feet.

10*th.*—Terrific weather all night and to-day; but as the tides are luckily now at the neap, we are pretty safe from flood.

N.B.—The Queen's wedding day; but I lost nothing by not being in town, as J. Hawker, *alias* Clarenceux King of Arms, told me he could get no admissions to the ceremony for me or anyone. So all I can do is to drink 'to the royal pair' among myself and myrmidons.

11*th.*—A letter from Peter dated December 20, when he had got quite well, thank God, and had been enjoying some splendid shooting and fishing, and had got a large alligator while on a visit at the seat of a Tobago planter or squire. Weather so much better this afternoon that I put my light punt afloat again and went off again, but had not gone far when the weather set in with all its fury, and continued all night.

17*th.*—A fine day at last, with a light air from the eastward, and no sun, the very best of times for gunning. I therefore got up by candlelight, and once more enjoyed the sea breeze in my light punt, but came home about one, after having gone many miles and seen nothing. Went off again about two, when it was quite calm, and rowed off in Channel, where I made a capital shot at 6 black velvet ducks. I floored the whole of them at about 120 yards The only dead one floated out past Hurst, where I dare not follow him.

18*th.*—A fine heavy gale from the east, though we fear too late to bring us any sport.

19*th.*—Gale from east. About 60 geese off; the most seen this year. Weathered a heavy sea, and was dropping smoothly down 'cock sure' of a good shot, when 10 more flew over and drove them all miles to leeward. The 10 flew past us in a heavy sea. I 'up gun' and down with 5 of them, and made my retreat with the first geese shot here this year. Came in at two and drove to Noah's marsh, where there have been some snipes, but found nothing but 1 jack snipe and 3 water rails, all of which I cleared off. In the evening 'Buckle' anchored a mile to windward of us, so that our further sport with these few geese will be done for either by his banishing them from the ground, or by his lying directly where he must have the first shot.

20*th.*—A prime north-easter, with a healthy black frost, and a few blossoms of snow, but, alas! two months too late to be of much service. Out from daylight till afternoon, and saw only a few geese far off at sea.

21*st.*—Out, but too rough to 'live' outside, and nothing on coast but a few geese, though as severe a winter's day as could be wished for.

22*nd.*—Hard black frost and furious east gale all last night and all to-day. Went off about four in the afternoon, and weathered some stiff breakers to a small trip of about 15 birds, and cut down 10 of them, a splendid shot for its extreme difficulty.

24*th.*—Intense frost and severe east gale all yesterday and all to-day, though nothing on our coast except one fine set of geese that remain where no boat could live.

25*th.*—Moderate. Out at daylight and saw the geese, but the gale sprung up again and I dare not follow them. Found the remainder of the 15 birds in the same place I fired on Saturday; there were 5 left, and I bagged 'every man John of them,' viz. 5 wigeon, and thus had the glory of annihilating the whole company.

26th.—Bitter cold gale and frost. Up at daybreak, having had the punt previously sent on to Pennington, so that I could walk to her after the tide was too late to float her inside. The plan answered so well that I fairly outwitted the grand army of geese, that had increased to about 300. The birds were all feeding under the lee of the mud at the edge of a most awful sea, and we popped on them from a place of perfect safety; but having only No. 1 shot in the gun they were about eighty yards too far, the consequence was I only knocked down 5. Had I been loaded with mould shot I think I must have bagged 20, as I caught the company all in a line, but at two hundred yards my shot was too light.

N.B.—Not another fowl to be seen. So much for good weather when it comes too late for fowl to migrate.

March 2nd.—The severe frost and north-easterly gale of wind never ceased all yesterday and all to-day, but not a bird has it brought on the whole spy-glass view of our coast. It's too late now for hard weather to do any good, and the gunning may be pronounced a blank for this season. I betook myself to the fields for exercise, and walked at least ten miles in search of golden plover, though never saw but 16; and some starlings and fieldfares spoiled my chance while I was crawling, by driving them up with their flutter and chatter. If I had been all day in the treadmill I could not have had a harder day's fag than I had to-day, and all for nothing.

4th.—Ash Wednesday. The most intensely cold north-east gale that ever blew into mouth and ears, and the coast looking as if uninhabited by man, and destitute of all living creatures except a few hungry gulls. My only reason for not 'cutting my stick' is the chance that either a calm would give me one fair trial at the geese, or a fall of snow might drive a few wild ducks from the private ponds.

6th.—Moderate. Went afloat outside and bagged 2 geese at about two hundred yards out of a little company of 14. As the geese were 'up to' the white punts I made my punt drab colour, with a wet of inland soil, as salt mud would stain the paint, and put on a drab gunning dress. This, by the way, should always be done in bright sun or moon, though at all other times white is the only colour.

7th.—A light breeze. Up with the larks, and cruised about twelve miles up Channel. Saw nothing the whole day but one small trip of geese that rose a quarter of a mile off, and thus convinced myself that all further attempts for this season would be only a waste of time, so came home by two o'clock, put my punt in store, and 'struck' for the season.

Sorry list of the past vile season: 30 wigeon, 2 mallards, 5 geese (most killed by anyone), 4 black ducks, 11 plover, 4 godwits, 7 curlews. Total, only 63 head. Add 11 snipes and 53 game, and my grand total is only 127 head, though I believe I've done the best of anyone. What a miserable display, though I never shot better or worked harder in all my life.

10th.—Left Keyhaven for Longparish, and on the 11th I arrived safe in Dorset Place, London. The train did the forty-eight miles five minutes under the two hours—the quickest passage I have had.

N.B.—No winter birds at Longparish, and complaints of scarcity even in the London market; so that the splendid weather (which still continues) has been of no service whatever from its having come too late.

17th.—London. At Chalk Farm (where I met all the leading gunmakers) to see a trial of cartridges invented by T. T. Berney, Esq., of Morton Hall, near Norwich, who had previously called to request my attendance. The cartridge consists of a spiral spring, which is filled with the shot and calcined cinders, and strongly wadded with about an inch of moss next the powder. The performance nearly doubled anything I had before seen, and these projectiles must be capital for open or for coast shooting; but, as the spiral spring is a deadly missile wherever it hits, they must never be used for common sporting. Mr. Berney promises experiments with a swivel gun in about six weeks, and was kind enough to show me his plan for firing his stanchion at plover by means of an elliptic spring attached to the saddle of a mule, he having one trained for this purpose. I never met with a more ingenious or intelligent gentleman than this thoroughbred old sportsman, Mr. Berney. I could, however, scarcely enjoy my view of his experiments as I was so unwell, and the weather was most piercing.

21st.—Not a wild fowl in London, except cartloads of rotten birds packed in boxes of ice from Norway.

23rd.—Took a copy of my sporting book to leave at Buckingham Palace (agreeably to his Royal Highness's permission) for Prince Albert, and then returned a visit with which I was honoured by Prince Napoleon Louis Bonaparte. After my attendance on these personages I went into our club, where I had the misfortune to receive a letter from Peter, dated on his birthday, January 19, announcing his alarming illness with yellow fever, which was, and I fear still must be, raging in Tobago. Out of six seized he was the only one alive, but, thanks to God, he gave me every hope that he has got out of danger, and when, please God, well enough to be removed, that he would use all interest to get home on sick leave, in which I fervently pray that he may succeed.

April 4th.—Being detained here by the postponement of Wednesday's Levee till Monday, the 6th, I had luckily not left town, when I had this morning the satisfaction to receive a letter from Peter dated 'Off the Lizard' (Cornwall) on board the 'Louisa Baillie,' West Indiaman, bound for London, announcing his safe arrival in sight of English land, and his amendment in health, after having been given over for death, by the yellow fever.

N 2

7th.—I was all day till six, cutting about and racing round the West India Docks; and then waiting on the pier in a pour of cold rain, with cutting north wind, to see if any of the ships coming in was the one in which Peter is, but no tidings as yet.

8th.—A postman's knock about twelve. Made sure it was a note from doctor about Peter, when 'Lo! who obeyed the knocker's rattling peal' but Peter himself! He had left the ship beating off Margate Roads, and very wisely flew up to town by the Margate steamer. His getting aboard this ship was a mere chance that decidedly saved his life; he could not have lived till the packet sailed, and the 'Louisa Baillie,' a first-rate West Indian of near 500 tons from Demerara, happened to put in at Barbadoes, and took him off the moment he got his leave. Thanks to God, all my fears are now at an end; and Peter is looking as well as ever.

May 11th.—London. One of the finest Philharmonics on record, at which we had the literally magic performance of the wonder of the world, Liszt, the Paganini of the pianoforte, whom I had previously heard on the 8th, when he made his *début* at Parry's concert; and whom I knew when a boy in England fifteen years ago. To describe his energy, effect, and execution, baffles all the public writers. In short, no one can compete with him in wildfire and electric effect; and his graces are of the highest order. So let us place him and Thalberg as the Gog and Magog of the piano, like two super-exquisite paintings; Thalberg as the sunshine, and Liszt as the storm, surpassing all other artists.

12th.—We made up a dinner party for Peter and friends, and on an appropriate day, which never occurred to me till the day came, for it was the anniversary of the 'Douro,' where my squadron gained the trophy for the 14th Light Dragoons in 1809.

June 4th.—Being apprised by Mr. Earle last night that judgment would be given to-day in my lawsuit, I went this morning again to the Court of Exchequer, where I had the great satisfaction to hear the judgment on every point given 'for' (me) 'the defendant.' Mr. Butt, however, after badgering the judges for near an hour, at last got a rule granted to have some legal points argued again at Michaelmas term. As my enemy in the country made so sure of swamping me, I only regret I could not send him a pigeon with despatches to give him an appetite for his dinner.

12*th.*—After leaving my name among the innumerable calls of congratulation at Buckingham Palace, I went to inspect the supposed two bullet marks on the wall near where the would-be assassin, Edward Oxford, fired two pistols at her Majesty and Prince Albert on the evening of the 10th. From what I could learn the villain was only about three paces off when he fired; and the bullet marks, if such they were, measured thirteen paces apart, and were evidently well directed, except rather behind. Her Majesty was driven at a quick trot; and by the blessing of Divine Providence, the scoundrel omitted to make the proper allowance for a cross shot.

20*th.*—Ran down to superintend the completion of, and pay for, some work at Keyhaven, where I arrived about seven in the evening, after having encountered a regular uproar, and seen a fine sight, during the three hours I had to wait for the coach in Southampton. It was a grand public breakfast to the Duke of Sussex, on the completion of the railroad; and what with guns, bells, bands, mobs, and processions, the city of London was comparatively quiet to the town of Southampton on this gala day. The Duke with the Duchess of Inverness, his wife, were close behind our train, with a separate engine; so that we were in the very thick of the great reception.

21*st.*—Sunday. Keyhaven. Thanksgiving for the Queen's providential escape, but no sermon on that subject. The singers, however, were determined to outdo the parson, and brayed out the four verses of 'God save the Queen,' to which the clerk appended an 'Amen' at the very top of his voice. All this was just previous to the last prayer after the sermon.

July 7th.—London. My lawsuit ended at last with a glorious victory on all four issues; the parties having declined the further litigation of a 'writ of error' before all the other judges, and agreed, as awarded, to pay all costs.

27th.—Battle of Waterloo, or family in uproar, preparative to our all leaving London to-morrow; a van of advanced baggage started, and the confusion and noise of tongues and door bell terrific. I raced on commissions till four, and then at all my intricate half-year's accounts in the midst of all the row.

29th.—I arrived in the charming air and quietude of Keyhaven Cottage.

August 4th.—Keyhaven. Anniversary of my purchasing a troop in the 14th Light Dragoons in 1804, when only 17 years 7 months and 11 days old. This to-day is just 36 years ago; as I am now these odd months and days over 53. *Tempus fugit.*

5th.—I was surprised to hear that a few months ago Lieutenant Harnet died; the man who, by his invention of mud 'launching,' has for some years ruined our coast, on the glory of which I made for him an epitaph.

PETER HAWKER'S EPITAPH ON LIEUTENANT HARNET.

Dedicated to the writer's esteemed friend, the Hon. William Hare.

1

Good reader, here Lieutenant Harnet lies,
  Who ruin dealt to all the Hampshire coast,
By 'launching punt,' a plan he did devise
  (Of which some imitating quacks now boast).

2

The ooze that once for authors formed a theme,
  On which our Gilpin and our Daniel wrote,
No more has geese, or swans, or ducks 'in team,'
  No sport we've now for shoreman, punt, or boat!

Inv.d & Sketched by P. Hawker. | Eng.d on Steel by H. Adlard.

MUD-LAUNCHERS, on the oozes, off LYMINGTON, shoving their PUNTS up to WIGEON.

London; Published by Longman & C.o 1844.

3

Lieutenant Harnet crawled upon his knees,
  And shoved this punt before him in the night,
Till all his kinsmen thus the birds did tease,
  And drove the fowl for miles at ev'ry flight.

4

Let's hope Lieutenant Harnet's gone aloft,
  For good he was, and all must wish him well ;
Though had he gone below, and ta'en his craft,
  I wot the devil he'd driven out of hell.

6th.—Insufferably hot. Nightingales in my garden within reach of a whip from the windows of the Cottage.

24th.—By way of a tonic I this day sailed to Alum Bay, ascended the heights, shot 20 wheatears for a delicious roast, brought home some nice little hen lobsters and prawns, blew myself out like a pointer, and found myself quite another man.

31st.—Left Keyhaven for Longparish after some baths, and sailing almost every day, by which I found myself much better than when I left. Three hours in Southampton, and went all over the colossal steamer, the 'Oriental,' previous to her starting to-morrow for Malta and Alexandria.

CHAPTER XXXIII

1840

September 1st.—Longparish House. Having only arrived here last night, and much to do, we could not throw off till near twelve to-day, when we had a broiling sun with a strong north-east gale, and the ground as dry as Lundyfoot snuff. But I did wonders considering this and the degenerated state of our once fine country, and the extreme wildness of the birds, having bagged, in little more than half a day, 24 partridges, besides 4 more shot and lost. Our combined bag was as follows:

Partridges bagged: myself 24, Peter 8, Charles 8 and 2 hares. Total, 40 birds and 2 hares.

3rd.—Bothered and hindered again till near twelve, when I went out with one old dog, and bagged 24 partridges without one miss. I gave up the 'Furgo' country, and all the markers, except Siney, to Peter and his friend Captain O'Grady, or I might have made a grand day. But they bagged only 8 birds between them.

6th.—Sunday. Heard all the shooting bulletins of my neighbours, by which I ascertained that, with my one dog, I had beat everyone in our country.

8th.—Plastered up my swelled face, and worked like a slave for the larder, but the birds were become so very wild I could only bring home 12 partridges. Mr. Fellowes shot over Tufton on Saturday, and his bag was one squeaker. What a pass our country is come to now the farmers mow the wheat, and destroy all the turf hedges for fuel!

9th.—Face no better, so laid myself up. This afternoon Buckle arrived from Southampton to enter my service, and to assist me in building a land-and-water punt, that I had some time ago invented.

15th.—Cold windy weather. Tied up my face and went out for about four hours in the afternoon, and brought in 8 partridges and 1 hare, making three doublets and three single shots, and missing nothing. No bad work for a cripple in the hands of the doctor.

16th.—Dragged the pond for 2 jack that had got through the grating when less than gudgeon in size. The one weighed $5\frac{1}{2}$ lb., the other $4\frac{3}{4}$ lb., and we caught also 12 small jack. We pulled out several brace of tench and perch; one of each we kept and weighed. The perch was 2 lb., the tench $1\frac{3}{4}$ lb. They were put in when about the size of sprats, in 1837. We took also, and let go, several trout from 3 to 4 lb. each, which were put in when about $\frac{1}{2}$ lb. in 1837.

26th.—Buckle left me for Southampton to prepare for a winter at Keyhaven, I having engaged him in my service.

29th.—For the first time for several days I've left the house and premises, being unwell, and busy with the punt. I went and killed 4 large trout that were wanted for dinner, the best of which was nearly 2 lb. This must end angling, as the fish, I see, are beginning to spawn.

N.B.—Never shot after September, except killing October 1st 2 pheasants and 4 rabbits, and December 2nd 3 jack snipes. Our game shooting was annihilated, so I laid aside my gun.

Game killed in September: 80 partridges and 1 hare. Total, 81 head.

October 1st.—Mustered an army, and scoured the whole of my liberty for the chance of a stray pheasant, and bagged 2 pheasants and 4 rabbits. We found but 3 pheasants the whole day, though we had fine calm weather and a good scent. The third pheasant was a grand old cock that rose out of bounds, a very long shot; but I hit him so hard that he most likely dropped dead, though we hunted for two hours and never could find him. Except this bird I bagged all I shot at.

5th.—Keyhaven. Still very unwell; at Batramsley, to see Captain Vere Ward on the subject of selling his gun, punt and gear. Coast literally swarming with birds, and even the clods killing wigeon with muskets. Buckle arrived this evening, and, on his passage here, this day killed and brought me for the larder 29 wigeon and 1 pintail in 2 shots. House in confusion at night, to get all in order for a daybreak start to-morrow. Most untoward arrival of fowl, as I came to take Mr. Price's cottage for Buckle and on other business, and not with the least idea that there was a fowl on the coast, much less the greatest October flight ever known.

6th.—Off at daylight, shot at about 40 wigeon across the line, got 5 wigeon and 2 teal. A better shot than I had right to expect. Got no other chance, as I had to come home with my punt leaking like a basket, from having had not a moment of daylight to overhaul her for this sudden turn-out. Weak as a rat, and no appetite. In the evening the easterly wind ceased, and the cock went to south-west: so I suppose I shall find that I have arrived just in time to be too late. Had I been here and in proper order to get afloat a week ago, I must have killed at least 200 or 300 birds, judging from the bags that have been got by the most contemptible bunglers.

8th.—Went off from six till six with the punt less leaky than before, but to no purpose, as the fowl were all gone, except a small trip off at sea.

11th.—Sunday. Green peas with a goose at dinner, my apple trees in blossom, and woodcocks in the country.

24th and 25th.—Longparish. A prisoner still. The latter day I got a letter from Mr. Berney to put me off from a grand pheasant shooting week at Morton Hall, Norfolk, in consequence of his fall from a ladder.

November 13*th*.—Keyhaven. An awful hurricane, and the most alarming flood that ever was known here. About twelve o'clock I had just begun a letter to Peter, when I was obliged to throw down my pen and fly in water boots for help to save my property ; had I not providentially been here, all my valuable guns, punts, and gear might have been ruined. The sea banks burst, and the water was soon a foot deep in all the lower rooms of the houses, and such was the torrent against the doors that, had they burst open, as we every moment dreaded, our house must have been swamped. Retreat was impossible, as no one could either wade or row against the violence of the current that swallowed up the road. About four the water suddenly abated, and we then opened the doors, and let it pour from the rooms as from a mill hatch, and we were then enabled to climb over hedges to lay in a night's provision from Milford. We were all on guard the whole night, and, as God's mercy had it, the wind flew from the south to the north-west, or heaven knows what must have become of us. This providential wind saved the whole village, by cutting the tide to only a moderate height, and at daylight in the morning all was well, except an awful breach in the bank, that will cause us to dread more than ever a south hurricane.

14*th*.—Half the boats in the harbour blown out over the banks into the marsh fields. Coots, rabbits, and fish lying dead among the general wreck of gear, gates, pales, and other property. Many floods as I have seen here, this one has been of all others the most awful and alarming. But, thanks to God and strong assistance just called in time, I saved the whole of my furniture and valuable gunning property.

15*th*.—Sunday. Called up at three this morning with a cry of 'The water! the water! for God's sake get up, sir!' This awful breach in the bank had let in even an average tide in such an alarming way that the water was again nearly up to my house, all owing to the sleepy indolence of a Mr. McLean, who neglected to stop the breach while a mere trifle. I went to him at his window, and with some difficulty persuaded him to send to a carpenter to make a temporary check by piles, gates &c. till the navigators could come on Monday. The carpenter, all asleep, could find nothing, and came down at his leisure, and condemned my idea. At a quarter past ten the break in the bank might have been stopped in an hour, but Mr. McLean was gone off to church and Sunday gossip, and I could get no authority. I offered a mob of clods a shilling apiece to turn in and stop the breach, but they would not hear of it unless they had 5*s*. each, so there it ended. In the afternoon the master navigator came and said I had advised admirably, but then it was too late, so we now remain at the mercy of Providence, with every prospect of alarming weather till to-morrow.

16*th*.—After our being on watch all night, there came on a serious influx of water before daylight, but at half-past six this morning it fell back without entering the house. Frightful gales all day, and nearly south. The navigators came at one, but could do nothing, from Mr. McLean having provided no marl or faggots, and it blew too fresh for a temporary stoppage with gates and such like. All operations at a standstill, and Mr. McLean riding out at his ease. No prospect of proceeding. So I took the postman's letter cart, flew up to Mrs. Whitby, who acted (like Buonaparte) in one minute. She instantly ordered all her men with teams to strike from their work, and to begin digging and drawing down six loads of marl preparative to to-morrow, and by four o'clock two loads had arrived, previously to which she came down herself followed by her bailiff.

17*th*.—A southerly wind having blown last night, we were in great alarm for the tide at a quarter before seven this morning, but a shift of wind about two checked the flood, and by nine o'clock the water had abated sufficiently to go on with ten men, besides Payne and myself, hard at repairing the awful breach. It poured with rain during the whole of the job, but, by dint of cheering on the workmen with good words and 'lush,' I had the place that had given way in the bank stopped up by two o'clock in such a manner as to put an end to all danger even in a gale of wind. The men had not left the place one hour before there set in a strong gale from the southward, that might have done us most serious damage. Had I not been exerting myself like a fellow fighting for his country the whole time, through the whole of this undertaking, Lord knows how the affair would have ended. But now our danger is over, and we may go to bed and sleep in peace.

18*th*.—Alas! little did I think yesterday afternoon, when penning the foregoing day's journal, that we were in one hour after to be visited with a more terrific hurricane than that of the 13th. But the navigators had not left us more than three hours in a pour of rain than there set in another hurricane, the most awful ever known here, and another flood over all the banks, and with still more awful appearance, as it kept increasing and washing against the houses from six till half-past nine, which was more than two hours after the second high water, and with the night as dark as the grave, and had not this breach been repaired just in time, the whole of the bank must have gone, and the village become a complete wreck. We were in absolute horror till near one in the morning, when there suddenly and most providentially came on a dead calm, and then a north wind that stopped the awful accession of the morning tide, which otherwise would have been over the banks again hours before daylight. After this the weather flew round again to the southward, and so threatened the place that we all turned out with the navigators in one incessant pour of rain the whole day to repair other parts of the banks that had been washed away by this second flood.

Two floods in one year, much less in one week, were never before experienced here, and, what is most extraordinary both of these came within the period of the neap tides. In the afternoon the rain continued to pour on us in torrents; but for the safety of life and property no one would strike work, till at last there set in an easterly gale that completely checked the sea for this evening's tide, and hope and joy then beamed on every countenance 'in spite of wind and weather.' To prove the suddenness of the floods I should name that poor Captain Symonds, who is ill in bed, had the tide all over his rooms, four feet deep, before he could save his furniture from saturating, and a duck, while roasting on his spit, was suddenly emerged into its former element. So furious was the sea last night, that it came over the beach, and the spray flew up to the top of the lighthouse. A general wreck last night of chimneys, windows &c. all over the neighbouring villages. This beats all we have ever yet had to weather.

19th.—A splendid easterly wind, and all comfortable, except having to clean up the messes that have been made by the late overwhelming floods and hurricanes. Received the thanks of the whole village for being their preserver, and went to Lymington to recruit my exhausted larder and cellar.

N.B.—I omitted to mention, when noting down this flood, that such was the certainty of our total wreck, had the morning tide (before daylight) not been checked by the change of wind about one o'clock on the 18th (just after midnight), that I had made up my mind to row all the punts out of the yard, which was under water, and lower the guns and the inmates of the Cottage out of the upstairs windows as soon as the 'ground ebb' should moderate the current, and then seek refuge inland with our lives saved and my valuable guns and gear rescued, leaving the Cottage and furniture to the mercy of the waves; for had the banks gone, as I made sure they would, one thousand men could not have made a new foundation quick enough to save the village before the return of the tide would have washed away their labour, even had the tide fallen low enough for them to work, which by all good judges was considered as very improbable.

22nd.—Sunday. A fine dry day, with a north wind and easy tides. What a contrast was to-day from last Sunday, when we were all in constant fear! The country papers of to-day gave a full account of the late flood and hurricane, and, I was flattered to see, did full justice to my exertions in saving the village.

25*th.*—All the London papers that come down here have, I see, an account of our flood &c. taken from the three county ones; all different reports, but still true, in substance, and I received congratulations on all sides.

29*th.*—Longparish. Another petrified fog, enough to paralyse a Newfoundland dog. Received this day the resignation of Buckle, to my great delight, as on trial he proved to be only live lumber, and his punt proved so unfit to weather a sea with two persons, that had I gone on the season with him I might have endangered my life.

December 7th.—Left Longparish, and went, for a change of air from the pestilential vapours of that low water-meadow country, to Keyhaven. During the thirteen days I was at Longparish I never was fairly warm the whole time, though we had fires in almost every room, and a stove in the gallery; and such was the illness in the village, that my family were busy every day in ordering little articles of sustenance for the poor sufferers.

10*th.*—Keyhaven. Out all day in a heavy sea, and the only chance I got was at the ground ebb, when I blew off, coming home, at 4 godwits. Read, who came to my employ, got this morning 2 wigeon.

N.B.—Got a hare for my larder, which was an animal of novelty. Mr. Sleet, the master of Squire Legh's yacht, saw something at sea which he supposed was a dog or a fox. He lowered his boat and chased it, and it swam so fast he could hardly row fast enough to catch it; and on coming to close quarters, he said it dived like a water rat; and, in short, he killed it with his oar, and it proved to be a fine fat hare, and he brought it to me for my dinner.

11*th.*—A splendid east gale all night and all day, but too furious to row against. Wild fowl of all sorts to be seen off in the foaming waves. This is as it should be, and a change that we have long wished for.

14*th.*—North-east gale and sharp frost. Up at six. Read put off on mud, and got 12 wigeon. I discharged but two rounds all day, and bagged 16 wigeon and 1 duck. I saw 15 dead ones floating in the heavy breakers before my face, which were got by other people. I should have had two more still better shots, where I could have got all of my birds, but a dirty scoundrel, named Dan'l Paine, of Southampton, the public nuisance of the Hampshire coast, came in his rough weather boat, and blew off his slugs and blunderbuss, and drove the fowl from the shore head, getting only a couple, that he disturbed the whole harbour in chasing.

15*th.*—Out from daylight till dusk, but the weather being moderate, though not calm, the whole Channel was in arms with blank-day poppers in boats, and consequently all I got was 3 wigeon, 1 pintail, 7 godwits, and 1 grey plover. Read got no chance last night, as the mud was frozen, and a heavy fall of snow all the evening.

16*th.*—Afloat at daybreak and off in Channel before the 'tormentors' had arrived; had one shot and bagged 20 wigeon, after which the water was full of boats all day. Harbour frozen, and a heavy fall of snow all the evening.

17*th.*—Under way again at break of day. Intense frost and heavy fall of snow, with a gale of wind; and after weathering it till it was useless to remain out any longer, I returned home without firing.

18*th.*—Up at daylight. Intense frost and heavy snow, with a gale of wind, so could not get afloat. Read crawled about all day in his mud-launching punt, and came in in a miserable mess with only 4 wigeon. I advised him not to go out, but nothing could keep him in.

19*th.*—Cutting weather again. Up at five, and off before daybreak. Got 4 wigeon that flew up at dawn before I could shoot sitting, 6 geese out of a small company at a long distance, and 1 dunbird. I never had more satisfactory sport, though the chances were small and my numbers few; because I did wonders in the face of old Buckle, who moored himself in my way to oppose me, and enlisted a chap of our village to help drive the harbour.

21*st.*—Intensely cutting gale of wind. Up and out as usual by candlelight; weathered some ugly seas, and then worked along the Channel's edge. Brought home 17 wigeon, 1 teal, and 1 mallard; best shot 12 wigeon and the teal. I fired in all three shots, and never used the popgun, having no opportunity. One shot was at 2 mallards and 1 duck. The gun flashed, and so good is my lock cover that the birds never jumped; so I pricked and primed, drew again, and knocked all three of them down.

22*nd.*—The coldest north-east gale I ever had to weather. No living outside in the Channel, and inside the harbour all frozen. We tried a few birds in the 'wash' just inside the breakers; but being to windward of them we had no chance to shoot, so I came home about two in the afternoon and just saved my blank by making one immensely long shot at 4 ducks, that I cut out of a company of 10.

23*rd.*—Hard frost, but wind more moderate; birds at sea, where it was too rough to shoot; and scarcely anything to be seen in harbour. I made a shot of 2 geese and cut down 5 burrough ducks out of 7—a very long shot on the mud. These are the only two triggers I pulled all day, not having once used the popgun; and in the evening we cleaned up all the gear preparative to my going inland to eat my Christmas dinner with my family.

24*th.*—Kept up late last night by the chimney of the

kitchen taking fire, which I extinguished by a wet flannel on the 9-foot ramrod of my long gun after much alarm.

29th.—Up at daylight, and by two in the afternoon got the great 'Petrel' punt and large double gun put together and in complete order, as Read's account of the increase of geese justified this trouble, though I find that all the birds killed in my absence at Longparish by all the gunners together did not exceed about 10 couple, and these only wigeon. We put afloat for only an hour and a half just before the day was over, and bagged 5 geese.

30th.—Off at daybreak. A looking-glass calm with bitter cold white frost. All the birds off for miles at sea, and Channel mobbed with float poppers. Drew but one trigger and picked up 10 geese out of a small company, and 2 more were sacked by Yarmouth water sharks. Came in early, and as clean as if I had been taking an airing in a close carriage.

31st.—The white frost of course turned to wind and rain, and the hard weather broke up. Everyone expected a grand day's sport, as is generally the case ; but, to the utter surprise of all, the birds remained all day for miles at sea, and not a fowl ever came inside the Western Channel.

1841

January 1st.—Off an hour before daylight ; but not a fowl in Channel or harbour.

2nd.—Wind north-west by north ; a splendid breeze to sail the punt all 'up along,' both out and back. Went all the way up to Need's-oar Point, about 12 miles, and saw nothing the whole cruise of the Western Channel except one very wild company of geese on the tide a mile from land, and a few ox-birds on the shore.

4th.—After a west gale, and then a white frost followed by rain and snow, the wind set in north-east again. I got one very long shot and bagged 4 geese ; and had not a sudden current 'slewed' my punt round when within ten yards of firing at about 300 geese, I should have made the greatest shot of my life. In the afternoon we had some light snow, and the birds were all on dry mud five miles to windward; and a bird frightener from Southampton brought up in Pennington, so we despair of the grand chance that was looked for to-morrow at the ground ebb.

5th.—Got but 3 geese and 1 scaup duck, as the whole coast was so infested with shooters that birds could scarcely pitch. No wigeon to be seen.

6th.—The bird frightener in Pennington, 'Buckle' in Oxey, 'Joe Parker' in Lymington leak, all the Yarmouth float poppers cruising up and down, and, in short, not a peaceable place for a bird to pitch. They all tried the geese, but 'no go.' At last about 10 birds pitched down just between the crafts of Buckle and the bird frightener, who were both on board. I put off from under Pennington walls and cut down 5 of them before their faces—the only birds killed by anyone the whole day; and though a trifling shot I had a great victory over the other gunners and the floating snobs.

7th.—Read, who had been crawling night after night in the mud punt and never getting a shot, at last came in this morning with some birds, viz. 9 wigeon, 1 mallard, and 1 pintail. We then went off for the day with the frost so intense that our beer froze in the bottle; and I did well, considering how the birds were persecuted by surrounding shooters. I fired three rounds, though with only one barrel, as there were no flocks worth a second pull. 1st shot, 36 plover; 2nd, 7 wigeon; 3rd, 8 wigeon; all in the view of my many competitors.

8th.—Up at daylight; and an hour cutting through the ice before we could row. None of the shooters had any birds except myself. I beat them all put together, though had but three poor chances, all long shots, and at miserably small companies of no more than the size of a covey of partridges.

1st shot, 5 wigeon; 2nd, 6 wigeon; 3rd, 2 wigeon, 2 ducks, and 1 mallard. Read had a blank night mud crawling.

9th.—Read came in with 16 wigeon that he got at one shot on the mud in the night. I pulled but one trigger all day, and came home with 3 ducks, 2 mallards, and 2 wigeon. The time at sea to-day was miserable, and even dangerous; so that we could follow nothing. A violent gale from the south, and all the ice for miles drifting to leeward in pans of half an acre large and four inches thick. On entering Keyhaven harbour, it was blocked by drifted ice, and that beat back by the river sluices; so that our only alternative to get home was to ship full sail, and cut our way through; which we providentially succeeded in, or must have been beat back to leeward, and at our wits' end to have escaped being carried to sea and swamped. In all my gunning campaigns I never encountered anything more formidable than this. It was tantamount to being in a field of battle. But my splendid 'Petrel' punt did her duty; and we got her hauled on the quay and well lashed, in case of a seriously high tide to-night.

10th.—Sunday. The gale of last night luckily abated in time to save danger to my punts, the three best on earth, and turned to a bitter white frost, after heavy snow. A pour of south-west rain all the time we were in church; and at night another white frost, enough to kill a Newfoundland dog.

12th.—Our harbour was in one pan of ice, half a foot thick, and our boats in danger every night. People defied the removal of the ice, because it could not be broken. I had it cut across with pickaxe and spade. Then I put a grappling iron into it, and pick hole; and, having sunk the buoys by poking them under the ice, so as to prevent their holding the ice, I, by means of a long towing line and powerful lever, got the whole field of ice under way; and off it went like one large island at the first ebb of high water; making our harbour as clear as in the month of May, and enabling everyone to resume his boat moorings in safety. This is the second service I have lately rendered to our little village. This job retarded my shooting so long that the Southampton bird frighteners had cleared the coast before I got off, and the only trigger I pulled was at 3 mergansers; I shot them all, and the splendid old cock merganser I sent off immediately to Leadbeater to stuff for my collection.

13*th*.—Torrents of rain, hail, and snow, with a gale of wind from the south-east, which worked round to the north-east, and was so cold as to scarcely melt a particle of the ice, but rendered every path and road like a piece of glass. I had put off in the morning early; but before I could get half a mile up Channel, was driven back by the furious weather. This is the first time I've got into my punt without bringing home something. In short, I've not before had a blank day, nor have I fired one blank shot with either stanchion or 'cripple stopper.'

14*th*.—Strong north-easter. Off at daylight, and came home in the middle of the day 'as wet as a shag,' it having come on to pour in torrents of cold rain. I got one shot and brought home 17 wigeon. Read has persisted in mud crawling every night, though he gets nothing.

15*th*.—A fine day and all the birds off at sea, except a small company that I caught on tide just under the Isle of Wight. I pulled one trigger and came home with 8 wigeon. Went ashore at Hurst, to clean up all my gear on the beach, after the saturating of last night's incessant rain on everything while moored, and then heard all about the flock of geese that had flown against the lighthouses on Wednesday night. Carpenter of the 'night light' got 5, and Page of the 'low light' got 4; and at one time the whole company of geese were sprawling about in the yards; but it was so dark that the lighthouse men could not see to knock down or catch more of them.

19*th*.—Though the wind got into the north, and I was off

at eight and out nearly all day, I never saw a chance to fire off even the popgun. In the evening, the Southampton bird frightener resumed his anchorage in the heart of our best 'feeding ground;' so I rigged up Charley Page, of Hurst, with powder and shot, in order to make this interloper's station too hot to be desirable; because, while this lubber is stuck up there, not a bird can pitch on the best place for killing either wigeon or geese.

20th.—A hard frost, and the cold more pinching than any day we have yet had. Out at daylight, but no chance while the bird frightener infests our coast. Charley 'served him out' with a popgun, as he was fumbling at the only few geese to be seen.

21st.—Intense frost, but too white and too pinching to be genuine; as, in one night, it froze the whole harbour half an inch thick, and we had a job to row out of it at daylight. The bird frightener kept the coast clear; and in return I hired a footman to follow him, so that he could not shoot; and Charley Page performed his part in this office, as well as in jaw, most admirably.

22nd.—The white poisonous petrifying frost of course turned to a south-wester and rain. I again cleared the harbour of ice with ease, by having yesterday sunk the buoys of all the moorings under it; and then made Peter Fifield cut it across, so as to be free to float out at the first ebb. Off at eight o'clock, but no chance of a shot of any kind. I had, however, some novelty and some fun. The one was seeing a battle between two ravens and a huge eagle, who dropped his grey plover that he held in the fight, and on which bird I dined; and I should have shot the eagle had not a second fight with some gulls made him rise again and fly up to the Isle of Wight cliffs. The other was a savage row between Charley Page and the bird frightener, who at last, with a mouthful of bitter curses, got his vessel under way and sailed off for Southampton. Joy go with him.

23rd.—Tremendous wind and rain from the south-west all night, and in the morning a strong northerly breeze. Saw the eagle again on wing, and sailed after him for miles, till we saw him pitched with five crows flapping over him, but he would not remain long enough in one place for us to 'settle his hash.' No sooner was the bird frightener blown out of harbour than a few geese returned to their station, though not more than about 18. I used them kindly by leaving them in peace till the ground ebb, when they began to taste the feed, on which I fired one shot and blew over 9 of them.

26th.—Up at daylight, but there came on wind and rain; so I worked for several hours to put all our stores, ammunition &c. in proper order, of which it was much in need, and about twelve the weather cleared up enough for us to get afloat. But the only bird I saw the whole day was a single laughing goose, which I killed dead as a stone at 125 long strides of Read on the mud, and I am sure every step he took was far more than a fair yard.

27th.—Not a bird to be seen off or in harbour.

28th.—A white frost. Never saw a wild fowl the whole day.

29th.—Availed myself of a fine day and a dead calm to make a long cruise all the way up Channel to opposite Cowes, and never set eyes on a fowl the whole trip, except a small flock of about 30 geese. I tried a new mould-shot cartridge at about 300 yards, and down came 2 of them; so I came home with 2 geese, and well pleased with this extraordinary shot. The whole coast is ruined by the Southampton fellows both for shooting and fishing, and these cadgers do so little that they are almost ruined by starving one another in opposition for everything. The once retired wilderness off Need's-oar is now swarming with vessels for gunning, eel picking, and periwinkling.

February 1st.—Extraordinary change of weather. Yesterday as hot as in June, with fog and small rain. To-day such a cutting north-easter that the water froze on the oars all the time we were out. I got one shot at a small company, and picked up 7 geese and 3 teal; the latter I never knew anything about till I bagged them, as the 3 were among the geese, and all came in for my charge. Got caught in a sudden gale off Pennington, and Read most dexterously let the punt drop down sideways, putting her bow to the heavy breakers, till we 'fetched' the safety of my leak; and, after shipping about twenty-five gallons of sea, we got out of the scrape most gloriously, though we resolved not to risk such a chance again.

2nd.—Intense frost and some trouble to extricate punts from moorings. No water inside, as tides were so dead and the mud frozen. Off from daylight till four, and obliged to walk Hurst Beach till birds dropped in outside; but, as the shooters had driven them all to the eastward, I got but one chance and brought in 4 wigeon and 1 pintail.

3rd.—The hardest frost I ever weathered. Harbour a sheet of ice and a cutting gale from the north-east, which knocked up such a feather-white sea outside that, after pacing Hurst Beach for five hours waiting to go afloat, we were obliged to retreat. I, however, saved my blank by knocking down with the popgun 1 wigeon, and also 1 brown goose,[1] an immensely long flying shot, with which I first tipped his pinion; and I put him alive in our garden in hopes he would survive for the Longparish pond.

4th.—Most bitter weather. Cut the punt out of the ice and secured her on the quay, and brought the gun up to the house. No one could row a boat, as the oars formed in clubs of ice, and the boats were like bodies of glass. All communication cut off from the sea, which ran mountains high with the furious easterly gale. In short, the whole place was a region of ice, without a living creature to be seen on it; and gunning, of course, at an end till the weather became

[1] Like the laughing goose, but with no bars on the breast. Leadbeater thinks it a variety of the laughing goose.

less severe. No one in the place had ever before experienced such cutting weather.

5*th.*—Weather for whales and white bears only. Water jugs in bedrooms so frozen that they were all one solid block of ice. Read would go out in the afternoon launching on the ice, and he came in half frozen and wet to the skin with 4 wigeon. He changed his clothes and would go off again. A furious east hurricane set in at nightfall, and we all feared Read was lost, and his wife was in sad alarm. I ran all the way to Highlea Dock, and the gale was ready to cut my nose off, and there I saw his punt turned up, and happily found that he was all right, and had missed me on his way home by having got into his house just before I started.

6*th.*—Annihilating weather. A most vicious petrifying tempest all night and all day, and all night again. Everything frozen, and a wind that one could hardly walk against.

8*th.*—Wind less violent, but frost harder than ever. Rain fell and froze as it lodged. Harbour in cliffs of ice. Read launched his mud punt over ice, and got 10 wigeon and 2 mallards. Yarmouth mail, frozen out of Hurst and Lymington, came over beach on foot. Thousands of birds off outside of the frozen region, which, as yet, nothing but a launching punt can be got over, and that with great difficulty.

9*th.*—Bitter weather, and everything like glass. Walked over beach to Hurst to see if there was any creek open to moor a punt, in case I put in there. The Camber was open, but the land passage (for punt carriage) in such a state that I could not attempt it, so I decided on waiting till I could get some passage by water. Plenty of birds and floating shooters out of number, though scarcely a bird killed, except Read bringing home 2 geese and 3 wigeon.

10*th.*—Found an open place off Highlea, and cut our way through the ice to it. Then got off for a few hours (while water served to get back again) and brought in 10 geese. The only shot I got.

11*th.*—A sudden thaw with south wind and rain. Went from our anchorage (to which we walked over the mud) to Hurst for a windward berth; but through fears of the drifting ice retreated to Keyhaven and anchored under the wall, as the quay was worse blocked up than before. Went off to some straggling wigeon about four o'clock, and just saved our water back again. Cut down 10 with the first barrel and 3 with the second.

12*th.*—Rain all night, and a fog all day. Went out with a compass on board and made two capital little shots; saw 7 geese, and floored the whole company; then saw 4, and floored them all. The ice was nearly all gone to-day, so we got a berth on our own quay again.

13*th.*—All in order for an early start this morning, but there came on a southerly gale of wind, with a pour of rain, that never abated the whole day. I, however, saved my blank with a good shot of starlings out of the drawing-room window.

15*th.*—Constant south gale and heavy rain all last night; off at daylight, and, after fighting through a heavy sea, got one chance and bagged 8 geese, after which it blew so hard and poured so heavy that I was obliged to go home and remain a prisoner.

16*th.*—Out at daybreak. Blew off both barrels, and picked up 15 geese. Afterwards was all but shooting into about 1,400 geese when a brute from Yarmouth popped off his rusty musket under sail, and sent the birds off for miles. Otherwise I was certain of making the greatest shot ever known. I really think I should have bagged 100 birds. About ten o'clock all was over for the day, as the mud was like a fair with periwinkle pickers and eel spearers. The only 2 swans I've seen this year would have pitched but for the crowd of people about. But they bore up and flew to sea for Poole.

17*th.*—Out at daylight, and in rain all the time; but the

geese never came to-day, and by eleven o'clock the whole coast was so mobbed with periwinkle men to freight the crafts for Billingsgate that not a bird would come to the mud.

18*th*.—Out at daylight again with my new-invented loader, which answered admirably. A breeze, with a fog. All I saw was 21 geese. Caught 7 in a lump and bagged them all, and on the others rising 3 were together, and I got all of them with a No. 3 shot cartridge, and thus brought home 10 geese out of nothing to expect. All were killed dead except 2, and both of those I floored with one barrel of the popgun. Thus have I done well in a fog, the very weather that I and every other gunner had hitherto discarded. At one the periwinklers and the beastly Yarmouth sailing boat, the 'Carrion Crow,' as I call her, drove both myself and all further chance away.

19*th*.—Started at daylight again, and went, with compass, in a fog, all the way to Pilewell Leak. Fell in with a company near Lymington, and picked up 8 geese. Then sailed into about a dozen curres, a good shot with the other barrel, and at the instant I drew they jumped up, and by this accident every bird escaped. This is the first blank shot I've fired the whole campaign.

20*th*.—Up hours before daylight, but such a gale came on we could not get outside. We had a rough day, and torrents of rain, and had only the recompense of 1 goose and 1 burrough duck.

22*nd*.—An intense white frost all last night, and such a dense fog the whole of this day that nothing could be attempted. Read got 5 wigeon after midnight, and we all turned out at six this morning, and after waiting till one in hopes of the fog abating enough for us to venture out, I gave it up and metamorphosed myself into a gentleman, and did some commissions in Lymington.

23*rd*.—Fog-bound till afternoon, and then the periwinklers

were all over the shore, so that, having no chance, we made our first blank day. Our morning, however, was turned to good account by making the punts tight after some leaks caused by fighting under heavy sail against the pans of ice in the late frosts.

24th.—The fog turned to a dark north-easter. Off early and cruised all day; picked up 13 geese at one capital shot, out of the only company I saw the whole day.

25th.—Up with the larks again. Saw one company of geese, as wild as wild could be; followed them all the way to Pitt's Deep, about seven miles, but the punt jumped so much on the sea with the strong north-easter that they would not stand the show and noise; at last they crossed me, flying rapidly, and down I dropped 5 with one barrel.

26th.—Out from daylight in a squally north-wester; brought home 11 geese in two shots, though never saw more than about two dozen the whole day; 5 more geese fell dead where it was too rough to venture, and another, winged, stole away on the mud, so that what I knocked down in all was 17.

N.B.—My shooting this trip has surpassed all I ever did, saw, or heard of; from December 29 to February 26, both days inclusive, I never had but one blank day, and then only out for a few hours after a day's jobbing; and, except firing at some curres that jumped at the instant I pulled, and trying an experimental cartridge at about 350 yards, I never fired one blank shot the whole cruise, though out every day that I could 'live' for eight weeks and four days. The show of birds this season has not been more than the tenth of what we had in 1837–1838, though the miseries of weather were tenfold greater, and the wear and tear of ourselves and gear the severest on record.

Wild fowl I have killed at Keyhaven up to the end of February 1841:

Ducks and mallards	19
Teal	14
Scaup ducks	2
Dunbird	1
Wigeon	185
Pintails	4
Burrough ducks	6
Brent geese	145
Curious brown brent geese	2
Merganser	1
Plover	23
Godwits, waders, &c.	13
Olive	1
Shore birds	179
Total	595 head

Nearly all killed with my large 200-lb. 'champion double duck gun' and with only firing two blank shots. Such a performance, I believe, is unprecedented in the annals of gunning. We had the most intensely severe winter on record; and yet not a tenth of the wild fowl that we had in 1837–1838. Not a single wild swan ever came to our part of the coast, and the only 2 I saw the whole winter were a pair flying over on their travels. Leadbeater never had so few fowl to preserve any winter as this; notwithstanding it was the hardest winter I remember, for the few weeks at a time that each frost lasted.

March.—London. I left my great 'Petrel' punt at her moorings in Keyhaven harbour, meaning to run down again for the chance of a few more geese (which birds rarely leave till April) before I took my gear into store, and 'knocked off' for the season.

8th.—With Eley, 'Uncle' Bishop, and all the crack gun fellows on logic and new experiments.

9th.—Keyhaven. On my arrival I heard that a good show of geese were still in the Channel; so I decided on making a few days' more cruise before I 'knocked off,' because geese are never so good as in March and April if you can get them.

11*th.*—North-east wind and cold again. Up at six and cruised all the way to 'Park Rails,' and never saw but 4 birds (geese) the whole day's trip. The 'winklers, it appears, have banished all the geese which otherwise would have abounded here in March, as they always used to do whenever the winter had been hard enough to bring them to our coast.

12*th.*—Took a cruise, but the birds appear to have left the coast altogether.

15*th.*—Summer come back again; and butterflies on wing.

16*th.*—Bade adieu to gunning for the season.

June 9*th.*—London. Went over the awful ruins of Astley's Amphitheatre, which was burned down yesterday morning. Having known Ducrow (through once offering to him a melodrama), I gained admittance immediately on sending in my card, and a more lamentable sight I never beheld.

19*th.*—Went down to Woolwich to see the launch of the 'Trafalgar,' about which there was more fuss and difficulty than in any other public exhibition. Sir William Symonds had kindly given a written order for myself and family; and this order was backed, in writing, by Sir John Barrow, Secretary of the Admiralty; but, after all, no one could pass the police without a ticket for each person; and these tickets could only be issued by Captain Hornby (Superintendent of the Dockyard), to whom I sent in my card and my order; and who, being too busy to see anyone, sent out a written memorandum that my name should be put down for tickets, which he could not promise. I then, after much difficulty, got on board the 'Trafalgar' under the shed. She was so low 'between decks' that I could nowhere stand upright; and her build was, in my opinion, nothing equal to the modern ships of my friend Sir William Symonds.

20*th.*—Received three tickets from Captain Hornby, which was an agreeable surprise, as I feared he had only given me some hope, to avoid the trouble that might arise from a direct negative. So far, however, from backing out of serving me, he kindly sent the tickets for the very best station.

21st.—Got down to the Dockyard soon after ten, by which means I had the choice of seats; and so well were I and the girls situated that we were close to the Queen when she named the ship. Of all the sights I ever beheld I never witnessed any so grand and splendid as the launch of the 'Trafalgar.' I had the offer of being on board while she was launched; but this I declined, because, for the sake of novelty, I must have been precluded from being able to see the christening. She was launched at half-past two; and nothing on earth could be better or more comfortably arranged than the whole of the superb sight and the accommodation. But the crowd afterwards was awful; and had I not put up the carriage nearly a mile off, I could not have been home till midnight.

July 5th.—Keyhaven. Up early and prepared for a sail to the cliffs, but became out of humour for sport by hearing of the horrible death of my factotum poor Eley, the cartridge man, with whom I was in perpetual communication, and who was the most punctual, respectable, and intelligent of all the sporting tradesmen under my patronage. He was blown to atoms by fulminating powder at his factory in Bond Street, where I was in the habit of repeatedly going to give him hints and advice; and often have I advised him not to extend his practice to the dangerous trade of making percussion caps. His loss will be irreparable to the sporting world; and no one will feel it more than myself.

8th.—London. Directly I set foot in town I went, with 'Uncle' Bishop,[1] to the factory of poor Eley, where I was astonished to see that scarcely any damage had been done beyond the appalling accident that blew him to atoms. His

[1] The famous manager of 'Westley Richards'.'

own son was within two yards of him, and people were working in the factory, at the time the explosion took place; but so little was the expansion that, although he blew up 2 lb. of fulminating mercury, not even a paper was burnt; and the walls were no more disfigured than if cold water had been thrown over them. In short, a few panes of glass being broken was all that could be seen in the way of damage. The usual quantity of fulminating mercury that people venture to mix at a time is from ¼ to ½ an ounce; and how so clever a man as Eley could have run the risk of mixing such a quantity was the surprise of everyone.

24th.—After an indescribable concatenation of worry and vexation in London, and after having waited four days till a succession of gales from the south had abated (with my passport signed and our things packed up), I this morning soon after two o'clock entered the Boulogne packet at London Bridge Wharf on our long-talked-of trip to pass a week or two in France. The 'Magnet' packet, for which I had secured berths, was so full that men and women were all huddled together like dead bodies in a cholera hospital; and a drizzling rain with a pitch-dark morning put an end to the superior comforts of remaining on deck. At three o'clock precisely we got under way; and such was the mess of sickness and suffocation that we were obliged to sit under umbrellas on deck for the whole of the passage after we had passed Gravesend. The stewardess was drunk, the steward a stupid fellow, and all the men on board, except the mate, a sorry 'ship's company.' The packet itself was good, a capital sea boat, and with fair wind, two lug sails, and steam, did the 140 miles in 10 hours to a minute, though two hours were absorbed by bustle and bother at the custom house before all was clear, as the *douaniers* now are become much more strict and tedious than they were in my many former trips to France. On landing we put up at a nice little hotel, recommended me by an old friend, Mr. Moscheles, called the 'Ship Hotel' in

Rue de l'Ecu, in which we had the luck to get the best apartments I ever had at any French inn. Nothing, out of England, could be more comfortable than they were. We dined at the table d'hôte with about twenty-one persons, and, to our surprise, all were either English, German, or Americans; not a Frenchman was there at the table. Being too tired to perform a long slow journey on the morrow, we decided on resting the Sunday in Boulogne, and booked for Lafitte's diligence on Monday for Paris.

25*th.*—Sunday. Went to the English church at eleven. Service performed by two fairly good parsons, and music nicely got up by the amateur English of the place, who are at the chief expense of this exclusive place of worship; and to which therefore there is a charge of 1 franc entrance to non-subscribers, and a very just one it is. After church we visited the celebrated library and museum of Boulogne; and the latter is, I think, without exception, the best I ever saw in my life for its extensive display of ornithology. It contains, in addition to all that museums usually offer, some good paintings and the finest statuary; but its greatest curiosity is an Egyptian mummy of some great personage, that is in such perfectly good condition that the hair and even the teeth are as perfect as when in life; and the printed inscription near it states its age to be 1511 years before Christ. We then made the best of our time to see the Catholic church, the cemetery, and the town in general, not omitting the magnificent harbour entrance, extensive sands, &c. And I have no hesitation in saying that, as far as I have yet travelled, I pronounce Boulogne to be the most desirable place in France.

26*th.*—We entered the *rotonde*—the only place to be got—of Lafitte's diligence at nine this morning, and arrived in Paris at six the next morning (the 27th)—140 miles in 21 hours. We had no fault to find with the pace that was travelled at, considering the hideous machine and the poor palfreys that were flogged before it, and the stoppages for changing were even too quick to be pleasant, but in other respects everything was most miserable. We had a beastly dinner at three at Abbeville, my old quarters, and could get nothing all the way from there to Paris but a bit of sour bread and a glass of vinegar wine, and the conductor locked us up and would never attend to us the whole night without my first lustily bawling out signals of distress. We were shook till our bones ached, and literally crammed with dust; never was there a more miserable 100 miles travelled than that through the famine land of Picardy, from Abbeville to Paris. On arrival, half dead, we had to be overhauled by the excise, which took nearly an hour, and we then got into Meurice's flash hotel, where there are now 150 English, and which is more like a barrack than an inn for comfort. We lay down, too tired for sleep; and, after cleaning up, took the morning to get rid of our first commissions and see the Louvre. All that was new to me here were the naval models, and an imitation of the original horses that I had before seen on the triumphal arch that leads to the Tuileries at the time when the Emperor was first banished to Elba; the eagle is renewed on everyone and everything, and a most elegant lady, the Duchess of Orleans, was surveying the pictures with us like any ordinary person. We at length mounted our six very high storeys to a seven o'clock dinner, and went to bed as tired as dogs.

28th.—Took a coach and saw Père-Lachaise, where the best monuments I had not seen were those of a Russian countess, Elizabeth Demidoff, Marshals Suchet and St. Cyr. No tomb as yet for 'Ney,' but the palisades and the flowers within them tacitly pointed out his remains. Next saw the fortifications (which were proceeding rapidly with 100,000 workmen) beyond the suburb called Belleville. Next the Invalides, where the greatest sight to me was the splendid tomb of the late Emperor Napoleon, with all the trophies of his glories around him, and his hat and sword at the foot of the marble coffin which covered those wherein were embalmed his mortal remains. All was within an iron railing, and shrouded in a darkness that was illumined only by the splendid lamp which was suspended above the coffin; and the regularity with which each person was admitted to pass was, like everything of the kind in Paris, admirably well arranged. We inspected the Place Vendôme, Place de la Concorde, Champs-Elysées, &c., all of which, with many other things, I had seen and noted down many years ago. The only new sights here were of a kind of obelisk, in the Place de la Concorde, presented to Louis Philippe by the Pacha of Egypt, and the enormous cannons taken at Algiers. Dined at Café Riche; then went to the opera of 'Le Serment,' in which Dorus Gras was splendid; and saw the ballet of 'Le Diable Amoureux,' which was the only ballet I ever enjoyed in my life. It was in three acts, and on a plot that made it not only interesting, but most exciting, and nothing could be more magnificent. Took ice and coffee at Tortoni's, and came home even more tired than yesterday.

29th.—The great annual fête to-day. Commenced with seeing the grandest fair imaginable in the Champs-Elysées, where, among other innumerable shows, spectacles, and little sights, we took about an hour in the newly built 'Cirque National'—the Astley's of Paris—which is, without exception, the most splendid amphitheatre that can be imagined. A Madame Cinizelli was the most distinguished equestrian of the day. This is one of the best evening spectacles, and was opened to-day only on account of the glorious fête of July. At seven we went to the front of the Tuileries, where all the bands of the garrison played in one grand concert before the good King and Queen, of whom we had a capital view when they came and stood on the balcony. The moment this was over, we adjourned to the illuminations, after which the best that ever were in London were no more than a few rushlights, and soon after nine there commenced a series of fireworks that no pen or tongue could describe. The one for the finish was

P 2

called a 'bouquet,' which threw the whole atmosphere into one gorgeous blaze with a fiery garland of flowers some hundred yards in circumference, and so well imitated in fire that the foliage was like a fine colossal painting. The fête having kept us worked hard from breakfast till bedtime, we could see no other 'lions' to-day.

30*th*.—On hard again at seeing the 'lions'—those for to-day were: the Eglise Madeleine, a church long ago begun and now nearly finished; the small chapel built by Louis XVIII. to commemorate his murdered brother, Louis XVI., of whom and of his wife are fine monuments or statues with the 'last will and testament' of each inscribed beneath; the magnificent triumphal arch on entering the Champs-Elysées, begun by the Emperor and finished by Louis Philippe; the Chamber of Deputies; the Chamber of Peers, with the Luxembourg, and the boudoir of Mary de Medicis; the churches of St. Sulpice and of Notre-Dame. During our many hours' drive about the town, I was struck with the wonderful changes that have taken place since I was here nearly twelve years ago, and for all these the French have to thank Louis Philippe, who has not only been indefatigable in completing all the works unfinished by the Emperor, but has wisely condescended to imitate the English by cleaning and paving the streets, and getting rid of all stinks and nuisances, for which Paris was formerly the most offensive place, next to Lisbon, that I ever had to encounter.

31*st*.—Visited the Bourse, the Jardin des Plantes, the Gobelins, the Panthéon, the Artillerie (or ancient armoury), and several other smaller sights. In the evening we went to the Théâtre Français, which, although the most fashionable place next to the opera, is, to my taste, the least amusing of any spectacle in Paris. I found the house much improved and far cleaner than our own theatres.

August 1*st*.—Sunday. Henri Bertini came from Versailles to see me about my patent hand-moulds, which I brought over with the improvements made since I had them in Paris some eighteen years ago, and I appointed Tuesday for him to meet me about them. At three we went to the English Ambassador's church, where my old tutor, Mr. Lefevre, was the reading parson. It was forty years since I saw him, and our meeting was quite an event. In the evening walked in the Champs-Elysées, which was a sort of fair, but no dancing, as formerly.

2nd.—Up early and off by railroad to St.-Cloud; but could not enter the palace because the King was there.[1] Caught a *fiacre* to take us on to Sèvres, where the chief specimens of porcelain are exquisite and are actually framed copies from the finest painters; and for which they ask from 30,000 to 40,000 francs apiece. The china in general is now but little superior to our very best, and nearly double the price. Our next 'lion' was the sight of all sights—Versailles, which took us the remainder of a long day, and worked us off our legs. After the gardens, we went over the whole of this most enormous and gorgeous palace, where there were all the victories of Buonaparte, restored to the walls by Louis Philippe; and these were, of course, all new (and not a little interesting) to me. This present King had expended an immense sum of money in putting the palace at Versailles in the highest order; and never since the days of Louis XIV. (who built it, and who was the only king that often frequented it) was this place in such a splendid state. We refreshed at a good *restaurateur*, Hôtel de France, and came home in the evening by another railroad. There are two to Versailles: one works round a half-circle on the right, and the other on the left of Paris; so that by going with one and returning with the other, you go round a circle outside the intended fortifications, and are so elevated that you survey Paris and the environs to great advantage nearly the whole way.

[1] Since the infernal attempts on his life, the attendants deceive the people as to his movements. It was given out that he would be at Fontainebleau to-day.

3rd.—Met Henri Bertini at the piano factory of Erard, Rue du Mail, No. 13, and presented him with a complete set of hand-moulds, book &c. to make what public use he pleased of. I then went with the girls to show them the royal library, and attended them shopping; and we ended the day with a 'lush' at Very's and a view of all the gaieties of the Palais Royal.

4th.—Made every preparation for leaving Paris to-morrow, on our return home, having got through all the best sights; and being heartily tired of the expense, noise, confusion and humbug of this place of splendid misery. I made a second sortie, and got permission to see the *salle* &c. of the Opéra Comique. Went over the whole of this new theatre, which is beautiful. The alternate boxes of the best class are fitted up with a private room. The theatre is very rich, chiefly in white and gold, and with some effective and fine statuary. The saloon is rich, and in great taste; and the floor of it is of various wood to imitate mosaic. To my taste the prettiest theatre in Paris, and well worth seeing. Dined at our hotel,[1] and concluded by going to the Théâtre des Variétés.

5th.—Left Paris at a quarter past seven this evening for Havre (all the day coaches being full for some days), and arrived in Rouen at a quarter past seven in the morning.

6th.—Havre. Such is the posting opposition in France now, that the changing of the horses is more rapid than in

[1] Specimen of charges here, which are a mere trifle more than at other hotels.

	fr.	cents
Tea or coffee	2	0
One small chop or cutlet	1	10
A bottle of claret.	7	0
Best Burgundy from 7 fr. to	10	0
Ordinaire (hogwash)	2	0
Picardon (the least acid and by far the best for its price)	4	0
Port	9	0
Sherry	8	0

Sixty-five servants, seven head men cooks.

N.B.—Judge what a scene of uproar for the whole twenty-four hours. A State inquisition—a Bedlam—I don't know what to call it.

England; and the diligence from Paris to Rouen (with a butcher and a savoury Dutch peasant for inside 'shipmates' in the *rotonde*, which here holds eight instead of four, and which was the only place to be got—I have not a laugh in me now, or should write the account in true colours) actually travelled about 2 miles with the off-leader's bridle off, and the head-stall and winkers dragging on the road and between the horses' feet, because the coachman would not stop, for fear of being passed; and racing is very properly forbidden. From Paris to Rouen we had the *coupé* and went the lower road; and having a bright full moon till the weather changed after daylight, we saw the rich country of Normandy nearly as well as if we had gone by a day coach. Our arrival at Havre was even worse than at Rouen, though luckily the weather cleared off again. The town was so full, owing to the cheap fares of contending packets, that we literally had to walk all over the place for an hour before we could get a hole to put our heads in; and, at last, we got into an inn with everything dirty, and sheets so wet that we dare not even lie down with our clothes on. This retreat from Paris beats all.

N.B.—I'm so bothered, and have such confused moments to seize a bad pen and ink, that I can scarcely write common sense; but still I must book, lest I forget. No alternative remained for us but lying on the sofa all night, or embarking in a packet that was to sail at ten, and with rough squally weather; so I engaged to go off with Captain Forder, of the 'Monarch.' After paying 16 francs for a filthy chop and three little soles at this execrable hotel, we bundled off, bag and baggage, just before dark, and got on board the packet; and had I not taken the double precaution to get my passport revised in Havre (which in Paris they told me was not required) the gendarmes would have taken me out of the vessel, and forbid my proceeding to England, having come on board expressly for that purpose. Well, at ten we got under way; and no sooner had we cleared the harbour than a strong wind with repeated squalls of heavy rain beset us for the whole night; and so contrary was this wind the whole way, that the captain was obliged to force the engines in a manner that was quite awful, in order to perform the voyage in any decent time; and to compete (as far as prudence would admit) with a dangerous narrow opposition packet, a Frenchman called the 'Hamburgh.'

7th.—We landed on Southampton pier at one, making a passage of just fifteen hours, and a more unpleasant one I never weathered, except that the packet was a first-rate sea boat, and the cleanest I ever sailed in, with the greatest attention and civility from everyone, from Captain Forder down to the lowest hand on board. After the usual bother and anxiety at the custom house, which I got clear of with great success, we proceeded by the four o'clock train to Winchester. Lord Adolphus Fitzclarence and another great yacht gentleman rode in the carriage with us, and we laughed at our change of company from the butcher and the Dutchman of yesterday. We luckily got a hack chariot that had just taken a family to the station, which saved some time, and we arrived at Longparish House a few minutes before six, making our journey from Paris to Longparish within the forty-seven hours. As if all our campaign was not enough, even here we had to meet with trouble. The whole of the servants and baggage that ought to have been here to receive us, and administer that comfort we so much stood in need of, had never arrived. They put off their start to this very day, and so slightly warned the rail police of their intended stoppage at Andover station that the whole of their heavy baggage was carried on to Southampton, and they had to remain at the station all day till an express got there for an up train to bring it back, and even then some articles were missing. This never happened with me, and I warrant would not have been the case had I been there. They all arrived about a quarter of an hour after us, and a precious mess of confusion it was for people who had been fifty hours in boots and without a change of clothes. Now all is over I am delighted that we took the trip, as the sights we saw and the miseries we had to encounter will be something to think of as long as we live.

CHAPTER XXXIV

1841

September 1st.—Lord Glentworth and I went out, from the middle of the day till a late dinner, and so few birds were to be seen, and those few so wild that I got only 6 partridges, and Lord Glentworth 1, and 1 hare. I expected vile sport, but not quite so execrable as this. The farmers, it appears, in addition to mowing all the wheat stubbles, and destroying for fuel all the turf banks, where birds could breed free from rain and the scythe, have been using a solution of 1 lb. of blue vitriol in a gallon of hot water to fortify each sack of sowing wheat from becoming smutty, and most people think that many birds have been poisoned by feeding on this corn. Our whole combined bag was only 7 birds and 1 hare. What a miserable first day! What a contrast with my bagging 52 brace, besides 6 birds lost, and 1 hare off my own gun, and with missing but two shots in the whole performance! If it's to be like this, I must either cadger for shooting at other people's houses, or send in my resignation as a field sportsman.

6th.—On approaching the house, after not firing one shot all day, I reflected that I never remembered a blank day before; so I turned round instead of going in, and tramped up to the inclosed country, where I worked till dark, and came in with 7 partridges.

8th.—Lame with my foot again. Poured some eau de Cologne over my stocking, and went off on the old mare with my gun, expecting to break down. But I so 'mended on it' by the friction of walking the turnips that I got on well till a six o'clock dinner, and had a capital day considering the vile season. I bagged 14 partridges, and missed but one long shot. This is the only day of this season worthy of record, and for my good luck I have to thank Mr. Henniker Wilson's party, who drove a few birds over from Barton Manor, though got but very few shots themselves. On the whole, however, my day was splendid for this lamentable season.

11th.—A sad, unlucky day. I got but 2 partridges, and missed a fair shot, a thing I have not done for many seasons, and on my coming home soon after three, in disgust at having found only 8 birds all the time I was out, I fell in with Charles, my keeper, who was weeping for his unrivalled dog that he had accidentally shot dead. I have been a sportsman for more than forty years, and never yet had such an untoward season at home or abroad.

22nd.—Wanting a brace of birds, I started about half-past twelve, hardly expecting to get them, and had the miraculous good luck to disperse a splendid covey that was driven to our home field by the Hurstbourne Park shooters, and to come home in triumph with 16 partridges. I killed all I saw, thanks to Eley's cartridges, with which I made such a succession of long shots as I never saw before in one day.

November 1st.—Keyhaven. Up at five so as to skim the coast before the Southampton lubbers. Cruised all the way to Pitt's Deep, and never saw but 9 wigeon, which a vessel put up, though a fine lot were seen by captains of vessels during the north-easter. Saw 18 geese off at sea, but had no chance to fire a gun, except at three dun divers on my way home, and I killed them all.

2nd.—Sport so bad that I took the gig and 'knocked off' some visits round Becton and Bashley, a savage country like the wilds of Ireland, and a cruel hard drive for my horse.

3rd.—Tried it on again, but the coast was almost barren.

Got 2 wigeon, all I saw, and 1 brent goose at above 200 yards out of the only 12 I saw. Not another fowl did I set eyes on in a very long cruise.

4th.—Read crawled on the mud (his filthy hobby) last night, but heard not a bird.

5th.—Out all day. Coast destitute of all wild fowl.

9th.—Up at four, and took a long cruise to explore the coast. Not a bird in the whole Western Channel, except the one small company of geese that have been so popped at by bullets that even 'on the ground ebb' they would not let me come within 400 yards of them. In short, I gave up gunning as hopeless till a change of wind.

18th.—London. I went to hear Adelaide Kemble in 'Norma,' and I think her quite the best English singer we have.

20th.—After having cut through business and commissions with railway speed in four days that many snails would have taken some weeks to do, I left town for Longparish. Had the Bishop of Winchester for a companion. The trip up, I had Commissioner Elliot, just landed from China.

December 2nd.—London. Busy about my new musket for Government, and saw Colonel Peel (Sir Robert's brother) at Ordnance Office. In sad suspense all night about the safety of my property at Keyhaven, lest the bank should burst as it did last year, when I saved the whole village by timely exertions.

3rd.—A letter from Keyhaven to say the floods had abated without entering my house, and that all my property was safe. Hard on again about my new musket, on which I had received a most flattering communication from Colonel Peel as to the Master-General's attention to my suggestions, and his intention of conferring with Lord Hill on the subject. Raced to death with divers business, and in the midst of it served with a summons for a special jury. Flew to Smith to buy me off if possible. But after a long dance to find the Philistine, his attempt failed, as he had been bribed so often that he was afraid of being 'blown' and ousted.

4th.—At musket again. Incessant rain morning, noon, and night.

5th.—Sunday. Had so many visits to pay after church that my cab hire came to *7s. 6d.*

6th.—Eternal rain all day. At Ordnance Office again about a conference with Westley Richards.

7th.—Served on jury. Only an hour at Westminster Hall. Got my guinea, and bolted like a scalded cock, lest I should be hooked for a second election, as several of our jury were, and on a case that stood fair for a week's work. Completed all my business and got my musket finished by bedtime.

15th.—Keyhaven. A lot of geese off yesterday, so was prepared for launching the light single-gun punt to-day; but there set in another south-west gale with pouring rain, so all I could do was to send a man about in the wet to try my new military musket, which seemed to defy everything.

17th.—A moderate day at last. Got 3 geese out of a small company at above 200 yards, and 2 curlews out of 3 that I fired at, a very long shot.

18th.—A pinching white frost with a north-east wind, cold enough to cut a feather. Got 2 geese, and gun flashed in pan at a company of 60. No sooner had we landed and cleaned all up than there set in the heaviest fall of snow I ever saw, which continued till about two in the morning, and then began to melt so fast as to fall from the house in such large pieces that I was woke up, and thought the chimneys were blown down and the slates breaking.

20th.—Intense frost and cutting north-easter all day, and yet I got no chance except just saving my blank with 1 wigeon. Read has crawled every night in his mud punt, and always came home with an empty bag. Poor show as yet.

21st.—Though a hard frost there were no birds, except

the few very wild geese that have been here since October. Buckle appeared for the first time this season, but has killed nothing.

1842

January 8th.—Breakfasted by candlelight, and got the champion gun and gear all in order for launching while it was daylight. No birds killed yet, but many said to be come and lying far off at sea owing to the moderate weather and the many gunners in our Channel.

10*th.*—Breakfasted by candlelight and launched at daylight. Brought home 2 tufted ducks, 3 golden-eyes, 5 ducks and mallards, and 1 wigeon. Splendid shooting and nothing missed, though a poor show of birds to shoot at.

N.B.—I have not been warm since a cold I took, Saturday three weeks, in spite of sudorifics, sulphur baths, &c., so I dreaded the risk of beginning the campaign to-day. But, instead of it making me worse, I got into a glorious perspiration from fatigue and excitement, and feel 50 per cent. better.

11*th.*—3 geese, the only chance I got, as a shift of wind to the south with a stiff breeze had filled the Channel with sailing bullet poppers, and the coast was cleared of all the birds, which went far off to sea. Old Buckle had arrived with an empty bag, and as savage as a bear.

12*th.*—3 geese again, the only chance I had all day.

13*th.*—A tremendous gale from the south-east from morning till night, with torrents of rain, hail, sleet, and heavy snow. Not even a dog could show his nose out of doors.

14*th.*—An extraordinary reverse of weather, a dead calm, with a day like summer. Not a bird to be seen, except 2 geese, both of which I bagged with the only shot I fired.

15*th.*—Took a long cruise over the whole Western Channel, and went as far as Need's-oar Point, off Leap, and then I went off Cowes, Hampstead, and Newtown, and (except a few ducks that rose before a steamer) never set eyes on a single company of fowl. Not even in summer did I ever go so far without a shot at something. Our log must have been fifty miles, as we were sailing in the punt near twelve hours.

23rd.—Sunday. Read all the week has crawled every night and all night on the mud, and never got a single bird. Not a fowl has been killed by anyone for days.

24th.—Read crawled all night in his mud punt, and he had the luck to get two shots just before daylight, and brought in 10 wigeon and 4 pintails. As soon as the water served I went off, but found no chance, and we were too happy to escape from a heavy sea and retreat by Pennington Leak.

25th.—A strong north-wester. Off from nine till one, but never saw a chance even for the popgun ; so, rather than have quite a blank day, I took off my gunning frock and walked ashore over a little bog in Mr. Pryce's 'mudlands,' thinking I might get perhaps one snipe. I had the good luck to obtain eight shots, 1 bird fell off in a field, and I killed dead and pocketed the other 7. This evening the coast was all alive with cannon and fireworks for the christening of the Prince of Wales.

26th.—A nipping white frost till near daylight this morning, when Read came in after his night's crawl without having heard a bird, and just in time to escape a violent change of weather. I made a most brilliant shot at a merlin hawk that flew over me as swift as an arrow, and though at least fifty yards, I cut him down as dead as a stone with snipe shot.

27th.—Read came home blank this morning, after a long mud crawl, on the winds abating. He fell in with old Buckle in the night, who had done nothing all the season, though eternally at it, and following the birds in his vessel with two punts on board.

29th.—Never set eyes on a bird all day, except 9 geese that I blew off at without success with mould shot at 300 yards.

31st.—Up directly after midnight, started about one, and

came in about seven in the morning. Was unlucky, or should have had plenty of wigeon. I had a miss-fire at one lot, and was just a quarter of an hour too late on the tide to bear the gun on a company of about 70. Came in with only 1. Lay down for an hour, and started about nine for the geese. Out all day ; the only shot I got was at 9, out of which I got 3 geese.

February 1st.—Prepared to go out again at one this morning, but it blew so hard one could not hear. After the tide was gone, Read mud-crawled and heard nothing. At nine we cruised as far off as Pilewell, and owing to changes of wind went from Keyhaven and back without using our oars at all. This is a very extraordinary occurrence. We found the whole army of periwinkle men on the mud for miles, so of course came home till the afternoon tide would wash away this rag fair rabble. All the wigeon on the coast were this day together on the sea off Hurst beach. I made out about 430 as near as I could count with a glass, which proves what lies have been told about the 'many thousands' that were every day off at sea.

2nd.—Up at two and out till daylight. Heard a few birds and lay under them for a shot without moving till I heard Lymington clock strike four and then five, but it came on too dark to fire at a small trip by sound, so I let them go, and moved down to Mount leak. Nothing there but a few single birds. On landing I had reason to rejoice at a blank, as Read, whom I trusted to load the gun, had forgotten to put the shot in, and had left the ramrod in one of the barrels for that purpose, so had I fallen in with a shot I should have come home *sine* wigeon and *sine* ramrod. So much for operations in very dark weather.

22nd.—Went to see the 'Kent' steamer, which was wrecked under the cliffs of Becton last Saturday morning before daylight. The master, Captain Lakeman, ran her aground about five in the morning, in a heavy fog, for want of using his lead-line to try the depth of water, having steered north instead of east.

23rd.—Got afloat. We saw about 300 geese, and had not the sea been so rough as to toss us about too much, we should have made a shot.

24th.—Afloat again, and got caught again in torrents of rain. Geese off again, but no doing anything in such weather, they would not rest a minute.

26th.—Bad weather again; that horrid brute Dan'l Paine has driven away all the geese with his blunderbuss and bullets, so that only about a score are left, and they went off in Channel under Yarmouth. I went after them, and bagged 3 geese as they flew off the waves, and 2 more came down that I dare not follow. The bad weather then returned, and we were too happy to fetch land in safety.

27th.—A terrific hurricane in the night and all this morning. My 'Petrel' punt, with the great double champion gun in her, rode out the gale at her moorings in gallant style.

28th.—Went afloat about ten and got as far as Oxey leak, where there were about 80 geese, but we saw bad weather coming and got home just in time.

Sorry list of the past barren season: Game total, 83. Wild fowl—5 ducks and mallards, 22 wigeon, 4 pintails, 3 golden-eyes, 2 tufted ducks, 20 brent geese. Total, 56. Other coast birds—1 merganser, 3 dun divers, 4 curlews, 7 plover, 48 shore birds. Total, 63. Grand total, only 202 head.

N.B.—I never shot better at game or wild fowl; but such was the scarcity of both that I regret having taking out a licence for the one, or knocked about my best punts and gear for the other, during this nasty, hoar-frosty, blustering, rotten winter.

March 8th.—Out early again, and at last had a chance to try the geese; but they rose more than a quarter of a mile off, so we voted it useless to cruise any more, and returned home, and thus wound up the most execrable season on record.

9th.—Another hurricane. Heavy rain nearly all day, with heavy squalls of wind. At about eight this evening the wind increased to the most furious hurricane I ever saw; but most providentially it came when the tide had ceased to flow outside, or Lord knows what might have been the consequence. This truly awful gale continued all the time the tide was ebbing; but, as God's mercy had it, a squall of rain 'hove' the wind into the west before the flood began to make. Such was the fury of this tempest that no one could walk against it; and we were so shook in our beds that sleep was out of the question. Boats out of number driven from their moorings, and two of Read's boats were blown about on the quay like a man's hat, and considerably damaged. How truly lucky I was to get all my valuable punts and gear safely housed yesterday!

12th.—Returned to Longparish; and in Southampton heard the report confirmed that Dan'l Paine, our mad and drunken frightener of wild fowl, was no doubt lost more than a week ago, as his boat, gear, and hat were picked up at Hillhead, and he had not been heard of since. He was recorded in the South Hants paper as a person patronised by me; but I never spoke to him in my life. Though he did more mischief to our coast than all the other gunners put together, and no good to himself, yet I sincerely regret the poor fellow's untimely end, and the only wonder is that he was not drowned long ago.

17th.—London. Busy in the City. Tortured with a toothache. Whipped in to the dentist, who ridded me of a tooth like a three-legged stool, which he hung fire at drawing. But I would have it out, and a blessed delivery too!

April 4th.—Went down to Keyhaven. Took the train at Winchester, as on Saturday, the day before yesterday, the long tunnel halfway between Andover station and Winchester, called 'Waller's Ash,' had fallen in and killed five workmen, besides wounding four more severely, and others slightly. By working all Sunday, however, the directors had got the line open again this day. When in Southampton I ascertained that the body of poor Dan'l Paine had been found in a place called 'Park Hole,' a few miles above Lymington Creek, and that he was taken home and buried rather more than a week ago.

5th.—Weather colder than in winter, with a cutting north-easter and frost; and some geese and even a few wigeon were still about; but having housed all my gear I took no trouble to go after them. A grand 'lion' to be seen. A whale about one hundred feet long was washed ashore in Totland Bay, nearly opposite Hurst. Boats, steamers, and all craft in requisition to see it.

6th.—Another lovely day for the whale; boats from all parts, and the Lymington steamer with a band of music. Went a second time, with General and Lady Elizabeth Thackery (who kindly invited me to take a passage in their boat), and took a sketch of the wonderful monster; and I cut out and brought home a few of the curious combings that are attached to his upper jaws, and which are the whalebones so general in use.

7th.—Company from all parts, this being considered as the last day of the whale, which, report said, was to be cut up for oil this afternoon and to-morrow.

8th.—The whale was sold for 24*l.* to a man in the island, who, instead of cutting it up on the spot, decided on towing it away with a steamer for exhibition, and then dissection. To-day the whale was high and dry, owing to the low fall of spring tides, and those who went had a famous view of him on the bare sands.

9th.—The steamer and all boats were prepared for a visit to the whale, and away I went with Read, but no whale. The purchaser had towed him off at daylight this morning, and all parties came home disappointed, particularly myself, as I had prepared for making a finished drawing of him on a large scale, to supersede the little hasty sketch that I took the other day.

30*th.*—London. Down to Woolwich about another committee which the Master-General had ordered on my new patent army musket, and for which I am waiting in town. Went over the Arsenal, the largest guns in which carry a hollow shot of 96 lb. and weigh $4\frac{1}{4}$ tons.

May 4*th.*—Down to Woolwich, and before the Select Committee with my musket, models &c. Having heard from everyone that this Committee made a point of rejecting everything that did not emanate from themselves and furbishers, I read to and left with them my protest against their own musket, now in use, and left a copy of what I said with Colonel Peel for the Master-General. The Committee never give applicants an answer as to their opinion, but concoct a letter after the party is gone, and send it in to the Board of Ordnance for the Master-General. So thus rests the musket job, on which I have taken so much pains, and all for nothing but a wish to do good to the service.

7*th.*—Longparish. Took the only three hours' recreation I've had for many weeks; killed 8 brace of tidy fish, besides lots thrown in. Received advice this evening that Peter was gazetted captain in the 'Gazette' of last night, May 6th.

12*th.*—Keyhaven. Took a sail to the cliffs at the back of the island. Put my little popgun in the boat for the chance of a shot, but saw scarcely anything; and there came on such a heavy sea and such a strong southerly wind that we sailed home against the tide, after being off a few hours. I got 3 willocks and 2 terns, all I fired at, in five of the most difficult flying shots out of a jumping boat, in which we got a pretty good wetting.

16*th.*—Took a sail in Read's boat in the Channel; and, to my surprise, saw the whole shore lined with godwits, all working to the eastward.

17*th.*—This afternoon we went off with an old leaky punt

of mine, and one single shoulder gun, and in a few hours I brought home 21 godwits, some red in their summer plumage, and some grey in their winter plumage. The two best shots were 6 sitting and 5 flying. Wind, heavy sea, and a vile punt. Had my grand set-out been in commission, I calculate I should have killed 150.

18*th*.—Off again with the same set-out this afternoon; but being fully aware that, as godwits rarely remain two days in the same place, I should find none where I shot yesterday, I went up with the flood tide about seven miles to the eastward, where I fell in with the rearguard of their army, consisting of a few small trips only. I, however, killed 18 godwits and 2 turnstones; my best shot was 9 bagged, added to 2 that escaped, out of not more than two dozen in the company. This afternoon I took No. 4 instead of No. 1 shot, and had I done so yesterday I should have trebled my number.

N.B.—A party, hearing of my sport yesterday, eagerly boated it to where I had been, and never killed a single bird.

27*th*.—Longparish. I went out for about an hour and a half with fly rod, and brought in 24 prime trout. Not being in an enemy's country, I left off when I might have caught, perhaps, as many more.

June 1*st*.—London. Presented Peter to the Queen, at the fullest Levee I have seen for many years, as it was the last of the season, and the first after the diabolical attempt on her Majesty's life last Monday.

7*th*.—An interview with Sir George Murray, the Master-General of the Ordnance, at the request of Colonel Peel. Sir George, on seeing my models, seemed fully to coincide with my views of the musket, and nothing could exceed his kind attention. But still the Select Committee and their armourer will have their own way.

21*st*.—Called at 70 Pall Mall to inquire for my kind friend and patron, Lord Rodney, who a few days ago was sitting with me in Dorset Place, but who had since been very seriously ill. The answer to my inquiries (which, of course, I had made every day) was, 'Sir, Lord Rodney is no more.' Never was I more distressed.

July 2nd.—Returned to Longparish, where on arrival I found the different official letters relative to the pay of the staff, the stores &c. of the North Hants Regiment, for which I now become responsible till a colonel is appointed, *vice* Lord Rodney, deceased.

4th.—At Winchester the whole morning, taking up the regimental stores, pay of staff &c.; and no sooner had I done all the needful, and posted my official to the Secretary at War, than I heard, and found to be correct, that the commission for the colonelcy of the regiment was signed by the Duke, and going for gazette by to-night's post, in favour of Lord Wiltshire, a young man, the son of the Marquis of Winchester. This is the Duke's recompense to me, who gained the trophy of 'Douro' for the 14th Dragoons, was severely wounded under his Grace in the Peninsula, major of 1815 in the North Hants, and lieutenant-colonel of 1821, having served six years major and twenty-one years lieutenant-colonel, and being more than qualified (by landed property, as by law required) for a colonelcy, and within a few months of twenty-seven years a field officer in this regiment.

23rd.—Keyhaven. Sailed to Alum Bay, and had a lovely day on the heights, after a swim off the rocks below. Got some wheatears for dinner in trying my new military musket. A bad show of them this year. All the rock birds gone some weeks ago. Saw Bill Coleraine, who told me he had got but twenty-two dozen eggs the whole season; whereas in former times he used to get his thirty dozen before breakfast in one morning. The worst season known for sport on the heights.

August 4th.—London. Down early this morning with Mr.

Godfrey, the bandmaster of the Coldstream Guards, to hear a practice of my march called the 'Prince of Wales's Quick Step,' which 'went' splendidly, though, of course, only a mere trifle. And this, by the way, is the anniversary of my being made a captain, as I got my troop in the 14th on August 4, 1804, when I was only in the eighteenth year of my age.

CHAPTER XXXV

1842

September 1st.—My daughter was married this morning to Mr. Charles Rhodes. If a man has any feeling in him, nothing, short of death, can more acutely try it than the parting thus from a child so dear to him as my darling Mary has ever been to me. May God be a Father to her wherever she goes, and inspire her husband with that ardent affection which she so justly deserves.

5*th.*—Took my first day's shooting, and, although far from well, fagged from ten in the morning until dinner. So scarce and wild, however, were the birds, that I came home completely knocked up, with only 5 partridges.

10*th.*—Better, but still in pain. Went out on the old mare, and had the worst luck on record. It blew a gale of wind, and I crawled about till I found a good show of birds, but old Don ruined my sport by running into every covey, and such vile retrievers were he and the old bitch that at one time I killed 2 birds with the first and 2 more with the second barrel, and lost 3 out of the 4, and I winged a stone curlew in some turnips, and even he got away. All I got was 5 partridges, 1 hare, and 1 landrail. I had three miss-fires, owing to a heavy shower, and all the good shots happened to rise after I had blown off at long ones. Had I been well and in luck, with good dogs and a reserve gun, I do think I should have killed 20 brace.

All I killed in September was 26 partridges, 1 hare, 1 landrail, 4 snipes, and 2 teal: 34 head.

October 5th.—Keyhaven. Took a long cruise, saw very few birds, and those so thin there were not two together, and as wild as in March.

8th.—Took another cruise, but never saw a chance, though the weather continued beautiful. Heard all the birds were gone to Poole, where they remain in peace, owing to the enormous quantity of herrings and other fish now occupying the whole time there of the coast gunners. Their profits in fishing are, I am told, enormous—one night producing more than a whole season's gunning.

December 19th.—Keyhaven. Not a fowl on the coast, and Read coming home every morning from his nightly hobby, mud crawling, without seeing or hearing a bird. I, of course, have not been such a fool as to put my punt afloat this visit to Keyhaven, nor have I even taken a popgun in hand, as there is literally nothing now by sea or land. Flowers blowing and blackbirds whistling.

29th.—Longparish. So mild was the weather that I put my fly rod together, and soon caught a large dish of trout (6 brace). We had all these fish broiled for dinner and breakfast, and they were quite as good as in the early part of the fishing season.

1843

January 16th.—Keyhaven. Not a single wild fowl in all the market of Southampton, and nothing whatever done or even seen in my absence. The news of the place on my arrival about a quarter before eight this evening was all about the damage done, chiefly to houses, by the hurricane of Friday morning, and that a flood was just avoided by the late raising of the banks, which would never have been done had I not constantly bothered about it. Sam Singer was all but drowned in the gale; as it was, his craft was washed aground, his punt and gun were washed ashore, and he had to swim for his life, and then to be laid up ill from cold and exhaustion, from the water he had swallowed in swimming.

18th.—Went to Lymington to see and offer assistance to Sam Singer, but found that he had recovered and left the place. On my return home, I boarded a Brighton mackerel boat, a thing I had for years wanted to see, and inspected the whole set-out. The nets, it appears, are a mile and a half long and only 4 fathoms deep, and are therefore worked on the surface of the water, as the mackerel always swim far from the bottom of the sea, which this kind of net never reaches, though when they come near land, as in Portland, then the common seines, which sink with leads, are used from the shore.

21st.—Heard of Sam Singer at Hurst. Sailed down and brought him up to spend the day and to 'blow' him 'out.' He told me that his loss in the hurricane was a spy-glass, a 'cripple stopper,' and his great-grandfather's compass, and was most loquacious and amusing about his late trip for duck shooting with two swell gents to Norway. He had done nothing on our coast this winter, and was quite sick of English gunning.

February 2nd.—My other dear daughter was this day married at Christchurch, St. Marylebone, to the Rev. Lewis Playters Hird. I never felt anything more acutely than parting from this dear child, and may God be a Father to her wherever she goes. My family are now all disposed of, and I remain as the mere scaffold on which has for more than twenty years been building, as it were, the edifice of their education.

19th.—Keyhaven. Rain! Wonderful how I turn the cock always when I arrive on the coast. Birds almost as scarce as before, in spite of the late intensely severe weather. Only 8 wigeon and 3 geese killed by all the punters put together during my four weeks' absence on business.

20th.—A butterfly day. Went afloat, but got no chance for a shot, though saw a few geese flying a long way off at sea, and a small trip of wigeon with them. I had only launched the small set-out, and went more for my health than with the expectation of having a shot.

27th.—Wild fowl only 32 for season. No shooting for anyone on the coast this year.

March 21st.—London. Took a lesson of Professor Richter in his new discovery for perspective, by which it is said a housemaid may, in one lesson, be taught to draw anything from a spoon to Westminster Abbey or a large landscape as correctly as a member of the Royal Academy.

May 16th.—My cause was tried to-day in that blackguard bear garden, the Sheriffs' Court, in an alley at the back of Holborn; and though the evidence, and the summing up of a counsel who sat as judge, were all as strong as possible on my side, yet the jury, a set of uneducated people, gave a verdict for the rascally plaintiff and his black lawyer. Instead of paying the least attention to the evidence on the summing up, this beggarly lot of jurymen were guided entirely by the nefarious lies that were spouted out after all power of reply was past by the most finished blackguard I ever saw as counsellor, a fellow who, I am told, was a journeyman tailor, who practises only in this court, and is hand-in-glove with all the low jurymen that are procured for it at a few shillings each for the whole list of causes for the day. Never, therefore, let a defendant go to this court if he would resist imposition. We, of course, moved to 'stay the writ' for the High Court of Exchequer, and the judge readily granted this request to us, which he had refused in two other cases. But, as the sum in dispute was under 5*l.*, we query if the Barons will grant us a new trial in their court.

July 10th.—In Hanover Square Rooms at half-past seven. Queen came at half-past eight; close to her all the evening. Her first turn at Philharmonic, and perhaps her last, as, in consequence of that dry mathematician, old Spohr, having the command, we had all noise and no melody.

August 26th.—Longparish. Licensing day, on which came on the grand fight, before the full bench of magistrates, relative to the spirit licence for my property, the 'Bullington Cross' inn. I had got nearly one hundred signatures, in opposition to which the black parson had enlisted all his own coterie, backed by some trumpery fellows whom he had humbugged; and never was there a harder fight. Old C—— held forth with a long speech; lying as fast as a dog would trot, and made out a case on which, to all appearance, we had not a leg to stand on. But when the brute had 'spun his yarn,' it was my time to administer the antidote, which I did in no measured terms; and the fellow looked as if he had been horsewhipped. The court was then cleared for decision, and out we went among the farmers of the market, before whom I told old C—— he was 'a liar;' and off he sneaked like a mongrel cur as he is. The decision was such that I gained the day and got the licence.

CHAPTER XXXVI

1843

September 1*st*.—Longparish. No shooting worth going out for.

5*th*.—Started about half-past eleven. I was five hours without getting a shot.

9*th*.—Slaved all day, and came home with 13 partridges, the most that has been yet done here with one gun; and I now long as much to get rid of my gun as I formerly did to take it up, for such is the sport here in these days, that it is slavery instead of recreation to take the field.

26*th*.—Went to Keyhaven. No joke going by steamer, as the delays at Cowes and Yarmouth, and the roundabout course she takes, keep you nearly double the time occupied by coach, and without anything to eat. I told everyone that the intense heat and long-continued dry weather would turn to rain on my approaching Keyhaven, as I never yet remember losing my charter. All laughed at me, but I was right, and the weather turned so wet and cold that we were obliged to have a fire.

September list for 1843: 50 partridges, 1 landrail, 1 hare, 4 snipes, 2 wigeon, 2 godwits. Making in all only 60 head.

N.B.—A miserable breed of game, and had there been a good one I had no time for pleasure this month; though, sorry as my list is, I did as well as my neighbours who had more time for sport.

November 1*st*.—Taken very ill, and was put into my bed,

which I did not get out of till the afternoon of the 3rd, when, thanks to Dr. Badger's good management, I was rid of the fever, though, having taken only toast and water, I was extremely weak.

4th.—Prince Alexander of the Netherlands, who is over here, sent to me to advise about a rig-out for gunning on the coast of Holland, so I secured him Sam Singer, and wrote about the famous gun that I built for the late Captain Ward; and on the 7th Captain Hudson (of the Guards) was to go off with my written prescription to Southampton, I being too ill to see to anything myself, and being also in the midst of troublesome business with my lawyer. It seems I'm never to have peace; and all this illness, as the doctor observes, is from downright worry and incessant excitement.

19th.—London. Up to this day I've been harassed, ever since I came to town, with the tedious expensive proceedings of an entail and trust, which could only be made strictly legal by lawyer's jargon, and which required a conveyancer. All the other parts of my new will, which I thought it best to make, is 'A B C,' and I did it in a few hours myself (and in a fiftieth part of the gibberish used in the lawyer's infernal rigmarole) by writing grammar, English, and plain sense, instead of technical jargon.

25th.—Got under way for Keyhaven, shut up in the close britschka; and having but one mare to draw this heavy 'trap,' I lashed on a carthorse to tow the whole concern through the rivers, up Withers's cruel hill, and through the slush to Barton, from whence the mare got on at an 'andante' pace to Winchester. At Southampton I secured Captain Ward's lovely gun, at the dirt-cheap price of 50*l.*, for Prince Alexander. Wrote a long letter of advice to his Royal Highness, and arrived at Keyhaven about nine at night.

December 4th.—Keyhaven. Our coast literally destitute of birds for several weeks; and the very few gunners who went out had nothing but blank days and nights.

13*th*.—In pain all day and in terror all night, and could not turn in bed without two people to raise my body, and a third person to ease my head; never in my life did I undergo such continued pain.

14*th to* 16*th*.—Confined to my bedroom, and for the greater part of the time to my bed, in spite of cupping, poultices, fomentations, colchicum and calomel.

21*st to* 23*rd*.—Keyhaven. Damp, rotten weather. Birds singing; flowers blowing; and doctors full of business.

24*th and* Christmas Day.—Weathercock with head where tail ought to be; dark, damp, rotten, cutthroat-looking weather; flowers blowing; bluebottles buzzing; doctors galloping in every direction; a Philharmonic of blackbirds and thrushes; an armistice from guns and shooting; the poor punters driven to oyster dredging, eel picking, day labour, or beggary; not even the pop-off of a Milford snob to be heard in that unrivalled garrison of tit shooters.

1844

January 1*st*.—Keyhaven. After a most furious night of wind and rain from the south-west, the weathercock this morning flew into the north, and occasionally to the east, with squalls of sleet, snow, and rain. This of course leads us to hope the new year will bring better weather.

4*th*.—Seeing no prospect of weather for a shot, and being liable to be called up to Longparish on the new year quarter business, I availed myself of a very high tide to bring my small punt ashore again, and stow her in the boathouse after her having been afloat about five weeks and never taken once from her moorings, as there was literally nothing to go out for to shoot.

15*th*.—On the whole day getting the great gun and 'Petrel' (with all the divers apparatus) afloat, as hundreds of foreign fowl had been seen in the Channel. Had a most satisfactory launch, as she and the cripple-catching punt, though laid up for, I believe, three whole years, were 'as tight as bottles.'

16*th*.—Off at daybreak and out till half-past four. But the fowl were not near so numerous as they had been yesterday. An intense frost; but it turned rather white, which is a bad omen. I got but 4 wigeon and 3 teal. The birds were off in the Channel, where there was too much sea to shoot, and I lost nearly as many as I bagged.

17*th*.—Off all day; but the birds were off under the Isle of Wight, and so scattered in a rough sea that we were obliged to put back and leave them.

23*rd*.—White frost, and then a beautiful day. Up at six and off. Went all the way to Need's-oar Point, having gone over nearly 40 miles of water; and, except a few straggling ducks that rose a quarter of a mile away, I saw nothing. A blank day, never even popped off the cripple stopper. Other gunners off all day, and all had blanks. A precious pretty gunning season!

31*st*.—Received a most kind letter from Prince Alexander of the Netherlands, expressing his delight with the gun I had sent him. His Royal Highness's first shot was 6 teal, his second 12 curlews, and his third 29 teal. A princely beginning. Heavy fall of snow all day; but no frost as yet.

February 2nd.—An intensely cold winter's day, with deep snow and a biting frost all night. Too severe and too sudden to last, I think.

3*rd*.—Keyhaven. One of the coldest days I ever weathered, and so slippery from the frozen snow that I did not reach my Cottage till near nine o'clock; having had scarcely a morsel all day, and being almost petrified with the cold.

4*th*.—Not a bird killed by anyone in my absence in London.

8*th*.—Began to work for my ninth edition, for which Longmans are crying out most lustily; having all but exhausted the eighth. No chance of more birds this season, I believe.

13*th.*—Another most vicious white frost. Dandy weather in the afternoon ; went afloat. All I saw was 2 brent geese and 1 duck, and which I put in the larder.

14*th.*—A candlelight breakfast, and afloat by daylight. Made a long cruise, and except seeing some ducks at sea found nothing but 8 geese all day. Got up to them, and should have had 4 or 5, but the gun was loaded by Read in the dark, and the right barrel missed fire for the first time for six years. They all split abroad as they rose, and I picked out one bird, a brent goose, and killed him handsomely with the other barrel. Mr. Childe, the painter, arrived here this evening to do some sketches from nature for my new edition of 'Instructions to Young Sportsmen.'

Mr. Childe busy sketching ; and I at his elbow every day hammering into his head the designs I wished for, and after such trouble as I would not go through again for 50*l.* I got rid of him and drove him off to the coach next day.

19*th.*—Was from morning till night 'hard on' with Read, Payne, and old Peter, housing my punts and gear, and putting away all my great guns in store, as it's now all over this season for a chance of getting a shot.

Sorry list of game &c. up to February 19th, 1844 (the worst year ever known in Great Britain, and even Ireland):

Game—50 partridges, 1 landrail, 2 hares, 3 rabbits, 17 snipes. Total, 73.

Wild fowl—1 duck, 7 wigeon, 4 teal, 3 geese. Total, 15. Other birds—14 plover, 4 godwits. Total, 18. Grand total, 33.

Grand and sorry total, 106 head.

Much illness and town business all the season ; but had I been well and at leisure, I could have done nothing, as scarcely a gunner has killed even a dozen wild fowl all this cruel season.

March 16*th.*—Longparish. A letter from Sam Singer, who

has come home from Holland with a gold watch and honours, and the Prince's gun, for me to get made into a detonator.

26th.—Went by Great Western Railway, the very best in the world, to Bristol. Went all over the leviathan steamer, the 'Great Britain,' while my dinner was preparing, and slept at a good hotel, the 'Cumberland.'

27th.—Up at daylight. Ascended the heights, and went over all the beauties of Clifton, and was down again about half-past ten before the steamer (the 'Victory,' Captain Parker) could be in, and in about half an hour in she came, and, thank God, with Peter on board. Worked him off by rail at one, and got him safe into Dorset Place at six. He was reduced to a skeleton, though not so helpless as I expected to find him.

May 1st.—London. Working hard at my ninth edition of 'Instructions to Young Sportsmen' up to, and on from, this day.

6th.—On hard, till late this night, every day, and baited with untoward domestic calamities the whole time I was slaving for the press.

7th.—By being up till twelve last night, and up at four this morning, I contrived to get ready a batch of my book business.

8th.—On like fury with Varley the artist, engravers, woodcutters, Longmans, lawyer, banker, gunmakers, agents &c. from the time I got up till night, and bound for ditto and ditto every day.

July 31st.—To Windsor to take the royal copy of the new edition of my book on shooting (that is published to-morrow) to Prince Albert, and also a copy for his private secretary, G. E. Anson, Esq., who was much pleased with the book. The Prince had a swarm of officials, or I should have seen his Royal Highness. Saw his guns.

August 29th.—Married to Helen Susan, widow of my old friend, Captain John Symonds, R.N., at half-past ten, at

Christchurch, Marylebone, and almost driven crazy with the death of one wife and marriage to another coming all at once. More fit to be buried than married.

31*st.*—At half-past seven boarded the 'Dover' steamer. Lovely day, and in Ostend at four. Scramble as usual, and a Jarvey man, who drove me to consul for passport, charged too much, and was taken off to prison, with a roar of laughter from the surrounding mob. No complaint of mine, but the police demanded information as to what I had paid. Put up at 'Ship' hotel.

CHAPTER XXXVII

1844

September 1st.—Left for Brussels at half-past four o'clock by railway, which was admirably well conducted, and reached Brussels at nine.

4th.—Left Brussels at a quarter before seven by railway, and arrived in Cologne (44 leagues) at a quarter before six, where our passports were revised on entering the Prussian frontier. Railroad admirably conducted.

5th.—Saw the principal sights of Cologne. Cathedral by far the best, and here we had the good luck to arrive in time for the last half-hour of a sublimely beautiful mass, in which the organ playing, by a Mr. Weber, was perfection. The treasure and relics in this most magnificent cathedral I've not time to enter into. After a very grand table-d'hôte dinner, which was somewhat ridiculous from the messes introduced, such as boiled lemons &c., we went by railway, as good as the Great Western, to Bonn. This town we were delighted with, having lost not an instant to explore all we could before dark. The two grand 'lions' were the Munster Cathedral, with the bronze statue of St. Hélène, and the birthplace of Beethoven, at No. 934 Rue du Rhin, over which we were shown by an old man who was bred up from a child with this immortal composer, and who was so eager to explain all that was interesting, that we could hardly get away from him.

6th.—Left Bonn with regret. The steamer started a little before eight in the morning, and, after a short stoppage at Coblentz, making 120 miles against the powerful stream of the Rhine, we landed about eight in the evening at Mayence, where we got into a huge hotel called 'L'Hollande.' We had dined on board the steamer at a large table d'hôte, where we had ices and all other luxuries. In this trip, for which we had a lovely day, we had the best possible view of all the celebrated beauties of the Rhine, to describe which would be impossible, even had I time to sit down and write. The passage from Bonn to Mayence gives you all the best part of this enormous river, as to rocky mountains, 'cloud-capped towers,' vineyards, country seats, and a winding course through almost every landscape that can be imagined, and absolutely bewilders you with one beauty crowding on another before you have time to sketch or even think of them.

7th.—Up early, and with a voiture and a commissionnaire surveying what was to be seen in Mayence, which is a large garrison town with about 8,000 troops, a mixture of Austrians and Prussians, then crossed the bridge of boats over the Rhine, and proceeded by railway to Frankfort, 22 English miles. Here we got into an enormous place, called 'L'Hôtel de l'Empereur Romain,' which from our entry to our departure proved to be the worst house I ever was in; dirty, dear, bad attendance, and no civility.

8th.—Sunday. Went to Homburg (about 12 miles), and back at night. Here we had a scene of the greatest gaiety imaginable; and not only that, but disgraceful scenes of gambling on the Sunday. The grand emporium for all this is a magnificent building called the 'Kursaal,' behind which there is a splendid range of walks to the mineral waters, with an excellent orchestra, and every kind of refreshment.

9th.—After a few hours about the town, we took the railway to Wiesbaden (about 30 English miles), not a little delighted to get out of the noisy, dirty, expensive town of Frankfort.

N.B.—Our move to Wiesbaden was the commencement of our return home; and, by my losing no time in our advance, we had just completed the little tour intended, when the dry and hot weather turned to wind and rain, which began this morning, and I should say with thunder; but such was the noise in Frankfort that I doubt if the thunder could be heard in our hotel.

At Wiesbaden, which is quite the pleasantest place we had seen in Germany, we put up at the 'Hôtel de Quatre Saisons,' a splendid house, with the best table d'hôte I had seen. After an early dinner, we hired a carriage and a commissionnaire, and were driven to the top of the mountain to see 'Die Platte,' the Duke of Nassau's grand hunting palace, from which there is a view that can scarcely be surpassed by any country seat in Europe. We had not time to see much of the town itself, which appeared so superior to the others we had been in, that, had I been in good health and with leisure to remain abroad, I would gladly have sojourned at this place for some time.

10*th*.—Went by omnibus (3 miles) to Beberich, on the right bank of the Rhine, and there embarked (about ten) in the Düsseldorf steamer; and about nine at night landed at Cologne in rain and utter darkness, and where we had a miserable scramble for our baggage; and I was all but getting my teeth knocked out by a porter meeting me with a huge box, that just grazed, and cut a little, my lip. Good hotels full; so had to take refuge in one called 'L'Hollande,' which seemed to be unrivalled for dirt, misery, rudeness and inattention, and where I had nearly broken my arm, and got a severe blow on the head, by falling out of a nasty little elevated Prussian bed.

11*th*.—Got off, by an early train, to Liège, which we found to be one of the best and by far the cheapest places we had been in. We went to the Hôtel de l'Europe, where we had a room fit for a prince: a superfluously good dinner and dessert, a breakfast, and a carriage to the railway (the next morning) all for one napoleon. I amused myself with visiting the two chief gunmakers (Monsieur Lessence Ronge and Mr. Vivario Plomdeur), where a 'first-rate' double gun cost but from seven and a half to nine napoleons to those who were bold enough to run the risk of using it. The Palais de Justice, the market square, and the arcade were three objects worthy of notice in this magnificent town, which I had expected to find dirty like Birmingham, and had merely taken refuge in it to divide the long journey of 68 leagues from Cologne to Ostend, which by rail takes at least sixteen hours.

General memorandum.—Railways in Germany, Prussia, and particularly in Belgium, extremely well regulated; and most particularly for the baggage, for which there are check tickets for every article. Hotels enormously large, and living quite as dear as in England. Tables d'hôte usually at one o'clock, with an endless variety of everything calculated to disorder the stomach, and wine little better than hogwash. All the beds so narrow as not to be large enough for one well-fed gent or lady. Attendance generally bad, on account of the enormous number of persons that one hotel will contain; and a general uproar, noise and confusion. People as a rule civil; but, of course, they play into each other's hands to pluck John Bull all they can, the same as in all other frequented parts of the Continent. Travelling miserably slow in all ways, except by railroad.

15*th.*—London. Arrived. Cleared off all German dirt with a good wash, and all foreign diet with a dose of blues. Weak as a rat, and much in need of a day's rest.

23*rd.*—Longparish. Having arrived on the 21st (after a series of such worry and confusion as no pen can describe, and then a tour in Belgium, Prussia, and Germany), I took a gun out of the armoury to-day, in order to see if I had nerve enough left to kill a partridge. This morning I started, in a cold easterly wind, and scoured the whole of my inclosed beat; and came home without a single head of game. I popped away twice, but too far to kill. Not wishing to lose my charter (of never yet having had a blank day), I went off to the hills for the whole afternoon, and slaved all the way to Bullington. I then used Eley's cartridges, as the only chance of getting a bird. I fired six times and got 6 partridges. Though half dead, I never made more extraordinary shots. Here is my first day, and not a very tempting one to make me wish for a second, unless the wind should change, or there should be better 'lay' for the birds.

October 1st.—Keyhaven. The long north-easter changed to a southerly breeze. Went on the water to try if I could recover my impaired health and appetite, and did wonders with what few plover were on our coast. I got three shots, and cleared off nearly all I saw. Never did I make a more lucky little beginning afloat. I brought in 8 grey plover and 8 knot plover.

November 4th.—Longparish. Scoured the whole country with a gang of beaters (as a grand finishing *chasse*); but the only shot I got was at one old cock pheasant, that had defied everyone since the 1st of October, and which I properly outmanœuvred, and killed in prime style.

5th.—Keyhaven. There had been a good show of wigeon, and Read had bagged 16 at one shot; so I bustled till very late at night, and then before daylight, to get my punt and big gun in order, as everything was laid up in store, except the light punt which Read had launched.

6th.—The north-easter flew to the west; and I had, of course, brought some rain as usual. We were off from very early till near three, but never saw a chance; though about 200 wigeon (all in one flock) rose before a steamer, close under Yarmouth.

16th.—A foggy breeze, which about four turned to a drizzling rain. Weathered it from that time till dark, and came in with 12 wigeon. Birds extremely wild, as they always are in foggy weather. Nearest of my two shots about 140 yards.

18th.—Out hours before daylight, but the wigeon were all gone. The only shot I fired was at a little bunch of mixed birds on a raft of weeds; and I literally cleared off the whole company. This day two new Keyhaven gunners made a grand start, to be on day and night, viz. Harry Troth and Harry Rook; and with two very fair turns-out, all on my system, but not to my advantage.

22nd.—Read out mud crawling all last night, and got but 2 wigeon. I out all to-day, and saw not a chance but 1 grey plover that I killed with the cripple stopper.

N.B.—The last week of November was such a failure that, although Read, Troth, and Parker were all on in hot opposition all day and all night without intermission, every bird killed for these last eight days and nights was 1 curlew and 1 wigeon. As for me, I had cleaned up my gear, and brought my gun ashore. It was high time, when all shooters and no birds.

December 4th.—A fine westerly wind. Many flocks of birds came down Channel, but only a very few would alight owing to our two new tyros being planted off all day like scarecrows, which prevented their coming in. I got 5 wigeon by going off in a heavy sea, and might have had a brilliant day if our little shore had been no more disturbed than usual.

5th. Off from before daylight till evening, and never pulled a trigger. An intensely cold white frost, and nearly all the birds had been driven away by the tyros. I should have had one beautiful shot at a little mixture of teal and wigeon, with 3 pintails, but a rascally boy with a popgun and a yawl rowed them up out of downright spite. These are the delights one must weather in big gunning.

7th.—Intensely cold with a very hard white frost, and yet an easterly gale. Up at five, and got 5 wigeon under the dying moon, and 11 more at daylight, making 16 wigeon.

9th.—Off before daylight, but the tyros had cleared the shore before me. Lots of birds, and, at last, some geese arrived. Went all the way to Pitt's Deep to get away from these disturbers of sport, but found they had made the birds so wild there was scarcely a chance to come in shot. Came home about three, and launched the grand set-out, the 'Petrel,' the big double gun and the following boat.

10*th*.—Off at daylight, and out till five. A bitter cold easterly wind and frost, and so much sea that we had a miserably wet time in getting six miles off to avoid the new tyros. Got but one shot all day with one barrel of the great gun; knocked down 8 brent geese, 2 wigeon, and 1 teal.

11*th*.—Up before daylight, and off to Pitt's Deep; but no good shot to be had. Got only 2 brent geese, with 1 plover and 11 dunlins, and did well to bag them.

12*th*.—Weathered a heavy sea, and bitter cold easterly gale up to Pilewell; beset with shooters in every direction. Made two shots, and brought in 14 wigeon, 1 tufted duck, and 1 brent goose.

13*th*.—A heavy gale all day from the eastward; went up to windward, and made one pretty double shot; 10 geese with the first barrel.

14*th*.—Frost and snow. All the birds driven away by the tyros to the outside of Hurst. Weathered it all day, and got but 2 wigeon; a long shot at a few scattered birds.

15*th*.—Sunday.

16*th*.—A wet day, and the frost all gone, though still an easterly wind. Weathered the rain for a few hours, and made one double shot, a very long one, and knocked down 5 geese with the first barrel and 5 with the second.

17*th*.—Out in the dark. Got at daybreak 4 wigeon; birds by hundreds at break of day, but so driven by all kinds of floating shooters that a good shot was impossible.

18*th*.—Out in the dark again. Harbour driven all night by strange gunners. No one got any birds but I, who brought in 3 wigeon, 1 mallard, and 4 brent geese.

19*th*.—Off at daylight. Cold easterly wind with heavy

rain. Got but one very long shot. Knocked down 2 geese that fell a great way off, and were 'prigged' by sailing boats. Came home after a long dull cruise.

20th.—Up at six, and went up to Lymington mud. Caught the grand army of geese near a creek at last, and was all but firing when off popped an infernal gun to windward. 3 burrough ducks came and pitched on the spot where the geese were, and I cut them all up quite dead. A tremendous east gale came suddenly on, and we had enough to do to reach home and save ourselves.

21st.—A tremendous frosty gale from the east all day. No boat could go off. Read mud-crawled, and got 3 wigeon, and crawled again in the day till he filled his punt, his boots, and his gun with salt water.

23rd.—Off before daylight, but so cruelly driven by rival shooters was our harbour that I never had a chance for a shot all day. Read had mud-crawled since twelve last night, and came in with 3 wigeon.

24th.—Read crawled all night in a bitter cold hazy frost, and came home blank. I went off at daybreak and had one long volley into the geese, with which I brought in 12.

26th.—Read came in after a night's mud crawling with 6 wigeon. I breakfasted as usual by candlelight, and was out all day; but it proved a farce to be off, as there were more than fifty poppers afloat for a Christmas spree, and not a bird could pitch. I heard at least 200 shots, and I am not aware that one single bird was killed.

27th.—Read came in with 4 wigeon, and had not his gun flashed twice he said he should have had 40, as the mud launching was never better than last night. I was out all day, and got but 2 brent geese, a very long flying shot, and the only one I fired.

28th.—Read had a blank night's crawling last night, and I a blank day to-day. The shooting is almost annihilated by green, greedy, unfair, bungling bird drivers.

1845

January 1st.—Up to Pilewell and back, but never saw a chance, as the birds were all driven to the eastward by the sheer bad usage of bungling bird drivers; but I saved my blank with a glorious brace of rare birds—2 barnacles. While my punt was at the quay, and Read mopping her out, and I just going to eat a second breakfast, these two birds came over and wheeled round over some popgunners, that would have scared them off by a useless discharge out of reach, but for my men, who prevented their firing. I ran out, jumped into the punt, and set off to the birds on the mud, just before the quay, and cut them up both quite dead before a multitude of spectators. I never saw or heard of but 3 barnacles so far south as our coast, one that I shot ashore many years ago and these 2 splendid specimens, one of which I shall send to Leadbeater to stuff for my collection. This was a lucky hit with which to begin the new year, and may our good luck continue.

2nd.—A calm, cold day. Went to within a few miles of Cowes, and never had a chance. Drove the grand army of geese down before me to near Keyhaven, but they went on the mud, 400 yards from any creek. I lay alongside them till near dark, when they rose, like a roar of thunder, to go off to roost at sea.

3rd.—Read got 1 brent goose early in the morning, but there was no chance for my gun till the very end of the day, when I went off; and just as I entered my own creek that I made, a large detachment of the grand army came from the east, and 'took the ground' about 150 yards from one of the 'spreaders' that I had cut. I had not put the shot in my gun, and was obliged to crawl out to do it, as we dare not rise. We then poled up the 'spreader,' but the water was too low to allow my gun to bear on the birds. I levelled the gun, and lay ready to fire when the tide rose; but before I had lain many minutes the geese all flew up without having seen us; I blew into them, and down came 20 in handsome style before a multitude of spectators, who were delighted. We never had a more amusing cripple chase, as only 5 birds were dead, owing to the immense distance at which I was obliged to fire; and, consequently, Read and I on the mud, and Payne in my following boat off at sea, were in full chase for nearly an hour in all directions.

4th.—2 brent geese, a long flying shot, and the only chance I got all day. The birds had enough of me last evening, and removed their quarters to Pilewell.

6th.—Up in the dark. Wet weather came on, and not a chance was to be seen. The geese were all to the east, but we dare not run too far to leeward with a stiff south-wester. Heard all the gunners' reports in Lymington, and found that I had killed more birds than all of them put together.

7th.—Up at six, and off the whole day, but never had a shot; so brought my gun and gear ashore for a thorough good furbish, putting the great punt to her moorings in order to be ready if there should again come a chance for some birds.

9th.—Busy all day ashore. Meanwhile the whole army of geese appeared under my windows, but I was not prepared, and the tyros flew out and drove them away.

14th.—As there were lots of geese about yesterday during a heavy south gale, I put my great gun afloat again to-day. I, however, saw but few birds in comparison to those of yester-day, and the only chance I got was 2 brent geese, at an im-mense distance, for want of water, which prevented my making perhaps the best shot I ever made this season, as the geese were all together, and, what is unusual, indeed very rare, they kept feeding till daylight was gone, instead of going off to sea at sunset. We both got out and pushed the great punt over the mud till we could move her no longer; so that had there been two inches more water we might have got close to these birds, about 200, all in a lump together. No such chance again, I fear.

15*th*.—Out again, but never fired a shot, or even heard the report of a gun all day. Weather mild, and nothing to be seen but a few geese that would not remain in one place long enough at a time to set up to them in the punt.

16*th*.—Up at a quarter to six and off till one, but neither fired nor heard a shot. Off again from three till six, and, after waiting on about eighty geese for near two hours, and then getting them in such a good place and so thick together that I must have stopped half the company, an infernal scoundrel ran in at them with a black sailing boat and drove them to sea for the night.

17*th to* 19*th*.—Sunday. South-westers and heavy rain. Not out, but kept great gun afloat and loaded for the chance of the geese, which occasionally appear in one grand company.

21*st*.—White frost and butterfly day; nothing about but one flock of geese that would not rest five minutes in one place. Got 6 shore birds with the popgun, and then blew off the large gun, in order to clean it out a little, and though the flint barrel had been loaded since the 14th and the detonator ever since the 13th, and left the whole time afloat in the most miserable wet gales that it was possible to weather, yet both barrels went as instantaneously as if fresh loaded in a sunny day. I once had this gun afloat for several weeks, and it went equally well.

N.B.—Not a bird had been killed while I was away; but on my arrival I had the delight to hear that Harry Troth, the man who ruined our Keyhaven harbour, was gone off, bag and baggage, into Norfolk to be under keeper of Hazeborough Lighthouse, for which appointment both he and I have to thank my own exertions with the Trinity Board, where I received the most polite attention from Mr. Herbert, the commander and secretary, on whom I waited the moment I got to town this last time. Never was there a better appointment.

It has put a starving family into comfortable independence, and ridded Keyhaven of a redhot young gunner, who did more harm in one week than our harbour had before suffered for nearly a quarter of a century. Troth's punt being a very pretty one, built by Sam Singer's workmen on my plan, I took care to secure her for *2l.* lest she may again be launched to the ruin of my amusement.

February 8th.—A hard frost and some easterly breezes. Afloat all day, and should have had some geese, but was 'flanked' all the afternoon by some greenhorn dandies, who spoiled me a capital shot in their Quixotic, and of course unsuccessful, attempt at killing a goose.

10*th.*—Saw some geese, but, as they were too far in on the mud, I left them to 'get a good haunt,' as the tyros were no longer in our harbour.

11*th.*—An easterly gale, with hard frost. Brought home 14 wigeon. Geese to the eastward, so had nothing to do with them.

12*th.*—The hardest frost this year, but so much white in it as to make it suspicious as to continuing. Afloat from morning till night; brought in 14 wigeon, and a splendid wild swan, the first heard of this season. I fell in with 4 swans off Pennington Lake. They were all scattered, and about to rise when we got within about 200 yards of them. I took one with the first barrel and 'floored' him, but he recovered and rose. In the second barrel I had swan shot, and cut up my bird handsomely. After bagging him, I took up the spyglass and saw the first bird lying sick on the mud. To make dead sure, I reloaded the great gun, and we paddled up close to him and were just getting the gun to bear when an old fool named Dagville, from Southampton, a notorious coast nuisance, fancied he could 'put salt on his tail,' and drove him from under our noses to where he may never be seen again. Always some lubberly ass about when a fine chance of a shot occurs.

14*th*.—A fine day, with a little frost again. Up before daylight and cruised all the way to Pilewell, but not a bird did I see, as the water was low, and the mud covered with periwinkle men for five miles to supply two vessels just arrived to get supplies for Billingsgate. Came home at twelve, dined at half-past two, and went out again from four till after dark, when the tide was up and the coast clear. Made a lovely shot, the first I got: 10 brent geese, at about 160 yards, out of the only little company I saw.

15*th*.—A sharp frost, and yet the 'winklemen were on the mud all day, so I drove into Lymington to leave a hamper with my last 10 geese, the fattest I ever saw, directed to Mr. Anson, for Prince Albert and her Majesty at Brighton.

17*th*.—Up at half-past four, out till eleven, when the 'winklemen mobbed the mud. Dined at five and went out from seven till ten under the moon; found some wigeon, but no water, so left them quiet for a higher tide.

18*th*.—Off at daylight again, but not a chance, as the tides were so dead that the 'winklemen were on all day.

19*th*.—Another early start, but no birds, though an intensely cold easterly wind.

20*th*.—A bitter cold white frost. Afloat early, and never felt the cold more severely. Not a bird to shoot at. In by twelve, and, after a second breakfast, drove to Barton, where I heard that the wild fowl were swarming under the cliffs, where no boat could venture with safety. Saw about 2,000 wigeon, covering about two miles of water, and consequently so thin that, had their legs been tied to an anchor, no gun could have killed more than two or three at a shot; and the coastguardmen there told me that most of them flew at night to the Christchurch rivers.

21*st*.—A bitter white frost. Not a chance all day. Afloat by moonlight from eight till near one A.M.; wigeon so scattered that we could hardly get two together. Brought in only 4.

23*rd.*—Sunday.

24*th.*—Out all day. Brought in 6 pintails, 5 splendid cocks and 1 hen, the first I had shot at this season. I fell in with 10 of them, and cut up 8 in fine style, but one beat us in a heavy sea, and another scrambled across the mud and got 'prigged' by a clod and his dog. A strong north-wester, but the beastly old 'carrion crow,' a boat-sailing bird pirate from Yarmouth, drove the place so unmercifully under sail that we lost all chance for some geese that again appeared. Prepared to go out from ten till two at night, but the wind set into the moon, so I went to bed.

25*th.*—Read crawled on the mud before daylight, after the moon had cleared itself from the wind, and brought in 5 wigeon. I went out till one, and then out again in the afternoon. Not a bird to be seen, and a wet south-wester after this morning's sharp white frost.

March 1*st.*—Easterly gale, winter again; about 300 geese off my 'leak,' a splendid place to steal on them. All but getting a fine shot, when that smutty old 'varmint' cadger Dagville, of Southampton, drove them all off with his trumpery set-out.

5*th.*—Intense frost. Pain in limbs and quite stiff. Shipped lots of poor man's plaster and went afloat; and, instead of getting worse, I found great benefit from the sea air and excitement, and should have had some fair sport had it not been for the Yarmouth blackguards who followed me on purpose to prevent my shooting. (N.B.—Such has been the ruin of our fine channel, by the sailing scoundrels from Yarmouth, the mud crawlers of Keyhaven, and the banditti of shore snobs, that at this moment about 2,000 wigeon remain for miles at sea under the cliffs, and betake themselves at night to all the fresh waters in the country.) The coldest night known for many years. Read, after crawling on the mud all night, brought in 1 wigeon.

6*th.*—Tremendous north-east gale, and water freezing to

the oars. Afloat early, and got one small double shot at the mouth of Pennington Leak, and then retreated for the safety of our lives.

7th.—Severest weather known for years. Harbour frozen up, and such a sea in the Channel as no punt could face. An absolute Siberia to weather, and yet not the chance of a shot for a recompense. Reade had a blank night and I a blank day, and glad to get home in safety.

8th.—The frost relaxed and the ice became broken, so as to leave the harbour clear at ebb tide. Very few birds, and all of them in the wash of the heavy breakers. Shooting impossible. Thousands of wigeon at sea under shelter of the cliffs, and now we want a south-wester to beat them out of this berth of defiance.

10th.—The bitter north-east wind kept howling away all yesterday and all to-day. Nothing inside the harbour, and an awful sea outside.

12th.—Cold, though moderate, weather; so went afloat all day, and was not in till past eight in the evening; got 2 brent geese at about 300 yards with a mould cartridge, and afterwards 9 wigeon.

13th.—The most bitter day that ever was weathered. Intense frost, with a north-east hurricane that one could hardly stand against. Prisoner for the day, of course. But in the evening tried 'the flight,' knowing the birds must fly low, wild and cunning as these were become after five months' incessant siege. But no! The birds actually fluttered against the tide all the way round Hurst rather than fly in their usual course, because they had not the power to mount up for 500 feet above ground as usual in order to avoid the popshooters. I was busy all the morning writing, and, among other things, sketching some amendments to the game laws, on which a committee has just been appointed in the House of Commons.

14th.—A north-east gale, with the hardest frost known

for years. Water jugs frozen in bedrooms, harbour blocked up &c. &c. Weathered a heavy sea, and bagged 3 brent geese. After I got home, and put the punt to distant moorings from the frozen harbour, I marked down 5 ducks and mallards in the Keyhaven river, and got 2 mallards and 1 duck, an immensely long shot, with my wonderful 'old Fullerd' shoulder gun that had not been used for two seasons.

15*th.*—A Siberian gale the whole day. Small birds starved to death with cold. No living afloat; and, in short, petrified with cold, and all for nothing. Too late to bring foreign birds, and all the stale birds blown farther westward.

16*th.*—Sunday. Heavy snow all day, and intense frost. Redwings and thrushes half starved, and rabbles of boys knocking them down with sticks in a bitter north-east gale.

18*th.*—Read came in with 25 wigeon, in two shots (16 and 9), the best mud-crawling shot for many years. Afloat myself all day, but never saw a chance.

24*th.*—Out all the morning, and again from nine till two under a lovely moon, and with a fine full calm tide, and never heard a bird.

25*th.*—Out from ten till two for the chance of the rough drizzling rain bringing in a few birds. All I got or shot at was 1 brent goose, and I then, finding all shooting was at an end for the season, mustered 'all hands,' and brought up to store all my gear, my great gun, and my punt, and bid adieu to the longest, though by no means the most successful, winter I ever had to weather.

Wild fowl &c. up to Lady Day: Wild fowl—6 ducks and mallards, 206 wigeon, 10 teal, 6 pintails at a shot, 3 tufted ducks, 3 burrough ducks, 94 brent geese, 2 barnacle geese, 1 wild swan. Total, 331.

Waders—37 plover, 14 godwits, 4 curlews, 1 olive, 2 ring dotterel, 196 shore birds. Total, 254.

331 wild fowl, 254 waders. Grand total, 585.

36 game, 585 fowl &c. Grand total, 621 head. A very long and yet not a brilliant season.

April 11th to 14th.—London. Laid up in bed unable to even sit up, and on the 14th (Monday) lost the Philharmonic on the Queen's night.

15th and 16th.—Laid up still, and on the latter day lost going to Charles Kemble's readings.

May 3rd.—Longparish. Better, and availed myself of the first two hours' leisure I had to hobble to the river with my fly rod, and caught 6 brace of large trout, but all so badly in season owing to the winterly spring, that one I threw in again, half starved, and the others proved unworthy of dressing.

12th.—Whit-Monday, and anniversary of our fight at the Douro in 1801.

July 15th.—Keyhaven. Up at six, and off all day and till nine at night in the 'Solent' steamer, first at Portsmouth, and then home round the island, after being all day in the thick of the grand naval review, and near to the royal yacht, in which were her Majesty and Prince Albert, with the King and Queen of the Belgians. The Queen Dowager and Prince George were in other yachts, and never before was there such a magnificent naval sight. The splendid ships reviewed were the 'St. Vincent,' 120 guns; 'Trafalgar,' 120; 'Queen,' 110; 'Rodney,' 92; 'Albion,' 90; 'Canopus,' 84; 'Vanguard,' 80; 'Superb,' 80.

These eight line-of-battle ships formed the experimental squadron under Admiral Sir Hyde Parker, and after the review majestically sailed off for their trial cruise in the Bay of Biscay &c. with a fine, fair, and brisk breeze. The day seemed made on purpose for the occasion, and in my life I never saw such a magnificent sight.

16th.—As busy as busy could be from morning till night.

22nd.—Busy every day up to this day with painters &c., having six punts to repair, and consequently such a prisoner (to keep them up to their work) that I've had no holiday except going to the royal show last Tuesday, and having now got all done that required my presence I booked my place to get away to-morrow. This afternoon the royal yacht, with the Queen and Prince Albert, passed Keyhaven, and possibly the Prince may have recognised the place, the engraving of which he so admired in my book on sporting that I dedicated and presented to his Royal Highness.

23rd.—Left Keyhaven for London per morning coach, and then on by express train. In the next carriage to me were the Duke of Cambridge and Prince George, and we went from Southampton to Vauxhall in ten minutes under the two hours.

CHAPTER XXXVIII

1845

September 1st.—Though taken so ill that I scarcely closed my eyes all last night, yet I contrived to weather the hardest day's campaign that we have had for many years. We were out from ten till eight in a dry north-east gale, and the birds, of course, as 'wild as hawks.' Nearly all snap shooting. Did miracles considering all things. I bagged 27 partridges, and not a small bird among the whole lot. On our return home the whole banditti were so dead beat as to be worked off their never-before-failing appetites.

3rd.—Another severely hard day, and not home till near eight o'clock. Brought in 29 partridges and 2 hares. Charles Heath, who joined us after beating the outskirts, got 11 birds and 1 hare; so that our combined lot of partridges was just 20 brace, on which old Siney petitioned for a 'butcher's halloo,' in which we indulged him, though our shout in good old times was always at every 20 brace from my own gun alone. All hands so dead beat again that we could hardly crawl home from the hills.

6th.—Another hard day, and still a cold easterly gale. Not home till eight. Never shot better. Brought home 19 partridges and 4 hares, and never fired a blank shot the whole day.

8th.—By blazing away at all distances I contrived to bring in 18 partridges and 1 hare.

19th.—Brought home my old master, the great 'lion' of

Europe, the Chevalier Kalkbrenner, and his wonderfully talented son Arthur, who came to pass a day with us.

20th.—Kalkbrenner entreated me to let his son see me shoot; so to oblige them I went out in a gale of wind. But I only got one very long shot, and by accident happened to kill and bag the single partridge that I fired at, and but for this lucky hit I should have had what I never before experienced —a blank day.

Game killed in September 1845 by myself: 134 partridges, 10 hares. Total, 144 head.

A fair breed of birds, but as wild as hawks on and from the first day. I was out but eleven times in all, and seldom for more than half a day. Though weak and unwell, I shot brilliantly, but could not fag as usual.

October 1st.—Up early, and scoured all our inclosed country, finishing with our little wood, before we came home to lunch. Not a pheasant to be seen the whole day. But after a fagging expedition on both sides of the river we came home to a seven o'clock dinner with 2 hares, 1 rabbit, 1 snipe (the only one yet seen), and 3 partridges. Most excellent shooting, and a satisfactory day, except not being able to find one single pheasant. All of us as tired as dogs, and a grand blow-out in the hall for all the beaters and markers by way of climax to the first of October.

6th.—London. While in town I took the opportunity of putting my name in a long list of other names petitioning the Queen for what the 'Duke' refused—some little mark of honour for the Peninsular war of seven years, similar to what was granted at Waterloo for three days. I entered myself thus at the 'United Service Gazette' office: 'Peter Hawker, Lieutenant-Colonel, formerly Senior Captain of the 14th Dragoons, and commander of the squadron that gained for the regiment the motto of "Douro."'

29th.—Keyhaven. Took a sail, with a brisk wind, all over our channel, and every bird that we saw was 7 wigeon, off in the breakers, and these were the very first Read had set eyes on this season, though out repeatedly in his punt. In times of old we had generally killed the best half our winter birds before the end of October, provided there was no hard weather to bring over a second flight.

November 1*st.*—Left Keyhaven for Longparish. On arrival at Southampton found that not a wild fowl had been killed there, though the wind was north-east. Having a spare half-hour I saw the magnetic telegraph at the rail station; and the gentleman who exhibited this wonderful invention, after he had conferred on all his official messages, asked me if I had any trifling question to ask for experiment. I said I would beg the favour of him to say, 'Are there any wild fowl at Portsmouth now?'

5*th.*—Longparish. Having heard that a pheasant had been seen on my estate, I sallied out with a levy *en masse* and scoured all the country side, and bagged 2 splendid cock pheasants, all we found. Never saw one hare all day, though the foxhounds drove Wherwell Wood in full cry, and passed us in gallant style.

7*th.*—Drove, for a day's business, into Andover. Best horse taken so lame that I drove her in jeopardy, and saved her from falling twenty times. When within a mile of home I turned round to bow to Counsellor Missing, and at that very instant down came the mare and broke her knees. Why was all this? Because we took Friday for a day of business, and, moreover, a single magpie foretold our disaster; but thank God it was no worse.

12*th.*—Took my banditti out all day in search of another cock pheasant that had been seen, but never found him.

15*th.*—Heard of the old cock again, but could not find him, nor could I get a shot at a single head of game.

1846

January 5*th.*—Bitter white frost again; and in order to shake off the shivers that I've had for a week, I shipped my long water boots and waded up the river. I killed in good style all that I shot at, viz. 3 jack snipes, 2 of them a brilliant double shot to front and rear, with 9 moorhens and 3 divers. I then shifted my boots, and beat all our wood and the rows, and the only head of game I set eyes on was 1 rabbit, which I bagged. The shooting here now is an absolute waste of time, but still I was well pleased to have such a satisfactory beginning for the new year.

13*th.*—Keyhaven. Afloat at daylight. Found that scarcely a fowl had been killed, though the increase of punt shooters was awful. I saw, off at sea, about 80 geese, and about half as many wigeon, and heard that many more were off outside the beach, but that all the army of gunners put together had not made up twenty couple the whole season.

15*th.*—Took a sail all the way up to Pilewell, and about the Western Channel; never saw a wild fowl, or even a plover, the whole day, so of course gave up all thoughts of launching a punt. The other gunners all complained that it was useless to go out.

My punts were all newly done up for gunning, and I never was better prepared for wild fowl; but I found the unprecedented scarcity of birds at Keyhaven to be such that I would not disgrace myself by putting a great gun afloat. A general complaint all over England about the scarcity of wild fowl, cocks, snipes, and all other winter birds.

February 11*th.*—London. The first Levee of the season, which I made a point of attending, as my bad foot prevented me from going last season, and I had not yet made my bow since the great kindness of Prince Albert on the dedication to his Royal Highness of my ninth edition. Coming home I found a lady's jewels in the cab that I hailed, and, of course, took immediate steps for their being restored to her.

June 17th.—London. Went with my old friend General Brotherton to Woolwich to see the wonderful effect of Charles Lancaster's new conical rifle ball, with which he some weeks ago hit a target five times in twenty-four shots at the incredible distance of 1,200 yards.

25th.—Went again to Woolwich to see another trial of Lancaster's conical rifle ball. For the first hour's shooting he had the disadvantage of strong wind and rain; but at last he overcame the want of proper elevation, and the weather moderated, and he then hit the target (nine feet square) six times out of nine successive shots at 1,200 yards.

CHAPTER XXXIX

1846

September 1st.—Longparish. A dry north-easterly breeze all day. Birds extremely wild, not only when together in coveys, but even after they were dispersed. The only good lay in the country was one large piece of high turnips. Here I found about 40 birds, all dispersed about the field; and yet, although my two dogs were over-careful, I never got a shot at one of these birds. However, by sheer slavery, and being out from half-past nine till half-past seven, I did contrive to do miracles by bringing home 20 partridges and 6 hares. Furgo Farm was without any lay at all, and almost destitute of game. I therefore went off to Bullington for the afternoon, or must have come home with only 4 brace and 1 hare. Having no appetite, I became so weak towards the end of the day that I could hardly stand, and consequently missed 2 fair shots. Except this momentary breakdown, I shot splendidly all day; and had there been lay for the birds and scent for the dogs, I should, no doubt, have bagged my 20 brace. We were all completely knocked up; and as for me, I was so dead beat that I scarcely slept the night. So much for the first day of '46.

3rd.—Another severe day with the wild birds in the dry north-easter. Out from ten till seven. Brought in 20 partridges. So dead beat that I could take nothing but some tea when I got home.

5th.—Out for half a day near home (being too weak for the grand beat round Bullington), and bagged 12 partridges, having made some very long shots, and fired but one blank shot, and that a long second-barrel one.

1st week, out two days and two half-days.—63 partridges, 9 hares, 1 rabbit, 1 snipe. Total, 74 head.

The country was never so bare, birds so wild, or scent so bad as this first week of September.

26th.—Took out my rod, and in my life I never saw the trout more kind. In about an hour I caught enough to have filled a large hand basket; but, not wishing to destroy trout at this season, I kept only 4 brace of first-rate large ones. If I had fished all day, and kept all I caught, I might have gone about bragging of my 40 or 50 brace!

N.B.—The barren state of the fields, and the dry easterly wind, made the shooting so bad for the whole month of September that I gave it up, and went to town after the first week. The birds would scarcely allow even the dogs to come within two gunshots of them; and even when dispersed would run all over the country, instead of lying for a shot.

October 1st.—Had the usual muster of all my myrmidons with the forlorn hope of getting 1 pheasant the first day; and left not a yard of my beat untried. After a fag, from seven till a seven o'clock dinner, I had the luck to bring home 2 pheasants; these were all I had a chance at. But we sprung 2 more pheasants that we chased for hours; till at last we got each of them out of covert, where we could have made dead sure of them. Unluckily, however, they were a few yards out of bounds, and there I declined going.

15th.—Started off in search of a rare bird that had been seen yesterday, but when I ran home for a gun he was gone. To-day I fell in with him, and, after following him about the river for near an hour, I crawled up to him, and did his business with Eley's cartridge. The name of the bird is the 'grey phalarope,' and though Bewick says 'it has seldom been met with in the British Isles,' yet I once before killed one near Keyhaven. The bird, as Bewick says, is a native of the Arctic regions, and is somewhat less than a snipe, with feet like a coot and partly webbed; it swims like a dabchick, and runs like a plover.

16th.—Went out to try a water dog, for which purpose I killed 3 coots; but the dog was 'no go.' The only sporting bird I had a chance at was a little jack snipe that I got; and coming home, what should I see and kill, but another phalarope!

21st.—The country being, just now, destitute of everything but wind, rain, and dirt, I returned to London.

31st.—London. Went to see Mr. Charles Lancaster after his miraculous escape in firing the new gun cotton, and the first-rate strong double gun that it blew all to atoms. This extraordinary composition, which everyone is eager about, strikes me as having more expansive than projectile powers; and therefore more dangerous and less effective than any gunpowder, except for blasting rocks and such-like uses, for which it is the best material in existence.

November 11th.—Having been unwell with the influenza, and the long batch of wet and unhealthy weather having changed to a dry north-easter, I this day ran down to Keyhaven for change of air.

12th.—Keyhaven. A brisk north-easter with a little black frost. Up at daylight, and not having launched a punt all last season (as there were no birds), it took me a long time to get even the small set-out in order; and what with caulking and other jobs, the day was gone. I went out from three till dusk. It blew too fresh to venture far, and I had no chance for a shot; but I saw 24 geese, the first that had yet been heard of.

13th.—Had prepared to go off before daylight this morning, but was taken so ill that I was obliged to give it up. Read therefore went instead of me; but he never saw the geese, nor did he hear any birds in the night, though crawling till past twelve.

14th and 15th.—Sunday. Laid up with the influenza, but lost nothing, as Read had been slaving to no purpose, day and night. My punt and loaded (single) stanchion gun remain afloat, and the east gale continues.

16th.—I was, thank God, so much better as to be able to go off, for a few hours, afloat; but the wind had hauled out to southward, and there were no wild fowl about; but I blew off my five-days-loaded charge in a glorious manner at smaller game. There were 14 plover pitched on some sea-weed; and I was just in time to get before some other gunners who were after them, but who behaved very civilly—not to spoil my shot (for which I gave them something to drink), and I had the luck to bag every one of the plover.

20th.—A furious hurricane all last night, from south by west (the very focus for a flood), and so fearful was I of the sea bursting over the banks about half-past ten (when there was yet an hour to high water), that I kept a fly nearly an hour at the door before I would venture away to Lymington, where I afterwards went. A wreck off our north shore. 'Hands' saved. Cargoes of railway timber rescued by our coastguard, who got a poor little goldfinch, drowned in his cage. A few wigeon swept into our harbour from their constant haunt of the open sea, which they could no longer live in.

21st.—Still rough, wet and squally. Out all day, but chiefly at dirty work in the mud; as the furious tempest of yesterday had carried away the bed of seaweed from my plover island, and nothing was left for birds to pitch on; so I lashed the new cargo within an old net made fast to the surrounding stakes of the fence.

23rd.—Up early, and by afternoon had completed another island (of reeds nailed with laths down to a large frame, and moored with an old chain and sunk post, so as to be always afloat, at one regular level, for the gun, at all tides—when there would be water over the mud), and my mock birds[1] answered so well that the curlews all came and sat with them for some time.

24th.—About five this evening I had a splendid chance for a grand shot, but had a most annoying disappointment. There came on a dead calm, and every curlew, plover and dunlin in the country had concentrated on my island. I put in a cartridge of small shot, and got almost on board them under cover of nightfall, and, to my great surprise (as it had never occurred since we got all the patent cartridges to perfection), the cartridge 'balled' and flew out to sea like a cannon ball, and, except one dunlin that lay dead (Lord knows by what means), I never touched a feather; and away went a cloud of birds, out of which I expected to fill two bushel baskets.

25th.—The westerly gales and rain having put an end to all chance of sport on the coast for the present, I had this day a grand furbish, and laid up what little gear I had put in commission.

28th.—Longparish. A stiff day to prove my 'pluck.' Went to bed last evening after dinner with a chill that I took in a deadly cold 'sniveller' coming home from Andover; and my sudorific did not warm me till near morning, when I got up at seven and breakfasted, in order to be ready by daylight. I then went off to the river for 3 teal that I did not find. Then off with a cry of dogs and followers in search of 2 cock pheasants that had been seen on my estate, and after our beating the whole country in despair, they at last flew out of 'Tracy's Dell' pit. Though a long and intercepted shot, I

[1] 'New Dodge.' Recipe for making a mock bird that I defy any gunner to distinguish from a living one at the distance of half a gunshot. Take a piece of wheat straw, and double it up to about the size of a curlew or plover. Tie or sew it up tight in some brown silk or stuff of any kind. Tie under it a piece of white linen rag for the silvery breast. Then roll up in a ball some pine tow (oakum has a smell of tar which wild birds may not like), and tie it up in the brown stuff. Run a wooden skewer through this ball, so as to come out like the bill. Sew this head to the body, and run two skewers through the centre of the body for legs.

hit one of them so hard, that after a chase as good as a fox hunt we put him in the bag. We then persevered till we found the other, which I blazed away at through a thick hedgerow, and which we had another long chase to get. Coming home, a hen sprung within a yard of me on the wrong side of a very little hedge. This artful bird gave me the hardest chase of all; but at last I killed her at about 75 yards with a patent cartridge, just as she was flying out of bounds. We were then all so knocked up as to need refreshment. Afterwards stormed the 'Moors' wood, though found nothing there. I then shipped my long water boots and waded the river for snipes; but the white frost had made what few there were as wild as curlews. I, however, cut down a miraculously long double shot with two of Eley's cartridges. I pocketed also the only jack snipe I saw; and then blew off my two barrels, by killing a double shot at 2 moor-hens. Here ended a most satisfactory little day.

If this is not a good day's work for a man who is weak and suffering and without appetite, I know not what is.

December 10th.—Received this morning an account of the death of one of the oldest and best of all my friends, Sir Charles Morgan, of Tredegar Park, who died last Saturday, in the eighty-sixth year of his age. Another severe blow for my valued friend, poor Lady Rodney (his daughter), and a sad embargo on all the princely hospitality of the Christmas at Tredegar.

15th.—Keyhaven. Up by candlelight, and on from seven till half-past one getting the great gun afloat, and also her tender the 'Feather' punt, both of which had been laid up for two years in store, as there was nothing to put any punt afloat for last year. Read, Payne, Peter Fifield, another and I were all in one furious bustle the whole morning to get through the jobs of caulking, powder drying, cutting through ice, to get afloat &c. We went out for a few hours to see that all was right; but it was the wrong time of tide to expect a shot, or even to see any fowl, though we heard that there were thousands on the coast.

16th.—Out from daylight till dark in as cold a north wind as could be weathered. Both water and land in one continued siege by bungling shooters afloat and ashore, so that scarcely a place could be found for the fowl to pitch and rest on till one could go into them for a shot. I got but two little shots the whole day, though did handsomely with them ; the first was 10 grey plover, the second 4 wigeon.

18th.—A nipping white frost ; out all day, and never had the chance of a shot. In the afternoon the sea under the Isle of Wight was like a mirror, and there were several trips of wigeon floating down on the ebb, where I should have got a good lot of birds ; but there were no less than seven boat-loads of popgunning blockheads, who destroyed all prospect of firing my gun.

19th.—The white frost (as I told everyone it would do) broke up at the spring tides of the new moon, and we had last night a westerly gale and rain. It blew and rained hard all this morning, and, as is usual on the break up, the wigeon came into the harbour. But the sport was spoiled by a greenhorn stanchion gunner, who frightened all the birds and nearly got drowned into the bargain. Read went off in self-defence, and got 1 duck and 1 wigeon. I, not choosing to run a race with opposition in a pour of rain, remained at home to write a batch of letters, and despatch a basket of fowl for Prince Albert at Windsor Castle. I went out in the afternoon, when the rain abated, but there was not a fowl in the harbour.

21st.—Up before daylight, and off in such a gale of wind and rain that the birds could hardly weather it at sea, and therefore I expected they would come inside at high water. They did so ; but in spite of wind and weather the shore snobs kept up such an incessant fire at birds a quarter of a mile off that it was folly to expect a shot. I was all but firing at about

50 ducks and mallards that I got all in a line, when a blockhead cracked off his popgun and put them all up. The coast here is absolutely ruined.

1847

January 1*st.*—Longparish. Began the new year with a capital shot from my decoy hut at 2 mallards and 1 duck, the latter a most extraordinary bird that I sent to taxidermist Leadbeater, with one of the mallards that had beautiful pink (instead of white) under his wings. I then shot at 2 more ducks and bagged them both. An excellent start for 1847.

11*th.*—After a bath nearly hot enough to scald a pig, and a dose of paregoric and sweet spirits of nitre last night, I was, thank God, so much 'to windward' to-day as to be able to put on my thick wild-fowl coat, and try my two large shoulder-duck guns 'Big Joe' and 'Old Fullerd'—two such guns as I think are unrivalled.

16*th.*—Having heard from old Read that there were again some birds on the coast, I this day started for Keyhaven. Old Read greeted me on my arrival, and said the birds were wild and much scattered; he had seen some geese.

18*th.*—Keyhaven. Up an hour before daylight to put the great gun anointed with neat's-foot oil and all the gear afloat, but could not get under way till near eleven, and the tide obliged us to be in by four. I brought home 11 brent geese and 1 wigeon. I should have had treble the number but for the bunglers afloat and ashore, who spoiled me two fair shots. A good show of birds and the weather most beautiful; an easterly wind, and a frost not too hard.

19*th.*—A dead calm. Under way about eight o'clock, and cruised twelve miles 'up alongshore;' but above Pilewell nothing but gentlemen gunners in all directions, and the weather being too fine the birds were all at sea, and would not venture in harbour, or even in channel. The only chance

I had was at a few stray ducks and wigeon, nearly under the Isle of Wight.

25*th.*—A tremendous gale all yesterday (Sunday) and all last night, which drove the wigeon from off at sea to the harbour and western channel. I had finished breakfast long before daylight this morning, but a torrent of rain kept me from going afloat till near eight, and then the tide was gone and the birds had got off in Channel. I took one shot and knocked down 15 wigeon.

26*th.*—Off again at daybreak. Saw a few wigeon, but they were so driven about by bunglers in sailing boats that I had only one passing shot at a few rapidly flying across at about 200 yards. I knocked down 2 in brilliant style, but the winged one beat us in a heavy sea, as the weather this day was very rough. I also punted up to a single goose with Westley Richards's extraordinary shooting musket, and killed him dead at above sixty yards.[1]

27*th.*—Another daybreak attempt, but the rain and hurricane of last night had blown away nearly all the birds, and I just saved my blank by popping off my pistol to put up some wigeon that were buried in the waves, and I knocked down a few of them at an enormous distance.

28*th.*—An awful hurricane all last night and till daylight this morning, and there would have been a flood had not Mrs. Whitby by my entreaties raised her banks fifteen inches, as the sea was even now within ten inches of coming over the banks. I landed my large punt, the 'Petrel,' in the road, and from there housed her in the boathouse. While the men were furbishing up the things I took the musket to blow her off, and had the luck to get the very bird I had long tried, even with the great gun, a huge saddle-back gull that was

[1] When I got home I weighed the barrel of this uncommonly good gun; and it proved to be precisely 6 lb.—the exact weight also of the two barrels of my unrivalled cripple stopper (called 'Bloody Burnett'), that none of my sporting doubles can compete with, although they all carry the same charge. This tells in favour of having plenty of metal, and particularly near the breechings.

blown by the raging tempest into the marsh close by; he measured 5 feet 3 inches from tip to tip of wings. I once killed 5 at a shot of these huge monsters when a youth, and a lieutenant in the 14th Dragoons, but had never killed one since that 'olden time.' The south-west gale had driven everything far to leeward, so that for the present all gunning was 'done for,' and I therefore prepared for a start away from Keyhaven for Longparish.

February 9th.—I got to Keyhaven again before six to-day. Read's report on my arrival was meagre as to wigeon, but rich as to geese. *Demain nous verrons.* Never could finer weather come for a gunner. A black north-easter, and all inland a region of snow.

10*th.*—Up by six, and saved high water to get the 'Petrel' afloat, and ship great gun and gear.

Afloat for about two hours, and never got a chance. And no wonder, as the shore snobs to windward were all day long making war on the scattered larks and thrushes, and I heard at least three hundred pops in the course of the morning.

11*th.*—Out the whole day, no chance.

12*th.*—Off at daylight. Such a savage white frost (the forerunner of wind and rain) that we had to beat our way through ice for nearly a quarter of a mile. I got a shot at 2 ducks and lost them both, and at 2 wigeon, and bagged them both, and these were my only chances from morning till night. There were several companies of birds off in channel, but the snobs would not allow them time to pitch, and the geese never remained five minutes in one place.[1]

13*th.*—Not a chance for a wild fowl, though out all day. But the onset (the first thing in the morning) amply compensated for what would have otherwise been a blank day. Having loaded one of my barrels with a 12 oz. (No. 6) cartridge of Eley, in order to be prepared for a large flock of dunlins that were generally seen very early in the morning, I

[1] Read, after mud crawling all night, brought in a wigeon.

made it my business to attend to them, and luckily caught them on a fine stage of floating sea-weeds. I cut a lane through them, and mowed them down as with a scythe, picking up 178 dunlins and plover. My other barrel being loaded with shot for geese, I would not degrade this great shot by discharging it with what would not have done proportional justice.

15*th.*—A gale of wind and heavy rain, which brought the birds into harbour. About half-past ten we weathered it and dropped down on them, and by using two cartridges of 'A A' shot I had the luck to bring in 5 of the best brent geese I've killed this season. We were no less pleased than astonished at the distance at which I killed these birds (about 300 yards). But a fair shot now is next to impossible, as all the birds are become extremely wild.

16*th.*—Off again in wind and rain, and should have had a better chance than yesterday, but the geese had no time to pitch for the shore poppers.

17*th.*—Afloat early as soon as the tide served, and left Read with a signal flag and the great punt to windward, and Payne and his punt with another signal flag to leeward, and waited at home for my letters and paper, instead of off in the punt. But no signal was made to call me, and when I walked overland to the punt about eleven I found that hundreds of geese and wigeon had come down with the high wind to drop in our flooded harbour; but not a bird of them could pitch, as they had a royal salute from the kill-nothing-poppers ashore, and the sailing about the harbour of the blank-firing 'snobs' afloat. The 'break-up,' therefore, which for a few days (if windy) was always our grand time to make great shots, was so completely 'done for' that I availed myself of the after-flood tide to get everything ashore. Here ends the gunning season, in the whole of which I've fired but one blank shot, and that out of reach.

18*th.*—The harbour swarming with birds, owing to the

constant wind and rain which had cleared it of the 'one-suit-of-clothes snobs,' and old Read had bagged 1 goose with his old rattletrap mud gun.

20th.—Game killed in the season: 87 partridges, 16 hares (all in September and all I shot at), 3 pheasants (all I saw), 40 snipes and jacks, 6 rabbits, 3 wood pigeons; total, 155. Wild fowl: 39 ducks and mallards (36 of them from my new decoy hut), 31 wigeon, 1 pintail, 2 teal, 1 sheldrake, 28 brent geese. Total, 102. Coast-waders: 2 phalaropes, 1 saddle-back, 39 plover, 313 dunlins. Total, 355. 102 wild fowl, 355 waders. Total, 457. 155 game, 457 fowl &c.; grand total, 612 head.

N.B.—No game shooting worth going out for after September, and Keyhaven ruined by 'snobs.' I never shot better, both by land and by sea, so am content.

April 11th.—Peter was married to Miss Fraser, of Stirling, N.B. I was married to Peter's mother on the 19th of March, 1811. God send him good luck, and less trouble than has, up to the present date, been inflicted on his father.

25th.—Went from London to inspect Tonbridge Wells, and never was I more glad than to get away from this pigeon-plucking watering-place, the only way to see which without a royal fleecing would be to bargain a fly man, and run on direct to 'the rocks,' with a basket of grub, then walk back and survey the town, and when tired, rest in the rail carriage till you were hurled back to the London Bridge terminus.

May 13th.—Longparish. Having a demand for fish, I brandished a fly rod. The trout were so sulky, owing to the cold storms, that it took me a long time to catch 10 brace.

15th.—Took out my fly rod and got 6 brace of fine trout, besides lots thrown in, in little more than an hour.

CHAPTER XL

1847

September 1*st.*—Longparish. A dry and strong gale of wind all day, with heavy showers after four o'clock. Birds constantly on the run and wilder than ever, and scent most miserable. Furgo Farm almost barren of cover as well as of game, so went on for the afternoon to Bullington. Did absolute wonders, considering all circumstances. I came home with 28 partridges and 3 quails, and out of all these 31 very fine full-grown birds there was not one old bird. This is what I never saw or even heard of before. We got home at eight o'clock quite tired, yet delighted with this extraordinary day.

List of game killed in September: 136 partridges, 8 quails, 1 landrail, 5 hares, 12 snipes, 1 teal, 1 spotted gallinule. Total, 164 head.

All my best shooting was over at Bullington, where I could only take a few hours' sport at a time, as I was too weak to go far and fag hard, and was much interrupted by business.

October 1*st.*—Only 2 pheasants on all my estate—both cocks, and both came home to the larder, after as hard and grand a chase with a village rabble as ever old Smith had, with his crack foxhounds. We had five hours of it, before the two birds came to hand. I got 1 very old cock pheasant, and Charles Heath, who went with me, got the other, a young cock, and also a hare, and these were every head of game we saw.

On my return home before three, I found that my new cloth kite had arrived from town, so, tired as I was, I went off to try the effect of it before the day was over, and it answered so well that in two double shots off near Bullington, I killed 4 partridges. A most satisfactory day, notwithstanding it was Friday.

8th.—The birds would not let us get into the same field with them. Determined to 'serve them out,' I loaded 'Big Joe' with Eley, started at five in the evening in the cart, and was in again by half-past six, with 10 first-rate young partridges. Nothing like a duck gun from a horse and cart on the road to fill a bag, when all popgunning becomes a wild-goose chase.

16th.—Keyhaven. Availed myself of the first leisure day to put my gear and small punt ready, in case this easterly wind should stand, and bring more birds. Some wigeon have been seen, and Read has got a couple. After seeing that my punt was all right and tight, I tried the experiment of the kite, and it towed the punt so well that we think it will manage my large one also. The one we tried was the mere toy that I got the 4 partridges with on the 1st.

November 8th.—London. A letter from Read to say he had just got 32 wigeon at a shot, besides shooting 9 more that he did not get.

10th.—Came Read's second letter, to say not a bird had been seen or heard of since he posted his first letter, so it's lucky I did not go down. This shows the uncertainty of wildfowl shooting.

December 16th.—Keyhaven. Tried a large new kite on my improved plan, and it flew and answered admirably on shore, as well as in propelling a boat. Coast literally destitute.

28th.—A beautiful black frost. Up by candlelight, and ran down to Keyhaven. On my arrival old Read said there were plenty of wigeon, but they kept far at sea, and he had seen none in bounds, but nevertheless I ordered the grand set-out to be launched early to-morrow.

29th.—Up long before daylight, and got my fleet all in order by ten o'clock; and no sooner were we prepared for action, than round flew the cock to the southward, and away blew the frost. It is quite laughable that whenever I come to Keyhaven, I turn the weathercock the wrong way. We took a cruise up the Channel, but it was so rough that, had we gone far, we could not have got home in safety. Not a chance for a shot.

31*st.*—Old Read crawled on the mud all last night. Got two shots and came in with 6 wigeon. The day being calm I went off early, and cruised till the afternoon, but never set eyes on a single fowl, as the wigeon had gone off to sea, where no punt could safely follow them.

1848

January 1*st.*—Out all day, and never saw a single wild fowl.

3*rd.*—Off at daylight and persevered till the middle of the day, but the only wild fowl I saw was 1 brent goose, which I brought home.

4*th.*—Breakfasted and off again at daylight; but never saw a wild fowl all day.

5*th.*—Heavy wet gale nearly all day, and yet there was not a single wild fowl blown from sea into harbour—an event worthy of record.

22*nd.*—The moment I got out of the fly, on my return to Keyhaven to-day from London, I proceeded to get the gun and all the gear into the punt, so that I may not have either to do work on the Sabbath day or have a candlelight job on Monday morning. The reports on my arrival were flaming ones as to quantity of birds, though few wigeon and not one goose had been killed.

24*th.*—Up and breakfasted by candlelight, and cruised all the way up to Pilewell in a sharp frost and fine easterly wind. Saw but one flock of geese (about 60), which were half a mile in on the broad oozes off Pilewell. The wind increased to a gale, and we had a job to get back. The birds were, as usual, outside the beach and far at sea, so that their abundance afforded us no advantage. Though I had no chance for sport, I was well repaid for my long day. I had been too ill to eat with an appetite for some weeks, and when I came home I devoured my dinner like a greedy pointer.

26th.—A furious easterly gale all day, and a cutting black frost. At half-past two we went afloat for a few fowls that were to be seen, and, after escaping such a heavy sea as I had seldom before weathered, we came in with but 1 wigeon and 1 mallard.

27th.—Most bitter easterly gale, with intense frost. Went off twice, and saw a decent company of mixed fowl (chiefly geese), but dare not face the breakers to shoot.

28th.—The hardest day's frost I ever knew. The harbour a desert of ice, and the snow falling the whole day. We put the 'Petrel' into the run of the sluice hatches after breakfast; and before two o'clock she was penned in with an inch thick of ice, so that we had to batter away before we could drag her ashore. Small birds starved to death, and chased by the boys to catch them. Water jugs frozen in bedrooms; and, in short, so over 'tight' (as gunners call it) that all sport was stopped for want of being able to get afloat; and we were absolute prisoners for the whole day.

29th.—The intense frost relaxed so much this morning that the ice became soft enough to cut through it; and we battered through the frozen region with our punts; and after sheer slavery from seven in the morning till half-past one in the afternoon, we glided into salt water off Hurst, where (the whole time that we were at hard labour) the 'snobs' of Yarmouth and the coastguard poppers of Hurst were blowing off their trumpery shoulder pieces, in sail boats and wretched punts, at a whole army of birds; and out of about 40 rounds, never got so much as a single dunlin. When we arrived the whole coast was clear; but at last a few geese came down and dropped in. We sculled off to them and bagged 9 brent geese. In the afternoon there came on such a sudden thaw (with a shift of wind to the south) that with the help of our sails we cut through the soft ice, and lodged our punts safely at Keyhaven. In my thirty years' campaign I never had a more severe day than this.

31*st.*—Wind flew back to north-east, with snow and sleet. Out early; came in at two with 10 brent geese, and ready to go off again, but a torrent of snow and a gale of wind prevented us.

February 1*st.*—Up soon after five, and afloat at daylight. A sharp white frost, and about nine there came on a light sailing breeze. The consequence was that every jackass was afloat, and we might as well have been in London as in our punts. Came in about three, never having pulled a trigger.

2*nd.*—Off at daybreak. In the afternoon the sailing snobs came on in nine boats, and drove away all the birds, of course killing none, and I had consequently a blank day.

4*th.*—A south-west gale, with thick drizzling rain all day. The very weather to keep off the 'snobs,' so brought in 9 brent geese. I had this day all but made the greatest shot in my life; about 300 geese pitched within eighty yards of Keyhaven leak, which I had safely cleared, and then lay under the mud, with the birds 'end on,' and, when within a minute of shooting, an ass, in a dandy's craft, popped at some rubbishy shore birds and sprung the company of geese.

5*th.*—A continuation of wind and thick foggy rain. Just what I wanted to choke off the snobs and dandies. Brought in 20 brent geese (6 the first shot, and 14 the second shot).

7*th.*—A thick fog, which brought out an army of shore poppers. Got 5 brent geese; and other people afloat got more from my shot than I did, as we could not see our 'cripples' and 'droppers,' and were obliged to take out a compass in each punt, to avoid getting lost.

8*th.*—A butterfly day, and every jackanapes out in a boat. Never had a chance, though out from morning till night; and should have come home empty, but for the recovery of 1 brent goose that I lost yesterday. This evening a large basket of pheasants came to me from H.R.H. Prince Albert.

9th.—A tremendous westerly gale. Kept, of course, to windward, and when the geese came from the eastward we dropped down wind on them, in an absolute sea that the tide made over the mud. My detonator missed fire, or I should have got 20 birds. I fired after them, flying, with the flint barrel, and got 5 brent geese.

10th.—Went off to an army of geese, but a sail boat sent them away miles to the eastward, and we came home for a time. About five the army of geese returned and pitched in a capital place; but a floating snob flew after them and drove them to sea.

11th.—A butterfly day again. Another mishap with the detonator, or I might have had 12 geese. Came home and again overhauled the tormenting lock, and found that the chief fault was want of power in the main spring. Overhauled my bag of extras and found an old spring that was put by as too stiff, but on trial it went very well and blew off six primers in succession; so we sallied forth again, though only just saved our blank with 1 goose; as a 'gent' had moored his yacht at Hurst, and sent his two myrmidons to drive the harbour all day with a huge machine called a 'punt,' and a stanchion gun like a barber's pole. Otherwise, in spite of the summer-like weather, we might have had some shots; as the geese were all day about our harbour by hundreds, and only required proper treatment to be heavily slaughtered.

12th.—The geese had been so persecuted all yesterday that we never saw but one lot of about 60 the whole day, and, after following them from morning till night, I caught them off near the breakers at nearly the dusk of the evening, and brought in 4 geese with one barrel, the detonator again having failed.

15th.—A heavy gale all last night, and a pouring wet day.

Off in rain to an army of geese, but my shot spoiled by two floating clowns.

16*th.*—No geese. All 'far at sea' in a white frost and dead calm. To-day I was obliged to get my great gun ashore and take out the breechings, in order to take them and the left-hand lock into Lymington, where I was the whole day with Clayton putting a new 'beak' to the cock that had worn too short, and had missed fire at the five best shots at geese I've had this season.

17*th.*—Up long before daylight, and got my breechings in again, with plenty of 'hands' to help lift the huge barrels into the vice, as yesterday the ropes slipped, and the weight had all but smashed my trigger finger and broke Read's neck. We escaped but by an inch. Got afloat again by twelve in high order, but neither birds nor tide to give us a chance this day.

18*th.*—Got 8 brent geese; the only shot I fired, as at last the detonator went as well as ever after this repairing of what was worn away by more than twenty years' hard work and rough usage.

19*th.*—3 brent geese; the longest shot I remember ever to have made. The birds were sitting, and such was the distance that I had to level about a yard over them, and consequently they were shot at sitting, but killed flying.

21*st.*—Up hours before daylight, and cruised all the way 'up along' to Pilewell. Not a bird on the coast.

23*rd.*—Yesterday being a wet day, with a gale of wind from morning till night, we could do nothing; but to-day we brought all our guns, gear, punts &c. ashore, and after a thorough good cleaning, with six men to help, I housed them all for the season. Though we have had but a tolerable season with the geese, and the worst on record with all other fowl, yet we have bagged more than all the other punters put together. The country is ruined by the enormous increase of tyro 'snobs' both afloat and ashore. Poole, Weymouth, Southampton, the same, as I hear from all quarters. Why won't Lord John take my advice, and have a *porte d'armes* tax like the French?

Game &c. killed in the season: 173 partridges, 8 quails, 1 landrail, 5 hares, 1 pheasant, 22 snipes: 210 head. Wild fowl: 5 ducks and mallards, 1 scaup drake, 3 teal, 12 wigeon, 76 brent geese: 97 head. Waders &c.: 1 spotted gallinule, 1 green sandpiper, 2 dun divers, 2 golden plovers, 2 olives, 5 curlews: 13 head. 210 game, 110 wild fowl &c. Grand total, 320 head.

March 30th.—London. I've nothing to note down during the past long, wet, and dreary month of March, except that just after I left Keyhaven there were some awfully high tides, and there had been no more shooting for Read or any one since the day I laid up my guns and gear. And, turning to more serious matters, all Europe has been, and still is, in a state of revolution.

April 3rd.—So intensely hot that we were obliged to put out all the fires, and yet I have not seen for the whole year so many wild fowl as were this day in the poulterers' shops and hawked about town. They were, no doubt, caught in the decoys on their way home to Norway &c.

5th.—Longparish. Tried experiments, in the course of which I proved that the coarse coast 'gunning' powder, even in a stout shoulder gun, shot more than one-fourth stronger than the No. 1 sporting powder, though the one cost a shilling and the other 2*s.* 6*d.* a lb. I always thought and argued that this would be the result; and now I've taken the trouble to prove it. Just before dinner I fancied a trout; but it was a dead calm, and a cold north-east wind, with a bright sun; so I turned poacher, and got 3 fine trout with a stick and wire.

8th.—Returned to London. All in commotion with the expected grand 'shindy' on Monday. Artillery and troops moving in all directions, in order to be prepared for the monster meeting of the rabble of Chartists.

10*th*.—The Chartist meeting, instead of a bloody fight with the military, as many timid persons were fearful of, was all over before two o'clock, and, as far as could be learned, no casualties occurred, beyond a few skirmishes with police and crowd, so ample and wisely managed were the preparations of the authorities, both civil and military, the latter under the Duke of Wellington. A very thin Philharmonic this evening, owing to the fear of many ladies to venture out; but a good concert, and a most inspiring effect produced by the appropriate performance of 'God save the Queen' by full chorus and the best orchestra in the world.

11*th*.—London all quiet again.

29th and 30th.—Intense white frost, and ice thicker than a penny piece.

May 18*th*.—London. To-day I received a letter from Longparish informing me that 'Squire Smith's' diabolical foxes had just destroyed five broods of spring chickens with 3 hens, 2 valuable ducks with their two broods, having in the winter cleared off every one I had (about 35) except these 2, and though last, not least, my 2 favourite brent geese that I had brought quite tame from Keyhaven. A curse light on all clodpoll preservers of foxes.

27*th*.—The fullest birthday Drawing Room that I was ever at since the days of George IV., who made one 'monster meeting' do for a season.

June 14*th*.—Returned to London again, after having passed at Longparish the most miserable ten days I've encountered for a long time. Heavy rain almost all the time I was down; trout so sulky as to show but moderate sport, and so poor as to be only fit for frying or broiling. Nearly all my poultry destroyed by foxes; three meadows of mowed hay lying 'done for' by the rain, and everyone looking as black and as miserable as the weather.

July 3*rd*.—Down to Longparish on further business, and also to clear off my quarterly accounts to midsummer. To-day the 'dog days begin,' and curious ones they are—a deluge of wet weather, and as cold as in winter. Further annoyances here as usual. The cursed foxes, in spite of dogs with long chains posted at every accessible point of the farm-yard, have had a further slaughter of what poultry they had left, and also took nearly 2 dozen of my pond-fed, pinioned wild ducks. The trout so cruelly swept away from the hatch hole below, that not a decent fish remained in the part of the river that I keep in hand. These are the blessings of being proprietor of a 'beautiful place' in the country.

CHAPTER XLI

1848

September 2nd.—Drove over to Bullington. Put the horses up at the 'Cross,' and shot over my manor. Had capital sport, considering the corn and the extreme wildness of the birds. I got 22 partridges.

4th.—I started for my usual beat over Furgo Farm. Here I fagged for nearly four hours, and got but 5 shots. We then ascended Furgo Hill to the part that borders on Tidbury and Bullington; and here we found a fine lot of birds. But it was then past two o'clock, and I was so exhausted with heat, fagging, and fasting, that my nerves were quite gone for shooting; and I was obliged to leave my sport for a little rest and refreshment. I renewed my shooting about four and kept on till seven, and arrived home about eight (dogs and all completely 'done for'), and brought in 22 partridges, 3 hares, and 1 landrail.

Charles Heath flanked us all over the Bullington side, and had capital sport, as he got 23 partridges, making up our combined bag to 49 head, which, since our good old days are no more, was an immense lot for our larder.

5th.—A general day's rest for ourselves and dogs, though a very busy one for me with basket packing, letter writing, &c. I was so 'dead beat' that, had I fresh dogs and fresh ground, I could not have stood another day's shooting.

6th.—Shot on the borders of Furgo and Bullington, and came home with 18 partridges. The most satisfactory day I've yet had, as I made four double shots, and never fired a blank shot the whole day. As the birds were wild this was good shooting.

8th.—Poorly and weak as a chicken. Crawled out a few hours before dinner with my rod, as it was a dark blowing day, and got 3 brace of trout.

9th.—Having quacked myself to windward with a tonic, I never shot more brilliantly even when without grey hairs.

I went over to Bullington in a windy day and brought home 18 partridges, 1 landrail, and 1 hare, without missing a shot, although I had but one close easy shot the whole day.

Game killed by me the first week: 84 partridges, 7 hares, 2 landrails, 1 rabbit. Total, 94 head.

Nearly all killed at Bullington, as the game at Longparish is not worth speaking of.

16th.—Went out between eleven and twelve; so weak I could hardly sit on the pony; but my 'pluck' carried me on to Bullington, and I came in with 12 partridges.

18th.—Busy at accounts till one; got to Bullington about three, and it was near five o'clock before I picked up a bird, as the fields were occupied by shooters in every direction, with a dry north-east wind, in which the birds were all on the run. I shot well, and killed 7 partridges, having slaved hard to make up this number, because it completed the general list to 100 brace of partridges up to the present time.

19th.—An extraordinary coincidence with fish. The weed cutters brought in a carp about $3\frac{1}{2}$ lb., a fish never heard of in our place. A jack was seen in our pond, and we netted him: he weighed full 6 lb.; and I wired a tench above 2 lb.

The very best partridge season we have had since the good olden time, thanks to my little manor at Bullington, as the shooting on my farms at Longparish is nearly 'done for,' and the breed of birds in general has been bad.

Game killed in September 1848: Specification of grand total—226 partridges, 16 hares, 4 rabbits, 2 landrails, 2 snipes. Total, 250.

October 2nd.—This being the first day of pheasant shooting, we kept up our annual 'blow-out' in the hall, with a muster of curs and myrmidons, for the almost forlorn hope of a stray pheasant on the estate, and made our usual early start to scour our woods, and every place in bounds. After some hard fagging for hours, with markers well planted, there at last sprung up an old cock pheasant. The old cock then made for our wood, which obliged us to beat it all over a second time, though to no purpose, till I luckily twigged the old rascal at perch, and of course blew him down, thus bringing to the larder 1 pheasant. A hen bird had been seen yesterday, but we could nowhere find her. We came home to lunch at half-past one, meaning to turn out again and beat the rest of the day for the hen; but there set in such a determined wet afternoon, with a gale of wind, that I dismissed my followers, and gave up all thoughts of being able to go out again. About five in the evening the rain abated, and I went off in hopes of catching the hen at feed, but without success. At one time I dreaded a blank, but got all right by bagging 3 rabbits.

N.B.—The pheasants are now so destroyed by foxes and rail 'navvies' that even Mr. Fellowes saw and got but 1, and Mr. Coles, I hear, 1, when formerly his first day was 7 or 8 brace or more among his party.

7th.—Made a couple of brilliant shots at 2 teal that dropped into our river this morning. I then went out for the day over Furgo and Bullington, and although the weather was so hot as to be quite oppressive, the birds were wilder than ever, insomuch that in spite of heading them they would not lie even in high turnips. All I could get was 3 partridges, all long random (cartridges) shots. I had, however, much diversion in another way by falling in with the Ethiopian Serenaders, whom I had before seen on the stage in London. They were at my public-house, 'Bullington Cross,' *en route* for Bath. They gave me a regular performance, which was a *chef-d'œuvre* of the kind, and then accompanied me a little way for the chance of seeing me shoot; but in this they were disappointed, as the birds would scarcely let us get into the same field with them; so they wished me good morning, and went back to the 'Cross' for refreshment, for which I had of course left a trifle with the landlord, who, it appears, had already been puffing me off to them as one of the 'lions' of the sporting world.

18*th.*—A wet north-east wind every day; and the weather became so intensely cold this afternoon that sleet and snow were falling, and everything seemed to predict a summons for wild fowl at Keyhaven.

23*rd.*—Ran down to Keyhaven, after an absence of fifteen weeks from this day, to settle all my little bills, poor rates, taxes &c. and to overhaul my craft and gear, though with no view of shooting, as even in the late north-easter but few fowl had been seen; and now we have a furious gale from the south-west, insomuch that I should have deferred my visit could I have foreseen the dreadful weather in which I was caught soon after I left my door at Longparish. It 'blew great guns,' and poured 'cats and dogs' till I entered Keyhaven Cottage, and kept on most outrageously the whole night. Old Read met me with a face as long as a double bass, and said he had been almost living on the mud night and day, and had as yet got but 6 birds.

25*th.*—Not a wild fowl could I hear of that has been shot, though some flocks had been seen off in the rough sea above Pilewell, and also in Sowley Pond.

26*th.*—The furious weather so far abated that I was enabled at last to inhale a sea breeze afloat; so I put the pop-gun boat in the water, and took a survey of the coast with a musket, in case of an odd bird *en passant.* To my surprise I got 1 wigeon out of 4, which were all I saw, and which I could not get together to kill more, though I waited patiently for hours under a pour of rain. I then went on shore and beat all the marshes, but never saw one snipe.

27th.—A gale of wind and driving rain again all day. About 100 wigeon were blown into harbour, but having no punt afloat I told old Read of them. I weathered it along shore to see him shoot; he, however, stopped but 3, 1 of which fell into other hands. I came home so wet that I had to change, and Read was like a 'drowned rat.' The weather is a downright misery; nothing but south-westers and rain.

28th.—Heavy gale, with drenching showers. 'Bolted' back to Longparish, having now done all I had to do, and it being impossible to get afloat or have any enjoyment of Keyhaven till there came some alteration of weather, and the deluge of fresh water had subsided. I don't know when I had a more unpleasant six days to weather. But it is well I went down, as my lock-up stores would have been much injured by the damp, which exceeded all that was remembered here before, except in the awful sea floods, which, if they do come, have always been in November.

31st.—Longparish. A report of a pheasant. Mustered 'all hands,' and beat everywhere all day, but never found him.

November 6th.—Just as I had breakfasted, old Jack the shepherd sent to say he had seen this rascally old cock pheasant I had tried for so often fly towards my wood. So I went quietly up to the covert, and after a long search up he got, and down I fetched him in brilliant style, and as dead as a hammer. Never was there a more satisfactory little day's sport.

7th.—Drove over to Laverstoke House (an old haunt of mine in bygone days, and where my son was born) to see my old friend, Sir Peregrine Maitland, who has taken this mansion for a year. He was born in Longparish House, which his father rented of my father while his command of the 1st Horse Guards obliged him to reside in and near London. Moreover Sir Peregrine was my brother sportsman when he resided with his sister, Mrs. Warren, in Longparish, at Middleton House, and was the very best shot I ever saw in all my life, and the person from whom I acquired a brilliant style of shooting, and of whom I am proud to call myself the pupil. This was about forty-five years ago, when he was captain in the Guards and I a lieutenant of Dragoons, so that we are now (both of us) a little the 'worse for wear' and the effects of Anno Domini.

11*th.*—Heard that a few more snipes were come. Went out and bagged 3 snipes and 5 jack snipes, all I shot at and all I saw. It was a dark, dull day, and therefore doubly difficult to kill everything in prime style.

14*th.*—Having received a good report of wigeon on the coast I ran down to Keyhaven.

23*rd.*—Keyhaven. Put off to a few stray geese that were scattered on the waves (the first seen this year), and knocked down 2.

28*th.*—During the whole of my sojourn at Keyhaven (where I've been just a fortnight from to-day) not a bird has been killed afloat by any gunner in the place; and, as far as I could learn, no birds have been killed all the way 'up along.'

December 24*th.*—Longparish. Sunday. Intense frost again, with a cutting east wind. Up very early in order to distribute my Christmas beef to the poor before church time. A satisfactory beginning for the new year of my birth.

25*th.*—Christmas Day. A total change of weather. The hard frost broke up with a south wind and rain. Read sent me a summons by to-day's post, but I withheld sending him orders till I heard further from him now that the wind was changed.

30*th.*—Though unwell with a cough and cold I sallied off in my water boots, and came in with 4 snipes and 6 jack snipes; a grand day, and I never shot better. I missed but one shot at the only other jack I found.

1849

January 1*st.*—So dark a day that we could hardly see without going to the windows. Very damp and cold, with a gentle breeze from the east. Capital weather for wild fowl if it should continue, and thereby lead, as is usual, to a black frost.

2nd.—Intense frost, with a cutting easterly gale. Went off to Keyhaven, where I arrived soon after four (high water), and just in time to launch the large 'Petrel' punt.

3rd.—Got the following punt and all in order, so as to get afloat about two; but it blew so hard that we got a wetting without being able to fire a shot, though there were clouds of wigeon on the breakers. I never felt such intense cold as with this very hard frost and bitter north-easter.

4th.—Read crawled on the mud all last night, and brought in 8 wigeon at five this morning—when he called me up to go out. But then there set in heavy rain.

N.B.—For the very many years that I have frequented Keyhaven it has scarcely ever been my lot to go down there without bringing wet weather. All the natives say, 'The frost is sure to turn to rain and drive away the birds when the Colonel arrives at his Cottage.'

6th.—Up by candlelight again, and out till three, when the tide would no longer serve; but never had a chance, as the geese were too much persecuted to venture near the shore, and the sea was too rough to come near them afloat, as the punt jumped like a rocking horse. Thus have I been out four cruises and never discharged a barrel. In the evening the weather cleared up, and promised to be fine and frosty again. In all my coasting career I never had such a hard and unprofitable four days' gunning.

8th.—Yesterday afternoon there set in a furious wet gale from the south-west (after a bitter white frost the previous night), and this day it poured and blew. I went afloat from nine till dark and got but two little shots; the first at a few geese near 300 yards, and bagged 2 brent geese, and the second at a few mixed shore birds that I cleared off. The stanchion 'gunners' were so numerous that the birds could find no clear place to pitch on, so went off to sea and would not come in again.

9th.—Up at five, and off at daybreak for a long cruise ten miles to the eastward. Here the coast was less infested with gunners, though equally disturbed by poppers in sail boats. The weather was fine, and consequently the birds were nearly all gone off to sea. We saw but one company of geese, and these birds were driven off by blank shots from the sailing boats. I blew off a barrel, and just before I got home had the luck to kill 8 brent geese out of a small and very wild company.

10th.—All in order and breakfasted by daybreak.[1] A furious westerly gale. The very weather for me, as it embargoed the amateurs. I, however, never saw so few birds in harbour as were driven in by this gale. My first chance was at 12 geese, 8 together and 4 detached. Pulled off one barrel at the 8, and 'floored' the whole lot. One was prigged by a pirate in a sailing boat, the other 7 brent geese I brought home. This enabled me (with birds in house) to send off 10 geese and 10 wigeon to Prince Albert. The only other chance I had was at a mixture of geese and wigeon, for which I waited two hours to let the tide 'pinch' in order to get them together, and when within a few minutes of shooting two rascally shore snobs popped off a blank and sprung the company.

11th.—A north-west hurricane all last night. Read crawled again all night on the mud and got 1 wigeon. Finished my breakfast an hour before daylight for the chance of the gale becoming less violent, and thereby enabling us to propel the punt to windward. The gale, however, increased to an absolute tornado, in which no craft could venture on the water, and the very houses and chimneys shook.

12th.—The gale abated after midnight, and Read went mud crawling about three this morning, and came in with 3 wigeon at seven, when I met him on the quay in a dead calm,

[1] When Read brought in 3 wigeon after a midnight mud crawl.

with moonlight and white frost. We then went afloat all day, and I never got but 1 wigeon out of a couple that I shot at in the rolling surf. Not a single company of birds to be seen in either harbour or channel, unless in weather where no craft could 'live.' All the birds frightened off to sea, which is now their constant quarter when it is possible to shoot inside.

13*th*.—Read got in the night by mud crawling again 6 wigeon, and at daylight there came on a stiff westerly gale. I went afloat at daylight and was off all day, and got but one poor long shot in a sea, and bagged 2 wigeon at 200 yards. Shooters innumerable, as is every day the case now. The coast is absolutely 'done for.'

15*th*.—A most unsatisfactory day. 'Done' out of one of the greatest shots that could possibly be made. After my being out the whole morning about 200 geese came in and pitched within a splendid shot of my own leaks, and it being half flood I got up to the head of a 'spreader,' all hid by the mud and there lay close to them, only waiting for the tide to raise the gun so that I could bear on them. About a quarter of an hour would have given me the chance of 50 or 60 geese at a shot, when no less than three other punts came scrambling in; and the result was that I could only get a long random shot after the birds had risen above the mud, and with which I shot 6, and (2 having got away and been bagged by a Yarmouth boatman) but bagged only 4 brent geese. In all my gunning career I never had a more bitter disappointment. I should perhaps have made the greatest shot that ever was heard of, as the birds were all clustered in one close column, through which my two great barrels must have mown them down like a swath of corn.

16*th*.—A dead calm. Read crawled all night, but got no shot. He knocked us up at five to go out in channel, but at seven there came on wind and rain. The geese came up about eleven. Went off in a heavy rain, but the shot of a 'snob' drove the birds away miles to the eastward. They returned again an hour before dusk. No water to get near enough. Tried one barrel, a very long shot, and luckily bagged what I knocked down, viz. 4 brent geese. Just in time, as two other swivel guns were advancing on them. Came in at dark in a miserably wet mess, as it poured and blew most cruelly.

18*th.*—Up by candlelight and afloat all the morning, but no fowl to be seen. Off again about two, when we saw a large flock of geese a long way to leeward. Had to go outside through a heavy sea to get round to them. Got up a creek, and lay under them for two hours. The gale kept other gunners in, so the coast was our own; but still we were destined to interruption; a cursed flock of large gulls attacked the geese and drove them away. On our arrival at the quay we saw nothing of our following boat with Payne, who had remained outside to intercept the cripples, if I had shot. It came on pitch dark with a frightful gale of wind, and no tidings of Payne for some hours. Both Read and I pronounced him to be swamped and drowned, and every preparation was ordered for a search with all hands, when practicable, which could be of no avail till daybreak. After having given him up for lost, in came Payne a little before eight at night, with his gun and all safe, and 1 brent goose in his hand that he had been rash enough to chase to the Fiddler's Race, where not another punt but mine, the 'Feather,' could have lived, and where no one but himself would have had the madness to venture.

31*st.*—Longparish. Availed myself of the first fine day to have one more trial at the game, and from all reports I almost feared a blank. I, however, had the luck to wind up with one of the most satisfactory days on record, considering the extreme wildness of the birds in a cold north-west wind. I did not start till past twelve, and came home at five with 5 partridges, which was all I saw, and, wonderful for the last day of January, 1 quail.

February 2nd.—Fog and drizzle all day. Country dark,

wet, and miserable. All equally flat on the coast just now, as Read writes that no birds whatever have been killed since I left Keyhaven.

10*th.*—Got 1 wild duck and 1 mallard from my decoy hut. No other chance, now, for the use of a gun. Wet, miserable weather, and the country destitute of all kinds of sport except hunting, which I've given up ever since I came to a sensible age.

20*th.*—Keyhaven. Up very early, when everyone remarked it was the first time for thirty years that the Colonel came down without causing rain (the weather had been splendid for ten days). Before the fly came to the door, however, to take me on my way to Longparish, there set in a determined wet day. On my arrival, among other letters there was a returned one from the General Post Office for Sam Singer, to whom I had written, but who has 'shot the moon,' without leaving an address, and who, it appears, had bolted to Holland as dry nurse in gunning to some dandy gents, in consequence of not being able to 'get a crust' on our annihilated coast.

22*nd.*—Game &c. killed in the season myself: 191 partridges, 14 hares, 3 landrails, 2 pheasants (all I saw the whole season), 1 quail, 11 rabbits, 32 snipes. Total, 254 head.

Wild fowl: 5 ducks and mallards, 1 tufted duck, 3 teal, 26 wigeon, 27 brent geese. Total, 62.

254 game, 62 wild fowl, 15 waders. Grand total, 331 head.

A good game season, but one of the worst wild-fowl seasons on record.

Charles Heath: 99 partridges, 2 pheasants, 3 snipes, 2 wild ducks, 20 hares, 12 rabbits. Total, 138.

Siney (with hare licence): 5 hares, 6 rabbits, 10 ducks, 3 teal, 1 wigeon, 3 wood pigeons, 6 snipes (caught in gins). Total, 34.

P. H. 331, Heath 138, Siney 34. In all, 503 head.

28*th.*—London. Sported my Peninsular medal this day at the Queen's Levee.

March 22nd.—Went with Mr. A. Lancaster down to the Redhouse at Battersea to try the effect of my new 'dodge,' and it surpassed all that we could expect; it beat every gun on the ground, and made both the Lancasters stare at the result. My plan was simply to throw away the solid breech for our grandfathers' old plug, and ignite strong cannon powder by a projecting platinum touch hole. The result was never failing fire, extra strength, closer shooting, no recoil, and a defiance to wet weather and bad usage. My plan is for single guns, as in double ones it would bring the locks as far apart as in olden times, and, moreover, it is here not so much wanted, because in double guns we can get a central fire without impeding the sight of the barrels.

April 11th.—Longparish. I devoted this day to experiments with my improved ignition of guns, and the result was magnificent, as the old patent breeching and fine powder were almost doubled by my saucer plug and 'sea gun' (largest cannon) powder. I wound up with a sally up the river and brought in 1 snipe and 1 magpie.

17th.—A heavy fall of snow.

18th.—A hard frost.

19th.—The severest wintry day, and one of the heaviest falls of snow that I have ever seen. Rooks and other birds taken alive, in a state of exhaustion, from being unable to get food or to fly. My prediction at Christmas came to pass. I said that for our spring in winter we should have winter in spring, though I never could have thought quite so late as this.

May 4th.—So intensely hot that we got rid of fires, and sent for ice to cool our beverage.

6th.—Sunday. A bitter cold north-easter, and fires renewed.

7th.—Ditto. I never remember such a change as this even in our changeable climate.

June 13th.—London. Went to the Horse Guards, and got old Monk (my servant in the Peninsula and ever since) his medal with six bars on it, viz. Orthes, Nivelle, Pyrenees, Vittoria, Albuera, Talavera. A glorious trophy for him to wear, when I've treated him to an appropriate uniform.

July 12th.—Keyhaven. Having lots of little commissions in Lymington, I sailed in there after breakfast. Old Read got under way to return with me here, but when off 'Jack-in-the-basket' he ran foul of a pile and staved the boat, with a hole large enough for three cats to run through abreast. She was a third full in no time, and we were all but sinking, when I made him shove in two pairs of huge water stockings that I had bought, as well as a spare sail, and we kept baling and sailing with splendid wind and weather, till we, thank God, landed at Keyhaven in safety. At one time I was fully prepared for the loss of the things I was bringing home, and a swim for my life.

August 4th.—London. This day, the forty-fifth anniversary of my being gazetted Captain in the 14th Dragoons, I had an interview at the Ordnance Office with Sir Thomas Hastings and Colonel Anson, by desire of Lord Anglesea, relative to my new ignition gun for the army, which I had left with Wilkinson to rectify the rough work of young Lancaster, and it was agreed that I should have a meeting and a trial of my gun with the new Ordnance musket in the ensuing autumn.

28th.—Keyhaven. Rain as a matter of course, which I never fail to bring, and there set in a wet evening.

N.B.—All the farmers had prayed that 'the Colonel may not come down till harvest was over.'

CHAPTER XLII

1849

September 1*st.*—A good breed of birds; but a hot, dry, easterly wind, that made them wilder than I ever saw them on the first day. About half-past two there set in a squall, with two hours' heavy rain, after which the ground continued so wet that birds would not lie at all. Considering all, however, I had excellent sport. I bagged 18 partridges and fired not a single blank shot.

3*rd.*—Had a long hard day and killed 24 partridges, in doing which my only two blank shots were fired when coming home dead tired towards the close of the evening.

Game killed the first week (though I never shot better or fagged harder than the few days I was out, my bag was far short of that of last season, owing to the want of lay for the birds, and the dry easterly winds that destroyed all scent):

71 partridges, 3 hares. Total, 74 head.

12*th.*—A pouring wet day. Mr. Longman drove up to the door from Farnborough for a few hours' angling, and, though a beginner in the art, caught the finest lot of fish that I have seen this year. He landed 9 brace, some of them near 2 lb., and caught all his trout with a fly [1] under heavy rain.

13*th.*—Went out at one o'clock, though so weak I could hardly fag, and in all my life I never saw the birds so wild. In spite of every dodge, I had been out four hours without getting a shot; and about five was coming home resigned to my maiden blank day when up sprung a wild covey, that flew towards me, and I made a most brilliant double shot; and

[1] The 'brown alder' fly.

afterwards cut down a bird that flew up in the road. So after all I did get 3 partridges.

14*th.*—Mr. Thompson, a good fly fisher, was here all the morning, and took but one trout, though a splendid fish of about 1½ lb. and well fed; while on the other hand, Mr. Longman, a beginner in the art, killed, the day before yesterday, 9 brace. Here is a proof of uncertainty as to the rising of fish, even in good weather.

20*th.*—A cold north-easterly gale all day. Such weather as would have called me to Keyhaven for early fowl, plover &c. had not the place been in a state of siege, by an army of red-hot green 'gents,' who scare away everything. No weather for partridges. I, however, went off all day; and by outflanking the birds I got 7 partridges and 2 snipes, without missing a shot.

24*th.*—A regular butterfly day, and I thought the birds would lie. But no; they were, if possible, wilder than ever, and would not let the dogs come near them even in turnips. Though I fagged all day and missed nothing, I came home with only 5 partridges.

This morning I had a letter from Keyhaven to say some wigeon and plover were come, but that the tyro 'gents' and 'snobs' were on so fierce that the place would no doubt be too hot to hold the birds for long. Otherwise I would have gladly left this treadmill partridge shooting and gone off to the healthy sea air, as I used to do.

26*th.*—Out all day; got two shots, and brought in 2 partridges. A north-east gale, and the birds up the moment you entered the field they were in. No recipe but charges of cavalry could make them lie even for a duck gun and cartridge; so, having no fleet horses to ride them down, I had no sport.

28*th.*—Attended church morning and evening, this being the day very properly appointed by our vicar to offer up our prayers for the cessation of the cholera, which has been raging almost everywhere, and our thanks for having as yet escaped this dreadful pestilence.

October 1*st.*—Kept up our old annual custom of a grand sally forth, and a 'blow-out' of cadgers in the hall; and had the great good luck to bring home the only 3 pheasants I saw. A very satisfactory day.

9*th.*—Up to London to take up my new model for punt gun; to see to the putting in hand my new ignition musket, which I've promised to show at the Ordnance early next month; and to do an innumerable lot of commissions.

10*th.*—Hard on again from daylight till midnight. My new model struck dumb the leading men. Wilkinson had just finished a stanchion gun with a boatload of iron, Lancaster ditto with a boatload of wood, while mine had nothing of weight except the large barrel.

11*th.*—The post brought a summons for Keyhaven, and a troublesome letter from the garrison chaplain, objecting to repairs or improvements in my record under ancestor's (Governor Hawker's) monument. Parsons always give ten times more trouble than any other set of men.

12*th.*—A splendid easterly wind, and all in a bustle to get free for the coast.

13*th.*—Started for Keyhaven, and before I got halfway there the beautiful easterly wind turned into a torrent of rain and southerly gale, that kept on all the evening and all night. Thus I emphatically kept up my charter this time of always bringing rain when I went to the coast. What birds had been here were all driven away, and but a very few couples had been killed by all the gunners put together.

15*th.*—The wet weather having left us, and the wind all yesterday and all last night having blown a gale from the north-east again, I this morning put afloat my small stanchion and light punt, in hopes that a few fowl may arrive on the coast; and, though suffering terribly, I sallied forth and cruised as far as a heavy sea would allow me to go, but, to my astonishment in such magnificent weather, not a single bird did I see. It is an absolute miracle that such a long series of easterly winds should have done nothing for gunners. Not above a dozen birds have this season been killed by all of them put together, and the popgun sportsmen complain that they never knew such a scarcity of snipes. The only way that I can account for this is that the incessant persecution of the few call birds that at first arrive and would call others down has banished all the birds from this place.

16*th.*—Old Read out all day, and never saw a fowl, though the weather was magnificent for gunning.

17*th.*—A total change of weather. Rain all night, and a strong south-wester all to-day. Wrapped up warm, and 'weathered it,' but not a bird could I see.

18*th.*—Out, and never got a chance even for the popgun. In the afternoon down came Sam Singer in his pretty little vessel, and we had such a 'yarn' for our mutual advantage as one seldom hears.

19*th.*—A fine warm south wind, and butterfly weather. Sam Singer sailed up for Leap and Cowes this morning, and I ill and a prisoner.

20*th.*—Better, and out to-day, and not a bird. At night Sam Singer returned from a fifty miles' cruise, and had got but 1 wigeon.

21*st.*—Mr. Wilkinson arrived from London at four o'clock P.M. for a general inspection of my arsenal and trials afloat to-morrow.

22*nd.*—Up very early, and went through everything, and showed Mr. Wilkinson the system of punt gunning, in order that he may learn all necessary for stanchion guns, as he is now the leading gunmaker of London. He returned to town not a little delighted with the lesson he had learned and the novelties I had shown him.

25*th.*—At Longparish, having returned yesterday from Keyhaven, from whence what few fowl had arrived were all driven away by the legions of tyro shooters both afloat and ashore.

27th.—An old cock pheasant came and dropped within ten yards of my window while I was writing. I threw down my pen and flew to my gun, but before I could get down stairs he ran away, and then flew off out of gunshot. I turned out 'all hands,' and though I beat the whole morning I never could make him out.

November 9th.—London. Much bother about my new Government musket, which Wilkinson undertook to get finished for me. But his myrmidons were so spread over the town that half the work was wrong, and must be done over again. These outskirt savages had spoiled all Greenfield's beautiful work, which will have to be altered over again at my expense. How can things be done right if a gun has to go east, west, north, and south, and the master is too busy with dandies to follow up his pack of artisans?

10th.—Having packed up all my models &c. I this day started for Birmingham. We left the terminus (the most splendid one in Europe) in Euston Square at ten, and arrived in Birmingham a quarter before two. The railway by far the most perfect of any I ever saw. To an item everything was perfection and first-rate. Great Western not to be named with it. Took up my quarters at the 'Stork' hotel, reputed to be the most comfortable one, and then sallied out in order to make the most of my time. After seeing my old friend Westley Richards for a short time, I proceeded to Clive's barrel-forging factory, a place more like the incantation scene in 'Der Freischütz' than anything else I can compare it to; and here I was happy to learn from Mr. Shardlow he would be all ready to forge for me early next week. I then went on gun business to Greener, the harpoon gunmaker. Dined at half-past six, and then 'cut off' for the evening to the new public 'Exposition of Manufactures,' a most interesting lounge, and brilliantly lit up as an evening promenade at *6d.*

admission. Went to bed as tired as a dog about eleven o'clock.

11*th*.—Sunday. Went with Mr. Westley Richards to his pew in St. Philip's Church. Service well performed, and a clever sermon from the Honourable Mr. Yorke. The evening service I reserved till half-past six, in order to see St. Martin's Church, and hear the celebrated Mr. Miller, the rector. He has great feeling, with most energetic eloquence, good logic, fine metaphor, and a most Christian-like manner. I am inclined to put him as No. 1 of all the preachers I have yet heard.

12*th*.—Went to Clive's barrel factory with my models of patent ignition for my new stanchion gun, preparative to the forging &c. Called on Mr. Parker, who makes the crested handles for my primers, and was interestingly amused by his showing me all the departments of his button and army accoutrement manufactory. I could see but little of Westley Richards, as he was the principal of the 'Exposition,' which Prince Albert came down to see this day. I explored many places, and was much pleased with the civility and industry of the people of Birmingham.

13*th*.—Nearly all day in Clive's factory, superintending the forging of my newly invented single stanchion gun. The noise and heat was terrific. The power of the beating hammer $3\frac{1}{2}$ tons, and it was a service of danger to avoid being burned or knocked down. A majestic old fellow named Talbot was the 'Lamiel' of this infernal region, in which men and boys were running about just like so many devils. Mr. Shardlow, the foreman, as well as Mr. Clive, kindly attended and explained everything, and Mr. Wilkinson arrived from town soon after we had begun work. I then dressed, and took a fly to go out to Mr. Westley Richards's country house, where he gave us a most excellent dinner.

14*th*.—On from breakfast till near two trying my new ignition gun at Mr. Westley Richards's splendid factory.

The performance of the gun satisfied him that I had not exaggerated about its effect. I then went all over his factory, which surpasses all the gun establishments I ever saw or heard of. He has his whole army of workmen, as it were, in a barrack, with spacious ground to try his guns from the very windows of the workmen. To have seen as many departments of gunmaking in London, I must have gone over twenty miles of ground. After lunch I went all over the electro-plate manufactory, in the company of Sir Robert and Lady Peel and daughter, who had run over with four horses from Drayton (fifteen miles) to see this splendid establishment, also the 'Exposition of Manufactures' that had brought Prince Albert here on Monday. I then inspected the grand papier-mâché manufactory, which was even better worth seeing.

15*th.*—This being the day for a general thanksgiving, I went again to St. Philip's Church, in Mr. Richards's pew, and returned with him to his villa, where we lunched. In the evening I went once more to hear Mr. Miller, who preached with great energy on our delivery from cholera, but as he this evening held forth extempore and preached for nearly two hours, I was not so much delighted with him as on Sunday last.

16*th.*—Up early, and off to Wolverhampton to see Mr. Brazier, the great lockmaker of Britain, about the lock for my new stanchion. I had a terrible job to find the right man, as the name of 'Brazier' here was like 'Smith,' too universal to be distinguished. After an hour's tramp in mud and filthy streets, I got on the right scent, and found him at his little country seat, called 'The Ashes,' and ascertained that 'Joseph Brazier, Esq.' was the precise direction to catch him. I had to carry my models on my back to show the whole concern, and lucky it was that I did, as Wilkinson had directed him all wrong about the lock, which luckily he had not yet begun. I left the models by his particular request, and after a most hospitable blow-out of Staffordshire pork-pie, and such a glass of strong beer as I had not tasted for years, I shuffled off to a fine old church, built in the time of Ethelred, where I tried the organ, and inspected a superb ancient stone pulpit, and various other antiquities. I got back by four, and then drove to Clive's factory; and lucky was it that I went there, as my direction and correction were necessary. But I don't find fault, because it's expecting impossibilities to ask my gunmaker, or rather gun merchant, to understand a stanchion gun.

19th.—On again, as busy as a bee. Saw to rough boring of barrel. Went all over the Government factory, where Evans (an old friend of mine, formerly at Joe Manton's, and who had worked at my 'Champion double swivel gun' in 1824) showed me the whole process of musket making, of which he is the lord lieutenant at Birmingham. Had a long chatter with Westley Richards and his men, who were delighted with my plan, which the editor of the 'Birmingham Gazette' kindly noticed in a long article. In the evening I went to the weekly choral concert in the magnificent town hall, and not a little was I surprised at the performance. Some of the choruses went far better than on our stage in London (except when we had the Germans there), and the organ was splendid. A Miss Stephens (pupil of Sterndale Bennett) played extremely well Moscheles' lovely fantasia on 'Au Clair de la Lune;' and all this for sixpence in the spacious gallery, and only threepence *parterre.*

20th.—On again at Clive's, proceeding with the new gun. Saw Evans at the Government ordnance factory, and had a minute inspection and dissection of a nondescript piece of intricacy, called the Prussian musket, fifty of which are ordered by the wiseacres at headquarters. Called on Richards to show him a letter from Clayton of Lymington, proving the superiority of my new ignition.

21st.—On at Clive's, boring the first cylinder of the barrel, and at Evans's ordnance office, to show him my new musket-sized gun. Then off to see the manufacturing of cut glass at Osler's, and from there to the rolling mills of Mr. Muntz, M.P., whose brother kindly showed me all the process for making copper for the navy (which has in it an amalgamation of zinc), and the old 110 horse-power engine of the great Watt. Came home so tired I could hardly stand.

23rd.—This being the day for grinding the barrel of my new stanchion gun, I was off duty with the men, so resigned myself for a morning's pleasure. Got in the four-horse 'bus at ten and went to Dudley (ten and a half miles) and saw Dudley Castle, one of the finest ruins in England. There were two novelties on the road, near West Bromwich: the one, two bridges that we went under, one a viaduct for a railway, and the other an aqueduct for the canal, and close together; the other was the gasometer that supplies the enormous town of Birmingham with gas at about seven miles' distance (a cheaper plan than drawing the coals from the pits at this place to Birmingham). I had a regular wet day for my trip, as an incessant rain set in just before we entered Worcestershire, where I had never been before. Except Herefordshire I've now been in every county in England.

24th.—Down to Clive's the first thing. Grinding not enough, so left the men to grind away to-day. Being then adrift I overhauled the fine Catholic cathedral and the magnificent market place, 123 yards under cover and splendidly built.

27th.—Busy directing Mr. Aston's men at the lock and screws of the big gun. Then at Clive's, afterwards with Mr. Shardlow at the proof house, where I saw the barrel proved. The proof, however, is but little more than a double charge. Mr. Marsh, the principal there, kindly showed me all over the establishment.

28th.—Stood over Aston's man to direct him. Then at Clive's and on to Greener's, after seeing Evans about my stock &c. He sent me to Messrs. Hollis and Sheath, the large wholesale gun manufacturers in St. Mary's Square, to see a large gun they were doing with my new plan of ignition. They were working from a Burnett gun copied from my 'old Moll;' and when Mr. Sheath found out who I was, the scene was rather amusing. He came away with me to see my models, which, he said, should be his standard for all future guns, if not expressly ordered to the contrary. Mr. Sheath, it appears, makes these stanchion guns up for the leading gunmakers in London to put their names on, and almost all their work in the large way is packed off by rail to him; and he has a sad difficulty to interpret some of their foolish directions. Aston makes locks for him, and the cost of a common cheap lock is 11*d.*; 4*d.* the iron, 6*d.* the work, and a penny profit for Mr. Aston.

29*th.*—A letter from Read to say birds were at Keyhaven, and that he was ill from a fall. On from morning till dinner with all my divers workmen, and we had a grand council together, at which I explained all my plans so far that my imprisonment in Birmingham was no longer necessary, and that all could now go on without my daily attendance over the workmen. In the evening, though all in a fuss for leaving, I could not resist attending the clever lecture by Lieutenant Gale, R.N., and his plans for an exploring expedition in search of Sir J. Franklin.

30*th.*—Having been up till past twelve last evening, owing to Lieutenant Gale's lecture, I had to turn out at six this morning on gun business, and finally arrived in London to-day.

N.B.—I must not take leave of Birmingham without doing the justice to this town to say that I never met with a more civil and obliging set of people than the inhabitants of this place, which is a town of unrivalled industry and mechanical genius.

December 1*st.*—London. Up very early, and on with Greenfield, Wilkinson &c. about my new military musket, which was, of course, done wrong in my absence. Run off my legs in order to get away after an early dinner, to take down my little tablet, and see it placed myself in the garrison chapel at Portsmouth, and to interview Sam Singer. I much wanted to see his new punt that he brags about so much.

2nd.—Sunday. Portsmouth. Went to church at garrison chapel, and arranged all for tablet in morning. The Governor, Lord F. Fitzclarence, had moved five miles off (while his house was doing up), so I had to hire a sailor to take a note for him, in a deluge of rain and gale of wind, and after all his lordship had bolted to London.

3rd.—Up by candlelight, and got the tablet well fixed before the parson was about, and then returned to London.

5th.—London. Heard from Keyhaven that a few geese and a fair show of wigeon were come, and that old Read had recovered from his fall that had laid him up.

11th.—I had a holiday at last, and so went to see the lamented Queen Dowager's coffin, and other things that I had no time for before.

13th.—To-day was the poor Queen Dowager's funeral, when there was observed in town all that respect which her exemplary conduct was entitled to, and at three o'clock there were, as usual on such occasions, the royal salutes of the Park and Tower guns.

14th.—Busy from nine till eleven at night, and among other jobs about a gun that had burst in the hands of Sir Claude Scott, Bart., the great banker, on the demerits of which I gave him a certificate, he having applied to me, though an utter stranger, as the first authority on the subject of arms.

18th.—A wet day. Down to the proof house in Whitechapel, with Sir Claude Scott and 'Uncle' Bishop, to go before the committee (where we met Purdey, Old Nock, and other eminent gunmakers), to present the shattered remains of Sir Claude's gun, with the view of taking steps to a more stringent Act of Parliament, as a check upon ironmongers selling guns, as well as the danger of introducing light steel barrels. A gun in Birmingham can be finished up for 6*s.* 6*d.*, and a 'tidy' gun, as they call it, for 9*s.* 6*d.*, and thus, by making the lock to feel pleasant and high ornament, it may be passed off to a green young lord as a 20-guinea gun.

20*th.*—On ding-dong blowing the rascally steel barrels in the 'Times' and other papers.

24*th.*—Longparish. Up by candlelight and run off my legs to cut through business between the Sunday and Christmas Day. In the midst of jobs, accounts &c. I had to run down to the river for a foreign tufted duck, at which I made a most lucky long shot. I tipped his pinion precisely in the right place for cutting, and turned him a-going on the pond with 9 pinioned ones that I had bought. I then attended my distribution of beef to the poor; partook of my usual birthday turkey, and got to bed, dead tired, about twelve o'clock.

25*th.*—Christmas Day. A torrent of letters, both private and in the papers, about my late war against the dangerous new-fashioned light steel gun barrels.

26*th.*—Got 1 duck and 1 mallard from the decoy hut, the only 2 birds on the river. Finished alterations in my 'Invisible' approach, and tried the 'Hornet' little stanchion in it, and it went beautifully. Erected a little tablet in the new-made island, and in short was all day 'as busy as a bee.'

27*th.*—Made up my mind for a holiday at last. But no. The post brought me in a batch of letters and papers that pinned me for nine hours to my writing desk.

28*th.*—There set in last night the most sudden intensity of bitter cold weather I ever experienced, with a heavy gale of snow from the north-west. This morning there set in a northerly gale of wind enough to perish one, and it froze hard all day. I got out with my gun, and was so cold even while fagging that I could hardly hold it. The country seemed destitute of every living creature. I worked all over the rivers, moors, and our wood, and had the great luck to bring home 1 jack snipe, or else should have had a blank day.

29th.—Got 1 wild duck that pitched in front of the house, where I had to crawl to her a long way in the snow. A bitter cold day, and everything freezing even in the house.

1850

January 1st.—Intense frost. Prepared for going down to Keyhaven. About four this afternoon I was sent for by my tenant, Mr. Goodall, who, poor man, was ill in bed, as he wished to shake hands with me before I went to the coast; and to my horror in a few hours afterwards, a message came to say he was dead.

2nd.—Went down to Keyhaven. On my arrival found that such an awful flood had taken place last week that Read has put all my guns &c. upstairs in my cottage, and this with a northerly wind which always keeps back the tide.

3rd.—We had all last night the most cruel white frost that ever bit a man's limbs. Up by candlelight, and got our fleet afloat before luncheon. Went off at half-past two, but never had a chance for a shot, and we had not been afloat half an hour before the wind flew to the south-west, and gave us a drizzling rain all the time we were out, so my charter of always turning the cock, and bringing rain when I set my foot in Keyhaven, was this new year most brilliantly kept up.

4th.—Up by candlelight, and hard on with Clayton, about his new stanchion on my plan for the Marquis of Hastings.

5th.—Up early and out all day, but saw nothing except 5 geese travelling in the air to the eastward, so I went up the creek and was in Lymington for some hours with Lord Hastings about his new stanchion on my plan, and again with Dagwell about the punt I prescribed for Mr. Wilkinson's gentleman gunner.

7th.—Up at six, and afloat at daylight, in the most intensely cold white frost I ever was bit by. Harbour frozen up in one night. Lots of boats off, but not a shot fired. Refused a fine shot of plover because a large company of wigeon was near, which two monkeys of boys put up with their sail boat, and in short I never pulled a trigger the whole day.

8th.—Up, breakfasted, and off by break of day. Harbour a sheet of ice, though a beastly white frost. Saw a company of about 1,500 wigeon, but so restless, owing to a fog, that they would not stay a minute in one place. Shifted my shot, and went at them, prepared for a huge distance. Blew off a barrel at near 300 yards, and got 4 wigeon.

9th.—Afloat at daylight, and saw nothing all day, though a good easterly wind.

10th.—Off early again, but not a fowl to be seen. Came back about ten o'clock.

About an hour after, who should land but my old and able satellite, Buckle, whom I had recommended for a gunning tutor to Sir John Carnac. But the Marquis, all hot of course, was gone off to try for birds, so I could not show the new gun to Buckle.

11th.—The beastly white frost burst itself into rain, of course, in the night, and this morning the harbour was released from the white ice and open again. Off early, as usual, but saw not so much as an ox-bird. In to lunch and off again, when the cock flew back to the east, and drove us home, by four o'clock, with a cold gale of wind and heavy snow. The coast appears to be destitute, and no wonder. There are ten stanchion guns within about ten miles of shore, besides amateurs and snobs innumerable. The fowl appear to be absolutely banished from Keyhaven coast.

12th.—Heavy snow and easterly gale. Very unwell, so sent out Read, who saw only a few geese out of shot. Went into Lymington in a shut-up fly to see Clayton about my new ignition guns that he is getting up for divers customers. Called on the Marchioness of Hastings, to make my excuse for not venturing out to-night for a concert to which she had kindly invited me, and just came in for a part of the rehearsal, which was a credit to amateurs.

14*th.*—Having been all yesterday a prisoner with illness, I got up this morning, feeling better, two hours before daylight, but to no purpose, as the tremendous easterly freezing gale embargoed every punt and boat. The sea was terrific, and I viewed with my glass acres of birds near the foaming surf on the Channel's edge. Snobs in every direction round shore, but not a fowl shot by anyone, as everything inland was a sheet of ice.

15*th.*—Tremendous easterly gale with biting frost all night, so despaired of getting afloat to-day. But about noon the wind abated, and we then 'shipped' our big gun and gear; but before we could get under way the tyros in every direction had scared away the army of fowl. We had one chance at a bank of birds, when a 'lubber' ran down on us and sprung them. So instead of a boatload of fowl, we came home without a pull of trigger.

16*th.*—Intense frost, but scarcely any wind. What was the consequence? The whole army of birds retired for safety to their old haunt at sea, and I never pulled a trigger all day except at a few geese flying past about two gunshots off. I by chance hit down 1 brent goose, and another fell off on tide.

17*th.*—Off early again, but not a chance, as a moderate and pleasant day brought out a boatload of snobs to every quarter of a mile of channel. A pretty pass our once splendid sport is come to. Not a bird got by anyone, of course.

18*th.*—Off as usual; channel so bombarded with boats full of bullet poppers, that I retreated about twelve and came home again. A white frost last night, which, of course, altered the weather, and soon after one o'clock the cock shifted to a determined south-wester, with a pour of heavy rain that never ceased all day. This drove in the wigeon and geese from sea to within a quarter of a mile of the quay, and we would have 'weathered it' and gone into them, but a snob in every furze bush kept popping off blank shots, and drove the fowl for miles away from the harbour, and to a distance that we dare not attempt to go in a heavy gale and torrents of rain. Keyhaven is now quite 'done for.'

19th.—Busy clearing tons of thick ice from our little harbour. Off in the afternoon, when a few geese came down; but the shore snobs drove them out to sea.

20th.—Sunday. Weathercock round again to north-east, with a black frost and breeze all day. How lucky that I badgered my men into clearing off the ice yesterday!

21st.—South-easterly breeze with small rain all day. The first good company of geese that I have seen this year pitched on our mud before tide was up. Went off and lay under them (and not out of shot); but as a fellow was after them also, I dare not wait for tide to flow, so made Read blow off the popgun in order to spring them above the bearings of the gun. But they skimmed away low till too far for small shot, and my barrel, which had large shot, missed fire through the cock catching in the lock cover; and I was thus at the loss of perhaps a dozen birds, as the company was about 700 strong. Was there ever such a run of bad luck as I've had this season? The birds went off towards Lymington creek. We went after them in a rainy day, but came home blank as usual, without any further chance.

22nd.—The grand company of geese came down again at low water. Lay under them, and a fellow opposite blew a ball into them at the risk of our being shot, and away they went. Sir John Carnac and Buckle came down in the yacht and were off to-day, but the snobs would not allow any gunner a chance. I blew off a mould-shot cartridge in despair, and hit down 2 geese at near 400 yards. What assassination of our harbour! With fair play 100 geese might have died this day.

23rd.—Up by candlelight us usual. Off all day. Isle of

Wight bullet poppers in every direction : no chance for anyone to get a shot. Out again in the evening, and brought in 2 brent geese by a mould-shot cartridge at above 300 yards.

24th.—Off early. A fair show of geese, but three boats to every company. A hard day's work for a blank.

25th.—Off at daybreak in fog and drizzling rain. A few geese in, but so wild they were off the moment we were in sight. We came home to lunch, and had a providential escape. Old Read, in cleaning up, accidentally fired the percussion barrel of the great gun, which blew a hole through both sides of the 'Feather' (my beautiful following punt) ; and singular enough I heard the report of this shot just as I had finished reading a letter from Mr. Guildford Onslow on a similar accident that had wounded him on the Lake of Como, from whence he had gone to Milan for surgical assistance. The chief object of his letter, however, was to report to me the extraordinary performance of the Austrian muskets with copper primers at 1,000 yards.

26th.—Off till two, not a chance for a shot.

28th.—Extraordinary weather. Yesterday a biting white frost, and then a day for ladies and butterflies. At night a south-west gale and rain ; and to-day such a ferocious tempest that no boat could row on end. An army of birds swept in from the wild ocean, but no one could do more than view them with a spy-glass. Attempted to go off, but it was impossible.

29th.—Foggy rain, dead calm, and remarkably high tide. Off early. Fell in with a fine company of geese, but the opposition scoundrels kept popping on purpose to prevent my shooting, consequently the birds were driven to sea, and I never got a chance to shoot.

30th.—A light easterly breeze. Got 1 brent goose, and devoted the remainder of the day to experiments, as it was of no use to be afloat with a few very wild birds only to be seen, and lots of slug-shooting stanchion-gun shooters to make them, if possible, wilder.

31*st.*—Read crawled last night in his mud punt and got 3 wigeon; but the mud was so mobbed with 'snobs,' as well as mud crawlers, that the birds were all dispersed like blackbirds and thrushes instead of being in good companies, as in former years. I persevered to-day again in a south-wester and constant thick rain; but the only company I saw (geese) would not stay a minute in a place, and at ground ebb we were washed off by a gale and torrents of rain. Here ends (January) the most execrable month's sport that I ever saw or heard of since the hour I was born.

February 1*st.*—Extraordinary weather; a dense fog with a gale of wind from the west. Out early and came home blank.

2*nd.*—A heavy west gale and blue fog, as yesterday. Off early for chance of flight as geese travelled by; but 'done' by winkle-boys infesting Shore Head. Out again at two, and tried the inaccessible geese with sail at the rate of ten miles an hour. By this change we got nearer to them than we had done before (about 230 yards), and I brought in 8 brent geese; and coming home I got a flying shot with which I picked up 5 curlews, besides one that dropped off on the breakers. The first bit of sport this trip, so let us hope our luck is on the mend.

4*th.*—Out early, and in about midday. Never saw a chance. Decided on 'knocking off,' and turned to 'all hands' to get furbished and laid up before dark. Started off the royal basket for their Majesties; cleared off a torrent of letters; and was run off my legs, though far from well, in order to get emancipated for a start to-morrow.

5*th.*—Up by candlelight in order to complete my furbish and the storing of divers 'traps,' &c., and left by the morning rail train. Got to Longparish in the afternoon; and never was I more delighted to get away from any place than from my favourite quarter, Keyhaven, now that it affords nothing but provocation in lieu of the finest of all sport in existence.

Game &c. killed in the season to February 10th, 1850:

Game—115 partridges, 8 hares, 4 rabbits, 1 landrail (all I saw), 3 pheasants, 15 snipes. Total, 146. Wild fowl—3 ducks and mallards, 1 tufted duck, 1 teal, 12 wigeon, 12 brent geese. In all, only 29. Waders—5 curlews, 1 godwit, 6 plover, 41 dunlins, 1 peewit. Makes 54 head. Grand total, 229 head only. One of the worst seasons ever known.[1]

11*th.*—A letter from Keyhaven. Not a fowl has been shot since I left, though the young red-hot marquis had been slaving every day, and as furious as a Scotch terrier among mice when the farmers are taking down a wheat rick.

March 11*th.*—Down to Birmingham.

15*th.*—All in a fair way to go on without me after four days' slaving with gunmakers, so prepared for my return home, and packed up my models that were no longer wanted. Had a little job with Mr. Osborne; and the reason it was not ready proved to be the burglarious entrance of a gang of ruffians in the night, and the pillage of 700*l.* worth of silver articles and other valuable goods.

18*th.*—London. Met Captain Lautour at Greenfield's, to whom I had recommended him for a new stanchion gun on my improved plan. He told me the Poole coast was quite 'done for;' though for this last week we've had an intense black frost, and London swarming with wild fowl from our north coast and Scotland.

30*th.*—Longparish. Paid the last wages to Charles Grayston, the very best servant I ever had, who left me with views of a literary situation; and my poor old dog 'Viper,' that always greeted me with his welcome, was no more, as some villain had shot him. Never did I arrive at Longparish under more sad circumstances.

April 6*th.*—Had a narrow escape from a serious accident.

[1] A general complaint that this was a miserable game season, and the worst snipe season on record, in spite of five weeks' hard winter. Moreover I was absent on my new inventions all the best time, both for sea and land, though the coast shooting was no loss, as Keyhaven is now annihilated.

Being engaged to be with Mr. Earle before twelve to-day, I put my favourite mare into my gig and drove off for Andover soon after eleven o'clock. As the mare was as quiet as a lamb I required no servant. When about two and a quarter miles from Andover, the poor mare was suddenly seized with megrims, or mad staggers, and in all my life I never saw any animal in such an awfully horrid state. She suddenly stopped and shook her head, and then lay down; she then sprung furiously up again, and violently ran back so as to throw herself and the gig into a quickset hedge on the top of a rising bank. With a still more violent struggle she precipitated herself down into the road, falling on her back and twisting the gig to what a sailor would call 'keel uppermost;' by further struggles she then got on her side and there lay, kicking and plunging in a desolate turnpike road, where, for near half an hour, I had not a soul to come near me. At last a waggon and cart came by, and the men belonging to them helped me to extricate the mare. She then ran about like a mad bull and fell down and got up again repeatedly; at last she made one finishing fall, and I made sure she was dying, when I proceeded to Andover with the man in the cart, and hastened off the veterinary surgeon to bleed her as a last resource. On completing my business I went back and found that the mare had been saved by bleeding, and was actually led off for Longparish.

13*th.*—Engaged every day on the business of re-letting my farms &c.; of course to a great disadvantage and loss in these deplorably bad times.

July 8th.—Dragged the river in order to clear off promises of fish to friends. We had but two draws; the second we took 104 fish, including some thrown back as not in season. The best haul for many years, though not more than a quarter of what we took twenty or thirty years ago. This evening came the intelligence of the death of the poor old Duke of Cambridge, and on which sad news I had the minute bell tolled.

August 5*th*.—London. At Woolwich before ten this morning. My new military musket never failed, and, in fact, all three (Lancaster's, the Prussian, and mine) went as well as could be, owing to the very fine weather. They are, however, to be left with 300 rounds each, at the Arsenal, to be further tested in all weather, and kept out at night. This is as it should be. Other new arms are coming, and it may therefore be many months before the committee can decide as to their recommendation.

15*th*.—Birmingham. On from morning till night, like a cat after a mouse, stirring up engravers, finishers, &c., or they would have put my new grand stanchion gun on one side for the work of other parties, who were all eager to complete guns for the 1st of September.

16*th*.—Very unwell, so hired a car for the day and rode about in state. As soon as I had got several parts of my new stanchion gun from the workmen, by means of standing at their elbows, lest they should put my work aside for other pressing jobs for the London makers, I drove into the country to see a splendid Catholic church (with images from Munich) at a village called Erdington, three miles from Birmingham; and then on to Sutton Park, four miles farther, which is a celebrated place for the picnics or gipsy parties of all the pleasure people in Birmingham.

17*th*.—As my workmen to-day had to do only the hardening and polishing of the stanchion gun, which did not require the help of my suggestions, I treated myself to a holiday in order to see the country 'lions,' lest I might not have to come again to Birmingham. At nine o'clock I started by a heavily loaded omnibus, and soon after eleven got to Warwick, twenty miles, where I went all over that most splendid of all baronial residences, Warwick Castle. To my taste it surpasses all the *châteaux* I ever saw in my life. Went on to Leamington Spa, where I saw all that was to be seen. After this I proceeded to Kenilworth Castle, six miles, where I spent an hour; and then was driven on a lovely road, surrounded by the finest oaks, to Coventry. Here I saw St. Michael's Church, the ancient figure of 'peeping Tom,' &c., and got to the rail station about six, soon after which the train brought me (eighteen miles) back to Birmingham, having seen in ten hours what some people would have spent ten days in doing.

20th.—Up at six and on to London, and off immediately to Greenfield about rectifying my new military musket, which had got broken at Woolwich, and consequently lost the remainder of its trial.

27th.—To Keyhaven, where I arrived at six; I felt much at not seeing my faithful servant, old Peter Fifield, to greet me as usual, he having lately died; and there set in a gale of wind and rain, as there always is on my arrival here. But this was all right, as I was thereby enabled to give my new musket a bitter night's lodging in the thick of it, on board a boat off in harbour, and after putting the weapon in a bucket of fresh water for a finish, she fired as well as possible after breakfast on the next morning. If this is not a waterproof musket, I know not what one is.

CHAPTER XLIII

1850

September 2nd.—Longparish. Had a severely hard first day. Found a very good breed of birds, and all as large and strong as the old ones; and as the country was cleared of the corn, the birds were wilder than I ever saw them in September. Not even the scattered birds would lie to the dogs, though driven into fine turnips, and moreover I never found the scent so bad. By sheer slavery, however, I contrived to bring home 22 partridges and 4 hares.

It was near three hours before I got my first shot; an extraordinary day on the whole. We had an army of volunteers, with a carriage full of grub, to follow us, and a stiff supper for 'all hands' at night.

4th.—Another severe day, and birds even wilder than on Monday. Came home to an eight o'clock dinner, with 21 partridges.

7th.—My bag was 12 partridges and 2 hares. Scent worse than ever, but no reason to complain, as I killed all that it was possible to kill, and took the lead of other parties.

8th.—I never knew the birds so wild, or the scent so bad. Shooting absolute slavery. Had to walk all day on dry, burning ground, and take snap shots, as the birds would not lie to my pointers even when dispersed.

N.B.—I have, however, every reason to be satisfied, when I hear how very little most other parties have yet done.

16th.—Not having been out since last Tuesday, from being too unwell to walk, I prepared for a quiet ride out with dogs and gun this morning, but was seized with such pain that I had to lie down instead of starting out. But in the afternoon I was a little better, and the sal volatile and camphor julep that I finished myself off with gave me such a fillip that I killed all I fired at, and not a shot but what was far beyond slow time or easy distance.

28th.—In want of some game, so went out, though not till past twelve, as I had no strength for a day's fag. I despaired of being well enough to shoot, though as things turned out I could not have shot better. I brought in 9 partridges, 2 hares, and 2 jack snipes, and lost also 1 bird, that I shot in a slovenly manner, for want of nerve to give him the bull's-eye. With this exception I bagged all I fired at.

Game &c. killed in September 1850: 71 partridges, 15 hares, 5 snipes, 1 teal. Total, 92 head.

October 1st.—The most brilliant 1st of October that my annihilated little beat has afforded for many years. I sallied forth, according to annual custom, with my army of beaters, expecting only about 4 head of game, and came in with 4 pheasants, 4 hares, 3 partridges, and 1 turtle dove, without missing a shot.

I bagged every pheasant I found except 1 old cock that I never saw. This splendid little bit of shooting was as usual wound up with a heavy blow-out in the servants' hall, and universal satisfaction over our home-brewed ale.

7th.—Availed myself of a furious gale of wind to accept of a day's fishing at Gavel acre. But such a failure did it prove that I only just saved my blank with 1 trout. There was scarcely a fish in the river. So I left the place in disgust and came home, after which I took my rod up my own river, where I picked out 4 brace of the largest trout, besides lots thrown in, as out of season. I took also my gun, and brought home 6 snipes in little more than two hours, having thus made ample amends for the time lost all the early part of the day.

9th.—Called away from my writing desk after an old cock pheasant that was actually seen flying across the meadow for our wood. Summoned all my myrmidons to the chase of him, and in spite of cavalry and infantry the old devil escaped, though we never failed to head him in advance and surround him in every way. We found him first about a quarter past eleven, and saw him last about a quarter before six, and he outwitted me and all my unrivalled army from morning till nightfall.

15*th.*—A fine day, so went off early to search for the artful old cock pheasant again; and in the very last field, as we were coming home at night, up he flew eight gunshots off, and mounted over our wood, but though we beat till dark, I never found him.

December 28th.—A holiday for me at last. Went off with Mr. Griesbach and three men and three dogs, and scoured the whole of our wood and inclosed country, and never set eyes on one single head of game. In my life I never saw such an utterly barren chase. But as I never had a blank day in all my life, I was determined to fight hard for the salvation of my character, so sallied off all the way to Furgo Farm. One bird happened to come towards me, a very long shot, and I knocked him down. So I came in happy with my blank saved by killing 1 partridge.

1851

January 9th.—Tried a gun of Moore and Gray, and nothing could be more satisfactory. It shot quite as well as my 'Old Joe' (Manton), that Lord Poulett once offered me 100 guineas for.

10*th.*—A letter from Keyhaven to announce the death of my old and faithful housekeeper for above a quarter of a century at my cottage, and also to say the coast was quite destitute of all wild fowl.

11*th*.—Sadly in want of brace of birds, so took out my duck gun, 'Big Joe,' at dusk, crawled up to 3 partridges that were feeding, and floored the whole trio at ninety-five yards with a 4-oz. Eley cartridge. This may be called poaching, but show me the gent who would not chuckle at such an extraordinary shot.

As the coast was so destitute of plover &c. as well as wild fowl, I never went to Keyhaven for any shooting this deplorable season.

Killed at Longparish.—150 game, 5 wild fowl. Grand total, 155 head only.

N.B.—The most destitute season for every kind of winter bird known in memory of man.

February 5*th*.—Keyhaven. Up long before daylight, and on till very late at night, in order to cut through the multitude of odd jobs I had to get quit of; amongst others to engage a *pro tem.* manager of my boathouse and garden, as poor old Read is nearly done for. Keyhaven has become overloaded with gunners, and not one of them has got enough in the whole season to make up a moderate shot for a common hand gun. In short the coast is literally destitute of fowl, as it is everywhere else; and it is sixty-two years since such a rotten and barren winter was known.

6th to 12*th*.—Bedridden and in agony. What with constant pain and incessant plague with fomentations, poultices, and medicine, I am almost worn out both in body and nerves.

20*th*.—Better; and I crawled out of doors after over a fortnight's imprisonment.

April 17*th*.—London. Better; but suffering in the place where I was wounded in 1809. Went to Mr. Grey's shooting ground at Kensal Green, where we all tried my first application of my new ignition to a dandy double sporting gun; and it even far exceeded my expectations. The conical breechings for large cannon powder shot quite as well as, or even better than, the usual patent breechings; and we made magnificent targets without one failure of the primers, and at forty yards put some of the shot through forty thicknesses of thick brown paper. Nothing could be more satisfactory; and all I wanted was the use of my limbs to be more active at the trial.

19th.—On all day at the Glass House putting on the crimson cloth to my counter, and unpacking and laying out on it all my things that came up some weeks ago (and luckily I took also my man-servant, for whom I had some difficulty in getting a pass), though I was too lame to help to lift the things myself. In short, I never met such an ill-regulated concern as this mighty Glass House called by many 'The Folly.'

24th.—Since Sunday I have taken no memoranda (through incessant bustle about my new military musket for the Great Exhibition) because on Sunday afternoon I lost the use of my right hand and could not even sign my name. To-day, thank God, I can write again, though very slowly; and I was on hard all this afternoon completing the arrangement of my things at the Glass House, with my servants.

30th.—Yesterday was the last day for exhibitors to uncover their articles for the exhibition; but I had the promise of a special entrée from Captain Westmacott, the director of our class, if I would send in my card to him. I therefore went to ask for the promised admission, but the doors were so fortified by a large body of police that I could not get near the entrance, and they refused to pass a card for anyone. After waiting above an hour, I chanced to see Captain Westmacott and holloaed out to him; and by his interceding with the committee he with difficulty got me in. But it was impossible that I could go back; so I had to borrow the few tools I wanted; and with the kind help of persons I knew, got all my things uncovered and set in proper order just before two o'clock, when a bell rang to clear out every person from the building. Thus I had a narrow escape from having my things roughly handled, and perhaps broken to pieces, by the rough hands of officials who would have torn off the cases and thrown them away. I never saw such a bear garden in my life; and all the exhibitors were refused admission to meet the Queen on the opening to-morrow unless they paid three guineas for a season ticket. They were almost in a state of mutiny at this rascally injustice; and for my own part, as I am still an invalid, I did not regret that I was emancipated from the awful crowd that there must be on the grand opening to-morrow.

May 1st.—Opening, by the Queen, of the Grand Exhibition.

Exhibitors, however, were not admitted but by three-guinea ticket; and I was lucky in not having taken one, as my exertions of yesterday had so crippled me that I could not have gone.

6th.—Longparish. Obliged to have a poor valuable horse killed owing to his accident, and we ordered him to be buried near the other old favourite animals. I was so cut up with one annoyance and the other, that I had no heart for anything all day. Having been for months a sufferer, I had hoped a little change of air would do me good.

14th.—London. All day at the Glass House, where, after paying 5*s.* to get in, I had some hours' trouble to obtain an exhibitor's ticket for future admission. My things were a little deranged, though I soon put them right again. Many foreign articles were not yet arrived. I stood this severe day better than I expected, but I was so weak I could hardly walk about the gigantic building.

16th.—Received an official letter from the Ordnance, with the Master-General's thanks for my exertions in small arms, but inclosing a report from the committee as to some failures of my primers. For this, however, I was fully prepared, as long illness had prevented my properly attending to the workmen, and I had consequently prepared another musket with superior primers on an improved plan, which I left in hand yesterday. I therefore wrote to Colonel Chalmer to state what I had since done.

29th.—London. A letter forwarded from Longparish, requiring my attendance at the Glass House every day till the jurors had passed my class. Went there for the whole day, and none of them came.

30th.—There again after breakfast, and kept an hour at the committee door till I could learn something as to the probable time of their inspection, which took place in about half an hour after I got to my counter. Nothing could be more flattering than the politeness I received and the compliments paid to my (original) productions; but, of course, I am not so sanguine as to suppose that such articles would be considered of such general utility as to justify the grant of a medal or any other premium. Other persons had copied my inventions and attempted to pass them off for their own; but here they were defeated by my luckily being present, and the jurors, therefore, were satisfied as to who was the inventor and who the imitators.

June 1st.—Longparish. Most unpleasantly situated. Just before we went to church I got a hasty summons from the Glass House to meet the Queen and Prince Albert at my counter there at nine to-morrow morning. Situated as I was I had no alternative but to fly off by the mail train after midnight; but I was so ill I was obliged to forego my attempt to get up to London to-night.

2nd.—London. The moment I arrived I hastened to Mr. Wilkinson, who told me I had 'missed the royal inspection,' of which he knew nothing beyond what concerned himself. I therefore proceeded, per 'bus,' to Glass House, all anxiety about what had taken place, and the only person who could give me any information was the policeman belonging to my class. He said that Captain Inglefield, R.N. (our superintendent, who had learned all from me), had explained everything, and that the Queen and Prince had paid marked attention and given some time to see my counter, and appeared to be much pleased with my new musket for the army and what else I exhibited. So far so good; and many thanks to the captain for his kind aid in my unfortunate absence. But still I would rather have lost one hundred pounds than not have been there myself.

3rd.—Went early to the Glass House. Found that most of our exhibitors had received their notices too late to attend the royal command for yesterday, so I acquitted myself and others by forwarding to Windsor Castle, for Prince Albert, a complaint against this shameful neglect of the authorities. I also posted this want of courtesy on their part in the newspapers.

5th.—I saw Captain Inglefield, who gave me an account of his explaining my inventions, and a flattering report of her Majesty's and Prince Albert's interrogations and approbation.

18th.—Got a holiday at last, and had a few hours' pleasure in hearing the six bands of the Household troops, added to that of the Artillery, at Chelsea Hospital, where a fête was given for a charity. The tremendous crescendos of 350 men playing together, and all the drums added, produced such an effect as I never before heard.

21st.—Busy at the Glass House cleaning up and repairing the articles exhibited at my counter, and then devoted myself to the lions of the exhibition for as long as I had strength to crawl about.

26th.—Keyhaven. Off behind the Isle of Wight all day in hopes that being at sea would do me good. Took my new musket to prove the ignition on salt water; nothing could go better.

29th.—Scarcely able to breathe for the intense heat, and so weak I could hardly get about. Lost my charter at Keyhaven. The first time for thirty years that I visited this place without having a drop of rain.

July 19*th.*—London. Busy all the past week, every day, about the finishing of my new ignition double sporting gun, for which I got an order of admission to the Glass House; but at the same time a letter from Mr. Digby Wyatt to say that 'the jurors were all dismissed from their labours,' and, consequently, there was no more chance for any more prizes being awarded. The Prince Albert started yesterday for Osborne, so I had not even the chance of showing the gun to his Royal Highness, unless he should have time to see me on his return to London, previously to the Court leaving for Scotland.

26*th.*—Run off my legs the whole week, and at last got my new double gun this morning into the Glass House, and had to work all day with the press to proclaim it by circulars and articles.

31*st.*—Indefatigable every day pushing my new plan, which the brutes of gunmakers tried all they could to suppress while I was ill and a cripple.

August 9*th.*—On from eight in the morning till a seven o'clock dinner every day in the past week at a multiplicity of callings on different subjects by the press. This morning, at nine o'clock, I was in attendance at my counter in the Glass House, by recommendation of Mr. Dilke, the Queen's factotum and cicerone, prepared to show my new double gun to Prince Albert, whom I had apprised of its completion, and who, I believe, would have made a point of seeing it, but her Majesty had been induced to stay so long over other articles in the transept that no time was left to go up to our gallery, and the royal party 'bolted' soon after ten o'clock, and went off direct from the Glass House *en route* for Osborne.

After giving long explanations of all my 'lions' (in my French) to a leading man of Madrid, and then a great man from Liège, I left the building, and was busy the rest of the day about my models for altering the disgraceful blunders of the new double carbines for the Cape service, and doing my best towards proclaiming a reform in the wretched arms of the Government.

16*th.*—On, for the last week, from morning till night every day, jobbing, writing for the press, &c.

23*rd.*—Not an hour's rest from Monday morning till this (Saturday) night. No time to take a journal. To-day hard on at Glass House and in City.

CHAPTER XLIV

1851

September 25th.—Longparish. Unable to put pen to paper till this day from severe illness, and now scarcely able to write, and consequently could make no daily memoranda; the use of my hand so gone that I had to be dressed and fed like a child. No great loss of shooting, as there is such a miserable breed of birds.

October 9th.—I removed to Keyhaven in order that I might try change of air. I was taken twice across to the Isle of Wight, and managed to get on the hills, as my legs are far less weak than my hands and head.

13*th and* 14*th.*—London. All day at the Glass House. On the 14th I was honoured with a special interview on the subject of my new gun, not only with Prince Albert, but with her Majesty also; and their affability was not a little flattering to a veteran amateur in gunmaking.

15*th.*—Attended the grand finale of the exhibition, which will be the leading subject of every newspaper in the world. And this evening my servants rescued all my property from the building.

16*th.*—There was one pour of incessant rain all yesterday, and then a white frost at night, which produced a lovely morning for the removal of goods, for which no packing cases were allowed till after the 20th, when the confusion was expected to be dreadful. I therefore went off about eight this morning with six assistants, and by means of having the great double champion duck gun carried across Hyde Park, and all the brittle articles taken in a large cab, I had housed everything that had been exhibited a few minutes before twelve in Dorset Place, and at three o'clock the bright sun had 'shut up shop,' and there was a return of wet weather. Nothing could have been better managed, all at no expense, except the mere fare for the cab, and I had therefore every reason to be truly thankful for this extreme good fortune.

25th.—My portrait and sketch of my life &c. appeared, by desire of the commissioners, and at the request of the editor, with other leading exhibitors, in the 'Illustrated London News' of this day.

December 1st.—As all other remedies had failed to make me warm, I had this day recourse to a desperate one, that cured a cold for me many years ago, and that was to sally forth in great heavy water boots, and slave in the river from island to island in search of snipes, and this, instead of the 1st of September, was my first sortie with a gun this season. I was too weak and unwell to shoot as I always had done, and consequently missed four shots that I ought to have killed; but I managed to bag 2 teal and 6 snipes. The full snipes were extremely wild, as they always are in white frosts.

N.B.—While fagging hard I got circulation, which I had not felt for the last fortnight; but when in the house I felt cold again.

3rd.—Started with Charles Heath and a cry of dogs and beaters, and scoured our wood, and all the home inclosures; and except getting a glimpse of two rabbits, I never set eyes on one single head of game. Determined not to lose my charter as to never yet having made a blank day, I proceeded to the river, and got 6 snipes and 1 teal without missing a shot.

6th.—Went out again to circulate my chilly limbs, and in spite of such a severe cold that made my eyes weak and dim, I killed all I shot at, and all very long quick shots, viz. 6 snipes and 1 teal.

22nd.—Got 2 mallards from my decoy hut at midnight.

1852

January 5th.—Went round the home beat, but never saw a head of game. Went to the river at three o'clock to save my blank. All I saw was 3 snipes and 2 jack snipes, all of which I killed dead and bagged, and I also made two very long shots at a wild duck and a water rail. I discharged my gun seven times, and killed my 7 head all quite dead. A satisfactory little bit of sport for one in bad trim and with damaged eyes.

8th.—Received the report of the death on November 6 of my friend Colonel Fordyce, who was killed in action by one of the savage Caffres. This was a sad blow to me, not only a subject of deep regret, but a circumstance of provocation, because my son, had he not retired on half-pay, would now, to an almost certainty, have come in for the lieutenant-colonelcy of the 74th. His junior, Major Seton, is now senior major, in command of the depot, where Peter would have been in safety; and his services would, no question, have gained for him this splendid promotion.

17th.—London. Had the mortification to see the appointment of my son's junior, Major Seton, to the lieutenant-colonelcy and command of the gallant 74th Highlanders on the death vacancy of the lamented Colonel Fordyce. Persons say, 'But your son might have been killed.' Not at all; Seton was snug in command of the depot, and by the time he gets to the Cape, the reinforcements now gone out, and the new constitution granted, will most likely render the war there now of infinitely less danger. While I was off in the City on a torrent of further business, who should call but Signor Vercellini from Liverpool. I had heard he was dead, and he heard I was dead. Old Sola also called, and him I had long lost sight of. A singular coincidence this visit of my Italian singers of olden time.

19th.—To-day Peter's birthday, which brings him to the age of forty. I had an interview with Lord Clarence Paget, and then with his excellent father, the Marquis of Anglesea, to present my new double carbine for the Cape, as an amendment to the ridiculous ignitions that have been just sent out there, ordered by the leather-headed people in office from young Lancaster, who objected to the construction of them, but dare not remonstrate, lest he should lose the order and the patronage.

24th.—Busy at the Ordnance for the last few days, in hopes of preventing further blunders in the new arms that are ordered for the Cape.

31st.—Much engaged all the past week about firearms &c., though so weak and unwell that I had scarcely strength to get about. Much to do with printers, editors &c. to prevent my being robbed of the credit of my inventions.

February 3rd.—After seeing the Queen's procession to open Parliament, I went to the club, where I saw conspicuously in the 'Times,' 'Herald,' &c. a notice of my advice on the Cape rifles and other arms quoted from the 'Birmingham Gazette,' so if my plans be adopted, the Government superficials cannot pass them off as their own suggestions, as is their custom.

6th.—Got a private admission to see the Crystal Palace, now that it is quite clear of all partitions &c., and no tongue can describe its symmetrical beauties. The building itself is even a greater 'lion' than all the valuables it had contained.

I omitted to state that I received my splendid prize medal several days ago.

10th.—Attended by command the select committee at the Ordnance, who, among many other things, sat on my new military carbine, which was decided *nem. con.* as 'by far the best that had been invented.' I took also a very clever French musket, to show how ours ought to be ignited, and had to hear much nonsense from Mr. Lovell, the inspector of small arms, who attempted to show that his was the best, and was absolutely uncivil when he met his match in meeting me. Other troublesome jobs, and a levee of lookers-in all at the same time, so that I could only compare myself to a cat thrown by the tail among all the cur dogs of Marylebone.

19th.—Had a long and most agreeable interview with Prince Albert, in order to explain to his Royal Highness my new primer and my carbine, that was approved by the Ordnance committee. I was honoured with the highest approbation, and the Prince was, as usual, most kind and affable, and entered, *con amore*, into all particulars.

20th and 21st.—On like a mad dog from morning till night with Captain Shrapnel, my old friend the General's son, with gunmakers, projectilists, general officers, Ordnance authorities, engineers, &c., on the subject of arms and national defence.

23rd.—Ran down to Keyhaven. Sorry reports; not one tolerable shot in the whole season. Universal complaints as to the scarcity of all kinds of birds on the coast.

24th.—A hard black frost, with a cutting north-east gale, but far too late to bring over fowl, though it may drive in the very few geese that have been about, as they rarely go home till April. Serenaded by Milford ringers and band, on my recovery from a winter's illness, and my arrival after getting the prize medal for big 'guns.'

26th.—Went with Buckle, Read, Parker, and Shuttler over the mud, from my leak to another one that I had nicknamed 'Molesworth's Spreader,' after an enthusiastic amateur that used almost to live in it with his punt, and we all agreed that to cut a channel across would be an incalculable advantage to Keyhaven gunners and boatmen by shortening the distance and avoiding heavy seas to the eastward. I therefore drew out and headed a subscription paper with 2*l.* on my own part, which I thought enough for me, after I had expended near 50*l.* on my large creek, which has proved such a universal convenience and accommodation, not only to gunners, but to the public at large. There were a few geese seen this morning near my creek, so I mustered three stanchions, as I had promised some geese to Prince Albert if they could be got. The birds, however, were all gone to the eastward before we had turned out, and it blew a heavy gale, so I left my small set-out afloat all night for the chance of a shot to-morrow.

27th.—Gale abated, and not a bird to be seen on the coast except 2 burrough ducks, both of which I brought home. I got well on board them, though the wildest of birds, by washing my punt with umber and water, as the tyros had so ill-used the white punts that even the ox-birds had become awake to them, insomuch that anything white had become a signal for every living fowl to be off. Furbished up and put all in store, preparative to leaving to-morrow.

All the birds I killed up to March 1852 were: Game, never shot at. 3 rabbits and 24 snipes. Total, 27. Wild fowl.—4 teal, 8 ducks and mallards, 2 sheldrakes. Total, 27 + 14. Grand total, only 41 head.

Illness nearly the whole season prevented my shooting, and at one time I was in danger.

March 3rd.—London. Attended the Queen's Levee, which was a very full one, owing to the numerous presentations on the happy change of Government, and our riddance from the Cobden-bullied ministers.

4th.—On with Captain Shrapnel, Uncle Bishop,[1] Mr. Elmslie, Lancaster and Grey, all more or less on experiments for the new engines of war.

13th.—Out again, and had a long, flattering, and interesting interview with Lord Hardinge, the newly appointed Master-General of the Ordnance under Lord Derby's Government, on the disgraceful apathy and monopoly of the officials, who have long had the control of the small arms department, and left with his lordship a wooden model of my suggestion for several improvements in the stock, ignition, ramrod &c. of the

[1] The head man and manager for 'Westley Richards.'

army musket, and found that the exertions of myself and others would be taken up and tried fairly.

Busy every day with Lord Hardinge, Colonel Chalmer, Purdey, Grey, Lancaster and Wilkinson up to end of March, and with divers other gunmakers on experiments, &c.

April 3rd.—A grand trial on Purdey's shooting ground, near Starch Green. Purdey went off in the morning, and at half-past twelve we had a meeting at Purdey's shop, of Lord Hardinge, the Master-General, Sir Howard Douglas, Colonel Chalmer, Colonel Gordon, Mr. Purdey, jun., and myself, with Sergeant Baker, the crack shot at Woolwich Arsenal, and then started off to try the Frenchman's Minié ball against a new conical ball of old Purdey's invention, and had the satisfaction to prove that we were no longer to be beat and laughed at by foreigners. Purdey's ball proved to be the best. We were hard at work till near five o'clock, and the result was this :

Through hard elm boards

Line musket (with four drams of powder and ball) through boards	9
Ditto with Minié	11
Purdey's 20 bore (with his ball and three drams of powder) .	12
Purdey's 1 oz. 32 bore (with only two drams of powder) .	14

We then tried for accuracy of range, and the Purdey 32 beat all others out of the field, so that on further trials there is every reason to hope that the Minié will no longer be the idol of the Woolwich authorities.

5th.—On from the time I got up till bedtime with all parties. Heard a flaming report of Lancaster at Woolwich, so between all my constituents I hope to see the Minié snuffed out, no matter by whom so long as he is an honest Englishman.

6th.—Heard of the awful wreck of the 'Birkenhead' troop ship off the Cape, where nearly 500 persons were launched into eternity, and among them poor Colonel Seton, who was on passage to command the 74th. Here would have been my son had he not retired on half-pay, so that all my regret at his losing this grand promotion was cancelled by his providential escape.

28th.—Had an interview with Lord Hardinge, with some models, &c., and among them a large model of my wheel-barrow stanchion gun artillery, with wool battery, for raking a close column of infantry with a pound mould shot goose cartridge. His lordship was pleased with my idea, and approved of introducing stanchion guns in future warfare.

May 6th.—Attended a grand meeting of gunmakers and riflemen, at the villa, Mulgrave House, Putney, of Lord Ranelagh, who deserves the thanks of the whole country for his zealous endeavours to encourage the art of projectiles, and who will have future meetings on a larger scale which will stimulate all the gunmakers to come forward in fair competition. This is what was long wanted, but hitherto no one has had the spirit for such an undertaking.

18th.—To Longparish for a day's business. Took down in my hand the dandy exhibition gun, in order to try that and the cannon powder at the rooks, which are now the only game of which our poor country will afford a rapid succession of shots. Got 125 rooks without cleaning the gun, so proved the humbug of this powder being too dirty to stand a hard day's shooting, and moreover proved that it shot much stronger than the fine powder. The only real fault of the former is, that it is bad for trade, being only 1*s.* per lb.

June 1st.—London. Went down with Mr. Lancaster, by desire of Lord Hardinge, to Mr. Lancaster's shooting ground, at Wormwood Scrubbs, to try the relative qualities of best fine powder and 'T.P.L.G.' cannon powder. Lancaster's new ground afforded quite a treat, and we had some fine sport shooting at his iron stags that fly up and down a railway similar to the 'Montagne Russe' in Paris.

21st.—Took the barrel and my new models to Mr. Lacy, 21 Great St. Helen's, near the India House, who does almost everything for Lancaster.

22nd.—The barrel was proved this morning, and then I set the foreman upon my job, which was to produce my style of musket for the Ordnance committee agreeably to an official letter that I had received.

July 1st.—Had a sad disappointment by missing a full-dress admission to hear the Queen's Speech in the Lords on a ticket from the Lord Great Chamberlain.

3rd.—Kept prisoner here in the dog days about this botheration musket of mine, having to go every day to the City, to prevent blunders and misunderstanding.

7th.—Much worry with the musket, owing to my directions being given by a middleman, and therefore I was obliged to see the workmen myself and correct divers mistakes. Had to go to Lord Hardinge's room, and bring away my perfect carbine as a guide to prevent more blunders. General Bacon caught me up and wished me to meet him and Prince George of Cambridge, to try Deane's five-barrel revolving carbine. Prisoner in the Palace from half-past two till a quarter past three. No one came, and no message left, so took a cab and returned to the City; first to Deane's and then to Lacy's, where I left the carbine in charge of Jones, a very clever 'screwer together,' after having waited an hour and a quarter in durance vile till he had returned from his tea. And all this in the hottest weather that had been known in England for many years. The thermometer about 112, and everything broiling, and all this too in the bustling nuisance of the City election. Did not get home till seven o'clock, and then completely knocked up. All this I go through from my anxiety to do good to the service, by superseding the vile rubbish that is served out to the army. But were a hundred guineas offered me, I would refuse it, rather than go through the worry I've had for this last month, and particularly this day.

8th.—On all day again about my musket, and did not get home to dinner till nine o'clock at night, as I was determined not to leave the factory till I could rescue the musket and all my models. The latter I left with Mr. Adams, in order to pit Deane & Co. versus Lancaster, on my way home to dinner, in a flying hansom cab, which cut along almost at railway speed. Thus, after eighteen days of perpetual pother, I got rid of Lacy's factory. The double carbine I left to have engraved on it the inscription which I had merely written and pasted on the butt, as to its being approved by the Ordnance committee last February.

13*th*.—Longparish. Went over to Andover on a multiplicity of business, and soon after one o'clock there set in the most awful storm of thunder, lightning, and enormous hailstones that I have ever seen. In one hour the town of Andover was in an absolute river. About four o'clock the storm abated and I started back for Longparish, but when I got about halfway home this dreadful weather set in again. My man and I were at one time in a stroke of lightning that passed between us and the splashboard of the gig, but, thanks to God's mercy, we just escaped this danger. The hail, larger than pigeons' eggs, continued to pour upon us, as it were, one incessant vertical volley of musketry, which the poor pony weathered as not one horse in 1,000 would have done. On our arrival home, drenched to the skin and with tattered umbrella, we found things in a sad state, and all the men we had clearing the parapets, lest the ceilings should burst in with the deluge of water that had overflowed the pipes, and, of course, windows out of number smashed to pieces. The storm did not cease till near six, when I went out and found the garden, greenhouse, and everything else in one absolute state of wreck. Fruit and vegetables beat level with the ground and scarcely a pane of glass left whole on the premises, the trees half stripped of their leaves, and branches blown off by the gale. The hail lay on the ground like a fall of snow, and we shovelled up as much as we wanted to make some ice, which was excellent and refreshing after our excitement. In short, no such a storm was ever known to old men of over ninety in our neighbourhood, and the consequence to crops and other property must be a severe loss to both the rich and the poor.

Dreadful reports from all parts as to damage to corn &c.

Broken panes in house	94
" " " greenhouse	286
Broken in all	380

19th.—Ran up to London to vote at the Middlesex election, and lucky that I did, as the fellows had put aside my musket to do rough work (for India), which I made them put aside by a little *douceur.*

20th.—Went to my district, Bethnal Green, and gave a plumper for the Marquis of Blandford, whose party was, of course, hooted at by the scum and rads at this dirty end of the town.

24th.—Up very early and down to Keyhaven, to clear off my bills &c. (after five months' absence from the place), to see to my new creek, and other work done, overhaul my flotilla, great guns and gear, after five months of such extremes of weather as had rarely been known before; and with a new man (Shuttler) to trust to, since poor old Fifield dead, and old Read retired and gone away to live the other side of Lymington. Found all things even better than I could expect.

A regular set in of wet weather at last, so I failed not to keep up my charter of bringing rain whenever I came to Keyhaven.

31st.—Intense heat up to this day, when I got a letter to say my musket was gone on with all wrong in my absence, so I flew at once up to town.

August 4th.—London. Saw Lord Hardinge for a few minutes, and gave a hasty explanation of the musket, which I then took away to be either made right or mended with a new one; and much regretted I had not gone to Birmingham, instead of being handed over to the barbarous gun butchers in the City.

7th.—Up very early, and went down to Waltham to the Government factory for small arms. Was received by Colonel Gordon in command, from whom I received the kindest attention and hospitality. Though my trip was a visit of demi-official business, it repaid me well as an excursion of pleasure, by seeing all the manufactory, splendid shooting ground &c. Here the machinery is worked by water as well as by steam engines, and 5,000 Miniés are being made from the forged, or rather rolled, tubes from Birmingham.

13*th.*—Up soon after four, and at Waterloo Station by half-past six to go down for the lord lieutenant's meeting at Winchester this morning. The Duke of Wellington had arrived when I got to the station office. This meeting of the lieutenancy of the county was relative to raising the militia, about which the old Duke is most active and energetic. The proceedings commenced before twelve, and ended soon after two; after which I had a fine opportunity to speak to his Grace about the muskets, and show him my models; and, what's more, tell him about the failure of the arms at the Cape, which he told me he had never before heard of, so it's high time he did.

19*th.*—London. Went early to Deane's factory, as the percussion hole was to be drilled to-day, and on that depends the well-going of my new musket. Captain Shrapnel's musket has just failed from this delicate job being blundered, and I had to throw away Lancaster's City job for the same reason. I then went to inspect Sydenham and the site for the new glass palace; it is to stand on twenty-one acres, surrounded by 300 acres, with a magnificent view from a lofty hill.

23*rd to* 26*th.*—Every day and all day at the factory over London Bridge, and after all my trouble had to order another musket to be got up, in consequence of the blunders of the City workmen. The scramble in preparing for the 1st of September put the whole factory in such a drive, that the men had no brains for any new and out-of-the-way job, and I was determined nothing should be sent to the board in my name with faults that were open to criticism.

CHAPTER XLV

1852

September 1*st.*—A wonderful day, considering the bad reports of game and the unusual wildness of the birds. Came home to an eight o'clock dinner, with 30 partridges, 1 rabbit, 1 curlew and 1 hedgehog. Made four double shots and missed but twice. Hardly credible after my being pronounced this time last year as never likely to survive another season. Thank God, however, the doctors were out in their judgment.

4*th.*—A sorry show of wild birds, and yet had another extraordinary day, bagging all that it was possible to kill, as the behaviour of the dogs, the marking and the shooting, were perfection. My bag was 21 partridges, 1 hare, 1 landrail, and 1 quail.

7*th.*—Out for a hard day again, but was so unwell that I missed three shots, and two of them very fair ones. The bag was 17 partridges and 2 hares, and should have been sure of a third hare, a most easy shot ; but both my barrels missed fire, a mishap that never occurred to me in all my life, unless in wet weather.

13*th.*—An extraordinary day's good luck, and first-rate shooting. I could not get away till twelve o'clock, but came home to a seven-o'clock dinner, with 15 partridges, 3 quails, and 2 landrails ; I only fired 21 shots.

16*th.*—This morning's paper in deep mourning announced the almost sudden death of the Duke of Wellington at Walmer Castle on the 14th. The event quite cut me up, as it was only on the 13th of August that I had such an affable interview with his Grace at Winchester on the subjects of the militia and my improvements in firearms. An immense flight of snipes having been seen by Lovelock while watching the fishery, I went up the river to try for them; but they were so extremely wild for want of wind, that though I saw above 20 couple, I could only bring in 4 snipes. Being thus engaged, I sent Siney off with my new exhibition gun, as I wanted game for the farmers; and he had the splendid luck to get 5 hares, 5 partridges, and 1 wood pigeon.

29th.—At Longparish House. List of game brought in up to Michaelmas: 125 partridges, 27 hares, 1 rabbit, 4 quails, 4 landrails, 7 snipes (and 3 caught in wires), 1 wood pigeon. Total, 172 head.

N.B.—The most extraordinary list on record, considering the bad breed of birds, and that last year I was too ill to shoot, and was pronounced as 'never likely to take the field again.' Thank God for my unexpected recovery.

30th.—Attended a large meeting with deputy-lieutenants at Romsey; and so much there was to do that I did not get home to a meal till about half-past nine at night. While waiting for arrival of parties, I had just time to inspect the celebrated old Abbey Church, the greatest curiosities of which were the ancient monument of the daughter of King Stephen, and a female human skull with long plaited hair, in a most perfect state and resting on a block of oak, 1500 years old.

October 1st.—Kept up my old charter of scouring our wood and hedgerows, and 'blowing out' my myrmidons in the hall. One old cock was the only pheasant seen or heard of on the estate. I had the luck to bag this said pheasant, with 7 partridges, 2 hares, and 1 rabbit; which performance, under all circumstances, I considered an excellent day's sport.

20th.—Keyhaven. Busy all the morning, and then afloat till dark to explore the coast; but saw nothing, though heard that a company of wigeon had been seen within a day or two.

Well repaid for a long day's cruise, by the delightful change to healthy sea air.

21st.—Off at six for anything to try a stanchion gun at, that I had made after my prize medal gun for the late young Marquis of Hastings, whose family gave it to Shuttler, who now goes with me; but the gun missed fire every shot but one, and then it hung fire at a cormorant, which, however, I bagged, after near an hour's chase in the channel. He regularly dived at about fifty yards; just twenty yards too far for the stripe of shot to catch his head in time. After several blank rounds most accurately fired, I tried him by firing enough before him for the cartridge to meet his head at right angles when in the act of 'shutting his port.' What was the result? He turned up as dead as a log of wood. Here then is a recipe for stopping a crippled 'parson.' Never too late to learn something.

November 4th.—London. Up at seven and on till night: First, with Lord Winchester on militia concerns; second, with Westley Richards on my new plan for a cripple gun; third, at Ordnance about committee; fourth, with Wilkinson on firearms; fifth, with Dingwall about my rents and leases; sixth, at Deane's factory on military arms and experiments; seventh, with Purdey and Brazier on locks and revolvers; besides doing a long list of commissions at West End and in City.

10th.—In a crowd and bustle getting tickets from Lord Chamberlain for the Duke lying in state at Chelsea on the 12th, and for getting into the House of Lords to-morrow.

11th.—I had the closest possible stare at the *cortége.* An incessant pour of rain all day; but it was fun to see the silk-stocking flunkeys (for whom nothing is good enough) obliged to trample through the mud like a brood of young ducks.

12th.—An awful gale from south-east, and torrents of heavy rain all day. Started at nine for Chelsea, where the lying in state of the Duke was the most magnificent spectacle I ever saw; and on this occasion the whole concern of carriage regulations &c. &c. was conducted as well as in Paris. This regularity, it appears, was but of short duration; so it's lucky I went early in the morning. In the afternoon the confusion was such that one-half of the select people could not get in at all; and the next day, Saturday, the first day for public admission, the crowd was awful. Two females carried off dead, and no one can tell how many cripples. Much damage done by the overflowing of Thames to-day. Such tides as had rarely been known.

15*th to* 17*th.*—Hard on at Deane's factory, as the Ordnance had sent word that they wished Captain Shrapnel and myself to prepare some specimens of arms, they not having yet had any on which they had not a difference of opinion. The City was like a field of battle, preparing for the monster 'black job' of the 18th, to-morrow.

18*th.*—The Duke's funeral. Up before four o'clock. Our retired part of town already in a roar with carriages. Got to the Club at half-past six, and had about the best place in all the house. To describe the magnificence of this, the most glorious of all funerals ever before heard of in the world, is superfluous because impossible, and every newspaper will feed on it for weeks to come. But I cannot help recording how much my feelings were excited at the last sight of the coffin, which was placed open to view upon such a car as eyes never yet beheld, and the poor old Duke's favourite horse following in the rear. The procession was above two hours long.

25*th.*—Went on private view to see all the orders, bâtons, swords &c. of the late Duke by permission of Mr. Garrard. A sight well worth seeing, as no man on earth ever held so many honours.

26*th.*—Went by tickets to the last view of the Duke's pageant—the interior of St. Paul's Cathedral, lit up with gas, and hung with black, precisely as it appeared at the funeral. Here ends what may be considered the last 'lion' of the grand and mournful exhibition of 1852.

December 6th.—At the factory again to-day, and to my great relief got my new military musket finished, all but polishing and other trumpery, which will be done by midday to-morrow.

7th.—Wet weather and a stiff day's work. 1. Went to the factory, where I had to wait till the rifle musket was finished. 2. To work it to the West End and then to the Horse Guards. 3. To wait till the Commander-in-Chief's levee of eighty officers was over, and then to show him the arm, with which he was much pleased, and directed me to proceed, officially, with it to the Ordnance Office. Here I left it, and then wrote from the Club an application for a committee. Several general officers saw the arm, and pronounced it to be the 'best yet produced.' A most satisfactory day.

8th.—Another wet day. Had an interview with Lord Raglan, the new Master-General at the Ordnance, and explained to him the advantages of my new arm. Nothing could be more satisfactory than my interview; but, unfortunately, the last committee had sat yesterday morning, when some very inferior arms were passed. Lord Raglan, however, wished me to see Sir George Berkeley; but he having left the office, I had to await the interview.

N.B.—While alone in the ante-room, I passed a good hour in overhauling every arm that has ever been sent in. I never set eyes on a worse heap of rubbish; not a new idea among all the gunmakers or Government officials.

9th.—After waiting an hour and a half among all the lot of firearms, which I overhauled again, I got my interview with Sir George Berkeley, who had only just arrived at the office. I explained to him my new arm, in juxtaposition with the 'Enfield' one that had been approved. He desired me to leave it with him, took down my address, and hinted about having another committee.

23rd.—Attended the Ordnance committee on my new arm. I produced and explained its advantages over those that had hitherto been brought before the board, and here the matter ended, till I received an official letter to my address in the country.

27th.—Longparish. The most terrific tempest ever known, all last night and till about three this afternoon. About fifty of my trees blown down, and among them the old lofty poplars in front of the house.

30th.—An answer to my letter of inquiry about Keyhaven. Thank God! the Cottage just escaped the awful flood and gale, in which, by help of old Payne, Shuttler, and others, all my heavy guns and property were removed upstairs. The damage done to boats on the quay &c. was extensive, as the raging sea came over all the walls and up to the houses. To-day I went out and viewed the awful wrecks of trees in my wood here, and finished with an afternoon's shooting, though expecting almost a blank. Had the luck, however, to come home with 3 rabbits, 1 snipe, and 3 partridges.

31st.—Proceeded to order labourers, sawyers, bricklayers &c. to clear the mischief done by the late ferocious hurricane. The number of trees blown down here proved to be seventy-six, besides those on the other side of the river, and on my estate at Bullington. Thus it appears that both in the summer hailstorm and in this winter tempest I was the greatest sufferer in the neighbourhood. While too busy to try for game, I espied that ever-intruding scamp-keeper of Mr. Coles going to his constant beat on my farm, and was just in time to have the ground well scoured before him, and gloriously finished the old year with 3 hares, 2 partridges, and 2 rabbits.

1853

January 5th.—Too busy to shoot, and wanting a head or two of game I sent my keeper Siney out for the whole day, and after slaving over all my best ground, he came home at night with (what I never yet had) a blank. I therefore exulted at my escape.

10th.—Received yesterday an official from Ordnance,

stating that a portion of my improvements in military arms would be adopted for the service, but, most unwisely, declining to adopt all my suggestions.

13*th.*—London. On from morning to night, and this day left my improved musket with Mr. Purdey, who was delighted with it, and kindly agreed to show it to everyone, in order to let the world see how superior this (my arm for 1853) was to the Enfield one of 1852, that the committee had obstinately fixed on, and had the impudence to send to Prince Albert. Captain Shrapnel was not even allowed a committee after his some hundreds of pounds expense. He is writing these people down ; I merely advertise in the papers.

List of game brought in up to February 1853 : 164 partridges, 39 hares, 9 rabbits, 4 quails, 4 landrails, 1 pheasant, 1 wood pigeon, 20 snipes. Total, 242 head.

N.B.—Not a shot at a wild fowl as yet this season. I beat all the neighbours for game this autumn, but the floods annihilated all winter shooting for coast or inland.

February 25*th.*—Bitter cold weather. Very unwell. (Tantalising reports of the sport at Keyhaven.)

April 23*rd.*—Longparish. I feebly take up the pen, which I've been unable to use ever since the 9th of March. I've had an awful illness, and been in agony for forty-two days ; repeated consultations with Sir Ben. Brodie, Dr. Bright, Dr. Pope, and Dr. Badger, and in very serious danger ; almost at the point of death more than once. Prayed for at Longparish and Milford churches. My son, telegraphed for from Scotland, came to my bedside before daylight on the 14th of March.[1] As all remedies proved ineffectual, Sir Ben. advised as a last

[1] He came from Inverary, N.B., sixteen miles by coach to Aberdeen, and from Aberdeen to London, 551 miles, in twenty-one hours. Coach fare, 2*s.* 6*d.* ; 2nd class train, 2*l.* 19*s.* 6*d.*, say 3 guineas, with 1*s.* to coachman. This cheap and quick record I made him write down for me to copy here. On April 21 a remarkable circumstance, a woodpecker came in shot of the window, and, a gun being loaded, I killed it ; and Mrs. Hawker sent it off to Leadbeater as a companion to the woodcock that I shot out of the parlour window (on Jan. 25, 1810) when on crutches with my Talavera wound.

resource, I should get removed from London to country air without loss of time. Being too ill to exist in an inn, or at any place without a nurse and all other attendants (in addition to my dear wife, who has never left me, day or night, since my first illness on the 14th of January), I, on the 9th of this month, April, got down to Longparish House, and, by the mercy of Almighty God, bore the journey better than I expected, and found my almost departed breath somewhat restored by total removal to a clear atmosphere.

10*th.*—My complaint is a violent affection of the heart, from having worked for years too hard, and had such a series of painful excitement on divers affairs.

20*th.*—I may venture to say that I am getting on (though of course very, very slowly) towards the chance of recovery, for which prospect I have to thank Sir B. Brodie and an All-wise Providence.

Another remarkable circumstance—and a lucky one for me, who could eat nothing more nourishing than fish—the trout in our river, which were not even eatable when broiled till near July, have come in many months before their time, and ate better than I have known them to be for these last twenty years. One of my fishery tenants, Mr. Macleod, in the first week of March, had killed, in a severe winter's day, 15 brace with a fly, and he kindly sent me a few as red and as good as salmon. This phenomenon is accounted for by the continued rains flooding all the low lands, and washing down constant winter food for the fish, which, notwithstanding the severe winter that afterwards cut up everything in March and April, never lost their high condition.

23*rd.*—I have been taken out for the last few days, for short drives in the carriage; but I am now a figure of skin and bone.

24*th.*—Another circumstance to record—Captain Duff and his friend came to my river to fish, and, in spite of the adverse weather, had a few days' good sport; and, what is a miracle, every trout was better in season (though in April) than, for these twenty years, I have seen them—even than in June and July, the only time they have hitherto been fit to eat. They were quite red, firm, and full of curd—in short, delicious. Thus my lamentable illness has 'cut me out of' the best angling season on record, as well as the use of my new ignition punt gun at Keyhaven, in the finest hard weather we have had there since 1838.

May 4th.—Winter again; bitter cold gale of wind east by north. As I made but slow progress in the low and water-meadow situation of Longparish, I had made up my mind to forego all the comforts of the mansion for the more healthy air of my dear little cottage on the coast, and therefore I left Longparish for Keyhaven this day, after having passed twenty-five days and nights at the former place, without strength or appetite. We arrived at Keyhaven Cottage about six in the evening, after my very long absence from the 26th of October, 1852, up to this 4th of May, 1853. My good people were all delighted to see me, which they had made up their minds they should never do any more.

5th.—Keyhaven. Stephen Shuttler has done me justice in every possible way in my long absence, and kept everything in the very best order, in spite of awful floods; and then a north-pole winter in spring.

N.B.—Found the air here far pleasanter than at the other places. Thanks to God for all blessings up to this Holy Thursday—or Ascension Day—for 1853.

7th.—A total change of weather to south by west, and a pouring fall of rain all day; in the afternoon the cock flew round again to the north-east with the most furious increase of cold rain, and a heavy fall of snow—lamentable weather for my poor eyes and limbs. Instead of having a fair chance to breathe the good air here, I've been, ever since I entered the cottage, a close prisoner; could not even step into the garden.

12th.—Anniversary of my Douro affair, forty-four years ago. Cold and piercing north-easter, which is comparative luxury to the deadly poison of a white frost, insomuch that I suffered far less to-day, and my eyes got better.

13*th and* 14*th.*—Bitter white frosts again. But two hours' fine weather on the 14th, when I got the sea air for the first time by being rowed down to Hurst and back. I came home refreshed, but much exhausted; and, on landing, who should be here but old Buckle, just arrived from Scotland? I was, however, not man enough to enjoy his 'yarn' as of old.

18*th.*—A beautiful day. Crossed to Yarmouth, and got driven to Freshwater for the fine sea air, but too weak to walk along the cliffs. Lots of 'gents' popping at rock birds and rifling the cormorants, and rookeries being stormed inland. All to tantalise me, like the gents having good sport angling the other day in view of my windows at Longparish, and I too ill to go out.

26*th.*—I sailed to Yarmouth, and got Butler's excellent phaeton to the high lighthouse, and returned by Groves's Hotel; but was so weak I could not enjoy my old paradise, Alum Bay, as before. The lighthouse is now kept by a Mr. Henderson, *vice* Coleraine, and the dangerous occupation of taking the eggs of rock birds is performed by a man named Lane, of the village below, called Weston, whose brother was lately killed in this awful pursuit.

29*th.*—Sunday. Being too weak to walk, I went in a donkey chaise to morning church at Milford (where, as well as at Longparish, Mrs. Hawker had me prayed for when expected not to recover), to return thanks to God for my escape from death in my long and dangerous illness, through which I had not been in church since the early part of last January, and never expected to be in church again, except on my way to the grave.

July.—Longparish. From the 1st I have been so dreadfully ill that I could do nothing. My nights have been as awful as before.

7*th.*—The thunder and lightning all night caused such

oppressive heat that no one could rest in bed. My sufferings could scarcely be conceived.

8th to 14th.—Too ill to get about save by quiet easy drives in the carriage, and to crawl out to look at all the grand repairs outside the house, which are now done. Attended by Dr. Hempsted twice a day, as my sufferings are alarming. We have had incessant wet weather ever since I returned to Longparish, and consequently the heavy water-meadow fogs oppressed me even more than those of London, from which I had retreated on the score of health. To-day, the 14th, Dr. Hempsted went from me to his other patient, the Earl of Portsmouth, for whom he had no hope, and who died this day at one o'clock. Peace to his soul!

[Colonel Hawker died shortly after the last entry (on August 7th) at 2 Dorset Place, London.—ED.]

SUMMARY OF THE BAGS OF GAME AND WILD FOWL RECORDED IN COLONEL HAWKER'S DIARY, 1802–1853.

GAME.

Partridges	7,035	Wood pigeons	20
Pheasants	575	Turtle doves	7
Blackcock	11	Stock dove	1
Grouse	16	Hares	631
Landrails	56	Rabbits	318
Quails	58		
		Total	8,728

Wild Fowl (Swans, Ducks and Geese).

Wild swans (hoopers)	38	Pochard (dunbirds)	64
Brent geese	1,327	Golden-eye ducks	21
Barnacle geese	3	Eider duck	1
White-fronted laughing geese	20	Scoters	2
Grey geese	3	Velvet scoters	4
Wild ducks	441	Curres (scaup ducks)	112
Wigeon	2,211	Shell ducks	37
Pintails	39	Mergansers	3
Teal	135		
Tufted ducks	27	Total	4,488

Riverside and Seashore Birds.

Curlews	118	Green sandpipers (ox-eyes)	8
Godwits	87	Sanderlings	2
Ox-birds (dunlins)	1,329	Oyster catchers (olives)	15
Redshanks	4	Avocet	1
Water rails	50	Moorhens	64
Spotted crakes	3	Coots	48
Sandpipers (stone runners and summer snipe)	13	Dabchicks	9
Stone curlews	5	Herons	18
Ring dotterels	28	Bitterns	3
Whimbrels (curlew jacks)	12	Phalaropes	2
Reeves	2	Total	1,821

Woodcock	68	Snipes	2 116

Plover, grey, green, and golden	351

Various.

Including great northern and red-throated divers		Night jars	5
Cormorants		Goshawks	2
Cliff birds—terns		Hoopoe	1
besides Grebes	3	And deer	3
		Total	181

Grand Total	17,753

SEASON 1

1802–1803.

Sept. 1 *to Sept.* 1.

(N.B.—Æt. 16½ years. Gun, Single-barrel flint.)

Partridges	198	Peewits	7
Pheasants	12	Stone curlews	3
Hares	17	Reeve	1
Rabbits	10	Nightjar	2
Quails	4	Black-headed terns	3
Snipes	99	Black tern	1
Wild ducks	2	Common terns	12
Diving duck (dunbird)	1	Black-headed gull	1
Woodcock	1	Cobb gull (great blackbacked)	3
Turtle dove	1	Kipps[1]	5
Wood pigeons	2	Ring dotterels	6
Moorhens	15	Sanderlings	
Water rails	10	Cuckoo	1
Heron	1	Redwings	2
Sea-gulls (common)	4	Brown owl	1
Dunlin	4	Woodpecker	1
Dabchicks	6	Missel thrush	1
Baldcoot	1	Fieldfares	8
Summer snipes (sandpipers)	7		
Ox-eye (green sandpiper)	1	Total	456

SEASON 2

1803–1804.

Sept. 1 *to Sept.* 1.

Partridges	38	Golden plover	2
Pheasants	8	Grey plover	5
Hares	8	Ring dotterel	12
Quails	4	Dunlins	30
Landrails	12	Windar (i.e. wigeon diver or dunbird)	1
Olives (oyster catchers)	4	Peewits	3
Woodpecker	1	Godwit	1
Stockdove	1	Stone runners (sandpipers)	5
Woodcock	1	Baldcoot	1
Snipes	32	Avocet	1
Water rail	1	Reeve	1
Curlew	1		
Curlew jacks (whimbrels)	12	Total	185

[1] A kipp is a genus of tern peculiar to the vicinity of Romney.

SEASON 3

1804–1805.

Sept. 1 *to Sept.* 1.

Partridges	55	Green plover	3
Pheasants	5	Dunlins	12
Hares	14	Olives (oyster catchers)	3
Rabbits	9	Diving wigeon (dunbird)	12
Landrails	3	Black duck (scoter)	1
Quails	1	Bittern	1
Snipes	35	Ox-eye (green sandpiper)	1
Stone plover	1	Coot	1
Turtle doves	2	Moorhens	10
Godwits	2	Turtle dove	2
Water rails	4	Nightjar	1
Golden plover	3		
Grey plover	1	Total	182

SEASON 4

1805–1806.

Sept. 1 *to Sept.* 1.

Partridges	93	Moorhens	11
Pheasants	8	Quail	1
Hares	24	Dabchick	1
Rabbits	16	Heron	2
Snipes	48	Green sandpipers (i.e. ox-eyes)	2
Wild duck	1	Peewit	
Teal	2	Summer snipe (sandpiper)	1
Landrails	2	Hoopoe	1
Water rails	8	Total	233

SEASON 5

1806–1807.

Sept. 1 *to Sept.* 1.

Partridges	182	Woodcocks	16
Pheasants	33	Landrails	2
Hares	43	Water rails	2
Rabbits	31	Quails	2
Wild duck	4	Moorhens	5
Teal	9	Heron	1
Golden-eye duck	1	Wood pigeons	2
Snipes	77	Total	410

SEASON 6

1807–1808.

Sept. 1 *to Sept.* 1.

Partridges	217	Moorhens	9
Pheasants	11	Dabchick	1
Hares	31	Dunlins	3
Rabbits	14	Ring dotterel	7
Wild ducks	5	Peewits	2
Woodcock	6	Redshanks	2
Snipes	72	Nightjar	1
Water rails	15		
		Total	396

SEASON 7

1808–1809.

Sept. 1 *to Sept.* 1.

Partridges	235	Snipes	22
French red-legged ditto	9	Turtle doves	2
Pheasants	33	Redshank	1
Hares	9		
Rabbits	5	Total	316

Left for Spain November 17, 1808, and returned September 28, 1809.

SEASON 8

1809–1810.

Sept. 1 *to Sept.* 1.

Woodcock	1	Peewits	4
Snipes	11	Wood pigeon	1
Hare	1		
Moorhen	1	Total	19

Only returned from Spain September 28, and had very little shooting this season, owing to severe wound received at Talavera last July 28.

SEASON 9

1810–1811.

Sept. 1 *to Sept.* 1.

Partridges	253	Bald coots	14
Hares	16	Water rails	5
Pheasants	24	Pochard	1
Rabbits	9	Dabchick	1
Woodcocks	6	Heron	1
Snipes	71	Wood pigeons	2
Quails	4	Peewits	2
Landrails	3		
Wild ducks	16	Total	428

Left on January 7 for Portugal, and returned home May 30.

SEASON 10

1811–1812.

Sept. 1 *to Sept.* 1.

Partridges	119	Snipes	65
Hares	36	Peewits	4
Quails	3	Heron	1
Landrail	1	Wood pigeons	2
Pheasants	41	Water rails	2
Rabbits	14	Ox-eye (green sandpiper)	1
Woodcocks	2	Nightjar	1
Wild ducks	9		
Teal	1	Total	303
Wigeon	1		

SEASON 11

1812–1813.

Sept. 1 *to Sept.* 1.

Partridges	119	Wild duck	16
Pheasants	41	Plover	5
Hares	18	Stone curlew	1
Blackcock	1	Wood pigeons	2
Grouse	16	Moorhen	1
Rabbits	11	Deer	1
Snipes	37		
Woodcocks	8	Total	277

SEASON 12

1813–1814.

Sept. 1 *to Sept.* 1.

Partridges	158	Coots	3
Pheasants	50	Dusky grebe (a kind of black and white sea dabchick)	2
Hares	19		
Rabbits	23	Green sandpiper (ox-eye)	1
Woodcocks	3	Ringed dotterel	1
Snipes	103	Dunlins (ox-birds)	32
Wild ducks	24	Curlews	4
Brent geese	14	Grey plover	3
Curres (scaup ducks)	7	Peewits	2
Pochard	4	Cormorants	2
Teal	3	Wood pigeons	2
Wigeon	6	Goshawk	1
Golden-eye duck	1	Heron	1
Sheldrake	4	Deer	1
Great northern speckled divers	3		
Water rail	1	Total	478

SEASON 13

1814–1815.

Sept. 1 *to Sept.* 1.

Partridges	126	Dunbirds	18
Hares	21	Curres (scaup ducks)	14
Pheasants	48	Brent goose	1
Snipes	63	Coots	8
Rabbits	11	Cormorant	1
Quails	3	Tippet grebe	3
Wild ducks	12	Deer	1
Wigeon	14	Total	342

SEASON 14

1815–1816.

Sept. 1 *to Sept.* 1.

Partridges	164	Teal	2
Pheasants	106	Woodcock	1
Hares	31	Godwit	1
Rabbits	15	Redshank	1
Quails	2	Heron	1
Snipes	40	Dunlin	15
Wild ducks	25		
Wigeon	4	Total	408

SEASON 15

1816–1817.

Sept. 1 *to Sept.* 1.

Partridges	308	Brent geese	6
Pheasants	40	Plover (golden)	3
Quail	1	Woodcocks	10
Hares	17	Peewits	6
Rabbits	9	Heron	1
Snipes	99	Grey plover	2
Wild duck	9	Knot	1
Wigeon	3		
Teal	1	Total	516

SEASON 16

1817–1818.

Sept. 1 *to Sept.* 1.

Partridges	178	Wild duck	15
Pheasants	20	Teal	2
Hares	12	Brent goose	1
Rabbits	8	Bitterns	2
Woodcocks	7	Heron	3
Snipes	230	Spotted crake	1
Quail	1	Water rail	1
Landrail	1	Total	482

SEASON 17

1818–1819.

Sept. 1 *to Sept.* 1.

Partridges	125	Wood pigeon	1
Pheasants	3	Heron	2
Hares	11	Peewits	4
Rabbits	3	Goshawk	1
Snipes	92	Landrails	5
Wild duck	27	Moorhens	8
Wigeon	1	Greenshank	1
Brent goose	1	Coots	2
Teal	2	Total	289

SEASON 18

1819–1820.

Sept. 1 *to Sept.* 1.

Partridges	216	Brent geese	7
Hares	10	Wigeon	1
Pheasants	2	Teal	3
Rabbits	3	Sheldrake	1
Landrails	4	Curlew	4
Snipes	90		
Wild ducks	17	Total	358

SEASON 19

1820–1821.

Sept. 1 *to Sept.* 1.

Partridges	103	Tufted ducks	2
Hares	7	Golden-eyes	2
Rabbits	3	Teal	1
Pheasants	2	Wigeon	6
Snipes	100	Brent geese	26
Wild ducks	8	Curlews	2
Curres (scaup ducks)	6		
		Total	268

SEASON 20

1821–1822.

Sept. 1 *to Sept.* 1.

Partridges	164	Teal	8
Hares	13	Wigeon	44
Snipes	8	Brent geese	9
Pheasant	1		
Wild ducks	6	Total	253

Illness and other matters prevented my shooting but very little this season.

SEASON 21

1822–1823.

Sept. 1 *to Sept.* 1.

Partridges	132	Wigeon	97
Quail	1	Brent geese	180
Hares	6	Wild swans	4
Rabbits	3	Peewit	1
Pheasants	4	Spotted crake	1
Snipes	43	Curlews	5
Wild duck	22	Godwits	5
Curres (scaup ducks)	5	Golden plover	1
Teal	5		
Pintails	3	Total	518

SEASON 22

1823–1824.

Sept. 1 *to Sept.* 1.

Partridges	216	Wild ducks	8
Hares	7	Wigeon	1
Quail	1	Curres (scaup ducks)	3
Rabbits	3	Teal	4
Pheasants	2	Grey plover	2
Snipes	46		
Brent geese	2	Total	295

SEASON 23

1824–1825.

Sept. 1 *to Sept.* 1.

Partridges	160	Wild ducks	4
Hares	8	Tufted duck	1
Pheasant	1	Teal	9
Rabbit	1	Blackgame	10
Landrails	2	Stone curlew	1
Quail	1	Coots	7
Snipes	42		
		Total	247

Very little shooting this and last season owing to illness.

SEASON 24

1825–1826.

Sept. 1 *to Sept.* 1.

Partridges	184	Pintails	3
Hares	8	Dunbirds	10
Rabbit	1	Curres (scaup ducks)	9
Wood pigeons	2	Grey plover	4
Landrails	3	Godwits	4
Quails	2	Coots	3
Snipes	46	Cormorant	1
Brent geese	2	Dunlins	120
Wild ducks	7		
Wigeon	64	Total	475
Teal	2		

SEASON 25

1826–1827.

Sept. 1 *to Sept.* 1.

Partridges	122	Pintail	1
Hares	8	Teal	3
Pheasant	1	Curlews	5
Woodcock	1	Coots	4
Rabbits	3	Godwits	16
Brent geese [1]	8	Plover	9
Wigeon	209	Dunlins [2]	146
Wild duck	12	Olives (oyster catchers)	2
Sheldrake	1	Herons	3
Curres (scaup ducks)	11	Total	565

[1] The most killed this winter by anyone. [2] In three shots.

SEASON 26

1827–1828.

Sept. 1 *to Sept.* 1.

Partridges	375	Brent geese	4
Hares	15	Black duck	1
Rabbits	12	Tufted duck	1
Pheasants	12	Curlews	2
Landrail	1	Olive (oyster catcher)	1
Snipes	22	Heron	1
Wild duck	3	Moorhen	1
Wigeon	80	Grey plover	2
Pintails	2		
Teal	2	Total	537

Besides many shore birds not here given.

SEASON 27

1828–1829.

Sept. 1 *to Sept.* 1.

Partridges	388	Wigeon	433
Hares	7	Teal	4
Quail	1	Curres (scaup ducks)	15
Rabbits	2	Great or velvet scoters	2
Pheasants	8	Dunbirds (pochards)	2
Woodcock	1	Plover	10
Snipes	70	Curlews	14
Wild swans	5	Coots	4
Barnacle goose	1	Olive (oyster catcher)	1
Brent geese	96	Moorhens	3
Wild ducks	25		
Pintail	1	Total	1,093

SEASON 28

1829–1830.

Sept. 1 *to Sept.* 1.

Partridges	122	Dunbirds (pochards)	2
Hares	14	Golden-eye ducks	3
Landrail	1	Pintails	2
Quail	1	Tufted duck	1
Pheasants	3	Scoter	1
Rabbits	3	Sheldrakes	12
Snipes	38	Brent geese	154
Wild ducks	11	Laughing geese	20
Wigeon	149	Wild swans	9
Teal	2	Plover	29
Curres (scaup ducks)	21	Total	598

Besides curlews, dunlins, coots, &c.

SEASON 29

1830–1831.

Sept. 1 *to Sept.* 1.

Partridges	173	Teal	3
Quails	7	Wigeon	103
Landrail	1	Curres (scaup ducks)	12
Hares	17	Brent geese	9
Rabbits	5	Pintails	2
Pheasants	10	Scoter	1
Woodcocks	2	Golden plover	4
Snipes	23		
Wild ducks	11	Total	383

No account kept of curlews, coots, dunlins, &c., shot.

SEASON 30

1831–1832.

Sept. 1 *to Sept.* 1.

Partridges	56	Dunbirds (pochards)	3
Hare [1]	1	Tufted ducks	10
Rabbit [1]	1	Pintail	1
Pheasants [1]	2	Wild ducks	7
Snipes	13	Teal	3
Wigeon	95	Curlews	2
Brent geese	38		
Curres (scaup ducks)	5	Total	237

Very little shooting this season, owing to an almost annihilation of game, and my own pressure of business.

SEASON 31

1832–1833.

Sept. 1 *to Sept.* 1.

Partridges	149	Wild duck	4
Hares	7	Wigeon	19
Quails	4	Brent geese	4
Landrail	1	Merganser	1
Rabbits	4	Tufted duck	1
Pheasants	3		
Snipes	7	Total	204

[1] All I saw.

SEASON 32

1833–1834.

Sept. 1 *to Sept.* 1.

Partridges	107	Snipe	1
Hares	5	Grey goose	1
Rabbits	2		
Pheasant	1	Total	117

Owing to trouble and business, only a few days' shooting this season.

SEASON 33

1834–1835.

Sept. 1 *to Sept.* 1.

Partridges	118	Wigeon	10
Hares	8	Teal	7
Pheasants	4	Spotted crake	1
Snipes	29	Grey plover	1
Wild ducks	7	Woodcock	1
Brent geese	2		
		Total	188

Illness prevented my shooting but very little this season.

SEASON 34

1835–1836.

Sept. 1 *to Sept.* 1.

Partridges	130	Pintails	6
Hare	1	Teal	6
Rabbits	3	Golden-eye ducks	2
Pheasants	3	Brent geese	8
Snipes	21	Plover	13
Wild ducks	20		
Wigeon	24	Total	337

I had but little shooting, and the scarcity of wild fowl lamentable; a general failure of all sport on the coast, and the geese appear to have been banished therefrom altogether.

SEASON 35

1836–1837.

Sept. 1 *to Sept.* 1.

Partridges	136	Shell duck	1
Pheasant	1	Curre (scaup duck)	1
Quail	1	Wigeon	81
Hares	5	Brent geese	33
Rabbits	5	Godwits	15
Snipes	24	Plover	3
Wild ducks	5		
		Total	311

As poor a season as ever was known. The coast is ruined, and we have now no game shooting after September.

SEASON 36

1837–1838.

Sept. 1 *to Sept.* 1.

Partridges[1]	106	Pintails	3
Hares	5	Tufted duck	1
Landrail	1	Pochards	4
Rabbits	4	Golden-eye ducks	8
Snipes	9	Shell ducks	6
Brent geese	310	Plover	56
Wild swans	19	Curlews	34
Eider duck	1	Godwits	5
Wild ducks	5	Dunlins	95
Wigeon	220		
Teal	2	Total	894

SEASON 37

1838–1839.

Sept. 1 *to Sept.* 1.

Partridges	58	Wigeon	5
Hares	6	Teal	1
Pheasants	7	Curlew	1
Rabbits	8	Godwits	2
Woodcock	1	Plover	4
Snipes	4		
		Total	97

The worst season in the memory of man, both on the coast for wild fowl, and inland for game. I never even launched a punt (it was not worth while) this winter, and did not fire a shot after November 26.

[1] Not a shot even at a pheasant this season.

SEASON 38

1839–1840.

Sept. 1 *to Sept.* 1.

Partridges	42	Wild ducks	2
Pheasants	4	Wigeon	30
Landrail	1	Velvet scoters	4
Hares	3	Curlews	7
Rabbits	3	Godwits	4
Snipes	11	Plovers	11
Brent geese [1]	5		
		Total	127

The game season was so bad I gave it up early as hopeless. The coast destitute of wild fowl.

SEASON 39

1840–1841.

Sept. 1 *to Sept.* 1.

Partridges [2]	80	Pintails	4
Pheasants	2	Shell ducks	6
Hare	1	Golden-eye duck	1
Rabbits	4	Grey geese	2
Wild ducks	19	Merganser	1
Brent geese	145	Plover	23
Teal	14	Godwits	13
Curres (scaup ducks)	2	Olive (oyster catcher)	1
Dunbird	1	Dunlins	179
Wigeon	185		
		Total	683

SEASON 40

1841–1842.

Sept. 1 *to Sept.* 1.

Partridges	53	Tufted ducks	2
Pheasant	1	Brent geese	20
Hares	7	Shell duck	1
Rabbits	8	Merganser	1
Landrail	1	Dunbirds (pochard)	3
Snipes	13	Curlews	4
Wild ducks	5	Plover	7
Wigeon	22	Dunlins	48
Pintails	4		
Golden-eye ducks	3	Total	203

Great scarcity of both game and wild fowl this season.

[1] Most killed by anyone at Keyhaven this winter.

[2] Owing to illness and business, I was only out five times game shooting.

SEASON 41

1842–1843.

Sept. 1 *to Sept.* 1.

Partridges	26	Wigeon	8
Pheasant [1]	1	Tufted duck	2
Landrail [1]	1	Teal	6
Hares [1]	2	Curlews	10
Rabbit [1]	1	Godwit	1
Snipes	31	Plovers	4
Brent geese	2	Total	95

No shooting for anyone on the coast this winter, and out only a few days in September, my health being very bad.

SEASON 42

1843–1844.

Sept. 1 *to Sept.* 1.

Partridges [2]	50	Teal	4
Hares [2]	2	Brent geese	3
Rabbits [2]	3	Plover	14
Landrail [2]	1	Godwits	4
Snipes	17	Grey plover	2
Wild duck	1	Dunlins	85
Wigeon	7	Total	193

Scarcely a gunner on the coast killed a dozen wild fowl all this cruel bad season.

SEASON 43

1844–1845.

Sept. 1 *to Sept.* 1.

Partridges [3]	10	Tufted ducks	3
Pheasant [3]	1	Teal	10
Hares [3]	3	Shell ducks	3
Rabbits [3]	5	Plover	37
Snipes	17	Godwits	14
Wild swan	1	Curlews	4
Brent geese	94	Olive (oyster catcher)	1
Barnacle geese	2	Ring dotterels	2
Wild ducks	6	Dunlins	196
Wigeon	206		
Pintails	6	Total	621

A very long and yet not a brilliant season at Keyhaven.

[1] All I set eyes on. [2] No time for game shooting in September.
[3] Had very little time for game shooting this season.

SEASON 44

1845–1846.

Sept. 1 *to Sept.* 1.

Partridges [1]	157	Rabbits [3]	4
Pheasants [2]	2	Snipes	21
Hares [3]	18		
		Total	202

Such an unprecedented scarcity of wild fowl at Keyhaven on the coast that I would not disgrace myself by putting a great gun afloat. A general complaint all over England that there were no wild fowl, woodcocks, snipes, and other winter birds this season.

SEASON 45

1846–1847.

Sept. 1 *to Sept.* 1.

Partridges [4]	87	Wigeon	31
Pheasants [5]	3	Pintail	1
Hares [5]	16	Teal	2
Rabbits	6	Shell duck	1
Wood pigeons	3	Phalaropes	2
Snipes	40	Plovers	39
Brent geese	28	Dunlins	313
Wild ducks	39		
		Total	611

Keyhaven ruined for coast shooting.

SEASON 46

1847–1848.

Sept. 1 *to Sept.* 1.

Partridges [6]	173	Teal	3
Pheasant [7]	1	Pochard	2
Landrail	1	Curre (scaup duck)	1
Quail	8	Spotted crake	1
Hares	5	Green sandpiper (ox-eye)	1
Snipes	22	Golden plover	2
Brent geese	76	Olives (oyster catchers)	2
Wild ducks	5	Curlews	5
Wigeon	12		
		Total	320

[1] I was out but eleven half-days, and then too weak and unwell to fag as usual.

[2] All I saw.

[3] All I shot at.

[4] No game shooting after September.

[5] All I saw.

[6] All in September.

[7] All I saw.

SEASON 47

1848–1849.

Sept. 1 *to Sept.* 1.

Partridges	191	Wigeon	26
Pheasants[1]	2	Tufted duck	1
Landrails[1]	3	Teal	3
Quail[1]	1	Curlews	9
Hares	14	Godwit	1
Rabbits	11	Plovers	3
Snipes	32	Dunlins	2
Brent geese	27		
Wild ducks	5	Total	331

A wretched season on the coast at Keyhaven.

SEASON 48

1849–1850.

Sept. 1 *to Sept.* 1.

Partridges	115	Wigeon	12
Pheasants[1]	3	Tufted duck	1
Landrail	1	Teal	1
Hares	8	Curlews	5
Rabbits	4	Godwit	1
Snipes	15	Plover	7
Brent geese	12	Dunlins	41
Wild ducks	3		
		Total	229

The coast shooting now at Keyhaven is annihilated, and we have had a miserable game season, and the worst snipe shooting on record in spite of five weeks of hard winter weather.

SEASON 49

1850–1851.

Sept. 1 *to Sept.* 1.

Partridges	95	Wild duck	1
Pheasants[1]	4	Tufted duck	1
Hares[2]	27	Wigeon	2
Rabbits	3	Teal	1
Snipes	21		
		Total	155

As the coast was destitute of every kind of winter bird, I never went to Keyhaven this season.

[1] All I saw.

[2] With the help of 'Siney' and 'Charles Heath' we made up to 53 hares this season, the most ever killed here for many years.

SEASON 50

1851–1852.

Sept. 1 *to Sept.* 1.

Partridges [1]	0	Wild ducks	8
Pheasants [1]	0	Shell ducks	2
Rabbits	3	Teal	4
Snipes	24		
		Total	41

Illness nearly the whole season prevented my shooting, and at one time my life was in danger.

SEASON 51

1852–1853.

Sept. 1 *to Aug.* 7.[2]

Partridges	164	Rabbits	9
Pheasant [3]	1	Wood pigeon	1
Landrails [3]	4	Snipes	20
Quails [3]	4	Dunlins	8
Hares	39		
		Total	250

Not a shot at a wild fowl this season, but I beat all the neighbours at partridge shooting in September.

The foregoing lists are epitomised from the original Diary of Colonel Peter Hawker, but they do not include many hundred shore birds that were, besides those given, killed by him, and, as stated in his Diary, unrecorded at the time. The wild fowl and marsh birds that were killed by the Colonel in his visits to Norfolk are also omitted in his Diary, though alluded to as having been numerous.

The bags of trout caught by Colonel Hawker in the river 'Test' at Longparish are only recorded occasionally, and the entries that are to be found under this head but roughly indicate the numbers taken by his rod. The trout killed in the fifty years of the Colonel's sporting life could not (from the allusions to angling in his Diary), at a low estimate, have been less than twelve thousand.

[1] None; never fired a shot. [2] Colonel Hawker died this day. [3] All I saw.

INDEX

ABBEVILLE, Hawker's visits to, and its hotel accommodation, i. 129, 166, 169, 170, 179, 181, ii. 210; wild fowl and sport at, i. 176, 177; its 'fever,' 182; Hawker's lawsuit there, 188–190
Abbey Church, Romsey, curiosities in, ii. 347
Abbot's Ann Marsh, sport there, i. 21; fire at, ii. 32
Abernethy, Dr, character of, i. 282
Adam, M., pianist, i. 334
Adelaide, Queen Dowager, her funeral, ii. 312
Albano, his pictures in Paris, i. 118
Albert (Prince Consort) and 'Instructions to Young Sportsmen,' ii. 179, 242, 261, 265; attempt on his life, 181; attends Naval Review, 260; Hawker's presents of wild fowl to, 256, 273, 296, 319, 339; the Prince forwards pheasants to Hawker, 284; visits the Exposition of Manufacturers (Birmingham), 307, 308; and Hawker's exhibits at the Great International Exhibition (1851), 330–332, 334, 338
Albertazzi, M., musician, ii. 131
Alderney cows in Guernsey, ii. 79
Alexander I. (Emperor of Russia) and suite visit London, i. 95; in Paris, 120, 128
—— Prince, of the Netherlands, ii. 238, 240, 242
Almondbury, anecdote concerning, i. 78
Alresford, sport at, i. 242, 243, 266, 273, 281, 288, 290, 307, ii. 36; military dinner there, i. 287; eel-spearing at, ii. 106
Althorp, Lord, Chancellor of the Exchequer (1831), ii. 32
Alum Bay, its sand pit, chalk rocks, and other beauties, i. 31, 313, ii. 49, 55, 125, 162, 183, 230, 355
Amiens, its cathedral, i. 129
Amsterdam, Hawker's visit to, i. 215; the king's palace, 215; Felix Meritus, 215; Nieuwe Kerk, 215; the Exchange and other places of interest, 216
Andover, march to, i. 7; sport at, 156; musical exhibition there, 172; election in (1837), ii. 126; accident at, 321; severe storm, 343
Anglesea, Marquis of, and Hawker's army musket and carbine for the Cape, ii. 301, 337
Anson, Colonel, and Hawker's army musket, ii. 301
—— Mr. G. E., private secretary to the Prince Consort, ii. 242, 256
Antwerp, its cathedral, i. 225
Appleby, scenery near, i. 49
Apvrel, Madame, of Barfleur, i. 110, 111
Ardencaple, sport at, i. 65, 66
Army, Hawker's career in, *see* 'Dragoons,' and 'North Hants (Militia) Regiment'
Arne, village of, i. 82
Arnwood, Hawker's visit to, ii. 99; shooting at, 153, 155
Arras, Hawker's experiences at, i. 185, 186
Arundel, Lord, establishes a convent at Stape Hill, i. 284
Ashridge Park, sport at, i. 7, 25, 34, 35, 36; oat harvest at (1812), 44, 45
Astley's Amphitheatre in ruins, ii. 206
Aston, Mr., gun-lock manufacturer at Birmingham, ii. 310, 311
Ath, inn accommodation at, ii. 210
Atworth, shooting at, i. 40
Aubert, M., performer at the Parisian opera, i. 117

Augusta, Princess, ii. 123
Avoset (cobbler's awl), its characteristics, i. 3

BACON, General, and Hawker's army musket, ii. 342
—— Mr., his horse race against Captain Coles, i. 67–69
Badger, Dr., attends Hawker, i. 299, ii. 238, 352
Bagshore, Hawker's servant, i. 314, 321
Baker, Major, of the 14th Light Dragoons, i. 69–71
—— Sergeant, of Woolwich Arsenal, ii. 340
Baldwin, Mr., coroner of Keyhaven, i. 314, 315
Bangor, inn accommodation there, ii. 57
Bank of England, visit of Prince Louis Napoleon to, ii. 153, 154
Barfleur, dangers of its coast, i. 100, 101; disturbance at, 102; customs officials, 107; market prices (1814), 109, 110; accommodation and sport there, 110, 111
Baring, Mr. Alexander, his preserves, i. 290
—— Sir Thomas, shooting on his estate, i. 241
Barnacle geese, wildness of, i. 62, 63; shooting in Pilewell, ii. 252
Barrow, Sir John, Secretary of the Admiralty, ii. 206
Barton Manor, shooting at, ii. 219
Bashley, wild character of the country, ii. 219
Bathgate, the dwarfs of, i. 57
Battersea, gun experiments at, ii. 300
Bayswater, double gun trial at, i. 308
Beaulieu river, shooting on, ii. 91
Beauvais, experiences at, i. 129; its church, 167
Beckford, Mr., his quinta at Mafra, i. 26; his Hampshire estate, 247–249
Becton, a wild country, ii. 219; wreck of the 'Kent' at, 224
Beer as a fire extinguisher, ii. 26
Beethoven, birthplace of, ii. 244
Belfast, Hawker's visit to, ii. 59
Belgium, Hawker's experiences in, i. 210–212, 226–234, ii. 247; revolution in, 20
Benedict, M., vocalist, i. 124
Ben Lomond, ascent of, i. 58–60
Benois, Captain, of the 'Henri Quatre,' i. 131
Bentinc, Countess, entertains Hawker at Laeken, i. 229
Béramendi, Le Chevalier de, Spanish Marshal, i. 225
Bere, Dorset, sport at, i. 81
Berkeley, Lord, shooting on his estate, i. 4
—— Sir George, and Hawker's army musket, ii. 350
Berleur, Mr., his gun factory at Liège, ii. 229
Berney, Mr. T. T., his cartridge invention, ii. 178, 179; shooting on his estate, 186
Bertini family (Madame J., and Mons. A., H., and J.), Hawker's musical studies with, i. 161, 169, 211, 233, ii. 173; Henri Bertini and Hawker's hand-moulds, 212, 214
Bethnal Green, polling at (1852), ii. 344
Bewick, Mr. (ornithologist), on the golden-eye, i. 360, *n.*; his work on ornithology, ii. 50; on the grey phalarope, 268
Bird, Mr., lawyer, ii. 67
'Birkenhead,' wreck of the, ii. 340
Birmingham, its manufactories, i. 200, ii. 307–311; its hotel accommodation, 62, 306; Exposition of Manufactures, 306; its churches and preachers, 307, 308; choral concert at town hall, 309; its gasometer, 310; Catholic cathedral at, 310; its suburbs, 322
Bishop, 'Uncle,' manager of Mr. Westley Richards's factories, ii. 205, 207, 339
Black game, greatest day's shooting on record, i. 283, 284
Black, Mr., his offer to Hawker, ii. 103
Blackmore, Captain, of the 'Lady Cockburn,' i. 208
Blandford, military horse race at, i. 67, 68
—— Marquis of, contests Middlesex, ii. 344
Blenheim Palace, Hawker's description of, i. 201
Blucher, Marshal, visits London, i. 95
Bond, Parson, plan of attack on his preserves, illustrated, i. 12, 13
Bonn, its cathedral and other places of interest, ii. 244
Boulogne, Hawker's experiences there, i. 129, 176; its English church, ii. 209; museum, 209; Hawker's impressions of, 209

Bourne-bottom, wild fowl there, i. 88
Bourne, fire at, ii. 32
Bouvancourt, fishing at, i. 167
Bowes, grouse shooting and sporting rights there, i. 47, 48
Bradford (Wilts), Hawker's army and shooting experiences at, i. 37–43
Braham, Mr., vocalist, ii. 101
Bransbury, sport at, i. 20, ii. 64
Brazier, Mr. J., gunlock maker of Wolverhampton, ii, 308, 348
Breydon Flats as a gunning ground, i. 274
Bridgewater, Lord, shooting on his estate, i. 7, 25, 35, 36; military relations with Hawker, 21, 23, 34, 69–72; harvesting on his estate (1812), 44, 45
Bright, Dr., attends Hawker, ii. 352
Brighton, customs and other experiences at, i. 171, 192, 340, 341, 343, 344; its mackerel fishing boats, ii. 234
Bristol, Hawker's experiences at, i. 38
Brock, Hawker's description of, i. 217, 218
Brodie, Sir Benjamin, attends Hawker, ii. 38, 70, 71, 92, 122, 161, 352, 353
Brotherton, General, inspects Lancaster's rifle ball, ii. 266
Brougham, Lord, at Longparish, ii. 149
Brownsea, Island and Castle, i. 88, 97
Bruges, Hawker's impressions of, i. 234
Brussels, Hawker's visit to, incidents on the journey, i. 208 211; life there, 211; its alleé Verte (Hyde Park), 212; the Cathedral of St. Gudule, 226, 227; parade of Dutch regiments in, 227; Grand Theatre or Opera House, 228, 229; compared with Ghent, 233; its railway, ii. 244
Buckle, Elijah, grand admiral of swivel gunners, experiences with, and services under, Hawker, i. 270, 273, 274, 280, 281, 320, 322, 366, ii. 5, 40, 48, 94, 97, 112, 113, 121, 132, 154, 160, 169, 176, 185, 186, 191, 193, 222, 223, 315, 317, 338
Bucklershard, lack of sport at, i. 132–134
Budget Farm, Longparish, deer-hunting there, i. 73–75
Buffin, John (Hawker's servant), i. 3, 8, 15, 20, 59, 73, 74, 86, 93
Buiksloot, wild fowl there, i. 218
Bullington, Hawker's estate near Longparish, sporting and other experiences, ii. 20, 40, 44, 110, 248, 267, 279, 280, 289–291, 351
Burnett, Mr., gunmaker, ii. 154
Burrard, Rev. George, of Yarmouth (Isle of Wight), ii. 106
Bury St. Edmunds, i. 274
Butcher's halloo, i. 285, 316, 343, ii. 108, 262
Butt, Mr., the plaintiff's attorney, ii. 164, 173, 181
Buttermilk, effect of, on a day's sport, i. 319
Butts, Mr., his gunpowder, i. 58, 146
Byron, Lord, funeral of, i. 275

CADAVAL, Duc de, his quinta near Cintra, i. 27
Calais, experiences at, i. 130, 166, 175, 176, 186–188
Calshot, yachting accident off, ii. 3
Cambridge, Duke of (1845), ii. 261; death of, 321
Campbell, General Sir Colin, dinner to, in Jersey, ii. 77
Canterbury, hotel charges at, i. 166
Capel, Captain, his shooting experiences, i. 251
Carlisle, agitator, and the threatened riots in London, ii. 31
Carlisle, Hawker's description of, i. 50
Carnac, Sir John, engages Buckle, ii. 315; his shooting experience, 317
Caroline, Queen, her trial, i. 203
Carracci, his pictures in Paris, i. 118
Carrickfergus, its castle, ii. 59; scenery from, 59
Casket Rocks, Hawker's sketch of the, ii. 74
Castleman, Charles (Hawker's servant), catches a hare, ii. 20; shoots a wild cat, 114; other experiences, 116, 117, 219
Chadwick, Mr., shooting experiences with Hawker, i. 77, 78
Chalk Farm, rifle shooting at, ii. 52
Chalmer, Colonel, and Hawker's army musket, ii. 330; and Purdey *v.* Minié ball, 340
Chamberlain, Mr., shooting over his farm, i. 81; his place on the Southampton river, 103
Chambers, Miss, benefit at the Southampton Theatre, ii. 152
—— Mr., banker, Hawker's visit to, i. 166; failure of, 279, ii. 169, 172
Champy, M. Maurice de, Mayor of St.-Crotoi, i. 170

Channel Islands, Hawker's visit to, ii. 74–82
Chappell, Mr., and Hawker's hand-moulds for the pianoforte, i. 175
Charlemagne, his crown, i. 116
Charles II., King, at Mount Orgueil, Jersey, ii. 75
Charlotte, Princess, death of, i. 157
Chartists' meeting in London, ii. 286, 287
Chatham, Hawker's experiences at, ii. 111
Cheesman, Captain, of the 'Wellington' and 'Eclipse,' i. 171, 340
Chelsea Hospital, military fête there, ii. 331; Duke of Wellington lying in state, 348, 349
Cherbourg, Hawker's visit to, and impressions of, i. 97–100
Childe, Mr. J., the artist, his sporting sketch of Hawker's party, i. 318, 319; illustrates 'Instructions to Young Sportsmen,' ii. 241
Chimney sweep's imp and the attorney, i. 78, 79
Cholera epidemics, ii. 40, 303, 308
Christchurch (Hampshire), shooting and other experiences there, i. 88, ii. 101, 102, 104; its church, 69
Chute, Mr., elected for Hampshire (1807), i. 7.
Cinizelli, Madame, equestrienne, ii. 211
Cintra, Portugal, Hawker's visit to, i. 26-28
Clanville Lodge, shooting at, i. 22
Clarence, Duke of, *see* 'William' (afterwards William IV.)
Clark, Captain, steward to Sir H. Wilson, i. 317
Clatford Marsh, sport in, i. 21
Clayton, Mr., the Lymington gun-maker, ii. 138, 285, 309, 314, 315
Clementi, Muzio, funeral of, ii. 37
Clive, Mr., his gun-barrel factory at Birmingham, ii. 306, 307, 309, 310
Clyde, shooting on the, i. 62
Cockerton, Parson, his action against Heath, ii. 135
Cohoun, Sir James, shooting on his estate, i. 58
Colaris, Portugal, Hawker's impressions of, i. 26–28
Cold-Henley, sport at, i. 162
Coleraine, Bill, his daring cliff feats, ii. 125, 230
Coles, Captain, his match against Mr. Bacon, i. 67–69
—— Mr., his shooting experiences, ii. 5, 291
Collingbourne Wood, sport in, i. 21
Cologne, its cathedral, ii. 244; Hawker's experiences at, 246
Colt, Captain, his gala, ii. 166
Coltatt, Mr., keeper and inn proprietor at Wraxall, i. 40
Combermere, Lord, General of Cavalry, and Hawker, ii. 132, 147
Cork Convent, near Cintra, i. 26
Cormorants (Isle of Wight parsons), shooting of, i. 30–32, 293, 294, 312, 313, 347, ii. 4
Cornet Castle, Guernsey, ii. 80
Coster, Jean Baptiste de, guide of Napoleon at Waterloo, ii. 12
Coutts, Messrs., bankers, ii. 38, 111, 154
Coventry, its ancient church, ii. 323
Cowes, tour around, i. 309; scenery, 310; Norris Castle, 310; regatta, 311, 312, ii. 107; accident to Hawker there, 88
Cramer, Mr. J. B., musician, i. 96, 247; banquet to, ii. 73
Cranborne, Hawker's experiences at, i. 86
Crawshay, Miss, her marriage, ii. 71
Crivelli, M., opera singer, i. 116
Crotoi, result of shooting excursion near, i. 178
Cruely, Priest, his hospitality, i. 109
Crystal Palace, Great Exhibition building, ii. 337; its Sydenham site, 345
Cudmore, Mr., pianist (Hawker's first music master), i. 96, 206, ii. 61
Curtis, Mr. Timothy, governor of the Bank of England, ii. 153, 154
Cuttlefish, peculiarities of, ii. 162

DAGUERREOTYPE process, ii. 169
Dagville, gunner, of Southampton, ii. 255, 257
Dagwell, Mr., punt builder, ii. 314
Dallas, Parson, snowbound, ii. 117
D'Aubertini, Mr., his musical academy, i. 172
Davies, Mr., excursion with Hawker, ii. 59
Davison, Mr., shooting and other experiences with Hawker, i. 314, 321, 325; death of, ii. 56
Deane, Mr., experiments with his carbine, ii. 342; his gun factory, 345, 348–350
Decoy birds (mock birds), recipe for making, ii. 340
Deer hunting, i. 73–75, 83, 84, 95
Delamere, M., commissaire de marine,

Barfleur, his hospitality, i. 100-102, 110
Delarne, Madame, her table d'hôte, i. 340, 343, 344
Delisle, Misses, accident to, ii. 8
Delme, Mr., his duck marsh, i. 267
Delvaux, Laurens, his carved pulpit, i. 232
Deptford railway (1836), ii. 103
Derby, Earl of, forms a government, ii. 339
Desabes, M., Hawker's shooting experiences with, i. 185
Devrient, musician, ii. 124
Dibdin, Rev. Dr., Hawker's opinion of his eloquence, i. 294; ii. 92, 126
Diddams, Farmer, sent to prison, ii. 160
Dieppe, journeys to, and experiences at, i. 170, 171, 339, 340, 343; Hawker's son attends the English school there, 344
Dilke, Mr. (afterwards Sir Charles), Queen Victoria's factotum, ii. 332
Dingwall, Mr., and Hawker's leases, ii. 348
Dinwoodie, David, Hawker's Scottish guide, i. 52-54
Dobson, Captain, Peter's 'Dominie,' at Eton, i. 331
Domenichino, his pictures in Paris, i. 118
Donald, Mr., Scottish lawyer, i. 61
Donaldson, Mr., his visit to Hawker, i. 172
Donzelli, M., opera singer, i. 334
Dorchester, shooting at, i. 56.
Dorsetshire, shooting in (1813), i. 81-83, 86; (1824) 283
Douglas, Colonel, shooting expedition, with Hawker, i. 63
—— Sir Howard, attends ball-testing experiments, ii. 340
Douglas, game and fish at, i. 54, 55
Douro, Lord, his wedding, ii. 161
—— trophy, *see* Dragoons, 14th Light
Dover, Hawker's experiences at, i. 130, 131
Doyle, General Sir John, monument to, in Guernsey, ii. 78
Dragoons, 1st Royal, Hawker's commissions in, i. 72
—— 14th Light, Hawker's connection with, i. 2-9, 14, ii. 182, 301; its services in the Peninsula, 15; its recruiting parties, 34, 37, 38, 44; Hawker's retirement from, 69-72; the 'Douro' incident, i. VII, VIII, ii. 161, 163, 180, 230, 260, 263
Dublin, Hawker's experiences in, ii. 58, 61
Dudley, its castle, ii. 310
Duff, Captain, his fishing experiences, ii. 353, 354
Dumbarton, accommodation at, i. 58, 65; sport there, 62, 63, 64
Dumfriesshire, wildness of the country, i. 50
Dunbird, rarity of, ii. 23
Dundalk, as a sporting resort, ii. 58
Dunlins, immense slaughter of, ii. 277
Dutch regiments, smart appearance of, i. 227

EARLE, Mr., Hawker's lawyer, ii. 112, 160, 164, 173, 180, 321
Edinburgh, Hawker's journey to, and impressions of, i. 56, 57
Edwards, Mr. George, of Castle Barnard, i. 48
Egerton, Sir F., of the United Service Club, ii. 88
Egg, Mr., gunmaker, Hawker's experiences with, i. 95, 137, 163, 172, 279, 280, 282, ii. 103
Electric telegraph, ii. 264
Eley, Mr., cartridge maker, his cartridges, i. 361, ii. 3, 11, 12, 15, 205, 207, 208, 219, 248, 268, 272, 276, 280, 327; his sad death, 207
Elley, Sir John, adjutant-general, ii. 132
Enghein, Hawker's experiences at, i. 210
Enham, sport at, i. 34
Epsom races, snow on Derby Day, ii. 161
Erard, pianoforte manufactory, ii. 214
Erdington, its church, ii. 322
Ethiopian Serenaders at 'Bullington Cross,' ii. 291
Eton, Hawker's visits to, i. 330, ii. 55; gala day at, i. 331
Evans, Mr. (lord lieut. of gunmakers), conducts Hawker over the Government factory, ii. 309, 310
Exhibition, the Great (1851), Hawker's exhibits at, ii. 328-334

FELLOWES, Mr. Henry (brother of Lord Portsmouth), his shooting experiences, i. 319, ii. 30, 36, 151, 184, 291; fire at his house, 87; Hawker dines with him, 149; his ball, 171
Fen district, Hawker surveys the, i. 139, 140

Ferrybridge, posting to, from London, and its cost, i. 45, 46
Fielder, Mr., constructs Hawker's portable ambush, i. 146
Fieldfare, extraordinary flocks of, ii. 25; as an edible, 25
Fifield, Peter (Hawker's servant), 272; death of, 323, 344
Fishing (1805–1808), i. 3-5, 7-9; (1809-1810) 16-18; (1810–1811) 32, 33; (1811-1812) 36, 37; (1812–1813) 73; (1813-1814) 94, 96; (1814–1815) 135; (1815-1816) 143, 144; (1816-1817) 147, 152-154; (1817–1818) 155, 158, 160, 161; (1818-1819) 163, 166, 167, 171; (1819-1820) 199; (1820–1821) 237, 238; (1822–1823) 267; (1823–1824) 273, 275; (1825–1826) 286; (1826–1827) 309; (1827–1828) 325, 331; (1828–1829) 346, 365, 366; (1831–1832) ii. 39; (1832–1833) 49; (1833–1834) 54; (1834–1835) 64, 73; (1835–1836) 84, 104; (1837–1838) 130; (1838–1839) 162; (1840–1841) 185; (1841–1842) 228, 229; (1842-1843) 233; (1844–1845) 260; (1846–1847) 268, 278; (1848–1849) 290; (1849–1850) 321; (1850–1851) 325
FitzClarence, Lord Adolphus, ii. 216
—— Lord F., governor of Portsmouth, ii. 312
Fleming, Mr., entertains a musical party, ii. 20
Fleuris, Hawker's visit to, i. 338
Flixecourt, experiences at, i. 182
Fodor, Mr., the Clementi of Holland, i. 216
Folkestone, sport at, i. 2
Fonthill Abbey, Hawker's description of, i. 247–249
Ford (Lord Portsmouth's keeper), his sporting experiences with Hawker, ii. 5
Forder, Captain, of the 'Monarch,' ii. 215, 216
Fordyce, Colonel, death of, ii. 336
Forsyth's patent locks for rock shooting, i. 31
Foster, Lieut., of the 14th Light Dragoons, i. 69
Foufoucourt, Hawker's experiences there, i. 183
Fowler, Tom (Hawker's sailor), his shooting surveys, i. 163
France, Hawker's visits to, i. 97-102, 106–130, 149-153, 166-171, 175-190, 331–340, 343, ii. 208-216; method of sport there, i. 107, 184; diligence travelling there, 112, 113, 129, 166, 168, 186, 209, 332, 336, 338, 339, ii. 209, 215; its cabriolets, i. 167; coach travelling in, 167, 169; post travelling in, 176; revolution (1831), ii. 22
Frankfort, hotel accommodation there, ii. 245
Fraser, Miss, marries Captain Peter Hawker, ii. 278
Frederick William (King of Prussia) and suite visit London (1814), i. 95; and Paris, 128
Freefolk, accident at, i. 138, 139
Frost, the case of, ii. 173
Fullerd, Mr., gunmaker, and his guns, i. 239, 299, 306, 308, ii. 259, 274
Furgo, sport at, i. 19, ii. 20, 184, 267, 279, 291, 326

GALE, Lieut., his lectures on the Franklin expedition, ii. 311
Galtz, musician, ii. 124
Game and wild fowl bagged (seasons 1802–1810), i. 1, 4, 5, 6, 7, 8, 11, 14; (1810–1811) 19, 22; (1811–1812) 35, 36; (1812–1813) 39, 44, 67, 78; (1813–1814) 80, 81, 83, 93; (1814–1815) 104, 111; (1815–1816) 136, 139, 142; (1816-1817) 146, 147, 153; (1817–1818) 156, 160; (1818–1819) 162, 165; (1819–1820) 174, 199; (1820–1821) 203, 208; (1821–1822) 241, 246; (1822–1823) 252, 265, 266; (1823–1824) 269, 274; (1824–1825) 278, 282; (1825–1826) 286, 294; (1826–1827) 298, 308; (1827–1828) 317, 320, 329; (1828–1829) 346, 349, 355, 364, 365; (1829–1830) ii. 3, 17, 18; (1831–1832) 20, 27, 36; (1832–1833) 42, 49; (1833–1834) 51; (1834–1835) 64, 71; (1835–1836) 85, 102; (1836–1837) 109, 112, 122; (1837–1838) 131, 144, 146; (1838-1839) 152, 159; (1839–1840) 168, 174; (1840–1841) 184, 185, 204, 205; (1841–1842) 225; (1842–1843) 233, 235; (1843–1844) 237, 241; (1844–1845) 259, 260; (1845–1846) 263; (1846–1847) 268, 278; (1847–1848) 279, 286; (1848-1849) 290, 299; (1849–1850) 302, 320; (1850–1851) 325, 327; (1851–1852) 339; (1852-1853) 347, 352; summary of game and wild fowl bagged during fifty-one seasons, 356–374

Game Laws, Hawker's work on, i. IX; suggestions commended by Lord Althorp, ii. 32; considered by House of Commons, 258
Garrard, Mr., grants Hawker permission to view Duke of Wellington's Armoury, ii. 349
Gathemare Lake, sport on, i. 107, 108
Gatteville, Hawker's visit to, i. 101, 107
Gavel acre, fishing at, ii. 325
Gaven, Mr., of Capel Curig, ii. 57
Geese, white-fronted (laughing geese from Hudson's Bay), ii. 11 *n.* (*see* also 'Barnacle geese')
George, Madlle., French actress, i. 127
—— Prince, of Cambridge (1845), ii. 260, 261, 342
—— Prince, of Cumberland (1828), i. 331
—— Prince Regent (afterwards George IV.), and Hawker's resignation, i. 69; grants Hawker a pension, 84; his Drawing Rooms and levees, 142, 199, ii. 287; his death, 22
Germany, Hawker's trip to, ii. 244–247
Ghent, Hawker's visit to, i. 230; collection of pictures at, 231; the cathedral of St. Bavon, 232; other places and things of interest, 233; its barges, 234; culinary art on board, 234
Girdlestone, Mr. C., his hospitality, i. 273
Glasgow, Hawker's trip to, i. 45; incidents and sport on the journey, 45–55; posts to (1812), 55; cost of the trip, 56; sport there, 57; from Glasgow to Edinburgh and back, 56, 57; lawsuit there, 61, 63; its climate, 63
Glentworth, Lord, shooting expedition with Hawker, ii. 218
Gobelins tapestry, i. 116, 119, 128
Godfrey, Mr. Dan, bandmaster of the Coldstream Guards, ii. 231
Golden-eyes, Bewick and Leadbeater on, i. 360
Gomont Farm, near Waterloo, i. 211
Goodall, Dr., of Eton, i. 331
—— Mr., Hawker's tenant, death of, ii. 314
Goodchilde, Mr., shooting experiences, ii. 41, 84
Goose (wild), a rare specimen, ii. 54
Gordon, Colonel, of Waltham small arms factory, ii. 340, 344
Gore, Mr. Montague, shooting experience, ii. 65
Gore, Mr. of Bullington, ii. 110
Gourey (Jersey), its castle, ii. 75
Gowan, Captain, of the 'Corsair,' ii. 60
Graham, Mr., his balloon ascent, i. 283
Grange Park preserves, i. 290
Grayston, Charles (Hawker's servant), ii. 105, 320
Greene, Rev. Mr., Vicar of Longparish, ii. 171
Greener, Mr., harpoon gunmaker, ii. 306, 310
Greenfield, Mr., stanchion gunmaker, ii. 306, 311, 320, 323
Greta Bridge, Hawker's journey to, i. 45, 46
Gretna, its hymeneal temple, i. 51
Grey, Mr., his shooting ground, ii. 327, 339, 340
Grey phalarope, characteristics of, ii. 268
Griesbach, Mr. William, and Mrs. Griesbach visit Hawker, i. 267; Mr. Griesbach's sporting experiences with Hawker, 267, 331, ii. 53, 104, 108, 326; their musical gatherings, 97, 115
Grisi, Madame, her operatic acting, ii. 72
Gronville (Jersey), its church, ii. 75
Grouse moors, coach expenses to, i. 46
Groves, Mr., shooting on his estate, ii. 49
Guernsey, beauties of its capital, ii. 74; absence of reptiles, 74; packet travelling, 77; places of interest, 77, 78; agriculture, 78, 79; language, 79; scenery, 79; general impressions of the place, 80–82
Guido, his pictures in Paris, i. 118
Gull (saddle-back) shooting, ii. 275, 276
Gun-cotton as an explosive, ii. 269
Guy, Mr., sport on his 'mudlands,' ii. 110

HAARLEM, its organ, i. 219
Haffendon, Captain, sporting experiences, i. 19, 20
Hague, The, the King's cabinet, i. 221; works of art in, 222; the palace, 222; the bells, 222; theatre, 222, 223; form of worship, 223
Halford, Sir Henry, consulted by Hawker, i. 283
Halton, Colonel, fishing experiences with Hawker, i. 286

Hampshire, the 1807 election, i. 7; riots in (1830), ii. 22
Hangings, near Mavey, sport at, i. 22
Hardinge, Lord, Master-General of Ordnance, ii. 339–341, 344
Hare hunt, a remarkable, i. 321
Hares (white) at Ben Lomond, i. 60; in Norfolk, ii. 159
Harnet, emperor of the Hampshire gunners, i. 323
Harnet, Lieut., inventor of the mud punt, i. 302; his epitaph, ii. 182, 183
Hastings, Marquis of, and wild-fowl shooting, ii. 314, 315, 348
—— Sir Thomas, Hawker's interview with, ii. 301
Havre de Grâce, its scenery, i. 111; hotel accommodation, 111; snuff manufactory, 111; customs officials, 331; Hawker's experiences at, ii. 215
Hawker, Colonel Peter: Sir Ralph Payne-Gallwey's sketch of his character, i. V–IX; his birth and parentage, VIII; ancestors, VIII, ii. 152; his first and second marriages, i. VIII, IX, ii. 242, 278; family, i. IX, 73 (*see* also 'Hawker, Misses,' and 'Hawker, Captain Peter'); his residence at Longparish, i. VII (*see* also 'Longparish House'); at Keyhaven, VII (*see* also 'Keyhaven'); prowess as a sportsman, V (*see* also 'Fishing,' 'Game,' and 'Shooting'); his relations with the Duke of Clarence (afterwards William IV.), 142, 287, 309, 329, 363, ii. 18, 49; with Prince Albert, i. VI, ii. 179, 242, 256, 261, 265, 273, 284, 296, 319, 330–332, 334, 338; Hawker's 'Instructions to Young Sportsmen,' i. V, VI, 142, 275, 276, 283, 295, ii. 18, 43, 45-47, 49, 148, 149, 170, 240-242, 265; and other literary works, i. IX, 15, ii. 56, 58; his patent hand-moulds, for the piano, i. IX, 175, 178, 202, 203, 216, 219, 222, 225, 229, 230, 239, ii. 37, 165, 173, 212, 214; and tambourine, 123; his new 'March,' 231; army experiences, i. VII, VIII, ii. 299 (*see* also 'Dragoons,' and 'North Hants Regiment'); proposal to amend the Game Laws, i. IX, ii. 32, 258; plan of attack on Parson Bond's preserves, i. 12, 13; trips to Spain and Portugal, 15, 21–30; his relations with Lord Bridgewater, 21, 23, 34, 69–72; his correspondence with Squire Jones, 41–43; trip to Scotland, 45–67; his relations with the Prince Regent (afterwards George IV.), 69, 84; and the Duke of Wellington, 69, 241, 242, ii. 32, 230; trip to Yorkshire, i. 77–79; trips to France, 97-103, 107–130, 166–171, 331–340, 343, 344, ii. 208–216; portable ambush for wild fowl, i. 145; trips to Belgium, Holland, and Germany, 208–236, ii. 244–247; on composition and critics, i. 238; his cure for smoky chimneys, 239; his relations with Lord Rodney, 241, 242, 265, 266, 273, 281, ii. 106; introduces French decoy system for wild-fowl shooting into England, i. 242, 243, 270, 273; invisible approach for fowl and game shooting, 365, ii. 313; his 'cripple net' for landing wounded bird, 46; trip to Ireland through Wales, 56-60; and to the Channel Islands, 74–82; his inscription for Joe Manton's tomb, 100; his claim for honours, 132, 133, 263; relations with Prince Napoleon, 153, 154, 179; writes epitaph on Lieut. Harnet, 182, 183; the Board of Ordnance and Hawker's efforts to improve military firearms, 220, 221, 228, 229, 301, 304, 307, 309–311, 322, 323, 329, 332, 337–344, 347; on the High Court of Exchequer, 235; his licensing experiences, 236; on writing his will, 238; his agitation against the sale of cheap guns, 312, 313; his exhibits at the Great Exhibition, 328–334; sketch of him in the 'Illustrated London News,' 335; severe illness, 352, 353–356; and death of, 356
Hawker, Captain Peter (Hawker's son), i. IX; sporting experiences, 342, ii. 30, 184; goes to school at Dieppe, i. 343, 344; gazetted lieutenant and presented at Court, ii. 29; quartered in Ireland, 32; illness of, 56, 59; in the West Indies, 155, 159, 175; return home, 179, 180; gazetted captain and presented at Court, 229; marriage, 278
—— General, with Hawker, visit Abbeville, i. 167, 188
—— General Sir S., and the Marylebone election, ii. 47; fishing experiences, 49; sent for by William

IV., 125; correspondence with Hawker, 132, 133; his death, 156, 157
Hawker, Honble. Col. Peter (Hawker's great-grandfather), Governor of Portsmouth, i. VIII., ii. 152; his monument in the garrison chapel at Portsmouth, 152, 304, 312
—— Misses Mary and Sophy (Hawker's daughters), i. IX, ii. 29; presented at Court by Lady Rodney, 123; their marriages, 232, 234
—— Mrs. (Hawker's mother), accident to, i. 17
Hawker's, Mr. Joe (the Richmond Herald), visit to Hawker, i. 96; proclaims William IV. king, ii. 18; sporting experiences with Hawker, 42, 52, 83, 108, 112, 129, 179
Hawkins, Mr., shooting expedition with Hawker, i. 77, 78
Hay, Colonel, visits Hawker, i. 247
Heath, Charles (Hawker's tenant and gamekeeper), action against, ii. 135, 160, 161; shooting experiences, 174, 219, 262, 279, 289, 299, 335
Heems, Jean David, picture in Ghent, i. 232
Hempstead, Dr., attends Hawker, ii. 356
Henry IV., his cathedral at Rouen, i. 332
Herbert, Mr., secretary of the Trinity Board, ii. 254
Heron (Jack), characteristics of, i. 315
Hervey, Colonel of the 14th Light Dragoons, and Hawker's resignation, i. 70–72
Hill, Lord, and Hawker's army musket, ii. 29; his levee, 220
Hinton, Viscount (afterwards Earl Poulett), fishing, shooting, and other expeditions with Hawker, i. 32, 33, 38, 39, 44, 80, 84, 96, 104, 148, 247, ii. 20, 326
Hird, Rev. Lewis Playters, his marriage with Sophy Hawker, ii. 234
Hoeckgeest, pictures in Holland, i. 222
Holland, Hawker's tour through, i. 21; incidents on the road, 213; description of the country and capital, 214-216; places in the North of Holland and customs of the people, 216–226; its waggons, 219; diligence, 219, 220; shooting, 221; the 'House in the Wood,' 221
Hollis and Sheath, Messrs., gun manufacturers, Birmingham, ii. 311
Holmfurth, sport near, i. 77
Homburg, the 'Kursaal,' ii. 245
Home, Mr. (afterwards Sir Everard), attends Hawker, i. 15, 17–20, 36, 37, 72, 73, 279, 283, 299
Honthorst, picture at Ghent, i. 232
Hornby, Captain, Superintendent of Woolwich dockyard, ii. 206, 207
Horne, Sir William, elected for Marylebone (1832), ii. 46
Horsey, Hawker's visits to, and experiences there, i. 143, 153, 158, 207, 273
Hosack, Dr., examines Hawker, i. 28
Hounslow, sport near, i. 3–5
Hudson, Captain, of the Guards, ii. 238
Huntingdon, Mr., Hawker's visits to, i. 143, 153; Hawker stands godfather to his son, 158; sporting on his estate, 207
Hurst, sport at, i. 360, ii. 7, 119, 138, 139, 197, 250, 282; sailing at, 150, 355
Hurstbourne Park, sport at, i. 18, 325, ii. 30, 219; fires at, 87; coach accident there, 153; ball, 171
Huskisson's monument in Liverpool, ii. 61
Hussey, John, gun borer, i. 308
Hutchins, Parson, his poaching hook, i. 166
Hyde, sport at, i. 82, 91, 194
Hyde Park, coronation fair in, ii. 149
Hythe, the 14th Light Dragoons at, i. 2; Customs troubles at, 106; boating experiences at, ii. 66

IGNACE and CAMILLE PLEYEL, Messrs., of Paris, i. 178
Influenza epidemic (1839), ii. 104, 120, 121, 160, 161
Inglefield, Captain, superintendent of the Great Exhibition, ii. 331
Inman, Mr. Thomas, punt builder, i. 262, 269
Ipswich, sport near, i. 9–13
Ireland, Hawker's visit to, ii. 56–60
Isle of Man, Hawker's sketch of, ii. 60
Isle of Purbeck, Hawker's visits to, i. 82, 269; sport at, 141
Isle of Wight, its 'Parsons' (*see* 'Cormorants'); sport there, ii. 48
Itchen, its floating bridge, i. 115

JENIERS, pictures at Ghent, i. 231
Jersey, Hawker's visit to, ii. 74; hotel accommodation, 75; places of in-

terest in, 75; customs and habits of the people, 75-77; military dinner there, 77
Jones, Squire, Hawker's correspondence with, i. 41-43
Jordaens, pictures in Holland, i. 221
Josephine, Empress, her palace, i. 120
Jouvenet, his visitation of Elizabeth, i. 115
Joy, Old, of Christchurch, his royal catch of mullet, ii. 104

KALKBRENNER, Chevalier (composer), i. 149, 158, 332, 335, ii. 263
Keil, Stephen (Hawker's carpenter), ii. 323, 366
Keiss, shooting at, i. 61
Kemble, Adelaide, vocalist, ii. 220
—— Charles, his readings, ii. 260
Kenilworth Castle, ii. 322
Kensal Green, gun-testing at, ii. 327
Keppel, Major, shooting experiences with Hawker, ii. 153
Keyhaven, Hawker's headquarters on the Solent for wild-fowl shooting, and other experiences there, i. VII, 103, 131-133, 135, 140, 141, 159, 163-165, 197, 198, 204, 205, 243-246, 253-265, 271, 272, 279, 288-296, 299-307, 309-315, 321-331, 347-364, ii. 3-6, 9-17, 22-25, 29, 33, 34, 39, 45-48, 53-56, 65-69, 88-90, 93-95, 98, 104, 110, 113, 117-123, 132, 133, 139-142, 150, 153, 155-158, 162, 168-170, 174-178, 186-189, 191-199, 203, 204, 219-225, 228-230, 233-235, 237-241, 248-250, 253-259, 263-265, 269-277, 281-284, 292-299, 301, 303, 304, 311, 312, 314-320, 323, 327, 331, 338, 339, 348, 349, 351, 352, 354, 355
King's Mill (Guernsey), orangery at, ii. 79
Klitz, Mr., the Clementi of Lymington, i. 310
Knight, Captain, of the 'Medina' packet, ii. 309
—— Mr., visit of the Hawkers to, i. 82; shooting on his estate, 194

LACY, Mr., gunmaker, ii. 341-343
Laeken, the palace of, i. 229; its orangery, 229
La Hogue, its dangerous coast, i. 100; view from Barfleur, 110
Lakeman, Captain, of the 'Kent,' ii. 224
Lancaster, A., and Charles, gunmakers, their experiences and inventions, ii. 29, 64, 103, 104, 266, 269, 300, 301, 304, 337, 339-342, 345
Langford, Charley, of the Middlesex Militia, i. 38
Langstaff, Mr. Tom, Hawker's musical friend, i. 172, 310, ii. 40, 85-87, 135, 165, 171
Langston Harbour, as a shooting resort, i. 311, 312
Lascelles, Colonel, inscription concerning, near Ben Lomond, i. 59
Latour, Captain, on Poole as a shooting resort, ii. 320
Laurie, Sir Peter, Lord Mayor (1832), ii. 47
La Ville d'Eu, its church, i. 170
Leadbeater, Mr. (ornithologist), i. 360, ii. 10, 54, 165, 197, 200, 205, 252, 274, 352
Leckford, sport at, i. 37
Leech, Mr., shooting experiences, i. 80; death of, ii. 55
Lefevre, Rev. Mr., Hawker's tutor, ii. 213
Leopold, King of the Belgians, and Queen, at the great naval review (1845), ii. 260
Lesuer, his paintings of St. Brunot, i. 115
Liège, hotel accommodation at, ii. 246; its gunmakers, 247; places of interest in, 247
Lille, its fortifications, i. 209
Lincolnshire, Hawker's journey through, i. 45, 46
Ling, Priest, the 'blacksmith' of Springfields, i. 50, 51
Liszt, his pianoforte playing, ii. 180
Liverpool, Hawker's impressions of, ii. 61
Llangollen, scenery around, ii. 56
Loch Lomond, its lake, i. 58; ferry, 59
Lock, Richard, gunner, i. 197
Lockey, guide and publican of Spittle, i. 47, 54
Logier, Mr. and Mrs., their system of musical education, i. 161, 172, ii. 58
London, visit of the Allied Sovereigns to (1814), i. 95; revolutionary rumours stop the Lord Mayor's procession (1830), ii. 21; scenes on Coronation Day (1831), 31; effects of the rejection of the Reform Bill (1831), 32; the Duke of Wellington's funeral in, 348, 349
London Bridge opened (1831), ii. 29

Long, Mr., gunmaker, i. 286
—— Mr., the crack shot, ii. 52
Longman, Mr., of Farnborough, fishing experience with Hawker, ii. 302, 303
Longmans, Messrs., and Hawker, i. 283, ii. 103, 240, 242
Longparish House, Hawker's residence in Hampshire, i. VII; sport there, 1–3, 5, 7, 16–18, 34, 35, 39, 44, 80, 83, 104, 135–137, 142–144, 146, 148, 149, 154, 155, 159, 160–163, 165, 166, 171, 173–175, 193, 198, 199, 203, 204, 238–241, 247, 250–252, 265–274, 275, 277, 278, 281, 282, 285, 286, 288, 297, 298, 309, 316–320, 324, 325, 329, 331, 342, 345–348, 365, 366, ii. 5, 17, 19–21, 28, 30–33, 41, 42, 49, 51–54, 63, 64, 70, 73–75, 83, 84, 87, 103, 104, 108–110, 113, 114, 129, 130, 151, 152, 155, 167–169, 184, 185, 218, 228, 229, 232, 233, 237, 247, 248, 260, 262, 263, 265, 267–269, 274, 278, 279, 290, 291, 293, 294, 302–304, 313, 314, 321, 324–326, 335, 336, 346, 347, 351; its fish and fisheries, i. VII, 160, 161, ii. 233, 353; building operations, fires there, and other experiences, i. 275, 276, 280, 290, ii. 21, 26, 27, 32, 40, 66, 67, 71, 72, 115, 120, 153, 155, 171, 191, 230, 236, 286–288, 300, 313, 314, 342, 343, 351; Hawker's last days there, 352, 353, 355, 356
Longstock, sport there, i. 21
Lorrain, Claude, pictures in Paris, i. 124
Louis XIV., Versailles built by, ii. 213
—— XVI., monuments in Paris, ii. 212
—— XVIII., not popular at Cherbourg, i. 97; at the Tuileries, 126; at Notre-Dame, 335; his Chapel in Paris, ii. 212
—— Philippe, present at the annual grand fête (1841), i. 211; improvement in Paris under his régime, 212; attempt on his life, ii. 213; and the palace at Versailles, 213
Lovell, Mr., inspector of small arms, ii. 337
Luss, sketching and shooting at, i. 58, 60
Lymington, Hawker's experiences there, i. 29, 103, 205, 206, 256, 257, 260–262, 269, 310, ii. 11, 25, 34, 48, 251, 285, 314, 315
Lyndhurst, Hawker's visit to, ii. 103, 245
Lyons, Mr., his yacht 'Breeze' wins the King's prize at Cowes, ii. 107

MACILWAIN, Dr., attends Hawker, i. 282, 283
Macintosh, Mr., shooting experiences with Hawker, i. 65, 66
McLaughlin, Mr., painting and shooting on his estate, i. 58
McLean, Mr., and the floods at Keyhaven, ii. 187, 188
Macleod, Mr., his fishing experiences, ii. 353
McNicol, Mr., innkeeper of Dumbarton, i. 58
Mafra, view of, from Cintra, i. 26
Magny, hotel accommodation at, i. 113
Maitland, Sir Peter, Hawker's account of, ii. 293, 294
Malawney, its wood, i. 339
Malibran, Madame, her singing i. 366, ii. 105; death of, 110
Mallard, Thomas, his presentiment, i. 253
Manchester, Hawker's impressions of, and experiences there, i. 199, 200; ii. 61, 62
Mantegna, his picture at Fonthill, i. 248
Manton, Mr. Joseph (gunmaker), his guns, i. 3, 5, 8, 32, 37, 63, 75, 84, 95, 107, 108, 132, 133–135, 137, 146, 155, 156, 174, 194, 239, 243, 253, 282, 308, ii. 64, 84, 280, 326, 327; his bankruptcy, i. 292; visits Hawker, 318; his quiet day's sport, 319; manufactory in the hands of the Philistines, 366; his epitaph, ii. 100, 101
Manvers, Earl, shooting on his estate, i. 42
Margate, Hawker's visit to, i. 295
Maria Louisa, her crown and mace in Paris, i. 116, 119
Marlborough, 1st Duke of, reminiscences of, i. 201
Marsh, Mr., his election for Andover, ii. 126
Martin, Mr., opera singer, i. 114
Marylebone election (1832), ii. 47
Mascot, Captain, of the 'Parfaite Union,' i. 130
Mathew, Mr. Bertie, Hawker's visits to, i. 103, 245; death of, 299
Mayence, Hawker's visit to, ii. 245
Mazocchi, Signor, bandmaster of the 74th Regiment, ii. 59

Menai Bridge, 'the eighth wonder of the world,' ii. 57
Menzies, John, of Craig-end, i. 63
Mermaid at Weyhill Fair, i. 35
Middlesex election (1852), ii. 344
Milbank, Sir John, his trial, ii. 159
Mildmay, Sir H., elected for Hampshire (1807), i. 7
Milford, the church at, i. 323, ii. 352, 355; sport of, i. 360
Miller, Rev. Mr., of Birmingham, ii. 307, 308
Miller's pond, fishing in, i. 77
Milles, Captain of the 14th Light Dragoons, i. 71
Minié ball, experiments with, ii. 340
Missing, Councillor, of Andover, ii. 264
Moeser, M., singer, ii. 124
Moffatt, its mineral springs, i. 52, 53; as a sporting resort, 52–54
Mole's Hole, fishing at, ii. 104
Moncey, Madame, and the French Customs, i. 331, 332
Monfarelle, its church, i. 101
Monk, Hawker's Peninsular servant, ii. 43, 44, 68, 91, 127; his medals and decorations, 300, 301
Montague, Lord, shooting on his estate, ii. 69, 70
Moore, Tom, the poet, i. 283
Moore and Gray, gunmakers, ii. 326
Morgan, Sir Charles, death of, ii. 272
Mori, singer, ii. 131
Moscheles, Mr., musician, i. 239, 247, ii. 20, 112, 124, 165, 173, 208
Moulin, Mr., his orangery in Guernsey, ii. 79
Mount Cassel, scenery at, i. 209
Mount Orgueil (castle) in Jersey, ii. 75
Mudeford, surveying experiences at, ii. 102
Mundy, General, of the United Service Club, i. 88
Munster, Lord, ii. 125
Muntz, Mr., M.P., his rolling mills, ii. 310
Murillo, pictures at Ghent, i. 232
Murray, Sir George, Master-General of the Ordnance, ii. 229

NAPOLEON BUONAPARTE, devotion of the French to, i. 97, 101; erects the Colonne de Place Vendôme, 114; paintings of his victories at Paris, 115, 119; his crown, 116; his château, 119; his billiard table, 119; his palaces, 124; triumphal arches, 125, 126; his tomb, ii. 201
Napoleon, Prince Louis (afterwards Napoleon III.), his visit to the Bank of England, ii. 153, 154; Hawker's visit to, 179
Nassau, Duke of, his hunting palace, ii. 246
Needles, rock-shooting and wild-fowling at, i. 30, 31, 312, 313, 360, ii. 7, 29, 55; diving operations at, 163
Nelson's monument (Liverpool), ii. 61
Nero, death of, Hawker's celebrated dog, i. 198
Netley Abbey ponds, fishing in, i. 77
Neville, village of, i. 109
Newbury, recruiting parties at, i. 34, 35
Newcastle, Duke of, game on his estate, i. 45
Newlands, sport at, ii. 2, 3
Nicholson, Mr., his hotel at Ostend, i. 236
Noah's Marsh, shooting at, ii. 176
Norfolk, shooting customs, i. 143, 159; sport in, 143, 153, 154, 158, 159
Normandy, shooting in, i. 107
Norris Castle (Cowes), its beauties, i. 310
North Hants Regiment, Hawker appointed Major, i. 142, 204; appointed Colonel, 241, 242, 244, 267, 287; dinner to, 287; proposed review by the Duke of Wellington, 31, 32; Lord Wiltshire appointed Colonel, 230
Norwood, Captain, of Talbot, i. 343
Noyelle-sur-Mer, sporting survey of, i. 170
Nyke, Dr., attends Hawker, i. 299

O'GRADY, Captain, his shooting experiences, ii. 184
'Old Harry and his wife,' i. 89
Onslow, Mr. Guildford, his letter to Hawker, ii. 318
Orford, Mr., of the 7th (English) Light Dragoons, i. 110, 111
Osler's cut-glass manufactory, ii. 310
Ostend, Hawker's visits to, i. 234–236, ii. 243; hotel accommodation at, i. 236; customs officials at, 237
Overton fair, ii. 105
Owl, a rare specimen, ii. 49, 50
Oxford, Edward, his attempt on the lives of the Queen and Prince Consort, ii. 181
Oxford, Hawker's visit to, i. 201

PAGANINI in London, ii. 29
Page, Captain, of the 'Prince of Waterloo' packet, i. 236
—— Charley, and the Southampton bird frightener, ii. 198
Paget, Lord Clarence, and Hawker's carbine, ii. 337
Paine, Daniel, wild-fowl frightener, ii. 99, 101, 113, 192, 225; death of, 226, 227
Painter, Mr., fishing experiences with Hawker, i. 286
Paisello's opera, 'Il Re Theodoro,' i. 116
Paris, Place des Victoires, i. 101; the Tuileries, 113, ii. 211; description of its interior, i. 118; State prayers in, 126; Colonne de la Place Vendôme, 114, ii. 211; the cavalry of France, i. 114; Champs-Elysées, 114, ii. 211–213; Fontaine des Innocents, i. 114; Palais Royal, 114, 125, ii. 214; the Théâtre Comique, i. 114; Parisian coaches in 1814, 114; the Invalides, 114, ii. 210; Museum Petit Augustin, i. 115; Luxembourg Palace, 115, 333, ii. 212; Senate House, i. 115, ii. 212; Ecole de Médecine, i. 115; Panthéon, 115, ii. 212; Eglise de Notre-Dame, i. 115, ii. 212; the festival of the Blessed Virgin there, i. 335; Italian Opera, 116, 133; Halle au Blé, 116; Bicêtre (madhouse), 116; Cabinet de l'Histoire Naturelle, 117; Cabinet of Anatomy, 117; Bureau d'Artillerie, 117, ii. 212; the Paris Opera-House, i. 117, 333; the Louvre, 118, ii. 210; Elysée des Bourbons, i. 119, 120; the Boulevards, 120; National Library, 120; Café Montacier, 120, 125; the gunmakers of Paris, 121; Parisian baths, 121; Franconie's Olympic Theatre, 121; suburbs of Paris, 122; bridge of Vienna, 122; Ecole Militaire and Champ de Mars, 122; St.-Cloud and its Palace, 122, ii. 213; royal porcelain manufactory at Sèvres, i. 122, ii. 213; Sceaux, i. 123; le Théâtre du Vaudeville, 125; boulevard du Temple, 125; l'Abbaye St. Martin, 126; Café d'Apollon, 126; Barrière de Neuilly, 126; the Bois de Boulogne, 127; l'Institution des Sourds — Muets, 127; Corps Législatif, 127, ii. 212; l'Eglise de St. Sulpice, i. 127, ii. 212; Théâtre Français, i. 127, ii. 212; Gobelins tapestry, i. 128; Observatoire Royal, 128; Mr. Véry's restaurant, 128, ii. 214; catacombs, i. 128; general impressions of Paris, 129; insanitary condition of, 129, 169; exorbitant prices in, 167–169; amusements in, 169; *combats des animaux*, 169; Hawker's second visit to, incidents *en route*, 332; Jardin des Plantes, 333, ii. 212; the Tivoli, i. 334; performance at the Conservatoire, 334; la Bourse, 335, ii. 212; manners and customs of the Parisians, i. 336, 337; Père-Lachaise, ii. 210; fortifications of Paris, 210; annual fête, 211; Cirque National, 211; the Eglise Madeleine, 212; Royal Library, 214; Opéra Comique, 214; Théâtre des Variétés, 214
Parker, Admiral Sir Hyde, at the Naval Review (1845), ii. 260
—— Captain, of the 'Victory,' ii. 242
—— Mr., army accoutrement manufacturer, ii. 307
—— wild-fowl shooter, experiences with Hawker, ii. 249, 338
Parliament, Houses of, destroyed by fire (1834), ii. 65
Parrot, Mr., experiences in France, i. 191, 192
Parsley, Joe, the 'priest' of Gretna, i. 51
Partridge eggs, wholesale destruction of, ii. 31
Paulett, Lords Charles, George, and William, their sporting experiences with Hawker, i. 44, 166, ii. 3, 5, 168
Payne, wild-fowl shooter, his experiences with Hawker, ii. 160, 188 241, 253, 272, 273, 277, 298, 351
Payne-Gallwey, Sir Ralph, his sketch of Hawker's character and career, i v-ix
Peacocke, General, and Hawker, i. 28
Pearson, Mr., his shooting experience with Hawker, i. 9, 10, 13
Peel, Colonel, and Hawker's musket ii. 220, 229
—— Sir Robert and Lady, visit Birmingham, ii. 308
Peninsular War (1815), Hawker's services in, *see* 'Dragoons'
Pennington, sport and other experiences at, i. 322, 326, 354, ii. 14 15, 88, 98, 223
Penrith, its scenery, i. 49, 50

Peronne, Hawker's shooting and other experiences at, i. 183–185
Perry, Dr., attends Hawker, ii. 43
Peyton, Captain Sir John, of the 'Madagascar,' ii. 107
Pigot, Major, shooting experiences with Hawker, i. 3
Pilewell, sport at, ii. 203, 250, 252, 264, 275
Pinnock, Mr., failure of, i. 279
Pisaroni, Madame, singer, i. 334
Pitt's Deep, as a sporting resort, i. 132, 322, ii. 48, 250
Pocock, Mr., stabbed by Sir John Milbank, ii. 159
Pollen, Sir John, Hawker's visit to, ii. 20
Pollington, Lord, shooting expedition with Hawker, i. 77, 78
'Pomore,' wreck of the, ii. 164
Ponton, Mr. J., Hawker's visit to, i. 144, 153, 174, 272, 283, 284; death of, 296
Poole and neighbourhood. Hawker's visit to, and experiences at, i. 86–94, 96, 97, 102, 140, 141, 149-152, 193, 194, 197, 198, 243, 244, 264, 269, ii. 69, 233
Pooley, its scenery and fishery, i. 49
Pope, Dr., attends Hawker, ii. 352
Port, on the banks of the Somme, i. 170, 176, 179, 181, 190
Portman, Mr., elected for Marylebone (1832), ii. 46, 47
Portsmouth, Lord, shooting on his estate, i. 76, 77, 84, 105, 137, 139, 156, 252, ii. 7, 17, 30, 35, 36; fires on his estate, 87; death of, 356
Portsmouth, Hawker's visit to, i. 311; Governor Hawker's monument there, ii. 152, 312; the Haslar Hospital, 152; naval review at, 260
Portugal, Hawker's visits to, i. 15, 26–28; distance travelled to reach, 30
Potter, Paul, his pictures in Holland, i. 222
Poulett, Lord, *see* 'Hinton.'
Poult shooting, i. 283
Poussin, picture in Paris, i. 124
Powell, Mr. Annesley, death of, i. 70
Prince's Tower (Jersey), view from, ii. 75
Prussia, impressions of, ii. 247
Pryce, Mr., his mudlands, ii. 46, 223
Ptarmigan, tameness of, i. 60
Purdeys, gunmakers, Hawker's experiments with, ii. 340, 348; and Hawker's musket, 352

QUARLEY HOUSE, Hawker's visit to, ii. 85–87

RADCLIFFE, Mr., his visit to the field of Waterloo with Hawker, i. 211
Radford, Dr., attends the Hawkers, i. 180, 181, 189
Raglan, Lord, Master-General of the Ordnance, ii. 350
Railway travelling (1834), ii. 61; (1849), 306
Ramsgate, Hawker's experiences at, i. 237
Ranelagh, Lord, grand meeting of gunmakers and riflemen at his villa, ii. 341
Raphael, pictures in Paris, i. 118
Ray, Mr., fire at his farm, i. 347, 348
Read, Mr., blacksmith and gunner of Dumbarton, i. 62, 63
—— James, grand potentate of all the gunners, his services and experiences with Hawker, i. 196, 205, 243, 246, 255, 257, 258, 260, 262, 263, 269, 271–273, 281, 287, 288, 293, 299–306, 313, 322, 323, 326–329, 350, 351, 353, 354, 358–360, ii. 5-7, 10, 11, 14-16, 23-26, 33-35, 37, 44, 48, 53, 54, 65, 68, 88, 89, 92, 94, 95, 97, 118–121, 134, 136-139, 142, 144–147, 157, 158, 160, 191-195, 203, 220, 221, 223, 224, 226–228, 233, 241, 248, 249, 251-253, 257–259, 264, 269, 270, 272–274, 276, 277, 280, 281, 292, 294, 296, 297, 299, 301, 311, 312, 315, 317-319, 327, 338, 344
Reade, Jemmy, 'priest' and 'blacksmith,' i. 51
Redbridge, 'march of intellect' at, ii. 52
Redmoor dyke 'bridge,' accident at, ii. 67
Reeves, John, ii. 89
Reform Bill (1831), rejected, ii. 32
Regent, Prince, *see* 'George IV.'
Regent's Park, skating on, ii. 83
Rembrandt, picture at Ghent, i. 231
Rettaville Lake, sport on, i. 111
Rhine, beauties of the, ii. 245
Rhodes, Mr. Charles, marries Hawker's daughter Mary, ii. 232
Rich, Captain, i. 166
Richards, Mr., sporting experiences, i. 251
—— Mr. Westley, gunmaker, his shooting musket ('bloody Burnett'), ii. 160, 275; Hawker's consultations

with, 160, 348; his gun factory at Birmingham, 306, 309
Richter, Professor, and perspective, ii. 235
Ringwood, shooting at, i. 5; Bagshore's experiences at, 314
Riots in London (1830), ii. 21; in Hampshire and other parts, 21, 23
Rising, Mr. Robert Hawker visits, i. 143, 153, 158, 207, 273
Rodney, Lord and Lady, their relations with Hawker, i. 241, ii. 123; Hawker's visits to, i. 242, 265, 266, 273, 281, ii. 106; entertains the North Hants Regiment, i. 287; sport on his estate, 290, 307; and the Reform Bill (1831), ii. 32; death of Lord Rodney, 229, 230; and of Lady Rodney's father, 272
Rogers, William, his shooting explorations, i. 207
Romney, sport at, i. 3
Romsey, the old church at, ii. 347
Rook, Harry, gunner, ii. 249
Rooks, extraordinary bag of, ii. 28
Rothsay, Lord Stuart de, ii. 104
Rossini, Signor, Italian musician, i. 275
Rouen, Hawker's visit to, i. 112; its scenery, 113; places of interest in, 113; hotel accommodation at, 113, 332; its cathedral, 332; view of, from the hill of St. Catherine, 338
Rousseau's tomb in Paris, i. 115
Row Ardenan, its inn, i. 59
Rownam's house, fête at, ii. 166
Rubens, his pictures in Gatteville, i. 102; in Paris, 115, 118; in Holland, 221; at Ghent, 231
Rue, its church, i. 180; sport there, 180
Rue de l'Ecu, hotel accommodation at, ii. 209
Russel, Mr., and the fishery of Pooley, i. 49
Rutter, his description of Fonthill Abbey, i. 248
Ruysdael, pictures at Ghent, i. 231
Ryde, its beauties, ii. 88

SAARDAM, Hawker's drive through, i. 218
Sachi, Madame, the rope dancer, i. 225
St. Catherine's Hill, the view from, i. 338
St.-Crotoi, shooting survey of, i. 170
St. Helier's, the town of, ii. 75
St.-Louis, burial-place of kings of France, i. 115
St. Malo, Hawker at, ii. 81
St. Paul's Cathedral, its aspect during the time of Wellington's funeral, ii. 349
St. Peter's Port, the town of, ii. 74, 79; its church, 80
St.-Pierre, visit to, i. 102
St.-Valery, shooting survey of, i. 163; Hawker's visits to, 167, 180, 181
Saltoun, Lord, his brass 'kill-devil,' ii. 161
Sark, the island of, ii. 75, 78
Schamps, Mr., his collection of pictures, i. 231
Scheveningen, its scenery, i. 220, 221
Schroeder, Madame, vocalist, ii. 124
Scotland, Hawker's visit to, i. 50; its marriage laws, 50, 51; posting, 54; where do the Highlands begin? 60
Scott, Sir Claude, and Hawker, ii. 312
Seine, beauties of, i. 113, 332, 338
Seton, Colonel, of the 74th Highlanders, ii. 336; his death, 340
Shakespeare, his birthplace, i. 201
Shardlow, Mr., foreman of Clive's factory, ii. 306, 307
Sheddon, Colonel, experiences with Hawker, ii. 97, 107
—— Mrs., her action against Hawker, ii. 61, 63
Sheldrake, peculiarities of, i. 96; Hawker shoots a fine specimen, ii. 9, 10
Sherrard, Mr. Hawker's visit to, i. 140
Shooting (seasons 1802–1808) i. 1–14; (1809–1810) 15, 16; (1810–1811) 19–23, 25, 30–32; (1811–1812) 34, 35; (1812–1813) 39 41; correspondence concerning, 41–44, 47, 48, 53-55, 57, 58, 61–67, 73–78; (1813–1814) 80–93, 96; (1814–1815) 104, 105, 107, 111, 131, 132; (1815–1816) 136–144; (1816–1817) 145–153; (1817–1818) 155–160; (1818–1819) 162–164, 172; (1819–1820) 173–175, 178, 180, 193–198; (1820–1821) 203-206; (1821–1822) 240–244, 246, 247; (1822–1823) 250–267; (1823–1824) 268–274; (1824–1825) 277–279, 281–284; (1825–1826) 285–294; (1826–1827) 297, 298, 301–308, 313–315; (1827–1828) 316–330; (1828–1829) 342, 343, 346–366; (1829–1830) ii. 1–18; (1830–1831) 19–25, 27–29; (1831–1832) 30–37, 40; (1832–1833) 42, 45–49;

(1833–1834) 51–56 ; (1834–1835) 63–71, 73 ; (1835–1836) 83–85, 87–91, 93–96, 98, 99, 101–103 ; (1836–1837) 108–110, 112–114, 117–123 ; (1837–1838) 129–134, 136–146 ; (1838–1839) 151–153, 155, 156, 159, 160, 165 ; (1839–1840) 167–170, 174–178 ; (1840–1841) 184–186, 191–197, 199–207 ; (1841–1842) 218–225, 228, 229 ; (1842–1843) 232–235 ; (1843–1844) 237, 240, 241 ; (1844–1845) 248–260 ; (1845–1846) 262–265 ; (1846–1847) 267–278 ; (1847–1848) 279–286 ; (1848–1849) 289–291, 293–299 ; (1849–1850) 302–304, 313–320 ; (1850–1851) 324–327 ; (1851–1852) 335, 336, 339, 341 ; (1852–1853) 346–348, 351, 352. *See* 'Game and Wild Fowl.'

Shoreham, Hawker in a gale at, i. 191

Shorehead, sport at, i. 351

Shotten, Ben, of the 14th Dragoons, ii. 76

Shrapnel, Captain, and the Ordnance Office, ii. 338, 339, 349, 352

Shuttler, Stephen, Hawker's gunner, ii. 338, 344, 348, 351, 354

Silva, Madame de, her residence at Jonqueira, i. 26, 28

Siney, 'ratcatcher,' Hawker's servant, ii. 52, 113, 127, 299, 351

Singer Sam, the field marshal of eastern gunners, i. 264, 272, 311, 312, ii. 34, 233, 234, 238, 241, 299, 305, 312

Sleet, Mr., his chase after a hare, ii. 191

Smew (Lough diver), a rare specimen, ii. 11

Smike, Mr., Hawker's lawyer, ii. 135, 173

Smith, Squire, his fox preserves, ii. 287

Snipe (jack) shooting, uncertainty of the sport, i. 1

Snowdon, view of, ii. 56

Sola, Signor, musician, his visits to Hawker, i. 155, 163, ii. 87, 135, 136, 157, 336 ; and to Quarley House, 85

Somerset, Lord Fitzroy and Hawker, ii. 132

Somerton Hall, Hawker's visits to, i. 143, 153, 158, 207

Somme river, as a shooting resort, i. 170, 176, 177 ; dangerous currents, 177

Sontag, singer, i. 366

Southampton, Hawker's experiences at, i. 106, 107, 172, 299, 300, 309, 323, ii. 44, 89, 152 ; opening of the railway to (1840), 181

Southaven, experiences at, i. 149–151, 194–197, 263, 264

Sowley Pond preserves, ii. 69, 70, 88, 95

Spain, Hawker wounded in, i. 15 ; game in, 15

Spitalfields weavers, grand carnival for their benefit, ii. 124

Spittle, near Bowes, grouse shooting at, i. 47–49

Spohr, musician, ii. 236

Springfield, hymeneal transactions there, i. 51

Stafford, Hawker's experiences at, ii. 62

Stape Hill Convent, i. 284

Starlings, tameness of Broek, i. 218 ; extraordinary bag of, at one shot, 288

Stephens, Miss A., musician, ii. 309

Sterling, Mr., shooting on his estate, i. 61

Steup, Mr., of Amsterdam, i. 216

Stockbridge, fishing at, i. 143, 144, 153

Stonehenge, Hawker's description of, i. 81

Storks, tameness of Broek, i. 218

Stratford-on-Avon, Hawker's visit to, i. 201

Strathmoor, shooting laws and customs at, i. 48

Stratton Park, sport at, i. 241

Studland, shooting at, i. 141

Sturney, Caleb, the fisherman, i. 86, 87, 89

Suffolk, shooting customs of, i. 159

Sussex, Duke of, fêted at Southampton, ii. 181

Sutton, Mr., purchase of his lease of the Test, i. 160

—— Sir Richard, ii. 149

Sutton Park, suburb of Birmingham, ii. 322

Swallow waterfall, ii. 56

Swans (wild), shooting, i. 353

Symonds, Captain John, shooting experiences with Hawker, ii. 2 ; illness of, 152, 190 ; marriage of his widow to Hawker, 242

—— Sir William, ii. 121, 206

TALAVERA, battle of (1809), i. 15, 32

Talbot, Major, shooting expedition with Hawker, i. 2

Talma, French actor, i. 127, 228
Test river (Longparish), Hawker acquires the right to fish in, i. VII, 160, 161
Thackery, General and Lady Elizabeth, ii. 227
Thalberg, musician, ii. 124, 131; Hawker on his playing, 180
Thompson, Mr., fishing experiences, ii. 303
Thoroughgood, Mr., the famous coach-driver, i. 274
Tichfield Haven, duck marsh there, i. 267
Tidworth, the village of, i. 157
Tiger, death of Hawker's favourite dog, i. 105
Tindall, Lord Chief Justice, his interest in Hawker's shooting gear, ii. 106
Titian, pictures in Paris, i. 115, 118
Tonbridge Wells, Hawker's description of, ii. 278
'Torbayman,' boarding a, ii. 39
Touchard, Mr., of Cherbourg and Havre, i. 99, 111
Tracey's Dell, shooting at, ii. 271
'Trafalgar,' launch of the, ii. 206
Tronchet, M., and his guide book, i. 129
Troth, Harry, gunner, ii. 249, 254, 255
Trowbridge, shooting on the liberty of, i. 42
Tufton, fire at, ii. 87; sport at, 184
Turner, Mr., head ranger of George the Fourth's park, i. 295
Turtle, Hawker's recipe for dressing, i. 29
Tuyll, Baron, his experiences with Hawker, i. 229
Tytherley House, shooting at, i. 19, 20

UDDENS Park, shooting at, i. 283, 284
Ulswater Lake, Hawker's visit to, i. 49
United Service Club, Hawker at the, ii. 88, 132
Utrecht, Hawker's impressions of, i. 214

VALCALVILLE, sport at, i. 109
Valognes, Hawker's description of, i. 109, 110
Van den Bergh, Madame, the female Clementi of the Hague, i. 222
Vandyke, his pictures in Holland, i. 221; at Ghent, 232
Van Eyck, pictures at Ghent, i. 233; at Fonthill, 248
Van Veen, master of Rubens, i. 233
Vanzon, Maarten, Dutch fisherman, i. 220
Varley, Mr. Cornelius, ii. 147
Vassal, Captain, shooting experiences with Hawker, ii. 141
Vast, its cotton mill, i. 110
Vaughan, Mr., the celebrated singer ii. 57
Verbruggen, Henry, his carvings at Brussels, i. 226
Vercellini, Signor, experiences with Hawker, i. 156, 163, ii. 57, 166, 336
Vernet, his paintings in Paris, i. 115, 124
Versailles, Hawker's description of, i. 123; its orangery, 123, 229; gardens, 123, ii. 213; the Bas d'Apollon, i. 123; Colonnade, great basin, 124; Palais du Grand Trianon, 124; whispering room, 124; Petit Trianon, 124; arms manufactory, 125; Louis Philippe's restorations at, ii. 213
Victoria, H.M. Queen, her Levees and Drawing Rooms, ii. 147, 148, 229, 265, 287, 299, 339; her coronation, 148, 149; her marriage, 175; attempt on her life, 181; attends the Philharmonic, 235; Hawker's presents of wild fowl to, 256, 319; attends the great naval review, 260; opens the Great Exhibition (1851), 329; her interest in Hawker's exhibits, 330–334
'Victory,' Nelson's flagship, i. 23, 311
Vilaire, Hawker's experiences at, i. 182, 183
Vinci, Leonardo da, his pictures in Paris, i. 118
Virgin Mary, the feast of the, described, i. 335, 336
Virginia Water, Hawker's visit to, i. 294, 295
Voltaire's tomb, i. 115; his statue, 120; his tragedy of 'Mahomet,' 228

WAAL river, modes of passing, i. 224
Wakeford, Mr., shooting expedition with Hawker, i. 19
Wales, Prince of, christening (1842), ii. 223
Wales, Hawker's journey through, ii. 56
Waller's ash tunnel, ii. 226
Waltham small arms factory, ii. 344

Walton-on-Thames, fishing at, i. 4, 5
Ward, Captain, yachting and shooting experiences with Hawker, i. 299, 311–314, ii. 13; death of, 71; Hawker purchases his shooting gear, 238
Warne, Mr. Richard, proprietor of Warren Farm, i. 133; sport there, 132, 133, 141
Warren, Mrs., of Middleton House, ii. 293
Warwick Castle, Hawker's visit to, ii. 322
Water-crakes, scarcity of, in this country, i. 35
Waterloo, Hawker visits the field of, i. 211, 229
Wearns, Joe, Hawker's sailor, i. 262
Webb, Mr. Robert, shooting expedition with Hawker, i. 40
Weber, Carl Maria Von, the composer, i. 294
—— Mr., organist of Cologne Cathedral, ii. 244
Weld, Mr., his yacht, the 'Alarm,' ii. 167
Wellington, Duke of, his official relations with Hawker, i. 69, 241–243, ii. 32, 132, 230; postpones the Lord Mayor's procession (1830), ii. 21, 22; death and funeral, 346, 348, 349
West, Mr., shooting and other experiences with Hawker, ii. 99, 153, 155
West Bromwich, its viaduct and aqueduct, ii. 310
Westhover, extraordinary flock of fieldfares at, ii. 25
Westminster Abbey, Hawker's visit to, ii. 149
Westmoreland, its scenery, i. 49
Weyhill Fair, curiosity at, i. 35
Weymouth, military revels at, i. 68
Whale at Totland Bay, ii. 227
Wherwell, sport at, i. 37, 104, 139, 147, 156, 157, ii. 3, 65, 264; burial of Annesley Powell at, 76
Whisky, illicit distilleries in the Highlands, i. 60
Whitby, Mrs., shooting on her estate, ii. 2; her action during the flood at Keyhaven, 188, 275
Whitchurch, sport at, i. 85; accident to Hawker there, ii. 43
Whitestaunton, sport at, i. 148
Wickham, Bill, his action against Heath, ii. 135, 173
Widmore, Mr., purchase of his fishery by Hawker, i. 160, 161; shooting on his estate, 240
Wiesbaden, places of interest near, ii. 245, 246
Wild fowl on the Clyde, difficulties in shooting, i. 62; at Poole, 86; at Bourne-bottom, 88
Wild-fowl shooting, a record week, i. 353. *See* also 'Game'
Wilkinson, gunmaker, ii. 301, 304–307, 311, 314, 340, 348
William, Duke of Clarence (afterwards William IV.), presents Hawker at Court, i. 142; Hawker's gifts of game and fish to, 287, 309, 329, 363; proclaimed king, ii. 18; 'Instructions to Young Sportsmen' dedicated to, 18, 49; accession to the throne, 22; opens London Bridge, 29; his coronation day, 31; his Drawing Rooms, 72, 123, 124; birthday celebrations in Jersey, 77; illness, 123; and death, 124
Williams (Hawker's sailor), i. 193; reconnoitres Keyhaven, 197; and the cormorant, 313
Wills, Mr., master of the 'Lord Nelson,' i. 97
Wilson, Mr. Henniker, his shooting experiences, ii. 219
—— Sir Henry, shooting on his estate, i. 317; fire at his farm, ii. 32
Wiltshire, shooting in, ii. 65
Winchester, Lord, consultation with Hawker on militia matters, ii. 348
Winchester, Hawker's drive to, i. 163; accidents to duck punt near, 175–193; Hawker quartered at, with the North Hants Regiment, 204, 241, ii. 31; military life at, i. 287; accident at, 295, 296; service at the cathedral, ii. 7; coaching experience at, 107; lawsuit at, 135, 164; meeting of military and other notables at, 345
Windsor Castle, Hawker's visits to, ii. 55, 242
Wolverhampton, Hawker's visit to, ii. 308; its ancient church and other antiquities, 309
Wood, Mr., negotiations with Hawker regarding Longparish House, ii. 71, 72
Woodstock, Hawker's visit to, i. 201
Woollard arrives with orders for Hawker, i. 39
Woolpit, shooting at, i. 13
Woolwich, Hawker witnesses the launch of the 'Trafalgar' at the dockyard, ii. 206, 207; the select committee on Ordnance examine

Hawker's musket at the arsenal, 228; testing of Lancaster's conical ball, 266; gun-testing operations there, 322
Wormwood Scrubbs, powder testing at, ii. 341
Wraxall, sport at, i. 40

YACHTING at Cowes, i. 312, 313, ii. 107; near Keyhaven, 3
Yarmouth (Great), Hawker's visit to, i. 158, 207, 208, 273, 274
—— (Hampshire), Hawker's excursions to, i. 323, ii. 106, 107, 355
York, the Hon. and Rev. Mr., his preaching, ii. 307
Yorke, Sir Joseph, of the 'Victory,' i. 23
Yorkshire, grouse shooting in, i. 77

THE END.